Life, Liberty, and the Pursuit of United

Life, Liberty, and the Pursuit of United

An Englishman's Quest to Remain
Connected to "His" Team from
the Other Side of The Pond

Gary B. France

Published by Fish Out of Water Books, Ann Arbor, MI, USA.

www.fowbooks.com

© 2018 by Gary B. France

ISBN: 978-0-9899087-2-6

Pop culture · Coming of age · Travel · Culture shock · Going against the grain · Adversity · Triumph · Extraordinary lives · Ordinary lives

We are all fish out of water.

We publish non-fiction, creative non-fiction, and realistic fiction.

For further information, visit www.fowbooks.com.

Cover design by J. Caleb Clark; www.jcalebdesign.com.

Author's Disclaimer

Certain creative liberties were taken by the author at times in regards to the timeline sequence of certain events. Furthermore, the names of characters and venues have also been changed to protect the identity/privacy of the real-life individuals populating the book. Additionally, some characters are composites of multiple people. Aside from these minimal enhancements, it all happened.

For Margaret and Brian

PUBLISHER'S FOREWORD

"Is this their moment? Beckham . . . into Sheringham . . . and Solskjær has won it! Manchester United have reached the promised land!"

The words of British TV commentator Clive Tyldesley—as Manchester United won the 1999 European Champions League final in the most dramatic of circumstances—describe what surely must be *the* soccer moment of a lifetime for millions of Manchester United fans the world over.

Aside from being inside the Camp Nou stadium itself—my sister, brother-in-law, nephew and niece were all there—witnessing those once-in-a-lifetime scenes live from Barcelona on a Wednesday afternoon in a packed out Irish pub in Ann Arbor, Michigan was as good as it gets. It was an unforgettable experience.

When you emigrate and start anew, you miss your home, your relatives, your friends—and, if you're a sports fan—you miss "your" team. You have to find a way to keep up with your team. It's a given. Nowadays, of course, it's simple; you open the NBCSN app. on your smart phone and choose any of the live games being played that day. But in the early 90s, and more than three thousand miles from home, it was a different kettle of fish.

"Life, Liberty and the Pursuit of United" could be my story. It could be the story of any number of soccer-loving expats. After my move from Manchester to Michigan in 1993, with the exception of World Cup '94, I lived in the soccer wilderness for three years before watching a live-via-satellite-from-England game—the 1996 FA Cup final between Manchester United and Liverpool. I will never forget the thrill of arriving at the Britannia Club in Warren, Michigan and seeing fans decked out in red and white soccer shirts and scarves. Talk about a home away from home! During my first three years in the States, I would receive occasional match day programs and newspaper clippings from my sister and brother-in-law. These two-week old clippings and programs were always very welcome—but they would bring with them a mix of emotions connected with cherished memories from the past and our numerous pilgrimages to Old Trafford—that powerful pull toward "home."

The four soccer seasons covered in "Life, Liberty and the Pursuit of United" represent a unique period in time. This was the cusp of the internet revolution—right before soccer began to gain a real foothold in the U.S. And it was also a unique period in the history of Manchester United Football Club: four seasons culminating in the 1998–99 "promised land" season of the Treble.

In this day and age we are all connected via smart phones and social media—but, in many ways, we are more isolated than ever. It's such a cliché—but it's so very true. If you wanted to see a Premier League game "back in the day," your only option was to go to the pub "early doors"—a 3:00pm game in England kicks off at 10:00am in Michigan. And that's how many longstanding friendships were forged—how a community of fans was born. Nowadays, it's easy to roll out of bed and watch in your pajamas, alone—a community of one.

Part soccer diary and part fish out of water memoir, if you like an "everyman" story that focuses on people, on characters, and one that is told with warmth and humor, with that northern English wit and charm, then whether you are a Manchester United fan or not, a soccer fan or not, you will enjoy this story of a northern English lad from Lancashire's green belt thrust into life in Michigan's rust belt.

Yes, this happens to be a book about a Manchester United fan. But it's about so much more; it's about home; it's about leaving home and adjusting to a new way of life; and it's about maintaining those important connections to home. It is about devotion to a team—to "your" team and the bonds created through that devotion. If it was written by a Liverpool or an Everton fan, a Chelsea, Arsenal or Tottenham fan, or a Detroit Lions or Seattle Sounders fan, I would read it with the same interest. And if it was written by a Manchester City fan—yeah, I think I could see myself being interested—*kind of.*

While it may not ultimately answer the elusive question as to why watching twenty-two grown men kick a piece of inflated leather around a field for ninety minutes (plus injury time) means so much, "Life, Liberty, and the Pursuit of United" provides us with plenty of insight.

We are thrilled to publish "Life, Liberty, and the Pursuit of United" and we hope you enjoy it as much as we do. Please drop us a line and let us know what you think: fowbooks@gmail.com.

"C'mon you Reds!"

Jon Wilson

Fish Out of Water Books
Ann Arbor, MI
www.fowbooks.com

PREFACE

On August 2, 2014, I sat with 109,318 soccer fans packed into the University of Michigan's "Big House" in Ann Arbor, watching Manchester United take on Real Madrid in what was—and still is—the largest crowd ever assembled to watch a soccer game on U.S. soil. Can anyone say that soccer has not truly arrived in the USA?

Rewind . . .

The year was 1995 and I had left my native Great Britain for a new life in the United States. I quickly realized that I was in a country that demonstrated no real affinity for the "beautiful game," and, more to the point, Manchester United! I even had to resort to calling my beloved football, *soccer*!

The thing is, when it's in your blood, it's in your blood. That's it. Done deal! Football, alright then, soccer, has always been in my blood. The America into which I arrived seemed to be in need of a transfusion in order for its sports fans to stand any chance of embracing the game that I appeared to have left behind in Britain.

Ironically, in those early days, I lived very close to an American high school and couldn't believe my eyes one day as I saw a soccer match in full flow. An immaculate floodlit stadium, huge stands, overhead play by play commentary, beautifully-groomed fields and, all around, top-draw facilities that the kids were enjoying—a far cry from anything I had experienced when growing up playing soccer in North West England. I was gobsmacked! I pondered how it could be that these kids were regularly playing soccer in such incredible settings, their parents so passionately engaged—and yet when the lights went out, they, along with most of America, didn't seem to want to know anymore. They would return to cheering for their Detroit Lions, Tigers, Pistons, and Red Wings.

Ah, yes, America's "big four" sports. I was initially enticed, trying to adopt a when-in-Rome mindset, a substitute sporting fix for my soccer void. I sampled Red Wings' Stanley Cup playoff mania. Ice hockey had a similar dynamic to soccer. Goalies, defense, attackers, offside, but it was on ice, had timeouts, and I won't lie, I couldn't see the bloody puck half the time. I went to watch the Detroit Lions play the Green Bay Packers on Thanksgiving Day at the Pontiac Silverdome but spent most of the match barely tolerating a three-hundred-pound Packers fan squeezed into the seat next to me wearing foam cheese on his head and yelling profanities whenever the referee made a call in favor of the Lions. I made it to Wrigley Field in Chicago. I enjoyed the catchy song in the middle of the seventh, but watching baseball, for me, was like watching paint dry. I took in some Detroit Pistons playoff games. The atmosphere at the bar was fun, but the last five minutes of a game could easily stretch into a full half hour. More of those time outs! Don't get me wrong; they were all great experiences and there is no country that does sport like America. It just wasn't soccer. I was kidding myself.

My blood remained as thick *red* as ever.

I refocused. I was sure I could unearth some semblance of love for the game in my new surroundings. I dug deeper. I heard stories of the North American Soccer League with world-class players such as Pele, Beckenbauer and Cruyff. Unfortunately, the league folded in the mid-eighties. The people I spoke with explained it as another failed attempt at trying to integrate soccer into a sporting culture that simply was not sufficiently interested. Despite my efforts to engage regarding the game, all I continued to hear was how soccer would "never catch on." People would say to me "why watch a game that ends in a 0-0 tie? What is the point in that?"

There was even little recollection of the year prior, when Diana Ross took a penalty and America launched a terrific spectacle, hosting the 1994 FIFA World Cup. Soccer had been placed front and center and mainstream television couldn't ignore it. The American public had been given another—albeit transitory—window through which soccer could be viewed. Again, it seemed to me like a case of "here today, gone tomorrow." Despite the fantastic effort made with that World Cup, the first MLS game was still roughly a year away and there were certainly no kids walking around wearing the Barcelona, Real Madrid, or Manchester United shirts that are so ubiquitous today.

Within a few months, my perseverance eventually did pay off. I achieved long awaited liberation. From the beginning I had been utilizing my only reliable source, a shortwave radio, to hear second half commentary of a chosen match from England's Premier League each Saturday morning. Despite the fluctuating reception, with matches tending to fade away during the crucial final minutes, those initial sound bites were all I had. I took to ordering two-week old British newspapers from a local bookstore, and made regular transatlantic phone calls to grab the latest reports and soccer news from my father and friends. Then, suddenly, out of the blue, came the moment—an unbelievable opportunity—to watch English Premier League games live via satellite at an early morning, one-of-a-kind pay-to-enter venue, the Britannia Club in Warren, MI. It was there that I met soccer fanatics from all over the world. Several have become lifelong friends. Roughly a year later, things got even better as we discovered our self-proclaimed "soccer pub" — Conor O'Neill's in Ann Arbor. A new soccer ritual in America had begun. At the two venues, we have shared in numerous, wonderful soccer moments over the years — the most memorable of all, for me at least, being Manchester United's glorious "Treble moment" in May 1999! Supply and demand had finally won the day. America maybe, just maybe, was beginning to wake up to soccer after all.

And so to 2018!

When it comes to the beautiful game, the United States is now a very different place. Right here in Michigan, we have stories such as the incredible rise of and fanatical following for supporter-owned Detroit City FC — one of the most talked about soccer teams in North America — where fans raised $750,000 so that their team would have its own home stadium. Moving up America's soccer ladder, the MLS continues to grow in popularity and, over the last few years, cable television has greatly expanded its soccer coverage as initially ESPN and Fox, and now NBCSN, provide an incredible package of English Premier League games with viewers able to watch their fixture of choice on TV, smart phone, or tablet.

Watching Manchester United play Real Madrid in that phenomenal gathering at the "Big House," a mile down the road from Conor O'Neill's, was a surreal moment for me. I couldn't help but reflect on just how far we have come.

It's Saturday.

Warming my hands around my early morning cup of tea, I stand alone appreciating the horizon, inspired by the winter landscape before me. It is a slow yet magnificent dawn as the sun begins its ascent above the waters of Lake Huron, Michigan, illuminating the atmospheric terrain.

I sense peace, yet somewhat fleeting, as my anticipation heightens, turning on the television at this early hour.

My attention immediately switches from the view outside my window to a high-definition picture of a rain-drenched Old Trafford, Manchester, England.

My worn and tattered Manchester United scarf is draped around the perimeter of the flat screen, ready for the match.

"Glory Glory Man United!"

An Englishman's breakfast in America!

Alpena, Michigan, 2018

Great Britain

1

Pain and Torture

I still recall the vivid, bellowing cries and commotion permeating the sanctity of my bedroom walls. My father's despairing groan. My mother's desperate plea. I was six years old. I was scared. "What was happening?"

The flashing lights from the ambulance parked in our driveway in the early hours of the morning intermittently illuminated the interior of our small bungalow. I felt a knot in my stomach. My mother's yell: "No. No! Please don't take my baby. Don't take my baby!" The knot in my stomach tightened. I placed my pillow over my head in an attempt to drown out the noise of the distress filling our home. My mother had given birth to her third child and something was not right.

My mother, Mattie, had the most beautiful Elizabeth Taylor eyes and dark complexion, and a laugh that sounded like the old Victorian Jolly Jack penny arcade laughing machine at the end of Southport Pier. Her own adoptive mother had blatantly dictated "You will go to the factory and put some money on the table" ending her dream of higher education, and inadvertently fueling my mother's trademark independent streak that remained with her for the rest of her life. My mother was all Rolling Stones, no Beatles. My mother, deep down, was a rebel!

My father, Jimmy, was the only child of a seamstress and a steam engine train driver. After completing his National Service, he forged a pathway into the Royal Air Force (RAF), eventually qualifying as an electrician. He was a good football player—earning a trial for Bury Town at one point—and even played in the FA Cup. My father did whatever my mother told him to, but he would then look over at me and wink. I loved it when my father winked at me!

The two of them were thrust together the night my father chose my mother at a friend's wedding rather than the bridesmaid with whom his friends had planned on fixing him up. "I'll be seein' you later," he had apparently whispered, closing the door on my mother's taxi that particular night.

My younger sister, Annie, had the misfortune of becoming my earliest playmate and, therefore, developed a love for the game of football—more or less forced upon her—as I needed a goalkeeper at the drop of a hat on so many occasions.

Ours was a family full of laughter, particularly during impromptu family car trips when we would all be crammed into a small Ford Escort van. Two young kids in the back storage space, each of us competing for our parents' attention up front. The aged shock absorbers must have taken a beating as we all rocked along to Diana Ross, Tina Turner, and Gladys Knight and the Pips with the volume at eleven!

"Go on love, give us some Tina," my father would request of my mother as he slipped into third gear, dragging our rusted chariot out of the village limits.

"Yeeeah! Yeeah! Yeah!" came my mother's immediate response as she emulated Tina Turner's high notes, her bluesy vocals rocking a ready-made audience screaming its approval from the back of the van. Our living room would often play forum to our performances and skits copied from television shows of the day. There was always music in the house. It didn't take much to convince my mother to bang out tunes on the piano, displaying her own musical prowess, providing a soundtrack to the chaotic events unraveling on the other side of the room.

Our family unit worked. It truly worked. We all loved being together— well, except for the odd occasion when my mother would lose it, slam door after door in our small bungalow and disappear up the road to the school playing field, climb the climbing frame, drape herself over the top of its metallic peak and gaze to the heavens wondering to herself: *what the hell is life all about?* There would then follow a couple of "dodgy days," several full trays of Embassy No.6 cigarettes, a tentative air about our home and a little less fun until the dial would once again be reset. Flowers from my father, our family's "calmer-in-chief," often did the trick!

That night in February 1970 tested our family's bond. My baby sister, Joanne, was born with a disabling spina bifida.

As the dust slowly settled my father made adjustments, leaving the comfort of working for a well-renowned electrical company to start his own business, freeing up time for the many demands of my sister's healthcare appointments. My mother worked on a local farm a couple of nights a week to bring extra money into the home. We began to attend several events each year in our county of Lancashire, enabling families of disabled children to connect and support each other. I vividly recall the dank, minimalist buildings, often the archetypal English village hall, playing venue for local support groups, the musty-smelling curtains atop a stage overlooking heavily-scratched hardwood floors crying out for some TLC due to the countless times metal chairs and tables had been dragged across them. In contrast, it was impossible not to feel the warmth and commitment to community on display during those gatherings. We soon realized that we weren't alone—ours was no solitary plight.

My father once told me that he and my mother had paid close to a thousand visits to the hospital, to doctors, and to physiotherapists during those early years of my sister's life. I attended a few of those physiotherapy sessions and to this day can clearly remember Joanne's therapist, Mrs. Calland, and her wonderful care. There is no doubt that those experiences during the formative years of my life led to my eventual choice of profession.

The British call it *physiotherapy*—a distinct gentleness to how that word seems to roll off the tongue—a soft and subtle suggestion of care. The Americans call it *physical therapy* or "P.T."—a harsher sounding moniker, implying a more direct physicality in its therapeutic approach to healing. Indeed, several of my U.S. patients claim that "P.T.," in fact, stands for "pain and torture"—administered by their very own "physical terrorist!" I guess one could say that I have, in effect, been "physically terrorizing" an injured population for the vast majority of my adult life.

2

How I Became United!

The village of Hesketh Bank lies in North West England on the Irish Sea estuary of the River Ribble, nestled between Southport to the southwest and Preston to the northeast. Both towns were targets for Hitler's bombs during World War II. The remains of an old air raid shelter from that era was situated in a field just down the street from our family home.

During the 60s and 70s, growing up in rural Lancashire's green belt "salad bowl," my friends and I would run for hours through farmers' fields, swam in rivers, and climbed trees. An old riverside church kept us fascinated with its gravestones, some of which went back several centuries. And, of course, young imaginations simply ran riot, playing in those archaic bomb shelters.

Knocks on doors frequently occurred and pots of tea were brewed, fueling lengthy neighborly chats among families. Any short walk to the store to restock my mother's "fag supply" took an age, as I would always be stopped en route by inquisitive neighbors rubbing my head, wiggling my ear lobe, or springing forth from their homes to exclaim "How's your mum doing, eh son?" or "By 'eckers, you aren't 'alf shooting up there, lad!"

A couple of miles to the south of Hesketh Bank lay the neighboring village of Tarleton, also renowned for its rich soil quality, vast mosslands, and a major hub of all things market gardening. Greenhouse after greenhouse situated closely beside canal way and river. Tarleton seemed a million miles away; the sanctity of Hesketh Bank was all I knew as a young lad. Despite all of the wonderful, adventurous childhood distractions available, it wasn't long before my existence began to center around one thing: "footy."

I loved having a football at my feet. Whenever we visited my Uncle Jack's house, I would be out in his yard slamming free kick after free kick, penalty after penalty against his wooden garage doors. I can still see the twisted slats of paneling. My uncle must have cringed each time his nephew came around. I was relentless, practicing "keepy-uppy" with both feet and my head. I was addicted to football.

At the age of nine, I attended summer school camps based at Tarleton's secondary school. We began to arrange home and away matches—"down at Tarleton" and then "home at Hecky Bank." These games soon started to become increasingly competitive. We became excited by any new skills or moves. It was a camaraderie borne out of a unified love of the game of football. A line of bikes would trail between villages—our mode of transport to and from games—with some of us giving "crossys" (crossbar rides) to any of our mates who didn't have bikes. The unpredictable English weather would never faze us, as we returned home on many an evening covered from head to toe in mud, having slogged it out until dusk.

We quickly began to idolize the football heroes of the era, using their names and adopting their ways and moves. Football cards, stickers, and collectable coins from petrol stations became hobbies we obsessed over, further aligning ourselves with players and teams. School breaks and lunches provided valuable time for "swapsies" in our haste to complete our collections. I would lie in bed gazing through my own collections, imagining how one day I too might become a famous footballer with long hair!

Even though England had failed to qualify for the 1974 World Cup, most of us still took turns arguing over who-would-be-who from the England team of the time.

"I'm Kevin Keegan."

"No way, I bagsied Keegan first!"

"You can be Rodney Marsh or Colin Bell."

"Fuck off! I'm not being a City player!"

"What about Billy Bremner then?"

"You daft twat! He's Scottish!"

"Yeah well so's Lorimer, but I'm still going to be him!"

The 1974 World Cup was the first major tournament that I really remember. My devastation at England not qualifying was short-lived as I became captivated by the the bright orange kit and flair of the Dutch, the so-called "total football" players, the likes of which none of us had seen before. I thrilled at the skills of Neeskens and was mesmerized by the Dutch captain, Johan Cruyff.

And so, for the rest of that summer of 1974, I became Cruyff.

It was around that same period that I began—whenever I was allowed to stay up—to watch highlights of English games with my father on the BBC's flagship show "Match of the Day," as well as "Football Focus" and "On the Ball," two shows that were broadcast on Saturdays at lunchtime, at a much more suitable hour for a young lad. I loved sitting with my dad and listening to his thoughts and opinions on the teams and players of the day.

I didn't follow any particular team that closely and continued bouncing around with regard to my player adulation. After the World Cup, and once the new season started, I immediately forgot Cruyff and I then became Malcolm Macdonald of Newcastle United one week and Kevin Hector of Derby County the next.

I dabbled with the football fashions of the day. My mother bought me an unlicensed nylon yellow Leeds United FC kit from Southport market for my birthday. Goodness knows where it was actually made. Probably just down the road in Chorley! It had been touted as the trendiest kit of the day by the market stall owner, with Leeds United being the high-flyers of the day. My new kit was a tight fit and did not feature the official team crest, nor did it have any of the official trimmings—even the collar was nothing like the one on the official shirt. I did, however, have a pair of official sock tags that only Leeds United had branded. My tags had "Lorimer 7" on them. Each time I wore them, I imagined that, just like the Leeds striker, Peter Lorimer, I too had "the hardest shot in football." But I soon realized that they made the knockoff kit look even more knockoff as I stuck out like a sore thumb. It was like wearing an expensive Rolex with a pair of pajamas! I appreciated my folks' effort of course—and my completely unofficial shirt inadvertently fired me up each time I wore it in those village rivalries—with the inevitable piss taking regarding my insipid yellow attire rousing my response on the pitch. Needless to say, it wasn't long before I fell out of love with Leeds United FC.

Along with Leeds United, the other teams hovering at the top of the English First Division table in 1974 included Derby County, Liverpool, Ipswich Town, Everton, Stoke City, and Queens Park Rangers (QPR). Any time I would see a terrific goal on TV at the weekend, I was *that* player for the following week. When QPR's Stan Bowles was flavor of the minute, declaring his name loudly after scoring appeared to increase my popularity.

During some of our evening games that summer, a "strange man" started to show up, watching us as we engaged in our "battle of the villages." My mother, true to form, had her antenna up, especially after

I told her how he would smile at any of the lads who went to retrieve the ball near to where he stood. Then, one evening, we were all stopped in our tracks as the man's loud hand clap and whistle beckoned us toward him—in the nick of time, I'd say, before my mother had got her hands on him.

That was the start of Hesketh Bank Boys Football Club. The man in question was Phil Wigton, a local electrician and football fan. He was soon to be accompanied by another local "sparky," Joe Slattery. The two tough taskmasters kept us off the streets and taught us the value of a strong team bond. From the very start, we were all on a mission. We planned local raffles, jumble sales, sponsored swims, walks, and cycle rides to raise enough money to run a grassroots football club: a few soccer balls, a football kit, training bibs, goalposts, nets, and the required equipment to chalk a line and stick a corner flag in the relevant corner of the footy pitch. Eventually we had enough funds to enable several local tradesmen—mostly fathers of the lads in our team—to build some changing rooms. No more discreet standing behind the strategically placed passenger door of a rusted old van or car to change into our kit. Having two electricians as our management team meant two vans with just about enough space inside them to "jam in" our team for away matches. As the exciting project began to gather momentum, several fathers and other family members became involved. The increased variety of transport options to away games not only swelled our support for each match, it also reduced prematch stiffness upon arrival at our opponents' ground. No more sitting on rolls of electrical cable or toolboxes. After only two years, we began to win league titles and cups, drawing attention from all corners of the North West. Our players began to represent district league teams and several professional team scouts began to show up to our games. Indeed, one of our players, Ian Ormondroyd, eventually went on to star for Aston Villa, having made his long journey from a muddied field in Hesketh Bank all the way to the English Premier League.

Up the road from us was the Hesketh Bank Association Football Club (the men's league side which had been around since the early 1920s) and, in 1995, more than twenty years after that first night when a bunch of local youngsters formed a village football collective, the two village teams combined. The football club still runs teams from under-7's through to the full senior first team squad. A ready made academy of young talent appears to have risen from those humble beginnings back in the early seventies. Whenever I return to Lancashire to visit friends, I always try to make time for an early morning stroll over to a small field in a corner of Hesketh Bank village. As I step onto the pitch, birds scatter from the hedgerow and, more often than not, rain drops fall upon my now graying hair. As I wipe the moisture from my brow, I take myself back to a wonderful time in my life as I picture a group of young lads playing the game they love.

As eight-year-old kids, we had no real concept of geography when it came to supporting teams. It was only as we spent more time around lads from other villages in Lancashire that we realized that a kid from the north couldn't possibly like a player from a London team. Arsenal, QPR or any other "southern pansy" team suddenly became "Cockney twats" in much the same way I am sure that the southerners considered anywhere north of London to be "caveman country" full of "northern bastards."

So, eventually, it was to be a "northern bastard" team for me. The fickleness of youth kept me bouncing from one successful team to the next. I couldn't seem to nail my colors to any particular mast—until, that is, the first week of April 1975. At the age of ten, I became completely entranced by the intense media build up for a *Second Division* game.

In the penultimate game of the previous season, Manchester United legend Dennis Law—"the King" of Old Trafford—back on his old turf but now playing for crosstown rivals Manchester City, scored one of the most memorable goals in English football history—a backheel that essentially sent Manchester United down to League Division Two for the first time since the late 1930s. In an incredible twist of fate, that famous goal proved to be Law's final touch in English football. The fact that a Birmingham City victory over Norwich City on the same day had already relegated Manchester United is often forgotten, or simply ignored, as "the Law goal" still reverberates with many of United's older supporters. Since I had no clue about any of this football history at the time, I didn't fully absorb the weight of the situation—one of the most famous clubs in the world was being sent down to the second division. Following the shock relegation, and as predicted by all Manchester United supporters, the team bounced back in style the following season, quickly climbing to the summit of Division Two.

My affections grew swiftly as I saw snippets of this youthful and exciting team surging magnificently back towards the limelight. With the season winding its way toward an exciting finish, Manchester United were to play Southampton at The Dell on April 5, 1975. Victory that day would return the Red Devils back to Division One.

Our next door neighbor, "Curly Scouse Stan," the fat butcher, was an avid Everton FC fan who always seemed to reek of pork and sage sausage.

He had a wicked perm and a habit of ruffling my own curly locks with his porky right hand before pointing a finger firmly in my direction, often declaring: "Gary, son, there's only one footy team to support, and that's the Toffees!" I knew who "The Toffees" were, of course, having seen "The Toffee Lady" on television prior to any Everton highlights, walking pitch side and throwing candy into the crowd before home matches. That was cool! Stan was cool! Despite his Everton allegiance and those annoying meaty head rubs, Stan totally threw me a "curve ball" when one day he actually admitted that "there really is only one great player that matters, Gary son. And that's George Best!"

But George Best was a Manchester United player!

As soon as my father came home from work that evening, I pestered him to tell me more about George Best. I had seen snippets on TV, but had never really connected. He told me all about the "holy trinity" of George Best, Dennis Law, and Bobby Charlton. I had heard about these players, but had always aligned myself with the contemporary flair of players such as Stan Bowles and Rodney Marsh. Manchester United had been viewed by all my mates as an insignificant team; a team in decline as they languished a division below the top flight. Youngsters more often than not attach to the excitement of success, not failure, right?

That night, I went to bed feeling even more confused: confused that such an apparent genius had played his last game for Manchester United and yet he was only twenty-six; confused that my next door neighbor and "Evertonian Toffee" loved him. Confused that Best, according to my father, had left Manchester United on New Year's Day 1974 after a final game against QPR which Manchester United lost 3-0. At a time when the team needed him, Best had gone missing. I couldn't get my young head around that, particularly having heard how brilliant he was from my dad and from "Curly Stan." Nonetheless, of course, the very next day in the school playground, I became George Best!

Manchester United's game against Southampton that first week of April 1975 was the first time I had felt truly attached to the build up to a game—the importance, the relevance, that it really mattered: that the result meant *everything*!

My father himself had never really tied his colors to any soccer mast, but I could tell that he had a soft spot for Manchester United. Any chance that he got that week he would sit me down and tell me more and more stories; stories that fueled my excitement for the big game that Saturday— a Second Division game that was occupying most of the sports pages.

He told me about the 1958 Munich air disaster claiming the lives of eight United players; about Sir Matt Busby's "Babes" and Duncan Edwards; more about Best, Law and Charlton and United's famous European Cup victory in 1968. As my father continued, something began to resonate. I could see the twinkle in his eye. I had never really talked with my father so intensely before, never really connected so strongly.

Saturday rolled around, and with it, the Big Match! I was glued to the radio that afternoon imagining every kick. Manchester United's midfield maestro, Lou Macari, scored a goal midway through the second half, which was enough to send Manchester United back to Division One. As the final whistle blew, I remember dancing for joy with my father. I had never seen him so animated! And in that instant, Manchester United became "my" team—"our" team! Just like that, our bond over the Red Devils from Old Trafford was solidified.

They say that you don't choose a team—that a team chooses you. Well, Manchester United had chosen me! From that day forward, the result of *every* Manchester United game became of vital importance.

United were back!

We were back.

Back in Division One!

It felt like the happiest day of my young life.

With four jackets and "Wiggy's" new leather football, around twenty of us played until the sun sank low that evening. I imagined with every pass, every touch, that I was in that Manchester United side playing at The Dell. No more Peter Lorimer or Malcolm McDonald; no more Stan Bowles or Rodney Marsh. From now on, it was only Manchester United: Lou Macari, Gerry Daly, Sammy McIlroy—and especially their star striker, Stuart "fist-pump" Pearson.

3

We're the famous Man Utd and We're Going to Wembley!

Manchester United began the following season in Division One, which meant I could regularly watch highlights of their games on BBC's "Match of the Day" and ITV's Sunday afternoon show, "The Kick Off Match." There were no live games on TV until the month of May and the massive football season finale—*the FA Cup final.*

In May 1977, Manchester United made it all the way to the final and were due to play their biggest rival—the mighty Liverpool, the team that left pretty much every other team in their wake. Liverpool FC had won three of the last five English First Division titles. Manchester United had not won a league title since the 1966–67 season and were clearly underdogs for the cup final. By now, I was well aware that a Manchester United fan's greatest nemesis, even more so than Manchester City, was Liverpool FC. *They* were the benchmark for all of English football and rammed *their* so-called "beautiful football" down our throats. I was sick of *them* winning—winning *everything.*

Despite Liverpool's dominance in all competitions, I was happy that Manchester United had "chosen" me. I felt a definite edge about how United played, how they wore the shirt. Liverpool hadn't even come close to luring me in. I didn't connect at all with their gangling defenders—not to mention the fact that most of them sported moustaches and seemed to resemble science teachers more than football players. My dad said that "footballers shouldn't have them bloody awful moustaches." How could I disagree with that? There was just something too "old man generation" about Liverpool for my liking. Manchester United was an exciting work in progress, the thrill of the "red tide" rising, and any chance "we" could topple the mighty 'Pool, so dominant for so long, became confirmation of "our own" belonging at the top of English football. It was boy wonder stuff to a young lad and I aligned myself with the next generation of Red Devils ready to defy the odds.

My uncle Jack bought me the most brilliant present in the history of presents for my birthday that year—my first ever Manchester United kit— and this time it was authentic; the red of an official Manchester United home shirt complete with an Admiral insignia and proper collar. There were no player names or numbers on the back of the shirts in those days; just to be able to wear the shirt of "your team" was enough.

In order to help United win, I laid my new United shirt flat on the floor, not a crease to be seen, extending out from the base of the television, in stark contrast to the cream shagpile carpet on which it lay. My United socks dangled from the corners of my parents' new pride and joy, a fake wood media center, all shine and short spindly legs complete with a side shelf—the perfect platform on which to drape my United shorts, after removing my mother's Jack Jones records from their usual resting place.

From late morning on, I lay prone, chin resting in my hands, transfixed on the day's events, flicking between the BBC and ITV for the best prematch coverage. The BBC's "Cup Final Grandstand" started around 11:30 a.m., beating ITV to the punch by a full half hour. After a brief glimpse of what the BBC had to offer, ITV's flagship "World of Sport" was where our Cup Final family viewing for the day began. Hosted by the supremely confident and brilliantly named Dickie Davies, the five-hour show landed full throttle, with a "reverse slam" right into our living room. Davies was all 70s flowing dark hair and moustache (another bloody moustache; he must have been a Liverpool fan!), notes in hand as he hunched forward fronting the back drop of row after row of typists, creating the impression that the ITV studio was the epicenter of the sporting world. Dickie never dallied in his smooth and clinical delivery and within minutes of his introduction he implored us to stay tuned for one of "World of Sports" regular features: *wrestling*—a turbulent tussle to get the prematch adrenaline pumping.

Wrestling did absolutely nothing for me. My Uncle Jack, however, loved it and his wrestling idol was none other than Mick McManus, "the man they love to hate." Jack would come over to our house most Saturdays after completing his early-morning milk round in Southport and sit watching his favorite sport. FA Cup Final Saturday was no different, except for the fact that he now had a special edition wrestling match in which to indulge.

My uncle was a curious bloke. At an early age, he had been clobbered on the back of his right shoulder by a cricket ball. This had apparently stunted his growth. He stood barely five feet tall with a most distinctive hunchback appearance. My mother would always provide an extra cushion for her older brother to give him a decent view of the TV screen.

"Ladies aaaand Gentlemen! We have a special bill for you on this Cup Final day. First up we have Mick McManus of New Cross, London vs Steve Grey from Peckham, London. We are packed to capacity here at Cliffs Pavilion in Westcliff-on-Sea hoping against hope that Steve Grey the lightweight can bring a surprise against the two stone heavier McManus, the Middleweight Champion of Europe. One fall, one submission or a knockout to decide the winner." As the MC made his introductory announcement, my Mother would turn the volume up to a piercing level, due to Uncle Jack's deafness in his right ear. Drawing hard on his cigarette, Jack would wave his nicotine-stained fingers at the television as he cheered on his idol.

"A first public warning to McManus"

"Boo!" screamed Jack. "Go on Mick son, give it to him!"

"Oh dear, Steve Grey's looking a little bit worse for wear after that reverse posting"

It was a foreign language to me: sleepers; half nelsons, reverse side headlocks, rollers, jabs, reverse double knee holds . . . all I wanted to watch was United and Liverpool in the Cup Final, and yet here I was watching two grown men in tight trunks prancing around a ring, one of them looking just like my Uncle Jack with his receding jet black hair doused in Brylcreem.

"Second and final public warning to Mick McManus!"

My uncle Jack went bonkers. "Yer bloody blind, referee! Haven't got a bloody clue!"

I temporarily repositioned myself further away from the television. A strategic maneuver as I was then out of the firing line of my Uncle spitting the remnants of his favorite tongue and lettuce "butties" all over our lounge floor as he continued his barrage of profanities. Our Golden Labrador dog, Bobby, loved it when Uncle Jack came over.

Then the moment. Thank goodness!

"A slam, reverse double knee hold from McManus on Grey!"

To me it looked more like greasy McManus had slammed his opponent to the canvas and sat his sweaty blue trunks right on Grey's face. McManus continued smiling into the camera as those same blue trunks, ass cheeks and all, nestled against Steve Grey's nose!

"Ladies aaand gentleman ... round three ... the one fall required for victory to Mick McManus!"

Yes! Finally!

"Mum! Can we switch it back over to the BBC now, please?"

"Go on then, son."

My prayers were answered and I jumped right up and switched channels—not before getting a manky old piece of tongue meat stuck to my left elbow.

It just so happened that in 1977, "BBC Cup Final Grandstand" was airing the very last "It's a Knockout" FA Cup Final special. Hugely popular with the British public, "It's a Knockout" would feature teams representing a town or city competing tasks in absurd games, generally dressed in large foam rubber suits, kind of a surreal school sports day for adults. You would have one team carrying buckets of water over greasy poles or rolling logs while the opposing team squirting water cannons or throwing custard pies at them.

"Oh I bloody love this! Give us a ciggie our Jack, will ya?" My mother appeared to be very happy with our return to BBC.

"It's a Knockout" host, Stuart Hall, would be in fits of laughter as competitors often succumbed to a despairing fall, legs akimbo, suffering the humiliation of several stewards having to right the costume surrounded by a nation of onlookers. There was even a "laugh-o-meter"—so very British—included to measure the intensity of Hall's outbursts of hilarity during the show.

The ITV/BBC battle continued on, as it was all about finding out which channel was going to feature Manchester United on the team bus coverage of the two vehicles transporting Liverpool and Manchester United toward Wembley Stadium.

"ITV are on United's bus, Gary. Lets switch back over again, eh." My father had bought both the *TV Times* and *Radio Times* special editions to ensure that we maximized our FA Cup Final viewing potential, particularly after we had got the wrestling out of the way. Indeed, by this time Uncle Jack's eyes were already beginning to glaze over. He had been up since 2:00 a.m. and his early rise was beginning to take its toll. Jack always fell asleep at our house—but not until the wrestling was over.

The Manchester United team bus came into view. I watched closely as fans ran alongside, cheering their heroes on, the vehicle slowing considerably as the crowds grew larger as it wound its way toward

Wembley Stadium. The pavements were a sea of red and white and black.

An ITV commentator had been placed on board the United bus and, with regular prompts from Dickie back in the studio, would immediately crouch down next to a player and shove a microphone in his face.

"So, are you ready for the final then?"

I mean come on, really? What a bloody daft question?

"No! I'm not ready at all. In fact why on earth am I sat here on this bus?"

"Do you think you can beat Liverpool today?"

Seriously?

"Err ... no! Liverpool are way better than us. We don't stand a chance. May as well turn the bus around and go home, actually."

Commentator to star striker: "Do you think you can score today?"

Are you kidding me?

"No! I wont even be trying to score. To be honest with you, I'm hoping that the manager picks me to play in goal today!"

Despite the idiotic questions, I was able to listen to my heroes talk and pretend that I was on the actual Manchester United team bus traveling to a Wembley FA Cup Final. What's not to like about that?

After the team bus had arrived at Wembley, we switched back over to the BBC to watch the players "inspect the pitch" prior to kick-off.

What were they going to do if it wasn't up to scratch? Call the game off?

Smartly dressed in coordinated team suits, a chosen few were pulled aside for more prematch thoughts and insight.

As 3:00 p.m.—and kick-off time—approached, the tension and expectation level rose to new heights as we all listened to "Abide With Me"—that beautiful hymn synonymous with the FA Cup final—over the Wembley Stadium PA system, rousing the crowd of over 100,000.

The teams congregated in the tunnel.

I pounded our shagpile carpet with uncontrollable excitement.

Then, the massive roar, as the two managers, Bob Paisley and Tommy Docherty, walked out onto the hallowed turf, leading their troops into battle surrounded by a cascade of color and a wall of sound. The obligatory shot of royalty, as Edward, the Duke of Kent meandered down from the Royal Box, his entourage close at hand. This prompted my mother's outburst: "Look at him! What an ugly bugger! He looks a right pillock to me!"

My mother was rather anti-establishment to say the least.

As the Royal Artillery band, decked out resplendently and at least two hundred strong, struck their first notes, some bloke on a dodgy public address system microphone rattled his tonsils to "God Save the Queen." We all watched in silence, as if it was our duty—yet I could sense that none of us was really that bothered. My father was quite possibly the exception, puffing his chest out proudly at the national anthem. I banged the floor again in anticipation, shouting "C'mon United!"

My dad flicked the channel over in another "let's just check ITV" moment to get a quick look at their commentary team of Brian Moore and Jack Charlton. And right on cue, Moore commented "… and there in the Royal Box, her Royal Highness, Katherine, the Duchess of Kent, who will be presenting the cup, in a beautiful yellow suit. And that is quite a tassel on her hat there Jack." Total on air silence—with Jack Charlton loud and clear in his "couldn't give a flying fuck" total lack of response! *Brilliant!*

"Oh my God put it back on BBC, Jimmy! Look at her! For goodness sake. What does she know about bloody football? We all know how she ended up with that ugly bugger now don't we?" My mother had once again made her thoughts quite clear. She then settled in, lit a fag, crossed her legs, tilted her head back, forcibly exhaling smoke and shouted "Come on United!" We had chosen our channel. Well—my mother had!

The referee checked with both goalkeepers, signalled for the start of the game and blew his whistle. We were off! *Game on!*

The first half flew by. It was a close affair. I kicked every ball and ran every yard with my beloved team. United's Brian Greenhoff was handling Liverpool's star man, Kevin Keegan, pretty well. Our wingers, Steve Coppell and Gordon Hill, were struggling to make an impact, and, of course, I was waiting for my hero, Stuart Pearson, to make his presence felt. As the referee blew his whistle signaling half time and a 0-0 scoreline, the players meandered off the pitch heading towards the Wembley tunnel. They had some maneuvering to do though as the Royal Artillery Band was already back out and stepping onto the turf to the right of the Liverpool goalmouth, keen to reclaim the spotlight. The rather chaotic scene made me smile. The musicians were not hanging around, not backing down, making sure that they grabbed every second of their allotted time in the limelight. It was a magnificent culture clash. Tuba's, trombones and big bass drums embedded among a compact bevy of ant-like marching uniformed servicemen confronting bandy-legged footballers. In the foreground, a commentator's voice was barely audible above the din. My smile tuned into laughter as I remained prostrate on the floor, inches from the television screen. I was just so bloody ecstatic, to be honest; United in an FA Cup Final again and holding the mighty Liverpool. My father stood up and gently kicked my thigh as he walked past me on his way to the kitchen to make us all a half-time cuppa.

"Hey, we'll get 'em second half, son, don't you worry about that!"

"Too right, dad! We're well in it," I replied, looking up at my father with a huge smile on my face. Uncle Jack on the other hand was now totally out of it, his snores echoing around the living room.

Manchester United began the second half well. "Come on you Reds," the loud and enthusiastic encouragement from United supporters rang out as goalkeeper Alex Stepney launched a long kick up field. After a short sequence of head tennis, Jimmy Greenhoff's forward header found Pearson, who beat the Liverpool defenders for pace and lashed a drive beneath the flailing Ray Clemence. We got to witness a "Pearson Pump" goal celebration as United took the lead early in the second half. I jumped to my feet and defiantly stood, mimicking my hero's gladiatorial stance. "My" United were a goal up against the all-conquering Liverpool.

The United supporters in Wembley Stadium rang out "We shall not, we shall not be moved." But then disaster struck. A mere two minutes after United's opener, a moment of pure genius. Commentator John Motson with the call: "there's a saying in football, that Liverpool are at their most dangerous when they are behind. Well that remains to be seen." The very next words from his mouth: "Jones. Case. Good turn. Oh yesss! A *brilliant* goal by Jimmy Case!" 1-1 and it was the Liverpool fans turn to announce loudly that they "shall not be moved!" Surely, someone was going to have to be moved!

The Red Devil's' fans immediately countered, "United! United! United!" Three minutes later, commentator Motson once more: "On by Macari. Smith slipped slightly ... Jimmy Greenhoff! United are back in front!" I jumped to my feet, ran and ran, arms aloft as the television reverberated to the roar of the United fans celebrations! My parents went nuts. Bobby ran for cover, opting for a crazy barking session by the front door, and Jack produced a seizure like thrust of his head, before letting out a volley of enormous throttling snores, seemingly unmoved by our jubilant celebrations. *Two grown men in tight trunks versus United taking the lead against their greatest rivals, Liverpool, in the FA Cup Final at Wembley — what planet was my Uncle Jack on?*

Manchester United had produced a moment of pure joy in our family home! My father and I eventually regrouped, right in front of the television screen, waiting for the slow motion replay. The shot from Lou Macari did indeed take a massive, king of all deflections off Jimmy Greenhoff's chest.

"Bloody hell! That could easily have landed on Wembley's roof, Gary" my Dad exclaimed.

"It didn't though, did it Dad!" I replied, as we both observed the bizarre trajectory of the Scotsman's shot.

"Get in thereeee!" I yelled again.

"Bloody hell you two, get out of the way. I can't see a bloody thing!" exclaimed my mother, calling for order as the referee came into view, poised to restart the match.

There then followed a very very long thirty-five minutes or so, as we all willed our team to hold on. As the final whistle approached with United still leading 2-1, John Motson one final time: "Agonizing wait for United fans this . . . and there it is! Manchester United have won the FA Cup!"

I could not believe it! United had won! "We" had won the cup!

As the United players began to organize themselves into a somewhat orderly line ready to move forward and climb the thirty-nine steps that lead to the Royal Box, I stood inches from the television, transfixed on the screen. It seemed like an age as I waited for the glorious moment when our captain, Martin Buchan, would lift the FA Cup trophy. I watched the close-ups of my idols receiving handshake after handshake, scarves around necks, United caps thrust onto their heads as they were mobbed by the lucky few who stood lining those famous stairs. I witnessed several meaty head rubs as our victorious players fought their way through to the top. We then watched as the Duchess of Kent struggled, making somewhat of a cock-up out of trying to lift the trophy by its base, in her attempt to hand it over to a poised and ready Martin Buchan. My mother couldn't help herself: "Oh God, Jimmy. Look at her. That woman again! She is bloody useless. Look! She can't even lift the bloody cup up right. Honestly! What is she doing there?"

And then, after what seemed an age, Buchan grasped both handles and raised the FA Cup high above his head. I stood arms aloft, victorious. Nothing had felt better in my young life than that very moment!

We had beaten Liverpool! We had won the Cup!

And my Uncle Jack was still asleep!

Later that night, the BBC aired an FA Cup final highlights show and my father let me stay up with him to watch United beat the mighty

Liverpool all over again. What made the victory even more special was the fact that United had prevented Liverpool from achieving something that no team in England had so far accomplished: "The Treble," comprising the First Division League title, the FA Cup, and the European Cup.

My 1977 FA Cup final experience had been such sweet redemption for the previous year's FA Cup final—the first ever time I had watched a live Manchester United match. Southampton from the Second Division, against all the odds, made it to Wembley that year to play Manchester United. Following their promotion in 1975, United had a strong first season back in League Division One, finishing third. For every United fan—and the vast majority of neutral fans, the 1976 FA Cup final was a foregone conclusion. All day long I anticipated United's victory. How many Pearson "fist pumps" would I witness? Which player, socks around his ankles, would don the famous trophy's lid on his head during the postmatch celebrations?

Despite numerous chances and continual pressure from United, the game remained scoreless up until the eighty-third minute. Brian Moore with the commentary: "Channon ... nice touch again ... McCalliog ... oh look at this ... Bobby Stokes ... hit well ... oh, and it's there!! Stokes has put Southampton in the lead!" In one of the biggest shocks in FA Cup final history, Bobby Stokes, the diminutive Southampton striker, scored and Southampton held out to win 1-0 and lift the trophy. It completed the worst week of my young life. A month or so prior, my sister Joanne had developed kidney problems. She was one tough little girl and our family all figured that her resilience would move her past her latest medical challenge. Unfortunately, it was not to be the case this time around. In the end, it all just became too much for such a small and fragile body. And so, suddenly, on April 27, 1976, Joanne quietly passed away.

4

School of Hard Knocks

As soon as the school bell rang for lunch, we would make a mad dash for the playground, immediately using our British sense of order to form a line. Two captains were duly elected for a swift team selection process with alternate picks until the line whittled down to the rather uncoordinated "leftovers." We would play our games with a tennis ball, since footballs had been banned after too many broken windows. Playing with a tennis ball certainly helped to hone our skills as we dribbled past the opposing team and around girls playing hopscotch. Football continued to hold its grip over us.

Toward the end of our primary school years, however, other temptations arose. After exclusion from all things that boys wanted to play—"Who's playing footy? No girls allowed!"—the opposite sex suddenly, overnight it seemed, became very appealing. A little chunk of our playtime spent in the company of girls became a necessity. The allure of a swift session of "spin the bottle," participation in a rather wet and messy snog as "the postman knocked," or stopping mid-game to listen to Alison Knowles tell me that Linda Hutton wanted to French kiss me behind the bike sheds after school, had become a very exciting part of the equation. Football remained front and center—but only just at times. Anthony Whiteman, alias "Tiger"—a right back in the making, ferocious in the tackle—often went AWOL in the middle of a game, tempted into the "ditch den" behind the swings the moment Karen Sidebottom came into view on her way home from high school. Trading a full bag of fizz bombs for a peep at her, by all accounts, huge knockers, we all had to admit did seem a pretty good deal. As Tiger's teammates, we learned to accept his frequent absences knowing that he would describe the whole juicy experience as soon as Ms. Sidebottom had left for home.

In high school, we progressed from a tennis ball to a "flatty" (an old, flat ball usually stolen from someone's older brother). Playground matches became more serious; skills more appreciated. School blazers were flung into a pile and school ties were wrapped around foreheads and wrists for team recognition. I was fortunate enough to be selected to play for Tarleton High, initially on the right wing and eventually as center forward.

In my penultimate year at high school in 1979, Manchester United, almost won the FA Cup final again after an incredible late comeback from 2-0 down to tie the game at 2-2, only to see Arsenal respond immediately with a late winning goal. I remember watching the match at a friend's house in a village close to Southport. Along with the despair of defeat, I also experienced new emotions, as my friend's rather drunk father returned home, immediately removed his trouser belt and, for no apparent reason, beat seven bells out of my friend's twin brother in front of our eyes. I began to understand why those same twins fought each other on a regular basis in our high school playground.

In the final year at Tarleton High, several of our playground renegades, including one of the twins, had progressed through the ranks of those early village football rivalries to form the bulk of the high school football team. We had formed our own "Class of '79" and reached the West Lancashire Schools District final. Our goalkeeper, "Wiggy," had played a blinder in the semi-final as we hung on to win against the tournament favorites, West Bank—no connection to the Israeli-held territory, the location of the school being in Skelmersdale near Liverpool. We had overturned a local footballing giant!

Around this time, I had become superstitious about my father coming to watch me play, as my game always seemed to suffer when he was on the sidelines. When it came to the final, of course, I had to back down. It was a huge event—our school never having gone so far before in the competition. The game was played at Burscough FC. It was a non-league stadium, but it was an actual football stadium with stands, terraces, a players' tunnel, dugouts for the managers, and floodlights; the whole shebang! With my mother and father in the crowd, true to form I had my usual "parents are watching" stinker of a game, but at least managed to win our team a penalty. According to my father, I was tackled "well outside the box" and "the ref must have been blind." My father has always been an unashamedly honest man. I recall having my legs taken from under me and immediately doing all I could to convince the referee that the foul had occurred *inside* the penalty box. The penalty was dispatched and we went on to score a second goal to become the West Lancashire District High School Champions. After the game, our team emerged from the ground to rapturous applause from parents and fans alike and we were ushered into the rather archaic, pale green mini bus that the school had hired, ready to be driven back to base by our PE teacher and football coach Mr. Topple. Topple ushered all on board and checked one last time that everyone was present and correct.

"Sir!" our solid, reliable center-half, Kevin "Kevvo" Young, yelled as his name was called last on the roll call. Topple continued to display his rigid classroom routine in the tight confines of the "rent a wreck" mini bus, instructing everyone to settle down—not easy after we had just won the cup! Topple checked his mirrors, honked the horn and drove us out of the ground to cheers from the gathered throng. Only then did he wind down the driver's side window and fist pump his right arm into the early evening sky!

"Yessssss! Get in thereeeeeeee!"

I don't think I had ever seen the man so emotional before. Was this really our normally strict, disciplinarian of a teacher?

"Well done, lads," he added, shoulders back as he drove out of the ground and on to the A59.

"Tarleton! Tarleton! Tarleton! Tarleton!" sang thirteen lads, arms aloft as we meandered through Burscough town center. A couple of miles or so down the road our elated driver pulled into a quiet country lane. Silence fell inside the bus. What the ... ?

"Hey, Wiggy, have a look under that back seat will you, son, behind those kit bags," he said to our goalkeeper, glancing at him through the driving mirror.

"Bloody hell, Mr. Topple! Nice one!"

"Yeaaaaaaaaaahhhh!" our team's chorus almost shattering the steamed-up windows surrounding us.

"Hey, don't be getting me in trouble now, lads. Let's keep this our little secret, eh? You've made me and the school proud out there tonight. All of you did! So, have a drink on me!"

Cans of Skol lager were eagerly distributed among the sixteen-year-old lads. We all drank together for the first time in our lives in celebration, Wiggy playing barman, still wearing his lucky green and very muddy goalkeeper shirt, which he had vowed not to take off until he got home.

My wonderful football journey continued, side by side with my mates, holding everything together amid the growing confusion of adolescence. At sixteen I left high school with an outside sniff at grammar school. Having obtained the minimum grades required, I wasn't that keen on going, but my mother encouraged me: "Just give it a go, Gary, just so's you won't regret it later." Prophetic words, most likely a reflection of her own adolescent past, making sure her son didn't miss out on a potential opportunity.

As the grammar school interview came to a close, I vividly remember one final question from the masters: "Do you prefer to play rugby or football, young man?" My answer was unequivocal. My chance of acceptance into the higher echelons of British academia immediately shot down the moment I answered, "Why, football of course, sir!"

In late spring 1980, Liverpool won yet another English First Division title. Manchester United finished a tantalizingly close second. Would I *ever* see "my" United win the league?

There was no official graduation from high school or prom night in those days; we simply had a party at Debbie Dunn's house. Debbie's parents were away for the weekend and they had a superb record player! A free and seemingly endless supply of her dad's homebrew complete with its heady sediment added to the allure. I took my brand new, limited edition, ten-inch vinyl of Orchestral Manoeuvres in the Dark's "Messages," which eventually provided a reprieve from the incessant repetition of "Funkytown" by Lipps Inc. Linda Hutton loved Orchestral Manoeuvres in the Dark, which, in turn, meant that I was intimately rewarded in the bathroom. Linda Hutton, blonde and beautiful, was certainly not backward at coming forward: a farmer's daughter who kissed like an angel and submitted without hesitation to my advances. I couldn't wait for Orchestral Manoeuvres in the Dark to release their follow up to "Messages"—hopefully with an extended twelve-inch version—and for my next rendezvous with Linda Hutton.

And so, off I went to WR Tuson sixth form college near Preston, and my first steps on a pathway to a possible career in physiotherapy. I was selected to play for the college football team and in my second and final year, the 1981–82 football season, the team spent autumn and winter battling through eleven qualifying rounds. After eleven straight wins, we were crowned North West of England regional representatives, reaching the last eight of the British College Football Tournament, a feat that the college had never before even come close to achieving in its history. In the quarter final match-up, we had been drawn against the Midlands representatives. It was a wild, rainy day—"chuckin' it down" as they say in Lancashire—and it made for an atrocious playing surface. I was closely marked by two mammoth, dreadlocked center-halves, complete with "Brummy-Nigerian" accents, screaming Rastafarian chants prior to every bone-crunching tackle they inflicted on me. After one particularly ferocious clatter from behind, the referee blew his whistle and awarded a free kick right on the edge of the Midlands team's penalty area. It was only a few minutes into the match. I had been practicing free kicks from outside the box for weeks and so I immediately demanded the ball, taking my time to secure my desired placement. A flashback to those nights of practice entered my mind. I stepped back and noted the spot, my window of opportunity, to the left hand side of the defenders wall. As the instep of my right foot made contact with the ball, my eyes fixated, watching the trajectory as it flew up and over, bending straight into the top right hand corner of the goal. I could not believe it! Our traveling supporters screamed their approval and I began to run, my teammates in hot pursuit. It felt absolutely incredible. I somehow managed to score two more goals that day, achieving a hat-trick that I will never forget, helping send our team into the semi-final of the British Colleges Cup.

To top it all off, as I climbed onto our rented coach, a most bizarre moment occurred as I received an inviting smile from Haley Thompson, a girl on our sports medicine course. Haley was slowly stroking the empty seat beside her, requesting that I sit next to her for the journey home. Err . . . okay then!

As I sat down, Haley moved in close and gently uttered the words "Gary, I was wondering if you would let me clean your football boots for you later over at my house?"

"Pardon?!"

Haley Thompson, "fit as owt," had singled me out, and was offering to clean my sweaty, soggy, mud-ridden football boots.

I couldn't believe it. Football is ace!

I blamed what transpired later that evening on the energy-sapping quarter final. I had been pummeled for ninety minutes by two Rastas, and now, less than two hours later at Haley's mother's house in Preston, I was receiving a different, albeit far more welcome, kind of pummeling. Haley was certainly not shy. She pinned me down on the sofa, yanked her top off, shook her hair out and unclipped her bra. I gasped in excitement.

Here we go, ready for liftoff, and . . . oh shit!

The sheer sensory overload had proven to be a tad too much for one day. No sooner than it had begun, fun time was over.

Possibly still in awe of my talents—football only, I regretfully sensed—Haley didn't seem to object as I quietly squelched my way to the bathroom, making sure to avoid Mrs. Thompson along the way as I attempted to render myself functional again. I was so intent on righting my all-embarrassing wrong that I completely forgot to retrieve my skimpy, post-premature ejaculation silvery blue Speedos, which now resided next to the family laundry basket. Who knows whatever happened to them? I never asked for them back and Haley never made mention of them. Needless to say, my relationship with Haley was short lived. On reflection, I am pretty sure that Mrs. Thompson may have suggested to her daughter that maybe, just maybe, she could indeed "do a little better" in the boyfriend stakes.

WR Tuson College had never had a more successful football team and I was its free-scoring center forward. Studying was surely never meant to be so much fun. The semi-final arrived and with it another humdinger of a match. 0-3 down at half-time against the Norfolk County representative team, we rallied back to 3-3, forcing extra time. We eventually emerged totally exhausted, yet victorious, 4-3 the final score. I had once again managed to sneak one in, although, this time around, it was my teammate Donny providing the other goals, with a glorious hat-trick. Unfortunately, I had to clean my own boots that night!

Despite a 4-0 defeat in the final to a team from Barry, Wales, the British Colleges Cup run had been the highlight of my young football career. The week leading up to that final, several of us had come down with the flu. We were running on empty and struggled to get through the ninety minutes. Plus, my parents were present, which, of course, meant that I played my usual stinker. I was beginning to understand why superstition and football were so inextricably linked.

Looking back on that final, we were all simply knackered when it eventually came around. We had little understanding of rest and recovery. We all just wanted to play, and by the season's end, the sheer number of games had taken its toll. Premier League players battle with the "club vs. country" conundrum. Most of us in the college team had a "village vs. college" football conundrum! The final round of games for our village Sunday league season took place only two days after the cup final letdown and we wished each other well in our various matches.

I had begun playing for the Tarleton Village adult team at sixteen years old. Any young lad from our local village, yearning to make an impression on the Sunday morning football icons he had grown up idolizing, wanted to be in that team. I was playing up front alongside a village legend, thirty-six-year-old Bill Bagott, aka "Shaggin' Baggy!" The man did damage on the pitch and even more off it! I will never forget one occasion when, with only minutes to go before a crucial battle at the top of the league was about to commence, there was no sign of my strike partner. Suddenly, the door of our changing rooms burst open. "Baggy" stumbled in, "fag" hanging from the corner of his mouth, and nonchalantly took his place among the haze of wintergreen, dropping his trousers to reveal two badly-scraped kneecaps. "Eh up! Sorry I'm late, lads. Debbie Cook needed a good seeing to in Taylor's Wood. Fucked me knees right up, though! Who the hell are we playing today?" My strike partner for the Tarleton Village team was once again ready to play Sunday league football.

I was a teenager hardwired to the "beautiful game," to playing football, and playing Sunday morning football had a vibe all its own. From that first moment, entering the dressing room and placing my kit bag underneath my usual spot on the wooden bench, I could feel the buzz: the suspense before the manager read out the teamsheet, hopefully confirming my place in the starting eleven; a withered, well-traveled old suitcase thrown down onto the middle of the floor, its lid pushed back to reveal the kit. I was always relieved when I managed to grab a pair of shorts that actually fit and a pair of socks with no holes in them. Wrapping electrical tape around my shins to keep my shin guards in place; not too tight, not too slack. The careful process of fastening my football boots, the smell of clean 'dubbin' filling my nose mixing with the aroma of the wintergreen liniment, stimulating my pregame senses. Soaking up the words of encouragement and instructions from management and teammates alike as kick-off time approached. And then, *the moment* — the moment that I pulled that number nine shirt over my head, rolling up the sleeves and making it my shirt. With that shirt came responsibility. Demand. My task was to score goals. To invent. I was a striker and I loved every second of it: learning to rely on my instincts; taking chances; making runs; holding the ball up; bringing teammates into play; trying to stay switched on; trying to outfox the often much older defenders as they attempted to kick seven bells out of me most games. I wore that shirt with pride, with intent, with a readiness to play well and give it my all for the team. Exiting the confines of the dressing room, boot studs clattering on the tarmac, carefully walking towards the grass. That first touch of the ball, controlling it, turning and running forward to the white lined perimeter of the pitch, stepping in, over the touchline, once again entering the field of play.

Sunday mornings: an early coating of frost dissipating and the smell of the fresh grass along with the cold breeze filtering through my hair; the thud of the ball during warm up, each and every time I attempt a shot on goal or a pass to a teammate; stretching, sprinting, receiving pats on back and recognizing our supporters—old man Dick and his aged Labrador, ever present, ever expectant, stood together in their usual spot right on the halfway line.

"Come on Gary, son. Let's be 'avin' one from you today, eh!"

The banter. The fantastic banter: "Ref! What the fuck?"; "Keep it tight, son!"; "Well in there!"; "Get fucking rid"; "Are you fucking blind, ref?" "Stay onside, Gaz!"; "Ref, you are a total fucking wanker!" Community united for the cause. The elation and the pride each time the ball hit the back of the net. Playing football on an early Sunday morning; there was nothing quite like it.

As I stepped out onto the pitch that morning for our final village game of the season, the ground was still muddy after a torrential rainfall overnight. I ran towards my usual starting position in the middle of the center circle. Loud cries echoed around the field. Managers screamed their final instructions. Then, that moment: time stops as I size up the opposition and focus my mind; the referee, whistle to his mouth, surveys his surroundings. He nods and blasts the high-pitched noise that signals the start of another ninety minutes of magnificent, marvelous joy.

It was tough going that particular Sunday, one of those games where I felt tired from the off, heavy legged towards the end of a season. We started well though and certainly had the better of the play against the team from Scarsdale—a bigger bunch of psychotic beer-bellied louts you would have been hard pressed to find anywhere.

Halfway into the second half, my striking partner and I were beginning to get a little joy out of the tiring opposition defenders. "Shaggin Baggy" played the ball into me on the wet surface. I knew in a heartbeat that I could turn the towering center-half grappling with me. After his short tug of my shirt I broke free and began to pull away from him as I bore down on goal with a single-minded determination, full of anticipation, ready to score. As I entered the penalty area for my face off with the goalkeeper, the ball stuck in the soggy marsh. I dug hard to release it, the noise of the modest crowd most evident. Then, in what seemed a flash, the aging defender, set on inflicting payback, clattered me from behind. I immediately heard a "pop" and was overcome with intense pain.

"Penalty, ref!" the chorus rang out as my legs buckled and my face slammed to the muddy turf, my open mouth instantly filled with a mixture of grass and sludge. I reached for my right knee, grabbing it tightly with both hands as I began an instinctive rocking motion back and forth, whimpering in pain.

Fuck the penalty!

My teammates surrounded me: hands on a shoulder, head rubbed several times, a muddled bunch of empathetic well wishes cascading around my ears. I lifted my head briefly and I noticed Baggy attempting a head butt on a Scarsdale defender before my eyes closed once again and my head fell back into the mud.

Just a second—one split second of madness and it had all came to an abrupt end.

No more.

Done!

It was the last game of competitive football that I ever played. I was only eighteen years of age.

5

"Under Starter's Orders
. . . and He's Off"

After graduating from sixth form college, I was given an opportunity to interview at Pinderfields College of Physiotherapy in Wakefield, West Yorkshire. I liked the look of Pinderfields. It had an interesting and unique history borne of the specialized care that the injured from World War II had required. After the establishment of the National Health Service in 1948, the Society of Remedial Gymnasts founded a training center at Pinderfields hospital. Eventually, it became more aligned with physiotherapy. The college had also established a reputation for the training and qualification of many soccer club physiotherapists—an obvious draw for me.

I awaited the outcome of the interview and dreamt of an acceptance letter. A letter finally arrived. I was not accepted. I was heartbroken, but I did not give up. I made it my mission to prove to the "powers that be" that I was worthy of a second chance and began volunteering at local hospital physiotherapy departments, committing myself to the cause.

During my time in the wilderness after sixth form college, I needed to bring in some type of income. My mother worked at a small factory in town where parts for a popular mechanized horse race were made and one day she noticed a job ad in the town's local newspaper, *The Southport Visitor*, looking for someone to run a Pleasureland stall in Southport for the summer. With microphone in hand I became host and MC of Pleasureland's Kentucky Derby. "The Kentucky Derby" — it sounded so American. So full of promise! Punters would roll a ball up a channel with holes numbered 1, 2, or 3 which would move their horse the corresponding amount of lengths along the track. Simple, ingenious, addictive, and fun!

"Under starter's orders . . . and they'rrre off"!

Southport Pleasureland had been operating since the early 1900's and was regarded as the "little sister" to the more famous Blackpool Pleasure Beach—Britain's Vegas of the North—further north along the Lancashire coastline. Both theme parks were based on the entertainment complexes created along the beach at Coney Island in Brooklyn, New York, where the earliest self-contained amusement parks from the late-1800s began to develop. I could sense American positivity each time I went to work that summer. The tall constructs and brightly colored death-defying rides provided an avenue to thrill amid the waft of the salty sea air mingling with the distinctive smell of candy floss. I had landed the perfect summer vocation; well, almost perfect. On several occasions, players from Liverpool FC showed up at Pleasureland, and wanting to demonstrate their competitive edge, they were drawn toward a "derby" victory. Small crowds would gather to cheer on their idols as I, on the other hand, began to revel in preventing victory to any player from Anfield: a gentle nudge of a ball; a subtle distraction thrown their way; even a disguised helping hand for an opponent. I used many tricks of the trade to deny.

The stall next to the Derby contained Mystic Martha—psychic/clairvoyant/fortune teller extraordinaire. Martha would often come out of her "psychic suite" and sit on our first horse stool chatting with me until I had pulled in enough punters to start a new race. One day when things were rather slow, Martha came over, sat down next to me and said "Garryy! Sit still for a moment and let me focus on your eyes; on your aura." The morbidly obese, ginger-mopped gypsy-like sixty-year-old, decked out in what can only be described as a set of my grandma's old shed curtains, had caught me off guard. Mystic Martha had me captured in her glow and wasn't about to relinquish her hold.

"Garryy, I am looking deep into your eyes."

"I guess you are Martha. I guess you are!" I replied, a freakish combination of trying to accept the bizarre moment and the queasiness engulfing my being of having to look deep into Martha's eyes for more than a split second.

"You are destined to leave these shores," she told me. "Ah, yes, Garryy. I see it now. I see you will travel far, far away."

Now for seven years straight, our only vacation had been to Anglesey off the north coast of Wales in a moldy, secondhand static caravan that my aunty Flo rented on the cheap for two weeks each August, so "far, far away" did indeed sound quite exciting. Had "Southport's Top Psychic" somehow ignited my internal wanderlust? Martha certainly was one of a kind. I also thought she was totally full of shit!

The following summer, I received a letter that was to change my life. I was finally accepted into Pinderfields College of Physiotherapy, Wakefield. I was on my way!

6

Celebrate Good Times . . . C'mon!

Arriving in Wakefield via the lesser-used of the city's two railway stations, Kirkgate, apparent from its moderate state of decay, I immediately considered the opportunity that lay ahead of me. As far as I was concerned, I had, indeed, reached the Promised Land.

It was only a matter of minutes before I experienced my first interaction with a real-lfe Yorkshire man in Yorkshire. He was sitting on a public bench close to the center of Wakefield. After hauling my oversized Adidas duffel bag through the city toward my new digs, I gladly slumped down next to the fella, my worldly belongings thrust onto the pavement between the two of us. The gentleman didn't even flinch. Flat cap, dour expression, most likely in his mid-sixties, he tilted his head and muttered "Naw then lad, how's tha doin?"

"I'm doing very well thanks," I replied. "How are you today, sir?"

"Eh up! Tha's not from round 'ere is thee?"

Struggling to digest the foreign dialect, I replied "No sir, I'm from Lancashire."

"Bloody hell, lad! Well, we all 'ave wur problems!"

An awkward silence followed, broken occasionally by my new friend loudly licking his lips. Then, after what seemed an eternity, he leaned in towards me, his expression stoic, no eye contact, the tip of his cap sharpening his forward gaze, and proudly proclaimed "Well then, young man, remember this. Tha's in Yorkshire now, see thee, 'n' in Yorkshire, men are men and women are grateful," the word *grateful* sounding more like "gllateful." My puzzled expression must have been glaringly obvious, astounded at the gentleman's kindness for sharing such a mindblowing nineteenth-century pearl of wisdom.

"Thank you! I'll do my best to remember that, sir!"

Seconds later, my ears were assaulted by a screeching howl, as a rather rotund middle-aged lady waddled out of a nearby shop. With her handbag tucked tightly under her left arm, she grabbed a chunk of cloth from the left shoulder of the jacket of my new friend before exclaiming "Bloody hell, our Clay! There ya're. Get a bloody move on! Us bus'll be 'ere any minute. I've bin lookin' for thee all over! Is tha bloody gormless or what?!" The lady then looked right at me, shaking her head as she yanked "our Clay" from the bench, and said "men, lad. I tell thee. Yer all bloody 'opeless!" I had been in Yorkshire less than one hour and I was already completely confused.

My time in Wakefield, however, was to prove a total revelation.

My roommate at Pinderfields College was Tom Skinner. Our room consisted of a sink, two beds, two tables, two cupboards, and, as we both unpacked our bags, much to our amusement, two identical copies of AC/DC's "Back in Black" album! The getting to know each other process quickly reached a rather more awkward juncture when Tom hung a Leeds United FC scarf above his desk around the same time that I unveiled my Manchester United scarf. Several pints that same night in the Fox & Hounds eased any sign of tension regarding football allegiance, and we wandered home from our new local both seemingly happy with our allocation of roommate for the next twelve months.

Father a miner and mother the undisputed queen of the Yorkshire pudding makers, Tom's background was trademark Yorkshire. He had been working as a hospital nightporter and morgue attendant prior to his acceptance into college. I was sharing a room with *the* single funniest human being I had encountered in my young life. Tom's sharp wit matched anything I threw at him. Daunting course revision sessions quickly evolved into comedic double acts utilizing any props we could get our hands on. Impromptu improvisations had us both rolling with laughter while trying to assimilate the location of such anatomical structures as the neurotendinous organ of Golgi, our answers verbalized via impersonations of famous characters ranging from Mick Jagger to Ronald Reagan, helping us tolerate the drudgery of our studies.

In the room next door to us was a cockney lad named Bill. Looking all of sixteen years of age with his soul-boy haircut, we thought he had arrived at the wrong building and that he should in fact be starting at the high school just up the road. "Soul Boy" had boundless energy, ran around like a headless chicken, and never stopped laughing. He was the first southerner I had ever met, his preference for lager shandy a notable contrast to "us northerners" who would always order a real ale. I found it quite ironic that Bill's football passion was Liverpool FC, but admired his choice of room decor—a huge half-naked poster of Debbie Harry which hung above his desk.

Then there was Soul Boy's roommate, Kenny—the "Scottish shag machine." A six-foot-something Billy Idol lookalike, Kenny defined the term "night owl." He loved a joint, a party, and had a habit of making a lifelong friend out of the latest stranger to cross his path on any given night out. Kenny loved to wear his kilt, along with a leather jacket, and was primed and ready to go mental when the nightclub we often frequented, played "Into the Valley" by the Skids or "Liberator" by Spear of Destiny.

I was sharing college life with three lads whose enthusiasm for living in the moment matched my own. The four of us were drawn together by our lust for life and an overwhelming desire to party hard at every opportunity in between the slog and grind of the tough medical curriculum. Nicknamed the Ground Floor Crew due to the proximity of our two rooms, the tag stuck and reflected our tight bond.

We totally embraced Wakefield and the "Westgate Run," a one-mile pub crawl consisting of twenty-four pubs, including the wonderfully authentic Henry Boon's and the rather more contemporary, and tacky, Rooftop Gardens with its 80's drunken disco vibe. Short skirts, high heels, stockings and plenty of cleavage was on display whatever the season, as local lasses paraded Wakefield's pubs and clubs. As if the visual wasn't stimulating enough, the verbal was never backward at coming forward, from those ladies of "Costa del Shakey Wakey." They knew what they wanted and they made sure that they got it.

I soon discovered that Old Trafford was easily accessible from Wakefield train station via Huddersfield and into Piccadilly station, Manchester. In fact, I attended more Manchester United home matches during my Yorkshire experience than at any other time thus far. Arriving early, I stood in the United Road paddock soaking up the atmosphere.

In May 1985, our student lounge created its own paddock. Tickets were allocated and drawn. I did not fare well, ending up with the back row on the far right hand corner. It mattered not, as I propelled forth from the lounge window and rattled Wakefield with my outburst the moment Norman Whiteside scored one of the most iconic goals in Manchester United history, with a step-over to savor. My sprint down Peterson Road, arms aloft screaming "Yes! Yes! Yes!" may well have had several onlookers considering me a patient of the nearby Fieldhead psychiatric hospital. United were once again FA Cup winners, beating First Division champions, Everton, 1-0.

During my second year at Pinderfields, in 1986, Manchester United made a management change, hiring a certain Alex Ferguson. Initially, I didn't know what to make of the appointment. I had witnessed the flamboyant "Big Ron" Atkinson win the FA Cup the previous season and had grown used to United managers being larger than life. The new manager appeared more measured. I was aware of his achievements at Aberdeen, breaking the Celtic/Rangers monopoly on Scottish soccer and winning the European Cup Winners Cup in 1983, against none other than Real Madrid. My father appeared happy with the appointment. "The fella has done brilliant up in Aberdeen, son. Maybe this is just what we need, eh?" he noted during one of our phone conversations.

In the summer of 1987, I finally achieved my goal, graduating from Pinderfields as a physiotherapist, quickly realizing that there was work in abundance throughout Britain. I chose a series of locum jobs to gain clinical experience while sampling various towns and cities throughout England. After several placements around the country, I took the opportunity to live and work for an extended period of time in York, a beautiful city by the edge of the River Ouse.

Nothing of note happened at Old Trafford for several seasons after Ferguson's arrival. The trophy cupboard was bare and patience was beginning to run thin. The tabloids had Ferguson marked as a "dead man walking" after five years without a trophy—until Manchester United's run to the FA Cup final in 1990. Mark Robins' third round winner against Nottingham Forest has been touted as the goal that saved Ferguson his job. United eventually made it all the way to Wembley to play Crystal Palace. After an entertaining 3-3 draw in the final, United won the replay 1-0.

That FA Cup victory provided qualification into the following season's UEFA Cup Winners Cup, where, somewhat surprisingly, they made it all the way to the final in Rotterdam where their opponents were Barcelona. I donned my United shirt and took my seat in the corner of Ye Old Starre Inn, York's oldest licensed inn, built in 1644. Bryan Robson—United's "Captain Marvel"—lifted the trophy that night after an enthralling match and a brilliant second goal from Mark "Sparky" Hughes to seal the victory. I had marveled in the tales of the '68 team from my father and now Fergie's United had achieved European glory.

I called my father at the final whistle and we both debated whether it was Steve Bruce or Mark Hughes who got the final touch for the first United goal. Before hanging up, my father said "that was one hell of a win tonight, son, but I tell you what, it's still not the Big One. The ghost of '68 is still there. One thing is for sure though. This team is on the up and up with Fergie in charge."

Several of United's youngsters were on the up and up too, with Lee Sharpe winning the Young Players Player of the Year for 1990–91 and a new player—Ryan Giggs—who was being touted as the next George Best.

The 1991–92 season gave my father and me further reason to celebrate as United won the League Cup for the first time in their history. A goal from Brian McClair was enough to seal the victory against Nottingham Forest at Wembley on April 12, 1992. I had made a visit back to Lancashire to watch the match with my father, enjoying the chance to spend time with family. United had now won a trophy for three years in a row!

Unfortunately, only eight days after that victory, a loss at home to Nottingham Forest and a subsequent defeat at the hands of Liverpool left the door open for Leeds United. The Whites seized their chance and in beating Sheffield United 3-2 became the 1991–92 league champions.

I suffered all summer long at the hands of my patients. Yorkshiremen have absolutely no problem when it comes to demeaning a Lancastrian, even more so when that Lancastrian happens to be a Manchester United fan. I focused on acquiring a thick skin during that particular soccer off season. United were still considered to be "a good Cup side," unable to achieve victory over the long haul of a full season.

As it happened, Leeds United had, in fact, won the very last English First Division title. A proposal was tabled for the establishment of a new league that would bring extra revenue into the game. The Founder Members Agreement, signed on July 17, 1991 by the game's top-flight clubs, established the basic principles for setting up the FA Premier League. The newly-formed top division would have commercial independence from the Football Association and the Football League, and therefore, be able to negotiate its own broadcast and sponsorship agreements.

In 1992, all of the First Division clubs resigned from the Football League, thus forming the English Premier League. This meant a break-up of the 104-year-old Football League that had operated until then with four divisions. The English Premier League would operate as a single division and the Football League with three. There was no change in competition format between the new Premier League and the new Championship (the former second division): three teams would be relegated from the Premier League and three promoted from the Championship. A new and exciting era in English top-flight football had arrived.

A poor start to the first English Premier League season, 1992–93, prompted Alex Ferguson to snag Eric Cantona from Leeds United in November 1992, a signing that seemed to invigorate everyone around Old Trafford. Aston Villa were flying high under the stewardship of "Big Ron" Atkinson, United's ex-manager and at the start of April 1993, the "Villans" sat atop the league, poised to become the very first English Premier League champions.

On April 10, 1993, I was in Bath for a weekend physiotherapy course, stuck in a slow crawl of traffic surrounded by the city's distinctive colored stone and beautiful architecture, the crescents and boulevards enveloping me as I listened to my battery-operated boombox on the back seat of my Ford Fiesta. The speakers propelled forth the drama of Steve Bruce's goal courtesy of BBC Radio 5. Six minutes of injury time had elapsed when the big man rose to score, beating Sheffield Wednesday. "Fergie Time" had arrived at Old Trafford. The continual, frenzied thrust of my car horn contrasted with the stagnant traffic and pedestrian swell, my vehicle motionless on the tarmac, echoes of my cheers resonating across to the beautiful Somerset countryside beyond the City's walls. With only two games left in the season, destiny loomed. United were now surging towards their first league title in twenty-six years!

Three weeks later—on May 2, 1993—it all came to a stunning conclusion. As dawn broke that morning, I awoke staring at the ceiling of my tiny, confined room, reflecting on events of the previous evening, desperate to watch the all-important match. It had been rather "Shakey in Wakey." The Ground Floor Crew from our college days had reunited, along with a couple of new members, one being "Big Bob," a physiotherapist from Newcastle and proud owner of a newly-acquired property on the city limits of Wakefield, aptly nicknamed the "Safe House."

At the end of a raucous night revisiting "Westgate Run," I found myself in an alleyway behind a kebab shop cornered by two police officers, arms aloft, index fingers applying horizontal pressure to their eyelids, both announcing "Ah, naughty boy! You no run from Chinese restaurant. Policeman always catch you!" What was supposed to be a fun joke among the four of us had not ended well. The bill was not paid and I ended up apprehended and put in a cell for the night, a stern-faced officer lambasting me with lectures on the consequences of my actions possibly jeopardizing my professional career. Every scare tactic in the book was used—his obvious aim being to teach me a lesson and "shit me up" big time. It worked! Needless to say it was a long night. Even when my associates in the "szechuan dash" put in an appearance at the station later that morning, all of us extending our repeated apologies, our pleas appeared to fall on deaf ears. The police were relentless in their message that we could all be in big trouble.

Eventually, I was released and later made it back to the "Safe House" for an unbearable amount of piss taking. The rest of the lads were sat watching the Sky Sports Sunday afternoon match and, of course, had ordered Chinese takeaway for dinner in recognition of my capture and remorseful return.

As the game at Villa Park neared its conclusion, the score was Aston Villa 0, Oldham Athletic 1. Ian Darke and Andy Gray, the co-commentary team for the match reminded us all "if this score remains the same, Manchester United will be crowned champions."

Let me repeat that: "If this score remains the same, MANCHESTER UNITED WILL BE CROWNED CHAMPIONS!"

Every sinew of my exhausted body was willing Oldham home. Then, with one single blast of the referee's whistle, the game was over!

Yes! It had finally happened! The team with whom I had signed a lifetime contract in 1975 had finally delivered, allowing me to witness them becoming THE NUMBER ONE TEAM in the land!

In one blast of a whistle, I went from feeling like a condemned man to mindlessly triumphant. Twenty-six years of LIVERPOOL, LIVERPOOL, LIVERPOOL (the odd Derby County, Nottingham Forest, Aston Villa, Arsenal, Leeds, and Everton as well, but you get the picture!) was no more! I grabbed the "Safe House" phone and called my father.

"Yes! Yes! Yes! Can you believe it, mate?! Champions! United are the champions!"

"After all of these years, eh son?! All these years! Absolutely brilliant," my father replied, adding "so how's your weekend going?"

"Oh, pretty steady, mate. Nothing too crazy to report",

"Enjoy it tonight, son. I know I will! What a moment, eh?!"

Sky Sports was changing the football landscape on many levels. Launched on April 20, 1991, Sky had outbid the BBC and ITV, acquiring live and exclusive English Premier League football broadcasting rights for the United Kingdom and Ireland for a five-year period. I could never have afforded Sky on my NHS physiotherapist's salary, but pubs around the country seized an opportunity. It didn't take long for Sky to take a peek "across the Pond" and start to broadcast their own version of "Monday Night Football."

The following day being a Bank Holiday Monday, I completed the M1, A1 and A64 traffic shuffle through the vehicle maze, dashing back from Wakefield to York in time to watch the "Sky Sports Monday Night Special." I took my seat in the pub, pint in hand, and transported myself to Old Trafford for United's final home game of the season against Blackburn Rovers on May 3, 1993.

"Sky Sports and the English Premier League proudly present a whole new ball game: Ford Monday Night Football, exclusively live. Manchester United versus Blackburn Rovers, only on Sky Sports in association with Fosters." Presenter Richard Keys' voice reverberated around the pub. "A moment in history when Villa slipped up yesterday. The long wait is over for United. They have produced exciting, explosive football all season. Tonight they are having a party and they will want to celebrate in style."

The celebrations commenced with the Sky Strikers cheerleading team. *Cheerleaders?* I had heard of them, but had never actually seen any in action. I considered it to be an America-only phenomenon, having read an article about the Dallas Cowboys cheerleaders. The photographs accompanying that article showed a magnificently coiffured, gorgeous group of athletic women. I vividly remember a picture of the ladies in formation, on field, synchronized stance, producing high kicks that were beyond belief. They looked incredible, their outfits stunning. The English version occupying my immediate attention up on a television screen as I stood, pint in hand in a North Yorkshire pub? Well, let's say it was an absolute world away—in more way's than one.

As the Sky Strikers crew began leaving the pitch—and not before time to be honest—I recalled the words of my grandfather: "When America sneezes, we all catch a cold here in Britain." I contemplated that the British game of football would be needing to take some very strong antibiotics to put that particular cheerleader cold to bed if it was to remain immune from such malarkey anytime soon. It was a prematch serving that simply did not work for me. It seemed to be a total disconnect from the British mindset. Almost comedic to be honest. They looked like fish out of water fronting an expectant northern English football crowd intent on one thing and one thing only—*football*.

I placed my pint on a table next to me and impulsively clapped and cheered as Manchester United took to the pitch. I noted a few glares from the other punters. I felt somewhat isolated, but it mattered not, as I transported myself to Old Trafford, Manchester.

There was a party atmosphere inside the ground. United were just ninety minutes away from becoming the first team to lift the English Premier League trophy.

Alex Ferguson had put out a full-strength side. The cameras picked up United's iconic manager from the 60s, Sir Matt Busby, as he waved his approval. It was a wonderful sight. What thoughts were running through the head of the last Manchester United manager to win the league back in 1967?

A mere eight minutes into the game, Kevin Gallacher's near post run and flick rocketed into the roof of United's net. Blackburn Rovers, it appeared, had not read the script.

United responded well. Cantona and Giggs both coming close. Then, with twenty two minutes on the clock, Ryan Giggs stepped up and produced a stunning free kick.

The quick reply as if to say "Not in our house! Not on THIS night of all nights!"

"Get in there" I shouted out instinctively, this time around to a small smattering of applause from inside the pub. I was, remember, in the land of the "White Rose."

United were level.

It remained 1-1 through to half-time.

United legend Bryan Robson took to the pitch for the start of the second half. Old Trafford roared its approval and within minutes added a Mexican wave to boot. Robson's impact was immediate. A volley from the edge of the Blackburn box after a beautiful piece of skill by Cantona, the Frenchman creating space for the chip to United's legend and Captain Fantastic. Minutes later, after more terrific work from Cantona, the "new guard" in United's midfield, Paul Ince, bravely slotted the ball home.

Sixty minutes gone. 2-1 to United.

After that goal had gone in, Giggs was producing flicks and tricks, and swift passing movements were being displayed all over the pitch by the Red Devils. The Old Trafford crowd produced "Ole" after "Ole" along with rapturous cheers for every touch by every United player. The cameras showed the Premier League trophy being lifted into place behind the United bench. An air of expectancy filtered throughout the stadium. The United manager and his staff could not help but smile in anticipation. I reacted likewise.

As the game wound down, whistles from the crowd could be heard, urging the referee to blow for time.

Cantona went on a run right side and released Robson who was quickly clattered by a Blackburn defender.

Free kick, edge of the box, into injury time added on.

Giggs? Kanchelskis? Cantona? A fitting finale for Robson perhaps?

Goal United!

3-1!

I shot to the payphone and made the call.

"Bloody brilliant, eh son!" was my father's immediate response, knowing exactly who it would be. "We've waited a long, long time for this moment. What a night! And what about Pallister with that bloody cracking free kick at the end? Hasn't missed a minute of playing time all season, son. The only player without a goal too. Bloody marvellous. What a way to end it. What a night!"

I once again contemplated my father's excitement, knowing full well that he had had to listen to the match on the radio. Somewhat of a blessing to be honest as he did not have to suffer the Sky Strikers.

"Busby was there to see it all, dad"

"So I heard, son. Bloody wonderful. Eighty fours years old. Eh up, they are saying on the radio that they're coming out for the trophy."

"Alright mate, I'm going to get back in front of the screen. Look after yourself dad and send my best to everyone up there."

"Will do, son. Look after yourself. Championes! Championes!"

I stood in front of the screen, watching the inaugural Monday Night Football broadcast in England.

Steve Bruce raised the trophy high.

Manchester United, CHAMPIONS for the first time in twenty-six years!

I could not believe it!

I took a quiet moment of reflection.

After a few more minutes watching the wonderful scenes at Old Trafford, I finished off my beer, put on my coat and headed out into the chilly North Yorkshire night.

With the season done and dusted, I returned to the routine that is summer without football, content in the knowledge that I had several months to relish United's victorious season. The only chatter from my

Yorkshire patients this time around consisted of Leeds United's glaringly swift demise.

Then, one day as I was lying in the back yard of my rented accommodation, relaxing to the peace of an English mid-summer's afternoon, I heard the phone ring. I wandered into the kitchen and picked up the receiver.

"Mr. France. This is Police Sergeant Tomlinson!"

Adrenaline shot!

"I trust you are well, sir. I am calling to inform you that no further charges will be pressed against you and your bunch of renegades after that silly prank you pulled. Take this as a warning, son. Do not do anything so stupid again!"

It was a stupid thing to have done and the police had made us all sweat for weeks. My first and only ridiculous attempt at a crime and I had totally cocked it up!

I put the receiver back and punched the air—Pearson pump-like in my delivery.

"Yesss! Get in there!"

7

Take Two!

And just like Manchester busses, you wait twenty-six years for one ... and two arrive together!

After the incredible end to the previous season, United hit the ground running in the following campaign. In the off season, Alex Ferguson did some shrewd business, securing the signature of Roy Keane for a national record transfer fee of £3.75 million We had our man, and along with the ever influential Eric Cantona, it felt like everything was falling into place.

On September 15, 1993, United travelled to Hungary to play Kispest Honvéd—their first European Cup tie in twenty-five years. Two goals from Roy Keane and one from Eric Cantona were enough to secure a 2-3 away win for the Red Devils. Progressing to the second round of the European Champions League, United then played Turkish champions Galatasaray to a 3-3 draw at Old Trafford. Before the return game in Istanbul, large numbers of Galatasaray fans kept the United team awake by making noise all night outside the team hotel. United were also subjected to the infamous "tannoy terror" tactics with the PA system blasting out Turkish throughout the match. The ploy proved effective as a 0-0 tie allowed Galatasaray to progress on away goals. United hadn't even made the group stages of the European Champions League.

Toward the end of the 1993–94 season, I went on an Irish road trip with my Geordie pal, Big Bob. Bob was a monster; cauliflower ears atop a six-foot-six frame. It was quite an experience though, to see such an imposing figure of a man suddenly turning green as the Stranraer-to-Larne ferry bounced around in the wild waters of the Irish Sea. Guinness and an Irish swell do not apparently mix well if you are Big Bob. The moment we emerged from the other side of a border checkpoint in Bob's sporty black VW Golf, our liberty still intact, we were free to roam Eire. We arrived in Cork on the evening of May 1, 1994.

"Sit yersel's down, la's! Ged de la's a puint!" Comforting words from the hotel manager after she had led us into the private function room at the back of the building, complete with big screen TV, her Irish hospitality abundant. Bob and I felt right at home and were eager for kick-off. Manchester United against Ipswich live from Portman Road. With three games remaining in the season, United were just one win away from English Premier League glory, and here we were in, of all places, southern Ireland! We had managed to make it to Cork just in time, minutes to spare before kick-off. What Big Bob and I witnessed that evening of 1 May 1994 was the sheer resilience and willpower of the Reds. After Chris Kiwomya put Ipswich Town ahead after twenty minutes, "King Eric" responded with a goal to level the score at 1-1. Cork's own Roy Keane was playing for United and we watched the match to a backdrop of "feckin' nutter," "yer feckin' eejit!" and the like echoing around the room whenever an Ipswich player touched the ball, a total contrast to the raucous cheers announcing any touch from the hometown Irishman. I willed the Red Devils forward in search of victory and was rewarded immediately with Ryan Giggs scoring just one minute into the second half. Our Irish den erupted! As the final whistle blew it erupted once again. Manchester United had managed a narrow 2–1 victory, enough to seal the title.

A rather disheveled local in his mid-twenties, looking like a reject from the Undertones, stood next to me, slamming pint after pint on the table, punching his right arm forth saluting his local hero every time "Keano" won a bone-crunching tackle. The lad claimed that he had grown up with Roy. "Da fella is a total feckin' legend is da truth really! Helluva player, so he is!" That evening, I realized that Cork had a lot of Manchester United fans as the city's bars sang in celebration of one of their own, and a second Manchester United title in two years: "Keano! Keano! Keano!"

Celebrations went on long into the night. Little sleep was had and we only just made our ferry connection up in Larne, Northern Ireland, very early the next morning. Driving north we once again approached the border and an army checkpoint, Big Bob making sure he didn't breathe on the soldier during the brief inquisition. Those checkpoints remained clear evidence of the ongoing troubles between Irish Nationalist Catholics and British Unionist Protestants that had escalated in Northern Ireland in the late nineteen sixties. The Martin Luther King civil rights marches over in America had apparently further inspired minority Irish Catholics living in the predominantly British Unionist Protestant North of Ireland to march in the hope of claiming a greater voice in the area. Clashes between government police and the protesters had erupted with atrocious consequences for all. Bombings, shootings, abductions all over the province, across the border and even onto the British mainland had ensued. Thousands killed and thousands more severely injured. As Big Bob and I exited the southern Republic of Ireland that day, we discussed the irony of having received such incredible warmth and Irish hospitality and contrasted that with the relentless hostilities and all of the lives lost after years of conflict. As we were granted safe entry back into Northern Ireland and the United Kingdom, we both wished for an end to the violence.

A slip by Blackburn Rovers the following day, losing 2-1 to Coventry, confirmed United's title! The Reds then went on to secure victory over Chelsea in the 1994 FA Cup final. As it happened, I had to attend a wedding reception the day of the FA Cup final. It was rather poor timing on behalf of the bride and groom, their post-nuptial speeches and dinner starting right at kick-off time. I had to consider a plan. As the match entered injury time, smiling and very satisfied, I returned a ragged blue cycling cap, complete with an old, yellowed earpiece hanging on the end of a weathered thin wire to my girlfriend's cycling-mad father. I had worn it throughout proceedings despite the poor color coordination with my suit. Competing with the clink of cutlery, speeches and polite conversation with guests, I had once again managed to remain connected with my beloved Reds in their victorious moment.

I had tried to remain incognito as best as I could, but, as the groom completed his speech, he looked over toward me in the far corner of the room, and his final words were: "and, oh yes, so what was the final score from Wembley then, Gary? Did United win?" Laughter broke out across the room and I stood to my feet and responded: "Manchester United 4 Chelsea 0!"

"Get in there!" the groom shouted, a "Pearson Pump" thrust of his right arm piercing the air as he celebrated the news. The entire room broke out into rapturous applause.

Manchester United had become only the fourth club in the twentieth century to win the league and FA Cup double. Only defeat to Aston Villa in the League Cup final in March had prevented United from winning an unprecedented "Treble."

Whatever it takes!

8

Hit the North!

Monday morning at Leith Physiotherapy Outpatient Clinic began with the sight of Betty Burnside's expansive and gravitationally-challenged rear end saluting me as she shampooed her hair over a tiny National Health Service sink that was designed for more clinically-inclined tasks, particularly obvious due to its strategic position, front and center of the Physiotherapy department. Betty had little shame.

That same Monday ended with a rancid stench signaling the arrival of local junkie, Charlie—declaring as loudly as possible that he hated all "FEB's"—blood slowly dripping from the gaping gash across his forehead. Charlie had fallen again. And he had mistaken our building for his intended destination—again!

"What's doin', ya fuckin' bunch a bastarrrds?!"

A rather shocked-looking Mrs. Morrison immediately turned pale as she sat quietly with her left shoulder wrapped in ice, looking to me for some explanation as to what the hell this monstrosity was doing walking into our department.

"Hey Charlie! It's been a while my friend."

The "softly, softly" approach often worked best when it came to Charlie.

"Aye, tha's been meanin to rattle yer feathers, doc. Come on now son, what about some stuff for Charlie, eh?!"

"I'm sorry, fella. No stuff here Charlie. Let's get you across the road, shall we, eh pal?"

"Och, yer's a black diamond, son. A black diamond. What the fuck's across the road anyway?"

Placing my arm around his skinny frame and trying to avoid contact with his blood stained neck and jacket, I escorted Charlie back to the entrance.

Now, for the culturally unaware, a "FEB" happens to be a "Fucking English Bastard." How ironic, then, for the rather disoriented Charlie that this particular "FEB" was the only one willing to offer a helping hand at a time when he most needed it. As usual, I escorted our friendly neighborhood addict across the road to the drug clinic, his gait clearly highlighting the fact that he was surely Scotland's elder statesman when it came to the joys of getting high. Life in Leith was never dull. And it was still only Monday!

I was now seven years into my physiotherapy career and had moved up the NHS ladder to become the manager of Leith Physiotherapy Outpatient Clinic—an opportunity to move into management as well as a prolonged stay close to the vibrant city of Edinburgh.

Kenny, the "Scottish shag machine" and member of the Pinderfields Ground Floor Crew, happened to be the lucky bastard whose parents had a fantastic tenement flat right in the heart of Edinburgh. Each August we would reunite for the Edinburgh Fringe Festival and weeklong artistic, binge-fueled bash. Edinburgh became a regular source of connection for four lads making their way through life. And, after several Scottish sojourns, I had set my heart on a more permanent stint in the city.

I simply walked into the physiotherapy department over at Leith Community Hospital one Saturday morning asking if there were any jobs going. Timing was everything it seemed, as the current man at the helm was planning to leave to become the physiotherapist at Hearts FC. I received confirmation of my new position and, within one month, left York and headed up the A1 for a new life in "the Athens of the North!"

A short time after I had made the move north, I had managed to hook up with a young student nurse. Suzie had caught my eye one night in the Halfway House, a tiny pub tucked in a corner of Edinburgh's Old Town. I quickly discovered that there was nothing "halfway" about Suzie. She was well into the club scene and we hit them hard for a while. "Madchester," with its blend of alternative rock and electronic dance, had relinquished its short-lived grip on the music scene as "rave" became the latest vibe. Suzie was more than "mad for it." She would drink and dance all night. She also had an addiction that was of a wonderfully more intimate nature—of which I became the exhausted beneficiary. Most club nights ended with me crashing at the student nurses digs close to the city center, facing the very unlikely prospect of achieving any sleep whatsoever. Mornings returned me right back to reality as I would leave the more upscale Morningside location and head slowly along the seedier Leith Walk and into Leith Port itself, the pounding of the street bars at 7:00 a.m. emphasizing its "24-hour pulse," a reminder of just how far one could go if inclined.

Only a few months into my new life in Leith and it was on one of those morning-after slogs back down into the old port town that it hit me. The excitement of Edinburgh life had been stimulating to say the least, but also exhausting. The initial excitement of my new position had worn off fairly quickly, thanks to the likes of Charlie, and I soon realized that NHS management simply wasn't the long-term answer. I could sense the physical and mental burnout on the horizon. Too many nine-to-fives becoming seven-to-sevens; the constant pressure to treat more and more, with less and less. I was twenty-nine years old and in a relationship that, in truth, was going nowhere. At the same time I was struggling to meet the monthly rent on my own modest apartment and still paying on a six-year-old Ford Fiesta, complete with leaky sun roof and battery operated boombox on the back seat due to the fact that I had just had my car stereo nicked, again. This particular "FEB" needed to make a change.

My usual short-term tonic and chance to decompress from the drama at work was to take a stroll along a rugged and blustery mile stretch of Portobello beach. The expansive beach and sandy coastline stimulated the senses as the wintery northeasterly winds blew away the politics of the day. In its nineteenth-century heyday, Portobello had been a thriving beach resort. Such was its popularity back then that it even drew hoards from Edinburgh's rival city, Glasgow, as they flocked for a seaside getaway. I would imagine its vibrant past each and every time I took my evening walk across that particular stretch of the Firth of Forth.

After one particularly restorative Portobello Beach stroll, the sea at its raging finest, I wandered back to my apartment on Leith Walk. I stepped into the hallway over the pile of mail stacked behind the door, grabbed a cuppa, and slumped down in my chair. It had been another long day of toil managing the NHS Physiotherapy clinic. Having sat and reflected a while, I noticed the monthly "Physiotherapy Journal" to which I subscribed. I reached down and grabbed it. I immediately flicked to the often interesting job vacancy section at the back of the publication. There were jobs posted in several locations around the country, igniting my wanderlust instincts. Then, I suddenly came across one particular advertisement. Jumping right out at me in distinctive italics, it stated:

> *American Midwest healthcare organization seeks young and enthusiastic sports physiotherapist. Experience in post-op orthopedic medicine essential. Excellent benefits package including medical, dental, vision, term life insurance, short and long term disability, 401K, paid vacation time, paid time off,*

and opportunity for professional development. [Oh, and by the
way, you won't be able to watch Manchester United anymore.]

I got right on it the very next day. I was eventually invited to Manchester
to meet representatives from a Florida-based medical recruitment agency.
Unfortunately, United had no home game that day. I emphasized the bad
timing, but the representatives had no idea what I was talking about. I
quickly realized that what I was contemplating may mean massive
sacrifices, including my ability to follow Manchester United.

The recruiter carefully rolled out a large map of the United States
across the table in the conference room educating me in the geographic
locations of the states most accessible when it came to credentialing and
educational requirements.

I was immediately drawn to Michigan. This Midwest state was
surrounded by the Great Lakes and it had Detroit—Motown—a gritty,
blue-collar industrial city that had breathed soul and raw energy into the
music scene of the States for decades.

Over the next few weeks, I was connected with a number of clinics in
Michigan. The interview process fueled my excitement as I would return
home from an uninspiring day at work to my summons from various clinics
around Michigan. On a cold and rainy January evening on Scotland's east
coast, the mere mention of a town called Kalamazoo, Michigan, got the
blood rushing—even though I had absolutely no bloody clue about the
place, its location, or how to spell it!

I quickly became excited about my potential career path once again.

Resigning a managerial post that had been given to me in good faith
by a very supportive and empathetic district manager couldn't have gone
any better. Angela's support and consideration for my cause was most
evident.

I walked out on Leith Physiotherapy department April 12, 1995,
locking the large, antiquated gates behind me for the last time. The
symbolism of those rusty iron eyesores that I had to deal with at the end
of every working day was truly poignant as I considered the sterility of
the UK National Health Service (NHS) at that particular time. I reflected
for a moment on the growing number of young and enthusiastic members
of staff across the country, becoming ever despondent at NHS policies
and lack of funding. Indeed, several members of my own peer group
with whom I had trained were already working in the private sector or
considering a move abroad.

Five weeks later, I was on Scotland's opposite coast, bidding farewell to my family. They had only recently relocated to Scotland's southernmost town of Drummore to escape the rat race, taking my gran and her sister who were both in their eighties. Renovating a rather decrepid stone cottage nestled close to the cliffs of the Mull of Galloway had been a success. As far as the move was concerned, my mother and father agreed that it was "the best thing they had ever done." My father also proudly mentioned something about being called a "FEB" by the locals shortly after his arrival in town.

That final weekend before departure, I spent time with my family, along with the added distraction of another possible Manchester United league title win. I sensed the perfect send off, despite the outcome being dependent on Blackburn Rovers faltering. United were at Upton Park playing West Ham and Blackburn were at Liverpool.

My father did not subscribe to Sky Sports and so we relied upon my old transistor radio for the BBC'S Five Live commentary. It made for thrilling, yet tense, listening. As the matches neared their conclusion, Blackburn were losing at Anfield. If it remained that way, then United simply required a win to clinch the title.

Snippets of radio commentary bounced back and forth from the two grounds as I wandered throughout our remote homestead on tenterhooks. Luděk Mikloško, the West Ham keeper, appeared to be playing the game of his life, stopping everything that was thrown at him, denying United the one goal they needed to be confirmed as champions.

The final whistles blew!

West Ham United 1 Manchester United 1.

Blackburn Rovers 1 Liverpool 2.

After a mere three years back in the top flight, Blackburn Rovers had won the English Premier League title, prizing it away from United's grasp by a single point.

I was gutted. My father was gutted. Our whole family was gutted.

I could not believe that I was about to depart for the U.S. with Manchester United ousted as English Premier League Champions.

Like old times, my father and I watched "Match of the Day" later that evening, both aware that it was our last chance for a long while to watch the football together. As we chatted, my father asked me how I was going to keep up to date with United's progress in the coming season.

"I have absolutely no clue, mate," I replied.

"Well, we'll think of something, eh son?"

Manchester United and football—the threads that tied me to life, infiltrated my soul, making sense of it all, and yet these two crucial components to maintaining my sanity could well be out of reach in less than twenty-four hours. As I sat there that night suffering the "highlights" of events on that final Premier League Sunday of the season, I contemplated further the huge lifestyle change that I was about to make. I was about to embark on my very own American dream, yet I was heading to a land that appeared to be devoid of any interest in football whatsoever.

To the sound of the all too familiar theme tune from "Match of the Day," I said my goodnights to my family and retired to bed for my last night on British soil for some time to come.

I was failing miserably in my attempt to get to sleep prior to an early rise for my flight when I heard a knock on the door. It was late.

"Yes?"

My father opened the door. His right hand remained clinging tightly to the door knob, ensuring that he barely set foot in the room. My father was old school, his emotions buried in that very British "stiff upper lip" and "brave face" way due to his emergence at a time when Britain had come back from the brink in the mid-1940's. After what seemed like a long time, he said "Are you asleep son?"

"No, not yet dad," I replied. "What's up?"

After a brief pause, he said "Oh ... err ... I just wanted to say ... I'm going to miss you son!"

"I'll miss you too, dad."

There was an extended silence as we acknowledged each other, both very aware of the huge step that I was about to take.

"Well ... good night son. Sleep well." And with that my father turned and gently closed the bedroom door.

The following morning brought with it a long, winding car journey towards Glasgow. Conversation between my parents and me flowed in the car. Despite our imminent separation, I reassured them both that I was in no doubt as to my choice and that I was excited about the challenges and adventures that lay ahead.

I took one last look at my folks and wandered to the boarding gate at Glasgow International Airport.

I was heading to America.

America

9

Touchdown

As I arrive in the U.S., it seems only fitting from here on out to refer to the "beautiful game" as "soccer"—widely considered to be the American term for the more universal "football." Ironically, it appears that the term "soccer" was in fact coined back in Britain—as a shortened version of "Association football." Nevertheless, since the U.S. already has its own version of football—you know, the one where you use your hands—it makes sense from here on out to refer to "soccer." And so, without further ado, onto "the soccer years."

May 15, 1995: I immediately spotted the fat Finn, complete with lazy eye, holding aloft a brown cardboard paper placard, the bold black letters declaring my name: "Gary French." The passport in my right hand read "Gary France." Close enough, I guess. I had one bag of clothes, a bag of medical books, and $600 to my name.

As the steady stream of passengers exited the arrival lounge to be greeted by family, friends, business colleagues, or lovers, I walked enthusiastically towards the rather portly gentleman, unlit cigar in mouth, right hand side of his shirt hanging out of his trousers, and his eyes obviously fixed on the blond female walking ahead of me, a gratifying chew on his cigar further highlighting his somewhat lecherous fixation.

After what in my mind seemed like an age, he eventually noticed me standing two feet in front of him. Unfazed and appearing fully entitled to his wandering eye, he exclaimed "Heyyy, welcome to America, Gaaary!" Mr. Jussi Kipli. My new boss and taxi ride.

A strong handshake was followed by a sharp vertical hoist of his trousers as he declared "Follow me, Gaaary. Let's get the hell outta here!"

I walked closely behind my new boss, racking my brains as to who he looked like. Then it dawned on me: Frank Cannon, the detective, played by William Conrad back in the 70s. He wasn't quite as bald as Cannon, but he possessed eerily similar facial features, along with a finely manicured tash. It was not quite the dynamic arrival into the United States of America that I had anticipated.

Things immediately began looking up, however, as my host escorted me to a huge Ford truck—a chariot so big, I was amazed there were no ladders attached to the side. The insignia on the front stated F-350. This meant nothing to me, but I am sure it translated as "Big"!

"Mr. Kipli, this is huge!" I exclaimed, mustering a somewhat modest British enthusiasm.

"Gaaary, please, call me Jussi," he insisted. "Welcome to the Motor City! I'm sure glad that this all worked out, buddy!'

"Thanks Jussi," I replied, attempting to board via the driver's side door.

"You wanna take the wheel already, buddy?" Jussi replied with a wide smile.

I turned swiftly, somewhat awkwardly banging into the Finnish Yank in my attempt to reach the passenger seat on the right side of the vehicle.

As I jumped in, Jussi hollered "Be patient my British friend. This coming weekend, this baby will be all yours!" I raised my eyebrows, accompanied by a nervous and somewhat confused grin.

With a swift downward crank of the gear stick protruding from the steering wheel shaft, Jussi hit the accelerator pedal and sped away from our parking space. Speaking through gritted teeth, his cigar wafting a steady stream of smoke into my pale jetlagged face, Jussi bellowed "This was my birthday present a couple of years ago, Gaaary. I guess I must have behaved myself, huh?! I looove this beauty. I really do!" he proudly noted, slouching back in his seat and accelerating like a bat out of hell onto the main road ahead, the screeching of tires making me feel like I was on the set of "The Dukes of Hazard"!

We were leaving Detroit Metro Airport in our wake and entering one of America's longest freeway systems—the very-significant-sounding I-94!

The chaos of the U.S. interstate highway jolted me to my core as cars of every shape and size jostled for position. I could not believe my eyes as a rust heap looking like a cast-off from an old series of "Kojak" appeared beside us. Apparently devoid of shock absorbers and featuring, of all things, a wooden bumper, the vehicle announced its arrival onto the stage bouncing up and down ferociously. A plume of black smoke trailed in its wake as the driver portrayed his proud "Detroit lean," window down and one hand on the steering wheel, with a glare to challenge anyone who might dare to overtake his trusted steed. He stared me down in a way that suggested that this was "his" freeway and that anyone who thought otherwise could "go fuck themselves!" It was a moment that further confirmed the huge step I had taken, leaving the familiar behind.

I continued to watch nervously as drivers aggressively weaved from lane to lane to pass anyone and everyone in their way. Lane etiquette seemed redundant as the "weaver birds" reigned supreme. I reflected back to the old public information announcements on British television, informing the public that "weaving from lane to lane in order to overtake was a definite no-no and that all drivers should only overtake using the outside lane."

I shuddered as a blast from behind announced the appearance of one of the biggest monsters I had ever seen. An American "semi" truck bounced at speed along the uneven terrain with a swagger all its own, casting a dark shadow over us as the driver claimed his right to the lane ahead with one final pump of his deafening horn. I focused closely on the truck's massive wheels, as big as Jussi's large vehicle, as the juggernaut hit stretch after stretch of uneven track. The 18-wheeler of a beast was taking a hammering. Its British cousin, the articulated lorry, was no match as I witnessed the sheer ferocity with which the "semi" claimed the road for its own. It was blatantly obvious that I was not on the A59 heading for Southport! Jussi, apart from the odd one or two "fuck yous," appeared completely unfazed by all of the high-speed chaos around us. Given the size of some of the vehicles, I could see why the road was not exactly the smoothest surface on which I had ever ridden.

"Hold on now, Gaaary!" Jussi exclaimed as he crossed two lanes of busy highway in about a tenth of a second. "This exit ramp is a little bumpy, bud!'

We exited the freeway onto a very straight road.

"This is Ford Road, Gaaary, named after the great man himself," giving his steering wheel a wee tap in recognition. "Always drive a Ford, Gaaary! Always drive a Ford!" I smiled wryly at the thought of my old 1100cc Ford Fiesta and its new owner somewhere back home in Britain.

After a few minutes on Ford Road, I spotted a sign that read "Welcome to Canton" and a nervous excitement bubbled inside me. "This is it," I thought to myself. We were entering the town I had been focusing on for the last few months; the town that had been mentioned in many a telephone conversation.

As I wound down the window, the spring breeze instantly caused my eyes to water. Jussi must have spotted my discomfort and commented "Jeez, those Michigan allergies man. You'll be needing some of that antihistamine medication soon, buddy!" I caught a glimpse of my reflection in the passenger side wing mirror. Canton was about to welcome a bloodshot Marty Feldman lookalike fresh off the plane!

We passed row after row of stripmalls, fast-food drive-thru's, and gas stations with logos and neon signs everywhere, all competing for the customer's eyes: Little Caesars, an ancient Roman cartoon figure dressed in a toga, head wrapped in ivy, declaring "Pizza, Pizza" from a cartoon bubble protruding from his mouth; Murrays Auto Parts, with a logo that featured a dreadlocked character who looked like Gnasher from the British comic, *The Beano*; Taco Bell; Big Boy; Denny's; Red Lobster. I felt like I had landed on another planet.

"All great places to eat right there, Gaaary. All filling that plate right up, buddy!" A smug and contented smile appeared on the rather portly Jussi's face, proclaiming his pride at the range of culinary delights on offer in his hometown neighborhood. I was sure that it would be a long time before I would once again see a sign for "Fish, Chips, and Mushy Peas!"

Blue boxes sporadically littering the sidewalk caught my eye. Jussi pointed out that they were US Postal Service mailboxes. Total contrast to the Royal Mail red to which I was conditioned back in Britain. The blue and white car registration plates up close and personal every time we pulled up at a red light were a much smaller rectangle compared to the elongated black and white UK version. Indeed, even the traffic lights themselves, resplendent in their yellow sheen, were suspended high above the center of the road, dangling precariously, swaying back and forth in the wind. And the huge billboards, row after row, in what appeared to me to be a relatively sparsely populated area. The monstrosities were advertising everything from food stores to "rock star" local lawyers, shoulders back and a defiant look, guaranteeing you "a result or it's free." I was on sensory overload attempting to align myself with my new surroundings.

Slowly, but surely, "retail row" began to diminish and as we continued our journey west, our surroundings quickly became less commercial. It seemed a sudden abrupt end to the urban sprawl that had been dominating either side of the road just seconds earlier. After a mile or two, we made a left turn onto the rather aptly named "Champaign Road," an unpaved road with unfinished skeletons of huge houses spread along the route. I had never seen houses of that size before.

Several of the dwellings were apparently still under construction, but already proud owners appeared to be occupying them, regardless of how sparsely constructed or presented they were. They had planted their flag poles in the ground, a pronouncement perhaps of their individualistic identity. The enormous central windows were reminiscent of homes from the 80s TV drama, "Dallas." I could see huge chandeliers, visible through the 70-foot tall entrance hall windows and imagined a sophisticated American alpha female, Joan Collins-like in appearance perhaps, resplendent in a ballgown taking an age as she descended the stairs, slowly running her hand along the spiral banister, declaring her presence to the crowd below. I realized that I was shaping most of these first impressions of America around the only real barometer I had ever had: American television of the 1970s and 80s. Growing up in a working class neighborhood of northern England, these shows had been my only window to how people lived "across the Pond."

The gardens, or rather lack thereof, were still only dirt, not a blade of grass in sight. I immediately sensed the unique pattern of each lot, distinct creations separating dwelling from dwelling and further proclaiming that obvious individualism to its closest neighbor. What also struck me was the fact that there were no fences. It was neighbor next to neighbor but with no actual material separation or boundary. Despite the distinctive difference from one home to the next, it was a continuum of acreage that blended them together en masse.

In my neighborhood in Lancashire, there had been very little that was distinctive about our own abode's exterior compared to the other houses on our street. The great British art of conformism had ruled the roost. But there was always a fence offering a border and protective wrap to what little property lay within its boundaries. The odd revolutionist's garden gnome placement or an old, decrepit caravan parked on the lawn, defied the "little England's" residents' sense of constraint: an escape to the open road at any time perhaps on the mind of the inhabitant.

As another mammoth construction became visible along Champaign Road, I tried to fathom why anyone would want or need such a huge house.

Five minutes later we turned right into a smaller sub division.

"Here we are then, buddy."

Jussi turned into the driveway of another impressive looking home with a pristine lawn and a carefully coordinated sprinkler system in full flow as dusk set in. I thought to myself "my grandfather told me never to water your grass at night. Maybe these Americans don't know *everything* after all?" Jussi reached for a small box the size of a cigarette packet from behind his sun visor and with the click of a button the twin garage doors began to open and we drove up the driveway and into a huge space. It was the first time I had witnessed a garage door open automatically. Jussi brought the truck to a halt right next to a bright red Ford Mustang. "Better be careful that I don't hit Diane's birthday present there, Gaaary."

My jaw dropped wide open at the sight of the incredible car parked next to us. "Wow, Jussi, what a beautiful motor, mate!" I exclaimed.

"Welcome to the Kipli household, my British friend!" Jussi said, a definite sense of pride in his tone.

It appeared on first glance that in America, birthdays were on a different level to back home in Britain. A specially-designated bank account, rather well funded, seemed to be required to purchase a gift for a loved one.

10

Wasted

I had certainly landed on my feet, with Jussi and his wife Diane kindly allowing me the run of their beautiful home. Diane was mid-forties and rather stocky, wearing white stockings under her knee-length skirt along with shoes whose heels were so high that they fully accentuated her rather solid Arnold Schwarzenegger calf muscles as she lunged forth into my personal space. "Well hello there, Gaaary. I'm sooo pleased to meet youoooowwaa," she said, her voice becoming increasingly high-pitched as she reached the end of her sentence. It seemed as though she was singing rather than talking.

"It's lovely to meet you, Mrs. Kipli," I responded.

"Oh gosh, Gaaary," Diane responded, "please call me Diaaannne. Oh my, what a wonderful accent you haaave!"

Prior to my departure, I had heard stories about British physical therapists arriving in the States and being dumped in motels for weeks on end and left to their own devices to find living quarters as they attempted to "make a start" in the U.S. I, on the other hand, felt very fortunate with my new boss offering to put me up in his home until I found my feet. There was only one slight drawback: potpourri! I developed a rather swift aversion to Hotel Kipli's overwhelming scent, with room after room of dried plants overwhelming my nasal passages at every turn. And my bedroom with its en suite bathroom, as grand and well equipped as it was, appeared to be the epicenter of the spicy herbal fragrance.

Evenings during my first few weeks in Michigan were a "beer and steak fest," as Jussi showed me around the various fine-dining establishments in the area. I discovered that he was the son of Finnish immigrants, and that after working as a physical therapist in a local hospital, how he had decided to venture out and start his own clinic. Jussi went to great lengths to ask me what I was expecting out of my time in the States and told me about the opportunities available if I worked hard. It wasn't long before the subject turned to sport and, of course, I chimed in about my fanaticism for Manchester United. Jussi's immediate reaction was "Bobby Charlton, what a player, man!" I commended the Finn for his astute observation.

"My father loved his soccer, Gaaary. He knew all about Manchester. I believe that they won Europe one time, right? In the sixties?"

"1968, Jussi. Bobby Charlton was in that team."

"Yes, yes, my father would have seen that match back in Finland, I am certain."

Jussi switched gears. "In truth though, Gaaary, there is only one sport that matters, you realize? That is ice hockey!" A combination of his Finnish heritage and Detroit's most successful sporting franchise, the Red Wings, made this a given.

One of our most frequent evening destinations during my first couple of months in Michigan was a sports bar aptly named Uncle Pucks. And if ever there was a moment I felt like an Englishman abroad, it was during my first visit to "Pucks." The long, narrow building with its low ceiling had an interior chaos all its own. A big-screen TV dominated one end of the room and projected the Red Wings game at a volume so loud I felt like I was wearing the skates myself. Jussi and I took a seat at the bar and focused on one of the smaller screens generously dotted around the place and I tasted an American "cold one" for the very first time. I had never seen so many goatee beards in one building in my life. I felt as though I had walked onto the set of "Northern Exposure." With my Budweiser in hand and a plate of chicken wings at an arm's length for that vital protein fix, I quickly became accustomed to the style and energy of Michigan sports fans. It was postseason playoff time and the Wings were flying high and favorites for the title, having won their Western Conference division.

I was immediately taken in by the cut and thrust of Canada's game. Players hit hard as the crowd roared its approval. The versatility of the six-foot-something, two-hundred-and-fifty pound plus warriors was a sight to behold. It was easy to forget the game was being played on such a slippery surface. It was a feast of body blows and body checks into the boards, skating prowess matched by thunderous hits into a thick piece of plexiglass, the only thing separating player from fan. Several mid-game fights broke out. It was reminiscent of Roman gladiators battling it out in front of a raging crowd with an appetite for blood. Jussi told me that the game on offer at Puck's that evening was being broadcast live from Detroit's Joe Louis Arena just 30 miles east—named after Detroit's hometown boxing hero. I found myself cheering loudly as my newly-adopted team hammered another puck beyond the outstretched arm of the opposing Dallas Stars' goaltender. The Red Wings were on their way to victory in this first round game of the Stanley Cup playoffs. Gary Glitter's

"Rock'n Roll Part 2" echoed around the pub as the screens in front of us pictured the players sliding in for a team embrace as slow motion replay after slow motion replay reminded us that another goal had been scored. After about the third replay, I was finally able to follow the puck as it flew into the net. Thankfully, I was able to master the "second response"—my celebrations mirroring those of the other punters each time a goal or near miss was witnessed, as in truth I had no clue as to where the puck was most of the time.

I couldn't help smiling at the irony as I realized I was supporting a team that played in red and white. Of course, the Wings were not Manchester United, but they were a team with a comparably passionate following: the "people's team"; the "working-man's team" from the industrial north. They were a team that played a game with a set of goalposts, scored goals and had attackers, defenders, and goalies. They even had offside.

I began to take note of the standout players, most of them Russian with names like Konstantinov, Kozlov, and the particularly skillful attacker, Fedorov. There was also a player named McCarty, who appeared to want to pick a fight with almost every opposing player. "He's our enforcer, Gaaary," Jussi explained. "He likes to protect our flair players and is never afraid of a fight."

"Yep, I can see that Jussi," I replied, having to yell over the loud reaction as McCarty got into more impromptu mischief, apparently for "highsticking" an opponent who was none too happy about it.

Jussi went on to educate me about things like line changes, faceoffs, and icing. As he downed more and more glasses of Michelob, he became more and more animated. I slipped into a moment of introspection: despite being enthralled by my new experience in my new American local, there was nothing at all familiar. There were passionate, dedicated fans cheering on their hometown heroes, my intoxicated host being one of the loudest, doing all that he could to convince me to join the cause. *But it wasn't soccer. It wasn't Manchester United.* I resigned myself to the fact that Detroit's Red Wings would most likely be the closest I would come to filling the sporting void I had left behind. I could only dream about watching a game of Premier League soccer on the big screen at Pucks.

As I surveyed the joy on the faces of the punters at Pucks, their Red Wings shirts declaring their own personal favorite players, I imagined how life was going to be without any chance of being able to salute my own team in red, my own sporting fixation. I felt a sudden craving for home, that first real pull confirming my separation.

After a couple more beers, Jussi said "Hey, Gaaary, you ever played darts, buddy?"

"Is the sky blue, Jussi?" I replied, a confident repost I felt, due to the countless hours I had spent in a local Lancashire pub, the Cock & Bottle, where a game of "501" or "Killer" and a cheap pint of bitter were par for the course on a Friday night out with the lads. Now, when I think of darts, I think of a set of three sharp metal objects each topped with a colorful feathered "flight," ready to be hurled at a cork dartboard held together by metal rungs separating the numbered sections, 1–20.

Not in Pucks!

As we wandered over to a quieter section of the bar, I was immediately struck by what can only be described as something from my Southport Pleasure Beach past. The only thing missing was the prize rack next to the machine! For a start I was handed plastic tipped darts. The board itself had hundreds of tightly woven pimples in it, rather like the surface of "stickle bricks," the rival to Lego from our childhood. Surrounding the board's perimeter was a digital LED scoreboard which looked so confusing I felt I needed a math degree before I could attempt to press any of its buttons.

"501"

"601"

"901"

"Cricket"

Mounted on a display next to the board there was an interactive, electronic heckler, which produced soundbites:

"Loser!"

"You da man!"

"He shoots. He scores!"

After Jussi had given me a quick overview, I stood before the line and was given a voice prompt to throw my dart. I was half expecting a surprise visit from Mickey Mouse or Pluto were I to land in "double top"!

"We have a bit of a simpler approach to this game back home, Jussi. None of these crazy bloody bells, whistles and this plastic stuff!"

I cast my mind back to the Cock & Bottle, with its thick, smoky haze, our boots sticking to the beer-stained floor tiles, the vision of a slouched local: black eyepatch, fag in hand, empty beer glasses surrounding him, grumbling about our youthful presence in "his" aged den!

Pucks' darts scene was definitely not the Cock & Bottle!

"Ah well, Gaaary, you're in the land of the lawsuit here in the States, buddy. Imagine one of these sharp babies landing in someone's leg if it rebowwwnded off the boarrrd," Jussi said, slurring his words as he attempted to explain the theory behind "safe darts." As I attempted to focus on the dart board in front me, I felt distracted by the foot-stomping thrust of a jukebox stuck in "80s-hair-band" mode, belting out "Livin' on a Prayer" and "Every Rose has its Thorn" along with a police-siren on the TV announcing the start of the third period of the Red Wings game. Talk about sensory overload!

After a couple more beers, Jussi declared it was time to leave. As we headed toward the door, Jussi thrust the keys to his truck into my hand.

"Izzz 'ad too many beers, Gaaaarrwyy. You will have to be my designated driver."

Designated driver? What the fuck?!!

I obligingly laughed and opened the door for Jussi.

As he wobbled through the exit, it became obvious that Jussi was loaded, drunk, as in "pretty much out of it."

"Honestly Gaaaarrwyy, buddy, you'll have to drrrrive. I've had one too many, my Brrritish ..."

I could not believe what I was hearing.

"Yeah, well I don't know if you noticed, Jussi, but I matched you all the way, mate!"

'Ahhhh, come on Brrritish buddy, drive my truck. Take us hooome!'

Jussi was deadly serious.

Unbelievable!

I had only just arrived in the States. We were pretty much in the middle of nowhere. It was pitch black. I hadn't taken my Michigan driving test and had never driven on the opposite side of the road before. And I had also drunk the same amount of beer as my new boss. I stood in the mild, late evening air, the muffled cheering from the bar colliding with the sound of crickets, holding the keys in my hand, a rather tired looking Finn slumped before me in the passenger seat of his huge F350 truck. As the new and unfamiliar nocturnal vibrations resonated around us, I contemplated my predicament. I decided there and then that even though we had drunk the same amount, I was more capable of getting us home than the wasted Finnish "Frank Cannon" next to me.

As I started the engine, Jussi stirred from his stupor assuring me that the road home was "safe and quiet at this time of night." I shifted the gearstick into drive, feeling somewhat disgusted at my actions. I had never driven a car under the influence before, let alone in a foreign country and in unfamiliar surroundings. I could have sworn that having to drive a fucked-up Finn back home was not in my contract!

After what seemed an eternity and after having to swerve to avoid the reflective stare of several strange nocturnal animals, I spotted Jussi's subdivision. Thankfully, and as Jussi had predicted, we had not passed or seen another vehicle.

"There you go, buddy! I told you that you had nothing to worry about. Great job, buddy! Great job!"

"Jussi, mate" I replied. "I am never doing that again! Why didn't you tell me beforehand?! I would have willingly driven you home and drank far less in the bargain."

"Ahh, come on Gaaary!" Jussi said, seemingly unfazed. "I knew you couldn't wait to get your hands behind the wheel of my baby." A wasted grin appeared on his weathered face as he added "'Besides, that wouldn't have been any fun would it?! Me getting buzzzed and my new British buddy sitting there drinking a diet," his rip-roaring laugh echoing through the truck's cabin as he went to undo his seatbelt.

Jussi Kipli , my passport to life in America.

For a brief moment that night, as I lay my head down on my pillow, my nose stuffed up by the wafting fragrant rose petal aroma, I couldn't help but visualize myself on a bracing walk along Portobello beach on Scotland's southeast coast, the troubles of my day fading away.

11

Separated by a Common Language

My new place of employment—Back to Motion Sports Medicine Clinic—was located in a modern medical building on the outskirts of Canton. It contained a plush foyer, and the registry of businesses attached to the wall read "First Floor: Sports Medicine and Physical Therapy." I had to get used to that term—*physical therapy*—having been a "physiotherapist" for so many years back in Britain.

I was the new addition to a team of three therapists. My caseload consisted of clients as young as twelve months to patients in their nineties; orthopedic cases such as knee, hip, and shoulder replacements; back surgery rehabilitation; and sports injuries. My work day began at 6:00 a.m. and finished at 4:00 p.m. I had never treated a patient as early as 6:00 a.m. in Britain. People in the States appeared to get up early and work long days, sometimes working two and three jobs. It didn't take long before my own working day soon began to gain a rhythm as I ventured into the building each morning around 5:00 a.m. I had been enrolled for the State of Michigan Physical Therapy Licensure examination for mid-July. I was required to attain certification as a Michigan Physical Therapist within a given timeframe, otherwise I would be on a plane back home at some point. This was a rather obvious motivator!

I have always been a morning person and find studying more productive at dawn compared to dusk and beyond. Besides, the pot pourri-free environment motivated me to study at work before the clinic opened. Confined to a small treatment room, I would focus hard on the study packs and multiple choice questions that would provide my passage into life in the States.

My work environment had a different feel to it than back "home." I was surrounded by a group of very welcoming co-workers; co-workers who loved Oprah Winfrey; who drove to work with gigantic cups of coffee perched next to the steering wheels of their monstrous vehicles;

who had no hesitation when it came to devouring donuts and cookies first thing in the morning.; co-workers who loved to shop—before work, at lunch, and right after work. They shopped at the mall, at Meijer, Kohl's, JC Penny, Macy's, Lord & Taylor, making sure they took full advantage of the "mega deals" and "special sales" constantly on offer. Co-workers who stayed up late trying to get their kids to pass something called their SAT's, before slumping on the couch to watch "the late local news at 11" and its non-stop reports of scams, beatings, burglaries, muggings, shootings, and murders. Discussions about baseball, Montel Williams, Ford Motors' latest stock prices, the Red Wings, euchre, and poker had me feeling like I was on a different planet as I adjusted to the daily grind of the American work day.

My first week at the clinic was as expected. Slow. Very slow. Initially, Jussi taught me about paperwork, procedures, office protocol, and the dictation process. No longer would I be sitting at my desk writing endless notes. I had moved up a notch and could call in my examination and treatment observations to a dictation service. Transcripts of my notes would be available within two business days ready to be checked before signing off. Wow! Now *that* was cool! I suddenly felt important.

The physical therapists I worked alongside were Rita and Dee, two very nice ladies in their early forties. It appeared early on, though, that if ever there was a stereotype of an American female's passage through adolescence to early forties, then I had the evidence right there working next to me every single day. From Prom Queens to young brides, they were both a page out of the textbook of the American dream. The same "guy" from high school prom, through college, and onto marriage; a different outfit every day, color coordinated with obligatory white or skin-colored tights whatever the weather; the 401K pension plan; the occasional visit to Vegas to escape reality, and, then, when all was said and done, plans to move down to Florida or Arizona to live a life of glorious retirement in the southern sunshine.

I thrived on our early exchanges, every bit as intrigued by their backgrounds as they appeared to be with mine. I considered the contrast: two Barbie dolls, fixed smiles and skinny frames, hair spectacular each and every morning, and me, a scruffy, scrawny lad with my broad Lancashire— and apparently "cute"—English accent. Immaculate appearances matched immaculate postures as the two belles professionally delivered physical therapy with a clinical execution. I observed Rita and Dee closely those first few days as they went about their business, imagining them as technicians in a state of the art government facility of vital importance to world stability and peace—a far cry from an apathetic middle-aged Scotswoman with poorly applied lipstick trying to rid herself of her dandruff before morning break in a bog-standard NHS sink! It appeared to me that the physical therapists at Back to Motion took their jobs very seriously indeed.

With that in mind, I knew that I was going to have to create a favorable first impression when it came to my initial treatment sessions. I knew that, niceties aside, they were eager to "see what the British guy was made of." Since I had yet to pass the Michigan State board exam, I was only able to treat clients under Rita or Dee's supervision. One of my first patients was Mrs. Stonovich, a frail old lady with one of the nastiest-looking elbow fractures I had ever seen. I was to take over her care from the previous therapist, who, of course, she had adored. No pressure there!

During the treatment session, I provided an empathetic ear for an obviously emotionally unstable lady, who appeared to be on the verge of a breakdown. I handed her tissue after tissue with which to wipe the many gentle tears that flowed throughout. As our treatment session wound up, I felt compelled to offer some words of encouragement to Mrs. Stonovich, who appeared to be comforted by the "very nice English gentleman." Still wanting to play well-wisher, I felt obliged to send Mrs. Stonovich on her way with some parting words of encouragement to ease her concerns. With my two colleagues and a physical therapy assistant deep in concentration in the treatment area, I pinpointed my charge as she was about to leave the clinic, head bowed and still reflecting on her delicate state. I said loudly "Always remember, Mrs. Stonovich, keep your pecker up, eh?!'

Silence fell upon the clinic, a silence that was shattered seconds later by an audible thrust of tears from my patient as she headed to the ladies room with a determined stride. Dee and Rita immediately glared at me, eyes wide open, aghast. I shrugged, confused at the collective reaction from staff and clients alike. Dee escorted me to one side, excusing herself from her own patient.

"Gary! I can't believe you just said that!"

"Said what, Dee?" I replied, mystified.

"Pecker! You can't shout pecker here, especially not to someone like dear old Mrs. Stonovich."

"How do you mean, Dee? What's wrong with saying keep your pecker up?"

"There's *everything* wrong with saying keep your pecker up, Gary! That's disgusting! I can't believe you."

"Wait! What?" I replied, fully committed to my defense. "Have we got the same pecker going on here, Dee?'

"What are you talking about," Dee replied somewhat agitated. "I can't believe you, Gary!"

"Pecker," I repeated, using the tip of my index finger to elevate the end of my nose with a rhythmical motion all its own.

"Keep your pecker up! Up, see?! Up!" My eyes were almost popping out of my head due to the sheer determination with which I had to convince Dee that I had not said anything out of turn.

"Oh my god, Gary!" Dee retorted in a high pitched staccato tone. "We don't, do we?! We don't have the same pecker at all!" And with that, Dee's laughter burst out across the department. As she laughed, she exclaimed loudly, "Oh my god! That is sooooo funny, Gary! We don't have the same pecker at all!"

Still somewhat confused, I said "Dee, what's this all about? My very first patient is in the ladies room in tears and I have no clue what you are talking about?"

Dee put her skinny, Barbie-like arm around me, shuffled me into the dictation room and then, quietly whispered in my ear:

"Gary, in America a pecker is a man's privates! His dick!"

Ouch!

And with that, I had cemented my arrival at Back to Motion Sports Medicine clinic. The ice had been thoroughly broken by my "tale of two peckers!"

12

Don't Forget the Motor City!

Jussi had been kind enough to loan me his F-350 for a short time each weekend and gave me a ride to work each day, but I didn't want to take advantage for much longer. It was time to get my own fully-fledged membership to the Motor City. I must have walked miles those first few weeks, cruising the massive car lots, trying to spot a bargain. I didn't have much money to play with until the paychecks started to come in and certainly didn't want to get embroiled in the payment plans and financing specials that I soon came to realize were a part of everyday life in America. Credit and debt were not in my British DNA.

I loved those exciting evenings. My stage was always set: the bright, blue evening sky, slowly fading as the distinct red tone to the west came to the fore. Jussi and I quickly developed a game plan as he dropped me at the east end of Ford Road—Michigan's car sales artery. Two hours later, he would return and position himself at the west end of the same road in anticipation of my imminent arrival. Of course, it was the time in between that I would relish, as I dreamt my way through numerous dealers' lots. I was looking at Mustangs, T-Birds, Pontiac Grand Am's, trucks and SUV's, the like of which I had never seen before: V-6's, V-8's, 3.5 and 4-liter engines, automatic transmissions. I was on another planet.

Each evening, Jussi would pick me up, and each time I had the same answer: "Nope! Haven't found one yet, mate!" Much to the annoyance of the polished car salesmen eager to coax a purchase out of me, I had mastered the fast track to test driving some of the most exciting new models available from Michigan's "Big Three." I was a scrawny Englishman with a five-dollar backpack trudging up to a salesman and asking "Hi! Could I take a look at that black Mustang?"

Then, one night, as the sun popped its chin down over the horizon and we were on our way home after another fruitless search, I spotted her: "For Sale: 1987 T-Bird, good runner, excellent condition, 80,000 miles, $2,000 OBO ("or best offer")!"

Jussi immediately had his reservations. And he was probably right.

Undeterred, however, I was truly taken by the beast of a machine. I had seen nothing like it before and couldn't wait to make it mine.

The transaction was swift. After a quick check under the "hood," I whipped out my checkbook and handed over a check for $1,700 to the scruffy garage owner. Chewing his tobacco in none too subtle a manner, and with an audible squeal emitting from his rear end as he leaned over the counter to hand me the title for the car, he turned to the side and spat out the chewed debris which landed with a "thunk" in the trash can. I guess you can't choose your dealer when you have a small budget, need a car, may only be in the States for a short time, and, more to the point, have suddenly become smitten by a beast of a motor at a price that answers your desperate need for wheels. The smell of the vehicle, the devilish black color, the shape, the wonderful curves, I had fallen in instant love with a car so different to anything I had ever seen, let alone being at an affordable price for a "fresh off the boat" Englishman whose only prior motor vehicle purchase had been a very distant, less endowed, cousin of the power rod that had caught my eye. My new baby was equipped with a V6 3.8 liter engine supercharged to 210 horsepower. As one popular motor car magazine noted: "nothing else in the price range offers the same irresistible blend of sporting performance and solid luxury." The T-Bird had been lauded as an icon of automotive technology. Did I ever, in my wildest dreams, contemplate that I would own such a car?

The next day was spent running around finalizing all the details such as visiting the Secretary of State to switch ownership of the car's title and registering new plates—all Greek to me. I was fortunate to have Jussi to help guide me through the whole process. When you buy a car in America for the first time, you find yourself on your hands and knees bolting your own license plate to the rear bumper and then placing a little color-coded sticker in the top right-hand corner to verify your car's registration.

As evening fell upon the sleepy Midwest town of Canton, Michigan, I edged my first-ever American car onto Ford Road and headed west for the Kipli household. The dashboard was a sight to behold, a menagerie of brightly-lit, digital green icons indicating my beast's reaction to the pressure on the pedals. It was a balmy spring evening and with the window down, I had another "American moment." I was driving my new supercharged monster without the requirement of a clutch! I went to sleep that night in awe of the fact I had just purchased a big, black "fuck off" American Ford Thunderbird!

The next morning couldn't come quickly enough. I was excited to drive my wheels into work. For a while there I was on a roll. The odd puff of black smoke and the occasional stall, but all in all a "cool ride" as I made my way along the local roads, acclimatizing to my surroundings and checking out available apartments. I even threw in the odd "Detroit lean," giving the boys downtown a run for their money. And then, not long after entering the freeway and getting up to full speed, it happened! I was cruising at 70 miles an hour on I-94, window down when my T-Bird decided to project from its rear a plume of the blackest smoke I had ever seen. And if that wasn't enough, it flat out stalled dead—right in in the middle lane of one of the busiest freeways in the Midwest!

"Check engine" light flashing, surrounded by clouds of black smoke, I was at the mercy of the traffic in my wake. Quite frankly, I shat myself! I stared into my rearview mirror, inhaling deeply and gripping the steering wheel so hard that my knuckles turned white. I battled to get a response out of the car trying to turn into the shoulder of the freeway and away from the oncoming traffic behind me. But the steering column kept locking! A swift introduction to power steering! The gravity of the situation hit me. I was a total sitting duck, frozen on a busy freeway. Car after car headed straight for me at ferocious speeds, swerving at the last second, the screeching of tires blending with the pulse of the horn, which I am sure drowned out the expletives, as each driver growled his growl. To say I felt vulnerable as I sat in my motionless vehicle, trying to find the hazard lights and restart the car while drivers "flipped me the bird," was putting it mildly. My eyes were staring back at me fixed in my driving mirror, attempting to subliminally notify the oncoming drivers that it was in both our best interests that they slow down and swiftly change lanes. After what seemed the longest few seconds of my life, I managed to start the car, and with a distinct nonchalance the black beast began to roll forward as if nothing had even happened. After a slow pick up, she was soon mixing it back up with the vehicles around her, her driver rather paler in complexion and still a tad light-headed, none too comfortable about the remainder of the journey ahead. A definite distrust had already developed between driver and vehicle!

I did manage to get her home, my smoking carnival arriving back at Jussi's early that evening. According to Jussi I had bought a "lemon" and at the end of the day there was nothing I could do about it. I could have gone back to "Oily Sid's" and threatened him, but Jussi explained the consequences and that I would probably become embroiled in legal affairs that would have taken forever and cost a fortune. I had to resign myself to the fact that I had been well and truly squeezed.

Working as a physical therapist, however, and treating a large number of patients had its advantages. Enter Quincy the Ford assembly line worker. Quincy was on "Workers' Comp" —a term that I had never heard of until I had arrived Stateside. I learned about it quickly though. Being so close to the Big Three auto manufacturers in southeast Michigan, I would come across many patients with that healthcare coverage. Workers' Comp struck me as a trade-off. The way I saw it was that it seemed to be an agreement between worker and company: should the worker be injured at work, the employer pays for treatment and also compensates the worker for extended time off and nobody sues. I began to realize that some patients on Workers' Comp were not always the most motivated to get better quickly. Quincy didn't seem that way though. He was itching to get back to work and had a genuine injury. A nasty rotator cuff tear. He was more or less fully recovered and only had a week or so left before returning to the line. I had been seeing him for pretty much most of my first few weeks at the clinic.

"Dude, I swear, it has to be your oxygen sensor."

"Do you think you can help me out, Quincy?"

"Brother, I'll fix you up. Come on down to my place early Saturday and my bro' and I will get 'er done, dude. We'll get ya, man!"

I wasn't sure about the "get ya, man," but the rest sounded terrific.

6:00 a.m. Saturday and I was driving into a rather dodgy part of west Detroit, dripping oil and spewing nasty emissions into the atmosphere. The street I was driving on was like a scene from "Escape from New York" as burned-out wrecks, rusted rides, and car parts littered the roadside, cradled by homes that looked like they had seen much better days. I bounced into Quincy's neighborhood. True to his word, Quincy was "up and at 'em" when I knocked on the door.

"Great to see you, dude! We should have her done and dusted in less than an hour, buddy. Hey, meet my brother, Coby." A huge bear of a fella emerged from the humble dwelling and practically broke my hand into pieces, such was the force of the grip of his handshake. I immediately sensed that Coby was none too happy about having his early Saturday morning disrupted by the pale white English dude his brother was helping out.

Coby did not utter a single word for the rest of the morning, as he went about his business, his eyeballs enlarging every few minutes. I swear he was one day away from a stroke, those bulging bloodshot eyes on red alert during the whole process.

Standing, holding a wrench at dawn with my two new best mates, all 500lbs of them combined, "hood" up and working like madmen, I realized that Jussi had obviously been right to question my impulsive choice of car purchase. To say I looked a tad pathetic would be an accurate assumption. To say that I continued to irritate the hell out of Quincy's brother for some reason was also very much on the money. Covered in oil and wearing a constant frown, I swear the man was about to grab a Colt 45 and ram it down my throat. However, I was indeed desperate. Putting my faith in the hands of my two new buddies, I did all I could to appear calm and grateful, chatting up a storm—as was my tendency—a real contrast to the stoic beast of a mechanic sending piercing glares my way at regular intervals.

Four hours and four bottles of Budweiser later, the suspect oxygen sensor and several other issues had been dealt with. It wasn't even noon. After a quick visit to the liquor store for a twenty-four pack of America's favorite beer, along with a bag of "super-sized" fodder from MacDonald's, a few greenbacks, and as many thank-yous as I could muster, I bid farewell to my Detroit saviors.

I suffered the "grip of death" once again as Coby bid me farewell, this time a glint from his gold tooth catching the early-afternoon sunlight. During that whole morning, the man had not uttered a single word despite my mile a minute banter. As my mother always said "you've got a tongue in your head, son . . . bloody well use it!" Well, I had used it—apparently a tad too much if Coby's rather tired and exasperated expression was anything to go by. Ours was indeed the swiftest of goodbyes, as before I knew it he had retired to his disheveled abode, having crushed my right hand once more, and leaving the parting words to Quincy and myself.

I eventually sped away from the "hood" that Saturday afternoon full of renewed hope that I now owned the automotive bargain of the year.

13

"Keep yer 'air on!"

I had the job. I had the car. I didn't, as yet, have the "pad."

I had saved enough for a down payment on an apartment, in no small part down to the kindness and patience of Jussi and Diane providing that initial roof over my head. I didn't want to fall into the trap of renting an apartment in one of the fancy Canton complexes with their "cool pools" and on-site fitness centers, and blow over $700 a month on a place in which I would essentially only be sleeping, due to my long work hours. Therefore I decided to opt for the most economical option. The town of Dearborn, home to Henry Ford and his motor car dynasty, just twenty miles from Jussi's place in Canton, and only fifteen minutes' drive from Metro Detroit airport, covered all of my requirements.

A cheeky visit to the Student Union office under the guise of being a mature student at the University of Michigan Dearborn gained me access to their rental agency list. This proved to be one of the best moves of my short time in the States thus far. Later that day, I was viewing a fully furnished "granny flat" at the back of a real life granny's house—a certain Mrs. Rhonda Cloak.

I didn't have many belongings. Indeed, that was something Dee had attempted to address by kindly offering to run me around a number of community garage sales during our lunch breaks or after work.

The garage sale: Americans love them. The concept is basic. You open your garage, sometimes your entire home and front yard, plant several signs outside, and even several streets away, directing the general public to come and take a peek. The village hall community jumble sale I had been accustomed to growing up in Lancashire England had, in America, seemingly morphed into a rather more individualistic sale of personal family possessions from inside the actual family home. Primed and ready in a rather large mini-van, Dee and I would enter each residential area fully intent on acquiring several giveaway deals on apartment necessities, perfect to set up an Englishman abroad. As it turned out, after several days of searching, the only item that I had acquired was a two-foot tall white bust of Elvis! It caught my eye at the very first garage sale. I wasn't even an Elvis fan, but it simply screamed "Americana." It was symbolic, a nod, if you like, to recognize the seismic shift I had taken to plant my feet on American soil. "Thank you very much!"

My new bedsit was a simple dwelling, with comfortable, if somewhat sparse, décor. All amenities were included and, in return, Mrs. Cloak received a good source of income. I was about to become part of a rather unique relationship and an arrangement that would serve both of us well. I signed a lease and moved in the following weekend. Jussi and Diane bid me a fond farewell. To be honest, I think burning Diane's white kitchen countertop with her new Tefal frying pan probably had me on thin ice, but politeness reigned and I appeared forgiven, Diane fully aware that her husband valued my presence at his clinic.

As Elvis and I sped east along Ford Road toward Dearborn, I reflected on the kindness of the Kiplis. That initial period of "finding my feet" with the cushion of their hospitality and support had provided me with a terrific foundation as I transitioned my way into American life. Jussi remained my boss and our connection would continue, albeit with a definite reduction in my cholesterol level and alcohol consumption.

There was no doubting that I had stumbled upon an original in Rhonda; seventy-nine years old, going on thirty-nine! Her youthful appearance amazed me and I was immediately intrigued as to her secret. Rhonda and I negotiated a few ground rules, one of which was that I would be able to use the washer and dryer in the basement of her house.

We agreed on a deal in which I would contribute some money towards the laundry component of the "Rhonda rental rules."

"I'll sort some kind of agreement out, Gary."

She wasn't kidding.

On my first weekend in my new Dearborn pad, I carefully stepped down the narrow staircase into the basement with my first dirty pile of laundry. Musty smelling American basements were still a new concept to me. The sheer size of the space beneath the actual house amazed me. I was used to attics back home, homes that had projections and extensions protruding out of ceilings, with nothing below ground floor.

Wandering through the basement maze, I eventually discovered a fourth sizeable room in quick succession and immediately noted, sat atop a tumble dryer and very clearly marked, a can labelled "Laundry Donations." The label was written in thick red marker, seemingly with the intent of making it as eye catching as possible. On closer inspection, I could see what appeared to be an old Folgers coffee can. As the Mrs Cloak version of the Folgers ad goes: "the best part of having a lodger is money in your laundry donation can!" I had heard the commercials on TV at Jussi's. The song had a sickly, albeit catchy, ring to it and the storylines were often rather corny to say the least. It was one of those "American moments" every time one of them had appeared on television, reminding me of my new alternative surroundings. As an ardent tea drinker it didn't hold a candle to any of the Chimpanzee PG Tips commercials or the classic Tetley Tea Folk ads that I was used back in the Britain of the seventies and eighties. My brand recognition skills were obviously working well, though.

The snuggly-fitting plastic lid of the can appeared original and featured a delicately manicured slit, providing sufficient space for both coin and folded US dollar bills to easily pass through. I quickly surmised that Rhonda didn't mess around. Still, it was better than the alternative—a lengthy stroll to Dearborn's main laundrette, or as Rhonda had already reminded me several times: "In America, it is a *laundromat*, Gary."

After emptying the washing machine of its first English load and stumbling over the basement drain, wet clothes in hand, I opened the door of the tumble dryer and immediately recoiled, stumbling backwards and dropping my clothes onto the floor.

"What the . . .?"

Gathering my courage, I cautiously approached the "thing" that was hiding inside the dryer. I was in a foreign country whose animal inhabitants were of a very different nature, and, at first glance, I had no clue as to what the beast that lay within could be. It was fairly small, very hairy and totally still. Gently lifting a mop from its bucket, I stood as far away as possible from the dryer and tentatively poked at the creature. It refused to move and so I tried again, finally managing to leverage the hairy mass out of the dryer and onto the floor. Still no movement. I sensed that it was most likely dead. I stood there for a few minutes to see if it was going to move before I approached. As I got closer, the realization hit me. This was no endangered species. This was, in fact, the answer to my question regarding my landlady's youthful appearance. Her wig! Her blue-grey mop had been washed and left in the tumble dryer. My "grundies" were about to share the same dryer as my seventy-nine-year-old landlady's wig. Mrs. Cloak had no idea that her new lodger had got to know her rather too well, rather too quickly.

After I had finished drying my clothes, I felt it was my duty to return Rhonda's "fountain of youth" to its previous resting place, thankful that Rhonda hadn't disturbed us in the process. Laying the stylish mop of hair in the warm bosom of a tumble dryer was quite a bizarre experience. Maybe the latent heat inside the dryer would add a little extra lift to Rhonda's curly locks? I returned to my pad, attempting to convince myself that this little episode had surely been nothing but a figment of my imagination and that I needed to keep the bizarre event tucked away in a quiet corner of my mind so as not to cause any further embarrassment in the future.

If only it were that simple!

The following morning was Sunday and just as I had arisen, I was summoned loudly by the owner of the hairy basement monster. I was invited to join Rhonda and her son's family for my inaugural "Cloak Family American Breakfast." I soon realized that my invite provided a chance for Rhonda's son to size up his mother's latest lodger, a chance for the family to rest easy, knowing that Old Mother Cloak was in safe hands. I spruced up, readying myself for the ordeal that lay ahead. Not that I could complain. The cheap rent and low overheads were more than ample compensation for having to oblige such an awkward invitation.

As I entered the room, I immediately struggled to compose myself. I did all I could to avoid eye contact with Mrs. Cloak without making it blatantly obvious, otherwise I think I would have totally lost it. I leapt at any chance I had to burst into a bellowing throttle of laughter to release the pent up hilarity within. It wasn't the dysfunctional appearance of all around that table—"dysfunctional" being the same word often used by Rhonda herself to describe her family—nor the totally over the top array of food that beckoned me. It was that bloody wig! That very same "mop" that I had poked and prodded with a rather more functional cleaning mop was now sitting—or rather, tilted precariously—on top of Rhonda's head. The hour that followed was agonizingly long, as I attempted to avoid too many glimpses of the blue-grey beast hovering on top of the hostess with the mostest, otherwise, it may well have sent me totally over the edge.

From that day on, I always made sure to pass a flattering, somewhat devilish, comment as to how well-dressed Rhonda was as she ventured out to one of her many social events. Her "hair" in its immaculately-groomed form would always gain the most respect. Her response to my compliments always seemed especially well received, judging by the pearly white grin thrown my way.

14

Summertime and
the Livin' is ...

My first summer in Michigan. Big blue sky all the way and a first sample of the humidity that saps your energy and leaves you drenched in sweat after taking two steps outside. Ferocious intermittent rains came and went. There was no moderate drizzle for days on end as was the norm back in Britain. In Michigan, it was all or nothing on the precipitation front. And, as the saying in Michigan goes: "if you don't like the weather, simply wait five minutes!"

I quickly learned that the only way to keep my new T-Bird in any way functional was to lube her up with a quart of oil every few days; 5W-30 was the code and key to my T-Bird's functionality. With a twenty-four-pack of "the black stuff" in the trunk, I was purchasing oil more frequently than petrol. My car and I quickly developed a high maintenance, love/hate relationship. And we had to make it work. In the urban sprawl of my new home town, you had to have wheels, since there was no "popping down the shops" on foot.

I tried to pull on the positives. Despite the constant appearance of the "check oil" light, the odd stall, and the occasional burst of black smog, with windows down, and a Michigan summer breeze ruffling my hair, I convinced myself that I was the newly-anointed King of the Road. Denial is an amazing thing! The wooden bumper car from I-94 now had real competition with my newly-rejuvenated beast of a vehicle, lubed to the hilt and ready to roam.

Out on the road in my temperamental beast, I began to properly focus on American radio. Cue another American moment! WWJ News Radio 950 for Detroit's traffic and weather "on the eights!" AM radio in Michigan appeared to have a sound all of its own as it fed the driving maniacs with all the information they needed as fast as possible, aligning itself with the juggernaut that was fast-paced America. WWJ News was the first station I tuned into and I was instantly captivated. Why on earth does anyone need to know the weather every eight minutes? And as for the traffic updates, I had never contemplated being told that a major road was temporarily blocked due to an abandoned barbecue grill in the outside lane; or, the fact that there was a fridge blocking the exit ramp of the Southfield Freeway onto Warren causing a two-mile backup. Wild! I became addicted to WWJ's traffic updates, delivered so dramatically that you would have thought that your survival depended on keeping that dial tuned to "Michigan's Biggest and Best News Radio Station!"

The drama was not confined to traffic updates. Take the weather for example: "I am at the corner of Wyoming and Warren where it is, as you can see behind me ... raining. It is actually raining so hard, I have to tell you all please, do not leave the house today without a waterproof coat." Thanks for that!

Meaningless interviews with passersby were constantly lined up, locals grasping the nettle to enter into "news radio stardom":

"Yeah I know it!" someone would declare eagerly responding to a reporter's loaded line of questioning.

"Sir. What do you think of this heavy rain today?"

"It's sure wet 'n' nasty, man." A most insightful response.

"Ma'am. It really is a cold one out here today, isn't it?"

"Ain't that the truth!"

"I'm tellin' ya, dude!"

Such riveting reposts.

"Ah, you sure got that right," a local resident would proclaim, before the on-the-spot reporter, proud of his or her soundbite, was happy to send it "back to the studio."

Another adjustment into American life was my weekend supermarket visit. I quickly became aware that I only had to open my mouth in line at the till and the floodgates would be opened. "Oh my God! What a cuuuute accent!" I was used to Northern English phrases such as "nice one," "dead good," "smart," or "top." But "cute"? "Wow! That accent is sooo cuuuute. Where you from?" My reply tended to be along the lines of "Where do you think I'm from?" "Oh, I don't know? Australia?" "Spain?"—that was the answer I received one Saturday afternoon as I was bagging my broccoli. I had heard that not too many Americans had passports, content to remain in the U.S. which had all that they desired in terms of diversity of climate and geography—which of course it does. Judging by the ability of most shoppers trying to recognize European accents I fully understood!

I contained my laughter, withheld my shocked reaction and headed home for a glass of Sangria in full anticipation of an afternoon siesta. Gracias for that!

Ah, yes, the American supermarket. It certainly is a place to behold for a new expat Brit. Talk about abundance. Indeed, why stock twenty types of cheese when one-hundred-and-fifty will do?! I had never seen so much in so big a space. As you enter most American supermarkets, it is almost impossible to avoid the scrum of people crashing their way through to the bottle and can return. The stench of old ale was a constant reminder that Michigan had a ten cent refund on bottles and cans—it was only five cents in the surrounding Midwestern states—and so, with carts overflowing, the empty remnants of the week's, or maybe month's, beer and Mountain Dew quota, shoppers would jockey for position.

Having fought my way through bottle returns, I would then be officially welcomed by the store's very own "greeter."

"Good afternoon, sir. Welcome to Kroger. How are you today?"

American customer service; nothing quite like it!

Funny folks, though, these "greeters." If I was to reply and act as though I wanted to start a conversation, the shocked look upon the face of "Missy Meet and Greet" would be priceless. The robotic greeting was where it stopped; anything further resulted in a dumfounded employee. In the "meet and greet" world, prolonged conversation was not a part of the job description. Besides, pretty much everyone appeared to be in a rush. Most folks would barely acknowledge the "Welcome to XYZ Megastore" greeting. A genuinely inquisitive Englishman, full of friendly Lancashireness, however, was different:

"I am fine today. How are you?"

"Excuse me, sir?"

"How are you doing today?"

"Oh? Me, sir? I am OK."

"Well that's good. So are they keeping you busy then?"

"Excuse me, sir?"

"I was just wondering; are they keeping you busy today?"

An extended silence.

"Beautiful day out there today, eh? What do you reckon?"

"Errm."

Silence, obvious brush off, and with eyes averted, as if to say "get outta here, dude," the greeter would eye the next customer. A swift side step, fixed smile, and the all-important corporate phrase is once again uttered:

"Good afternoon, madam. Welcome to Kroger. How are you today?"

Despite having been shunned by my new friend, with my personal "meet and greet" having been brought to an abrupt and unseemly end, I was ready for my several-mile stroll around the store. I would then head over to the checkout line and wait for the customers in front of me to dispense their shopping cart loads onto the conveyer belt. I was amazed at the sheer volume of items in the trolleys. There was enough food to feed a small army and enough cans of Pepsi and Mountain Dew in one cart to fill a vending machine. As my wait in line continued, I noticed rows of glossy magazines right next to the checkout tills, carefully positioned for that final impulse purchase.

"Fast Track to Becoming the Next Millionaire"

"Hillary Clinton Adopts Alien Baby"

"Bigfoot Kept Lumberjack as Love Slave"

"Best Tips for Trimming Your Fanny"

For a conservative Midwestern state, I was surprised at how seemingly liberated the women were, given the content of these magazines. I hadn't imagined a Michigan female desperate to purchase her ninety-nine cent booklet enlightening her on the correct way to trim her hairy crotch, let alone a publisher considering there being a market to sell such a magazine, furthermore placing it front and center next to a public checkout in a supermarket. I recall a lady behind me in line perusing the magazines and reaching for a copy of the "fanny trim" booklet. Our eyes met for a split second and I noted a definite defiance; her eyes-wide-open glare aimed in my direction, staring me down as she placed said magazine into her trolley. I could tell that there was one "fanny" that was about to get well and truly "trimmed" and she wasn't concerned in the least who knew it!

It was a few weeks later that I found out that a British "fanny" and an American "fanny" are two very different anatomical sites! I was still new to the States and was still struggling with my "peckers" and "fannys"! I imagined how the next time I tuned into WWJ 950 News Radio there would be a reporter placed in some way out location informing listeners just how cold her "fanny" was, as she reported on the fact that it was, once again, actually starting to rain.

I was rarely homesick during my first weeks in Michigan. I didn't really have the time to be. With so much that was new and with everything moving so quickly, the anticipation and excitement at what lay around each and every corner dominated my mind. The buzz of relocating and adapting to a new culture kept the thrill of a challenging new path alive.

America's impact is sudden. Opportunity beckons. It has the blood racing a little more when getting out of bed each morning. Its vitality grabs you by the balls and gets you believing that maybe your dreams can indeed become a reality. Still, my Lancashire upbringing, close ties, and respect for friends and family resonated at all times. I made sure to keep in touch with everyone. Letters were written, which took at least a week to arrive on UK shores. Replies were procrastinated over, eventually arriving in Michigan at least a further two weeks after that. Snail mail for sure. Old news by the time I ripped the letters open, but those connections were so valued. I purchased international phone calling cards to remain further engaged with the folks back in the UK.

Starting a new life abroad, far removed from all that I had known, highlighted that detachment along with the occasional guilt that I felt, having moved more than 3,500 miles away. Prior to coming to America, even during my early UK wanderlust years, I had always had somewhere that I had belonged to, people to fall back on, my inner nomad being satisfied, but with that important, constant support network never too far away. However, had I truly been fulfilled with my life at the time? The answer of course had to have been no. That itch, that recurring fidgety itch, had always been my driver.

I was fast realizing that maybe America, the last place I could have possibly imagined a short time ago, was actually making me more aware of how I could really challenge myself, push myself with an impetus that was providing happiness in the moment. A good sign indeed! Then again, America seemingly has made a habit of doing just that.

In the midst of such free and fun-loving trailblazing abroad, I always took time to remember where I came from and the huge step I had taken. I just had moments—anyone would. Those moments that sometimes made me feel as if I had done a runner from the people that meant the most to me. However, we should all go our own way, of course, and my mother's prophetic words, hammered into me from an early age, echoed loudly in my head once again.

"It's your life, son. Don't you worry about us. As long as you're happy doing what you're doing, then we're happy."

The freedom granted by that statement, the value of release, to be able to move forward and follow my own instincts. I so appreciated that.

Those same words remained poignant so many miles away from home. I was, indeed, continuing along my own instinctive path forward in life. My mother simply wouldn't have had it any other way!

15

"You Can't Win Anything with Kids"

My move to Hotel Hairpiece was going well. I had adjusted with relative ease to life in a rather unique twenty-five-by-fifteen-foot, window-lined, greenhouse-like bedsit. I had developed a surprising yet instinctive minimalist mindset, a rage against what I had quickly recognized as the American consumerist machine, resisting the abundant temptation at every turn. Indeed, my pad was so small that you couldn't even swing a proverbial cat in it, although Rhonda's pampered feline, Mr. Mozart, unneutered and every bit the "midnight rambler," did have me contemplating that thought most evenings as his high-pitched call to all female queens in the surrounding neighborhood drove me nuts. There was certainly nothing C minor about that cat's ear-rattling tone. Mr. Mozart was Rhonda's pride and joy. And Mr. Mozart was Gary's pain in the ass.

The location of my greenhouse proved perfect for work and amenities. The I-94 freeway on ramp was only two miles away. Entering the freeway from Dearborn's south side, I noted the sign for Chicago, which was 248 miles away. Big Bob of the Wakey Safe House and Soul Boy Bill from my college days had recently relocated to Chicago, and the thought that I was on the road that could take me all the way to the Windy City excited me each time I jumped onto the freeway, driving the short twenty miles west to work. I was sensing that a Midwest road trip could well be on the horizon, but without any late night Chinese on the menu.

I began to co-exist with my landlady with the minimum amount of fuss, as we both showed a mutual respect for each other's space, our communication extending to a brief "evening," or "how was your day?" During my first weeks at Hotel Hairpiece, I had no desire to purchase a TV. There was only crap on the 118 channels from what I had witnessed over at Jussi's. Any sporting events of significance—the Detroit Red Wings, Pistons, Lions, or Tigers—offered a chance to get out and explore the various bars dotted around the neighborhood.

I reveled in my reading and gobbled up CD after CD after discovering the BMG Music Service mailorder catalog with their "Twelve CDs for the Price of One" deals. I was a kid in a musical candy store. CDs were expensive back in the UK. Suddenly, I was able to stock up on albums for next to nothing: Pixies, Nirvana, REM, and Canadian bands like Cowboy Junkies, Sloan, and The Tragically Hip.

I worked hard to resist the multitude of fast food choices, with row after row of bright neon signs tempting all passersby to stop and consume. Instead, I developed my culinary skills on a thirty-dollar twin plate stove top, learning as much as I could about nutrition. I enrolled in yoga classes at the nearby hospital. Before leaving England, I thought yoga consisted of shaving your head, putting on a tightly-fitting diaper, and murmuring "ah, grasshopper"! The antiseptic smell of the adapted hospital conference room dissipated each time I focused on the gorgeous nurse come yogi, demonstrating her poses. Michelle's very own downward dog was my particular favorite, a pose that she, too, seemed to enjoy holding for what seemed a blissful eternity. Having taught me some zen insight, I was quickly inspired to turn my room into my very own tantric temple, a sanctuary from my daily surroundings.

My newly-discovered yin, of course, required the obligatory yang as I ventured upon a small bar at the end of the street called the Fall Sports Lounge. It was the perfect venue for Detroit sports broadcasts, along with live music from local bands each weekend, fulfilling another music fix. Slowly, but surely, I was rooting myself, attempting to establish a new normal thousands of miles from home.

I felt good. I was happy. But despite my smooth adjustment into American life, there was still that ever-present void: that one vital, missing component; a void that was present each and every weekend; one that left me pining as if for a long lost love. I had no "beautiful game"; no soccer fix; more specifically—and most importantly—*no Manchester United*!

And then, by chance, a sort-of solution presented itself. I had discovered a bookstore in Dearborn called The Little Professor. There were wall-to-wall books of every genre and a decent selection of art and music thrown in for good measure. If that wasn't enough, tucked away in a back corner, I discovered a small row of the familiar: *The Sunday Mirror*; *The Independent*; *The Mail on Sunday*, and *The Guardian*. These newspapers, imported from England, were a couple of weeks old, but they contained the all-important British sports pages. They were the last thing I had expected to find in a bookstore in Dearborn, Michigan.

Dearborn was home to the world headquarters of the Ford Motor Company, and I figured that The Little Professor offered this selection of newspapers for the British engineers who had moved to Michigan to work for Ford. There is a distinct sense of the surreal, sitting in a coffee shop in a small Midwestern town, drinking tea, and purusing the print pages from London's Fleet Street, while surrounded by the sensory overload of local activity, its quirks and accents on full display. I quickly came to depend on my regular order of "one of each." Ten dollars well spent, thank you very much. It was all I had. It was more than I had anticipated. It was a start.

Once August rolled around, however, and with it the start of the 1995–96 English Premier League season, my craving for soccer and Manchester United brought me right back down to earth with a bang. As they would say in Detroit, "shit just got real!" I needed to find a way to reconnect, to support my Red Devils, live and as it happened. For the first time in twenty years, ever since I first pledged my undying allegiance to Manchester United, I was resigned to no other option than living it in retro. I began to face the reality of a lengthy spell on the sidelines.

And then, one day, out of nowhere, right at the start of the season, Rhonda—most likely sick of my constant bellyaching—came up with an off-the-cuff suggestion.

"Is there any chance you could pick up the games from England on shortwave radio, Gary? I think my ex-husband left one down in the basement. He was quite the radio enthusiast and I'm sure he used to listen to a radio show from England."

"Yes, Rhonda! You beauty!" I gave her an impulsive hug before becoming overpowered by the smell of old lady lavender.

And so, lifted from the "this is my ex-husband John's stuff" section of Rhonda's musty basement, an antiquated piece of plastic measuring five inches by five inches became my potential lifeline to English soccer.

God bless you, Rhonda Cloak!

God bless you, John Cloak, whoever and wherever you may be!

And so, just like that, August 19, 1995 became resurrection day!

I wasted no time readying myself for the start of the new English Premier League season. I soon realized that my new Saturday ritual was fully dependent on essential placement of my portal. Reception was not easily attained; trial and error and a dogged determination in pursuit of any semblance of soccer news "live and as it happened" was my focus. The small plastic engine room to a global broadcasting machine hanging precariously from my fridge belied its significance as the central player, the doorway through which all the twists and turns of an epic Saturday's soccer could enter. Duct tape, that infamous American DIY necessity, held the radio securely in place as the faintest hint of reception latched onto a weathered and rather crooked looking antenna rendering my "church of the soccer mind" audible.

On the stroke of 10:00 a.m. U.S. Eastern Standard Time in Michigan (3:00 p.m. in England), I heard the distinctive high-pitched sound familiar to me from my time growing up in Britain. "The Pips," live from London reverberated around my pokey Dearborn bedsit. First introduced after the original broadcast of the chimes of Big Ben to usher in the New Year of 1924, this official time signal aligned in Greenwich Meantime had been utilized ever since—the last five seconds of each minute followed by a longer extended sixth and higher pitched "pip." It was signature BBC. Saturday, August 19, 1995—and the pips had ushered in the exciting start to a brand new English Premier League soccer season.

"Aaand welcome to Sportsworld on the BBC. Over the next couple of hours, we will bring you the main sporting news from around the world. But first here is a summary of today's world news read by ..." Cue the usual articulate British accent announcing the main news headlines of the day. As I listened, I sauntered over to top up my morning cup of tea, spilling a little as I reached over to turn the volume up as high as possible—not an easy task as the small unit still hung freely from its anchor point on top of the fridge. I felt immediate comfort as I was transported back to my homeland, a decent amount of tea still remaining in the cup in my left hand as I sat on the edge of my bed, contented with my efforts.

World news updates completed, there then followed a further introduction by presenter of the day, Martin Fookes.

"The start of a brand new Premier League season and we have it all covered for you here on Sportsworld. Let's straightaway take you around the grounds."

Get in there!

I smiled as I listened to enthusiastic commentators describe the "early goings" in game after game to the familiar backdrop of the roar of the crowd.

Manchester United were opening the season away at Aston Villa.

Sportsworld host Fookes once more: "We will continue to bring you all of the goals as they happen along with full second half commentary from one of our featured matches of the day just after 4:00 p.m."

Programming then swiftly changed gears to an editorial on fly fishing in East Anglia. Not exactly my cup of tea, but I had to stick with it, not daring to mess with the radio reception. After the last line had been cast off the East Anglian coastline, next up was a five-minute slot reporting on the German Bundesliga. It was a tad too early in the day to tolerate a Scotsman with dry accent attempt to wrap his tongue around the words Borussia Mönchengladbach. Soccer reports came and went as commentators delivered their very own signature spin about how goals had been dispatched. I listened intently for one reason only—news from Villa Park, Birmingham, England. And then . . .

"There's been a goal at Villa Park! Here's Alan Green with your commentary."

Yes!

That sentence was my first live connection with Manchester United since my move across the Pond.

The BBC producers liked to keep their listeners guessing and so my immediate concern focused on which team was in possession. The commentary started with United; a very good sign—or so I thought. In an instant, however, the Reds had lost possession, Villa had seized their chance and suddenly, there it was, Aston Villa's Holte End hero, Ian Taylor, had scored after just thirteen minutes.

What the . . . ?

And it wasn't long before I heard "and there's been another goal at Villa Park."

Ever the optimist, I sensed a United equalizer.

"And it's now 2-0 to Villa!"

Mark Draper had scored Villa's second goal with only twenty-six minutes gone. I still, of course, believed.

"And back to Villa Park again where a penalty kick has been awarded."

Peter Schmeichel had fouled Milošević in the penalty area.

"Dwight Yorke steps up. Dwight Yorke ... scores! 3-0 Villa!"

David Beckham scored a free kick late into the second half, but there was to be no comeback for United that day.

I glared over at the poxy plastic box dangling from my fridge and flipped it the bird.

Later in the day, I called High Glen Cottage in Drummore, Scotland to chat with my father—who I now referred to as "Des," in reverence to

Des Lynham, the one-of-a-kind BBC Match of the Day TV presenter—my father's newly-designated nickname reflecting his important role as chief United correspondent for his expat son. I had caught him in the middle of Match of the Day, late in the evening UK time.

Des delivered as only he could. "What's his face, Gary?"—a definitive trait of my father—his memory for names never coming too easily. "You know, Gary ... the ex-Liverpool lad ... lanky fella ... center-half ... likes to run with the ball. Oh, bloody hell. What's his name, son?"

"Alan Hansen, mate?" I threw him a lifeline.

"Aye, that's him. Well, you know what he said after the United game?"

"Go on, dad."

"He's just said that you can't win anything with kids! He was insisting that Aston Villa must have taken one look at that United teamsheet at quarter past two and been given an instant lift. He said that will happen every time Fergie plays kids and that he's got to buy more experienced players." United were missing several of their star names that day: Cole, Giggs, Cantona, and Bruce. Des continued. "Hansen reckons it's still not enough though, and that if they are to go on and win the league, they need strength in depth. And he said United just don't have that!"

"You can't win anything with kids!"

I sat back and considered those words conveyed to me via a telephone in a remote corner of southwest Scotland. United were fielding "kids" and these kids—according to one Mr. Alan Hansen—were out of their depth. Hansen's opinion certainly seemed justified after the outcome of the game at Villa Park. United had taken a good beating and the season opener had not gone well for sure. But then I thought to myself: *you know what? He's an ex bloody Liverpool player. Fuck that!* The most important reaction would be that of United's manager, Alex Ferguson. Would he hit the panic button and dispense with his "kids" after just one game?

Shortwave radio transmissions provided the all-important commentaries and scorelines during those first few weeks of the season. Reception would often fade on some of the bleaker autumn days that followed and it became an all-too-regular occurrence with only a couple of minutes to go in a particular match for the commentary to become a frustratingly garbled mass of sonic shite. More often than not, I would have to rely on Des to deliver the news from around the grounds, my father holding the telephone receiver next to the television in Scotland as the BBC's *Grandstand* reporter reeled off the results. My soccer world abroad was off and running, thanks to John Cloak's old radio, the BBC's *Sportsworld*, and my transatlantic roving reporter.

Alex Ferguson did indeed ignore Mr. Hansen, continuing to encourage youth as United blended the old heads of Bruce, Keane and Schmeichel with the likes of Nicky Butt, Ryan Giggs, Paul Scholes, David Beckham, and the two Neville brothers, Gary and Phil.

After that awful start at Villa Park, United put together wins against West Ham and Wimbledon, followed by a very significant result beating previous season's champions Blackburn away by two goals to one. After another victory at Everton, a home win against Bolton, and a draw at Sheffield Wednesday, it seemed like United were doing pretty well with those "kids." after all. The biggest game of the new season was up next, with Liverpool due to visit Old Trafford.

I continued to socialize with Jussi, meeting up with him every couple of weeks for beer and wings. One particular evening, Jussi handed me a cutting from a local newspaper and said. "I think you're gonna like this, my English friend." I wiped my hands free of the sticky BBQ sauce, leaned back on my stool and, most intrigued, analyzed the article in front of me.

"Live Soccer from the English Premier League at the Britannia Club, Warren, Michigan."

Huh? Let me read that again.

"Live Soccer from the English Premier League at the Britannia Club, Warren, Michigan."

"What the ...?! Blimey mate! This is incredible! Jussi, you beauty!"

I couldn't believe what I was reading.

That newspaper clipping was about to change everything.

16

King Eric Rules the Britannia

I surveyed my weathered map of Michigan, a relic of Jussi's from the first time he had let me use his truck. The gridlike layout of Michigan's main roads allowed for a relatively easy understanding of the important route ahead. I was relishing my journey—my very first visit to the Britannia Club in Warren. Manchester United were playing Liverpool and Eric Cantona— "King Eric"—was returning from the soccer wilderness following his unprecedented lengthy suspension. Could there be a better game to see live? Shortwave radio soundbites or telephone calls to Scotland would not be required today. I was in my element.

I set off early, heading east on Dearborn's Rotunda drive. I had decided upon a three freeway jaunt in order to sample some of southeast Michigan's main arteries. I loved hitting the open road in the U.S. There was such a sense of freedom to it, the open expanse all so new to an Englishman abroad. Turning onto the Southfield freeway I immediately felt as though I was driving on the surface of the moon, due to the severity of the potholes and dilapidated state of the aging concrete. The road surface was so bad, I actually began to laugh. Plumes of black smoke coordinated with the crunching of my chassis as pothole after pothole inflicted more stress on my old T-Bird. Crossing over 8 Mile Road, Southfield's southernmost border, I surged north and hit I-696, otherwise known as the Walter P. Reuther Freeway. As I blended with the speedy flow, I could see why Michiganders apparently nicknamed it "Detroit's autobahn" due to its reputation for fast drivers. The huge multi lane highway packed with traffic, even on an early Sunday morning, continued moving me further northeastwards and I became one with the race track, praying for a stall-free passage. Several minutes later I managed to hit the correct exit and merged onto I-75 north. I only spent a short couple of minutes on the Interstate but it was long enough for me to contemplate the fact that I was driving on a road that actually starts in Miami Florida and finishes at the northern tip of Michigan and the Canadian border. My tiny footprint on what is almost 1,800 miles of road was another "American moment" for sure. I had gone a tad around the houses, but being new to the area, it was a purposeful move, allowing for more familiarization with districts surrounding the vicinity in which I had chosen to live. I had called the club for directions, so as I left the I-75 Freeway, shifting onto Twelve Mile Road heading east, I began to zone in on the suggested landmarks. With my compass again set directly north I knew I was getting close. Suddenly, I spotted it. Sitting next to a small patch of wasteland and sticking out like a sore thumb, there it was: The Britannia Club!

The exterior of the building with its brick base had a subtle nod to the British Tudor era, its upper siding and wood finish emphasizing a hint of that familiar white back paneling with black wooden slats. A small montage of British and American flags encased in a glass window box was mounted to the left of the front door—a front door that announced "entrance at the rear." I drove through to the parking lot in the back and my black beast rocked gently to a standstill. The smell of burning oil lingered heavily in the air.

I trotted up to the back door, fumbling for my seven-dollar cover charge in single notes crumpled in the inside breast pocket of my jacket. I was greeted at the entrance by a tiny South American doorman who introduced himself as El Tico, mumbling at a fast pace with his head down, himself holding a wad of dollar bills. I bid him a good morning and attempted to make polite conversation, discussing the big game that lay ahead. El Tico lifted his head up and smiled, muttering something I couldn't understand, already concentrating on the next punter in line. I returned a smile and headed inside. As I wandered through a long, dark corridor, the smell of meat pies, bacon, and toast immediately filled the air. The dimly lit interior cradled me into the main auditorium, which instantly reminded me of a typical British working men's social club. The main floor was filled with tables with all of the chairs facing toward a main stage which featured a large projection screen. I stood for a moment and surveyed my surroundings. To my surprise, I was not the only one to arrive ridiculously early. Several people were already in their seats and I allowed my instincts to drive me toward a table just left of center, occupied by two lads who appeared to be around my age. I offered a polite inquiry as to availability at their table and was greeted warmly.

"Sure, no problem, dude. Sit yourself down. I'm Chin-ho. Chin-ho Lee. No relation to Bruce."

"Hey, Chin-ho. Gary France. Good to meet you."

"Love the accent, man! Is that English?" Chin-ho enquired.

"Certainly is!" I replied. I then turned my focus to the second fellow already maneuvering over to greet me.

"How you doing, Gary? Frank Rock!"

"Wow, that is quite the surname, Frank. Great to make your acquaintance, mate."

"Likewise" replied Frank. "So, we've got Gary France, from England, currently residing in the U.S. of A! Now that is quite something. I dig the accent, man," a smiling and enthusiastic Mr. Rock replied.

"Not only that Frank, but my middle initial is B. G.B. France, just to add a tad more allure to the name thing. Lancashire born and bred, Frank, about forty minutes from Old Trafford," I responded, immediately signifying my soccer allegiance.

"Awesome! A real injection of authenticity on the day of our Lord and Savior's return!" Frank replied, shaking my hand with even more gusto a second time around.

"Oh Jeez!" Chin-ho chimed in, shaking his head, "not another Man U fan!"

Ours was an instant connection, as I learned that both lads were Britannia Club regulars. With plenty of time to go before kick-off, I settled in and posed the obvious question: "So how on earth did two Michiganders become so enamored with English soccer?"

Chin-ho explained how he had moved to the States from South Korea at the age of twelve, originally settling in New York City, then moving to Michigan in 1989. "Gary, the only thing that kids wanted to do in my town was to play soccer and watch games from England." An athletic-looking lad, I sensed an honesty about Chin-ho and was instantly gripped by his passion for the game. He went on to tell me that he had first heard about the Britannia Club a couple of years earlier via an article in a freebie magazine, but since he had had no wheels at the time, he had had no way to make the fifty-mile journey from Ann Arbor. He also explained how frustrating it had been to follow soccer in the States. "We could read about the games from England in magazines, but there was never any chance to see any action first hand. I relied solely on purchasing old soccer videos which became my main way to experience the thrills of the game."

After I spent several more minutes listening to this enthusiastic Korean American, Chin-ho confirmed his allegiance. "Liverpool!"

"Ah, that's too bad, mate," I responded jokingly. "We all have our issues."

"Come on, man," Chin-ho countered. "There's only one team that matters in this world and that's my Anfield Gods. Gary, man, my prize possession is my *Robbie Fowler's 100 Goals* tape."

"You have got to be joking, mate!" I replied laughing, shaking my head in mock disgust.

After a brief announcement from the chefs in the back corner, Chin-ho cut short our conversation. "You'll have to excuse me a second, man. It's time for breakfast. That English fried bread is the best!"

"Don't come between Chin-ho and his full-English, Gary!" Frank warned me.

As Chin-ho bolted to satisfy his craving, Frank began to tell me how it was through Chin-ho's soccer video obsession that they had met. Frank Rock, I learned, was a freelance writer from Ann Arbor. He was a tall, gangly fella, fair haired with Lennonesque glasses hovering over his nose. He struck me as a scholarly gentleman with a definite warm, welcoming disposition. Frank explained how Chin-ho had been peddling tapes of soccer matches in Ann Arbor back in the summer of 1993. He continued:

"I bought a Johan Cruyff tape from Chinny. Couldn't get the goddamn thing to play so I had to track him down to get my money back. He was cool about it and gave me a Best of Liverpool tape instead. Hey, how was I to know any better?"

Frank further explained how they eventually became good friends through their shared passion for the game and through Chin-ho's offer to drive him to the Britannia Club.

As kick-off approached, Frank's account of how he came to love the game of soccer further intrigued me—more importantly, his recollection of how he came to support the Red Devils.

"Manchester United are the only relevant team on this planet, Gary!"

"Gooood laaad!" I responded with an American high five.

"Red blood pulses through my veins, Gary!"

My very first visit to the Britannia Club and I had already met a fellow Red. This was a good sign.

Frank continued. "The first soccer game I ever saw was England against France in the '82 World Cup. England scored in the first minute and the crowd went insane! *Really insane.* I had never seen anything quite like it and I was immediately hooked. I didn't know squat about the game and had to look up the rules in one of my encyclopedias. The games were broadcast on CBC from Canada, and since we weren't that far from the

Canadian border, our antenna would pick up CBC. Canada, having a larger Commonwealth contingent, was well ahead of the States when it came to soccer coverage. The matches were presented by this dweeby little dude sat at a desk. A little television next to him showed the inside of the stadium while he commentated. As kick-off approached, the studio camera would zoom toward the television and then the network would switch to the actual feed. It was like a Monty Python sketch! Only the England games were broadcast live and the rest were on at midnight via tape delay. I ended up watching most of those midnight broadcasts and would stagger downstairs the next morning to catch the train to my job in Detroit."

As a new Brit abroad, I was reveling in Frank's introduction to the beautiful game. He continued: "The 1990 World Cup was the first coverage on mainstream TV over here. However, it did come with arbitrary commercial interruptions and insane commentary, such as 'the Czechs are down 3-1. They'll need 2 to tie!' I know Italia 90 gets pegged as the apotheosis of negative football but I thoroughly enjoyed it. And, yes I still watch England vs Germany nearly every year, though I skip the penalties! I'd spent the summer of '92 starved of soccer until I heard the announcer mention Euro 92. I knew I had to at least watch the final. I saw Denmark beat Germany and I still think that remains the greatest exhibition of goaltending that I've ever seen."

Frank also mentioned a definite affection for the savvy and swagger of Serie A, after watching highlights from the Italian league on a local station on a weekly tape delay format. Our conversation was absorbing, so much so that I hardly noticed Chin-ho return to our table and begin drooling over his fried bread "top up."

I remained engaged in conversation with Frank.

"In the fall of '92, our local station switched to coverage of the Premiership. I was pretty bummed. I had seen Leeds play Sampdoria in a preseason match where David Batty provoked Roberto Mancini into a shoving match. I didn't know anything about English soccer except that I knew I wasn't going to like it. Leeds played pretty rough and they gave away the ball too much. However, the first English Premiership match I saw was a thriller between Leeds and Liverpool and, to my surprise, that game pretty much instantly converted me into a Premier League fan."

The Britannia Club was starting to fill up when I noticed an older fellow milling around the stage, tampering with a projection system suspended from the ceiling. I asked Chin-ho what was going on.

"Oh that's Reggie," Chin-ho replied, a line of ketchup now dribbling down the left side of his mouth. "He won't stop messing around with all that stuff until it is time for kick-off."

"Reggie! Now that is brilliant, mate! How British is that? I never thought I would come across a Reggie out here. That sounds perfect, mate. A club called the Britannia with a host called Reggie. Superb!" I enthusiastically responded.

As the volume increased over the PA system, I leaned in closer to listen further to what Frank had to say. "Of course none of the games in the early days were broadcast live, but for us soccer ignorant Americans they were at least a window to the game. I still didn't like Leeds—and certainly not Liverpool—a jibe that resulted in a jovial nudge from Chin-ho—but I do remember being particularly impressed with Leeds' French player, Eric Cantona. My first glimpse of Manchester United came against Leeds. I remember going nuts when I placed Schmeichel as the "goalie god" from the Euro 92 tournament, and was instantly convinced that Ryan Giggs was the single most spectacular player I had ever seen. I started to care desperately about the outcome of the games I was watching. I could no longer wait to watch United on tape delay. My wife got me a shortwave radio."

It was at that point that I chimed in regarding my own recent experience with the BBC World Service.

"Oh yeah, Gary, those World Service broadcasts are awesome, dude. There was one particular morning where the commentator spoke at length about United's history: the Busby Babes, the Munich air disaster, the European Cup final in '68'. I was enthralled. I'd heard none of this before."

The big Yank continued: "Gary, I could hardly contain my glee when I heard that United had signed Cantona. I remember my son immediately settling on the Frenchman as his new favorite player. Needless to say when Cantona helped United win the Premier League, we celebrated wildly. By this time, things were really getting out of hand as I had installed a goal frame in the back yard, shredding what little bit of lawn existed by playing all hours of the day."

I smiled as I listened to Frank telling me that he would have the shortwave radio playing loudly in a corner of the garden, creating the right atmosphere, while his son Todd ran around the yard smashing the ball into the goal and leaping into the air in a frenzy of celebration. There was something very Pythonesque about Frank!

Our banter continued—an effortless flow of conversation between three soccer enthusiasts from three very different backgrounds. The prematch conversation had been non-stop and a superb warm up for the big game. Then, with about twenty minutes to kick-off, a young Willie Nelson lookalike appeared. Chin-ho stood immediately and offered his hand in "hood-like" fashion, complete with a gentle shoulder push, as the red-headed, ponytailed new arrival parked himself on the other available chair next to the Liverpool fanatic. Chin-ho introduced us.

"Hey Gary, meet Eddie. Unfortunately, he's a United fan, but of course that's his problem right?"

"Hey, Eddie. How's it going, mate?" I replied.

"Nice to meet you, man. I hope Chinny didn't try to turn you to the dark side before I got here." I immediately picked up on his British accent, softened with some American drawl.

"Not a chance, mate! Frank here has my back, so I reckon the Korean Scouser is totally outnumbered."

"Yeah, Frank is always good for biggin' up the Reds—aren't ya, Frank?" replied Eddie, giving a firm slap to the tall one's shoulder before sliding his seat next to mine.

"So, you ready for the return of the King?" Frank enquired.

"Ooooufff! Too right, Frank! What a game to make your come back in, eh lads?!" Eddie replied, rubbing his hands together in anticipation.

Yes indeed. After nine months in the wilderness for his *moment de folie*—his kung fu-style attack on a rival fan, where he narrowly avoided jail time—this was to be King Eric's return, ready once again to light up the English Premier League. You couldn't have written a better script: our hero returning to face Liverpool at Old Trafford!

With several minutes to go to kick-off, Eddie talked about how he had ended up in Michigan and how he had first met Chin-ho. With a piercing glare and hunched torso, he leaned in and began to explain in his seemingly unflappable, slow-paced drawl: "Yeah man, Chinny and I met a couple of years ago."

"At least," Chinny chimed in. Chinny explained how he had been riding his bike aimlessly through Ann Arbor when he noticed a guy kicking a ball around as he passed by the main soccer fields. "He was practicing shooting so I asked if he needed a goalie." After chatting for a while, Eddie had asked Chinny if he wanted to try out for his team in the Ann Arbor Premier League.

Chinny made me smile as he went on to explain, "He hadn't even seen me kick a ball yet, and it was apparently a very competitive league. Anyway, I made it onto the team and played for a couple of seasons."

Chinny and Eddie had remained friends ever since even though they both began to miss games due to work and family commitments. Eddie told me that he had been in the States for several years and was working in a bakery in Ann Arbor.

At the very last moment, an American lad with a college frat boy air to him rushed in and plonked himself next to Chinny, his rather rotund girth for a man in his early twenties most evident as he removed his sweater, revealing a tight-fitting yellow and gold shirt with the unmistakable Crown Paints sponsorship logo front and center. Another one with that unfortunate Anfield affliction. Some obvious Liverpool brotherly love was in evidence as both men gave each other a mutual shoulder slap. I leaned in and gestured to him, "Good luck, mate!"

"Oh yeah, Gary, sorry. This is Jacob."

"Hello, Gary. Very nice to meet you"—an overtly polite prematch opposition meet and greet, I thought, particularly from a Liverpool fan minutes before a United/Liverpool clash.

Kick-off had finally arrived.

I was more than three-thousand-five-hundred miles from home, about to witness a huge game for Manchester United, and sharing the experience with a Korean Liverpool fanatic, a six-foot-six gangly, Lennonesque United fanatic from Michigan, a die-hard don't-fuckin'-mess-with-me United fanatic, and an overly polite American Liverpool fanatic—all squeezed around a small table in Warren, Michigan. Quite a change from the usual company I had come to expect at our corner pub back in North West England. We were a newly-formed "band of brothers"—soccer fanatics brought together through our love for the game.

There was a mad dash as a number of fellas rushed back to their tables, having squeezed in a plate of the club's "full English."

Silence fell.

It appeared we had an obvious "captain of the ship." Reggie, the Master according to Chinny, made his appearance, front and center, demanding everyone's attention as he turned off the volume and abruptly announced: "Ladies and Gentlemen, welcome once again to the British Britannia Club" (the irony of Reggie's strong Michigan dialect was not lost on me). "We have a fantastic offering today. Manchester United (cue an instant, raucous response from all of the United fans present) versus Liverpool (an equally raucous response from the Liverpool fans, along with a well-placed smattering of boos!). I'm so happy to see such a terrific turn out this morning. Thank you all so much for making the effort! Don't forget to thank our two chefs on kitchen duty this morning. Those pies are delicious. And enjoy the complimentary tea and coffee on offer at the back of the room. And so, without further ado, I give you Liverpool and Manchester United!"

A huge round of applause, table-top slapping and whistles escorted Reggie as he leaned forward and, after a few final audiovisual tweaks, sent the volume soaring and the room plunging into darkness.

The stage was set!

My thoughts immediately turned to my friends and family back home. What was my dad—Des Lynham—feeling at that very moment? The build-up from the media in Britain must have been intense due to the Cantona storyline. We, of course, were totally detached from that, reliant upon our own unique prematch build up. Our band of fanatics in that building north of Detroit were feeling the tension, that was for sure. I was loving it! I sensed a laser-like focus from our clan, understanding not only the massive implications of the game, but the privilege of being able to witness such an iconic moment in Premier League history: Manchester United's "King Eric the Great" once again ready to go into battle at Old Trafford, against of all teams, the nemesis, Liverpool FC.

As the scenes from Old Trafford appeared on the big screen, I not only saw a football match between Manchester United and Liverpool—I saw the home that I had left behind.

At that very moment, I felt that I was home.

Game on!

United made a flying start. With only a couple of minutes gone, Cantona was straight back in the thick of it as his first class control and beautifully floated cross found Nicky Butt who chipped the ball past a couple of Liverpool defenders before lobbing it past the on rushing keeper and into the net.

1-0! Absolute mayhem! A dream start!

Frank Rock punched the air, lost in the moment, mobbed by two ecstatic fellow Reds!

Chinny? Emotionless, silent, not even batting an eyelid as all around him saluted the boys in Red.

And then . . .

Robbie Fowler was played through on the left side of the United area, and just as we all expected a cross to Ian Rush in the middle, he let loose with a ferocious drive that left Schmeichel for dead.

Enter South Korean Crazy! "Oh man! Yes!! What a goal! That guy is unbelievable, man. Unbelievable! Did you see that?!"

The lad was in awe as his hero hit the back of the net. Jacob's celebration was a little more measured, his reddened pallor suggesting he may just burst out of his tight-fitting Crown Paints shirt at any moment!

1-1. Half-time.

I decided to mingle with some of the other fans at the club and was quickly drawn toward an older couple sitting at a table across from us. Archie and Isabel introduced themselves. Archie's weathered features had "Braveheart" written all over them and a face that would certainly not have looked out of place in the Mel Gibson Oscar-winning classic. Dressed in a pair of tatty old jeans and tartan shirt, the Scotsman seemed very much at home in the Britannia Club. I received a warm welcome and even an instinctive kiss on the cheek from his wife, Isabel, as Archie told me that the two of them never missed a game.

"We've been coming here for a good number of years. Being able to see the matches regularly now is just magic," the Scotsman proudly announced with a broad smile.

"You could call it our second home, Gary," added Isabel, her left arm now gently wrapped around my waist, suggestive of the warmth of my comrades from the northern most part of Britain. In a short ten minutes or so I learned that Archie and Isabel had been in Michigan since the mid-50s. An avid Glasgow Rangers supporter, Archie told me that he had at one time been a scout for the U.S. Soccer Federation, beaming with pride as he showed me his old business card. This was a man who obviously loved the game, so much so that even on shores far away from his home he had pursued his passion to such a degree that he was able to contribute to the progression of the game in the USA. We continued sharing our views on the match.

"How do you think the second half will play out, Archie?"

"Och, United will win this one, son. No bother," Archie's calm and deliberate words were reassuring for any Manchester United fan—perhaps a nod to his fellow Glaswegian, Mr. Alex Ferguson.

At that moment, the lights once again dimmed, signifying that the second half of the match was about to commence.

"On yer go, son. Get back with yer pals now."

Having just returned to my seat, and with the second half barely underway, Robbie Fowler once again beat our "goalkeeping god" with an exquisite chip, after brushing off Gary Neville on the edge of the United box.

2-1 Liverpool!

"He's done it again, man! Fowler! He's incredible, man! What a player!" Chinny was in his element.

Time ticked on as the afternoon sun began to fade behind Old Trafford's famous Stretford End stand. Then, as the pace of United's attacks began to intensify, Cantona picked the ball up just inside the Liverpool half and ran at Liverpool's central defender, Neil "Razor" Rudduck, turning him inside and out. King Eric then floated a beautifully-weighted ball into the path of Ryan Giggs and just as "Giggsy" was about to shoot, he fell to the ground with Jamie Redknapp in close proximity.

"Penalty!" We all yelled in unison, as did the rest of the Red contingent in the club. The referee, David Elleray, responded just as we had hoped, blowing his whistle and pointing to the spot. Cool as a cucumber, King Eric stepped up and sent the Liverpool keeper the wrong way.

Eight months, five days and 70 minutes since his kung fu madness, King Eric had scored a vital penalty to salvage a 2-2 draw.

Frank Rock saluted his hero. "The King is back! Long live the King!"

Chinny was once again silent.

The final whistle blew. Manchester United 2, Liverpool 2.

Handshakes all around confirmed our gratitude to each other for the excellent company we had all experienced throughout the match. Our host, Reggie, center stage, requested an air of quiet to announce the upcoming live action and thanked us all for attending another soccer Sunday at the Britannia Club. The members of our paddock were swift in their goodbyes, everyone appreciating the conversation and looking forward to the next time soccer would pull us back through the door.

I walked out from the club with Frank and Chin-ho, the midday sun startling to our eyes, which were still accustomed to the darkness inside the club.

"Great to meet you, Gary. Until the next one, eh?" Frank shook my hand before hunching down into the passenger seat of Chinny's car. "Glory to our Reds, my friend," were the tall American's parting words.

"2-2, Gary!" Chin-ho proclaimed. "That means it's going to be a pleasurable drive back to Ann Arbor for us both," he smiled. "Glad you made it out here, Englishman. See you next time."

"Take care, lads," I responded, before making my way over to my car. A blast from Chin-ho's car horn made me turn around to see the two of them with awestruck expressions, pointing toward my T-Bird. I acknowledged them with a tilt of my head, palms to the sky and a wee tap to the rear of my beast. My gesture was greeted with a second blast on the horn and Frank shouting out of the passenger side window "Hey, nice wheels, man," a decent dose of sarcasm evident in his voice as the Ann Arborites pulled away.

I stood in contemplation in the early-autumn afternoon sun, enjoying the peace and calm of the moment after a morning of raucous noise inside a darkened den.

I smiled to myself. Did that really happen?

Here I was in Michigan. Manchester United had just played Liverpool at Old Trafford, Manchester, England—and I hadn't missed a kick!

17

A Home from Home

After leaving the UK with Manchester United stumbling in that final game of the 1994–95 season and handing the league title to Blackburn Rovers, it felt great to jump right back in. Games were broadcast most weekends, with the Britannia Club attracting an increasing number of soccer-loving maniacs from every corner of Michigan and beyond. The time difference of five hours was perfect for catching the English Premier League. Up "early doors," watch a match, back home by lunch, with a large chunk of the day remaining to explore what Michigan had to offer.The fact that the club offered soccer via satellite was all down to one man: Reggie.

Reggie was somewhat of an enigma and seemed to maintain a tad of distance between himself and the punters. I imagined him to have a military background. It seemed to make sense as there was a definite authoritative squadron leader look about him. He certainly was not afraid to step out onto the stage and declare his agenda in his cool, assertive manner, but when those brief moments of order were dealt with, he would once again step back and drift into the shadows and focus on nothing else other than ensuring soccer from England's Premier League played out live and uninterrupted to his flock. Reggie thrived on producing the best possible watching experience for everyone present. Within that building, among our subculture, it seemed that "us punters" were clearly comfortable with the fact that Reggie was indeed our commander-in-chief.

As kick-off approached, the lights would be dimmed and a hum of anticipation would fill the room. Striding up to the stage, his microphone placed front and center, the moment was pure "Reggie time" as he would welcome one and all to his emporium. He never said too much and limited any extensions of his personality. It was all about the soccer for Reggie.

Reggie's true forte appeared to be the audiovisual department. On one occasion, as I was entering the building, I was able to peek into the back office. It resembled a NASA command center with all its high-tech satellite and recording gear. If the sound clarity wasn't up to scratch, there would be a pause and Reggie would immerse himself in the stack of audio equipment, manipulating the knobs and dials, and we would be good to go once more.

Mid-game, if all was not well . . .

"Turn it up Reggie!"

Reggie would oblige.

"What's wrong with the friggin' picture, Reggie?"

No problem. Reggie would sort it out.

I remember on one occasion when reception had become particularly dicey, all of a sudden there was a clatter from a corner of the club as Reggie emerged with a tall set of ladders to the sound of enthusiastic applause. Bouncing on stage, full of purpose, he performed his death-defying act while adjusting the satellite box which dangled precariously from the ceiling. On completion of the task Reggie looked for no recognition, discreetly retreating to a dark corner of the room.

Despite those odd hiccups, most often as a result of unpredictable weather patterns, there was always a groundswell of belief that it wouldn't be too long before our host restored connection with sound and vision from across the Pond.

I soon noted, however, that Reggie had one distinct personality flaw; he *loathed* Manchester United! This became obvious as the weeks passed by. The look of disdain on his face was a dead giveaway, whenever he reluctantly announced the game the following week would feature the "Reds." I knew Reggie appreciated good soccer, so how could he not appreciate Manchester United? His emporium would have a guaranteed full house whenever the Reds were playing, assuring him of a fine taking in his half-time raffle. The kitchen would be going full throttle and the bar would be a haven for those early morning draft beer loving punters. Regardless, Reggie would still exhibit that look of torment due to the fact that his cash cow was the team he most despised. A fantastic goal would rip the back of the net at Old Trafford, but Reggie would remain stoic in some dark corner of the club as the fans celebrated. What made this dire situation even more apparent was that the person responsible for bringing live soccer broadcasts into our lives was a closet Liverpool fan! The adopted American "Scouser" could otherwise do no wrong in my eyes. After all, he delivered the Reds to my Michigan doorstep—and for that I was truly indebted.

I learned more about my new home from home from Chinny.

"Reggie told us all about it one Saturday morning right before a match, Gary. It was fascinating listening to him explain all about those humble beginnings. He told us how it started back in the fifties when a bunch of British expats who had relocated to Detroit for motor industry jobs began hanging out after work. People from similar backgrounds, building community, looking for that home away from home I guess."

"Human nature, eh mate? Look at us sitting here today," I chimed in "I mean I was here like a shot when I heard there was a chance of watching some footy and in a place full of my own you know."

"Very true man. For sure!" Chinny replied.

"Sorry mate. I interrupted. Please, carry on Chinny" I apologized.

"No problem, man. Anyway, according to Reggie, the British group continued to grow and by the late sixties, after meeting at each others' homes and various venues here and there for many years, they actually raised enough money to buy a property and start an authentic style British social club across the Pond. Reggie and several of the other members seemed to think that it was some kind of old tool shop they bought. It must have taken months to renovate it."

"Bloody hell, that is quite some story, mate. More to this place than first meets the eye, eh Chinny?"

"I guess so, man. It's hard to believe that Reggie hasn't been a piece of the furniture from the beginning, either. He's the man, dude!" Chinny noted.

I quickly came to realize that Reggie, "the man," and his clan were doing a great job of advertising the availability of live games, and this attracted fans from far and wide. On one of my visits, I had secured my usual spot and quietly began to peruse the tabloids, reflecting on the previous week's results, when an Indian lad in a United shirt approached me and asked if he could borrow my week-old Sunday Mirror. We began to chat. His name was Jai and he had relocated to the States from Leicester. Jai and his wife lived in Grand Rapids on the west side of the state, approximately 200 miles from the Club, yet they made it to a high percentage of the United games. Grand Rapids was closer to Chicago than Warren, but Jai had heard about the club and its dedication to live soccer coverage. Having paid an initial visit, he soon came to realize that the unique atmosphere was well worth the journey. Bear in mind that most games started at 10:00 a.m. Michigan time, sometimes even earlier, so here was a couple who, on the back of a work week, got up at 5:00 a.m. on a Saturday or Sunday, hit the freeway and made a mad dash across the state to catch their team in action.

"Gary, you can't get anything close to this at 3:00 p.m. on match day back in England, right?"

I began to look for Jai on subsequent visits to the club, sharing some fine celebrations with the lad each time a Red Devil hammered the ball into the back of the net. Like many of us, he had been contemplating a return to the UK sooner or later, but his job as a dentist had been going very well out in Michigan and that made a return to UK shores all the tougher. Not having to wait hours for Match of the Day's highlights possibly another good reason too. "What more incentive do you need to stay out here in the States, right Gary?" he joked.

After several more visits to the Club, I began to notice a definite, unspoken order as to where most individuals of my newly-discovered soccer haven sat. I was very happy with how my own "season ticket" had worked out: left of center with a fine view of the proceedings. Several rows of tables behind us was the main bar—an important structure in the scheme of things, to say the least. The very back row, directly in front of that, with a clear, central view of the screen was what I called "the Committee"—a bunch of lads who appeared to be well catered for in the drinks department. Among the posse of VIP members, one fella in particular stood out, a large bloke, always decked out in an authentic, albeit several sizes too small, Everton F.C. shirt. He had his own place at the very end of the long table and seemed to own the respect of all the other members. Hardly ever moving from his seat, I observed the man receiving handshakes and nods of consideration, before, during, and after matches.

The man's name was Sid Stone.

Mid-fifties, ruddy complexion and with a rather jolly appearance, Sid had apparently become a soccer fan after making friends with his son's English soccer coach. That same coach just happened to be an Everton fan which had sparked Sid's interest in and devotion to the Toffees ever since. Sid had kindly volunteered to be the Britannia Club's unofficial roving reporter, creating his own small cottage industry by way of an outstanding newsletter, "Sid's Soccer Weekly." It wasn't a fancy publication by any means, just four sheets run through a xerox and held together by a single staple. The content on those pages, however, provided some valued contemporary soccer opinion: the soccer world according to Sid. Our Yankee Evertonian would crank out his weekly fanzine for only a couple of dollars. The prospective reader had a great way to keep up with all the latest soccer news. I quickly jumped on board for a first month's subscription, such a bargain at less than a dollar an issue. Sid was beating the two-week-old British newspapers hands down, often with a full week to spare. Those reports of Sid's were the most up to date yet, other than a postmatch phone call to Des back in Scotland.

Fast forward to April 3, 1996—a Tuesday evening—Reggie had organized a "special evening showing of the crucial game between Liverpool and Newcastle United," the outcome of which would have huge significance in regard to the possible destination of the league title. Newcastle had been flying high all season and at one time were twelve points ahead of Manchester United. However, a Cantona-led United revival was underway. A positive result for Liverpool would dent Newcastle's title hopes and fuel United's race to the crown. I had to see the match. It had been a hell of a busy day at the clinic, so I headed to Warren for some Britannia Club relief!

Joining the early evening chaos of the back end of rush hour on the Southfield Freeway, I took a second to concentrate on the view in my rear view mirror. The sky was illuminated by a blood red sun slowly descending into the west's horizon behind me, another beautiful Michigan spring day slowly coming to a close. The dominant sunset accentuated the satisfaction of the journey. It seemed strange to think that it was already Wednesday back in Britain and that the game I was about to watch already over.

As I arrived at the club, I was greeted once again by El Tico. His usual "good morning" was replaced by a "good evening." I attempted to strike up a conversation about the match that lay ahead. As usual El Tico made a passing comment that I was unable to decipher, smiling as he handed me my change, full concentration on the next punter in line. The dimly-lit interior cradled me into the main auditorium which on this occasion had its truest appearance yet of a typical British social club, albeit with a rather obvious gender change. The room was full of ladies, pens at the ready, cocktails in hand and completely focused on the stage. There above them stood a smartly-dressed gentleman—who was most definitely not Reggie. He was holding a microphone and had his large velvet "bag o' balls" open on the table. You could hear a pin drop as the man's right hand gently dipped into that velvet bag, caressing small ball after ball, ladies besotted, yearning for the moment that a number was to echo around the room via the microphone clasped tightly in his left hand. Bingo was a very unique pastime. My mind suddenly wandered back to attempting to play Bingo caller in a small pub in west Yorkshire. None of us physiotherapy students were in the same league as the man on the Britannia Club stage that night.

I refocused my attention to the main reason I was in that building that night. I contemplated my phone call to the club just two days earlier when I was told that the Liverpool and Newcastle game would definitely be shown via tape delay. Apparently, however, Tuesday night was Ladies Bingo Night. As I stood somewhat confused, yet admiring the old British crests adorning the walls, I felt an arm on my shoulder.

"Good evening young man. Are you here for the game?"

"Oh hey, Reggie. Yeah. Liverpool and Newcastle right?"

"That's right, buddy. Follow me around here to the left. And your name is?"

"Gary ... Gary France."

"Reggie," a firm shake of the hand announcing his presence. "I have seen you around before Gary. A Manchester United fan, right? Watching a Liverpool match? Well, we're glad to have you with us this evening."

"Thanks, Reggie. Truly appreciate you showing the game," I replied.

"Of course young man! You'll no doubt be cheering Liverpool on for win a then, eh?"

"Well, I won't tell if you won't, Reggie," I replied. And that was where our conversation ended as Reggie continued to usher me through a rather ragged pair of red curtains. I could see that he had already shifted his focus, on the lookout for other soccer strays mesmerized by the "two fat ladies" and their "legs eleven" in the main auditorium.

As I passed through the curtains, I was immediately enveloped in a smoky haze. The small back room was packed with soccer fans, old and young alike, perching on any piece of available furniture. All eyes were focused on a small TV screen in the back corner above a bust of Queen Victoria. It appeared that Britain and America had different ideas when it came to "bust adoration." I considered how my own recently-acquired Elvis bust would look nestled cozily next to the venerable British monarch. It was a vision that exemplified my current Anglo-American existence in a most bizarre, yet somewhat relevant manner. The Queen hanging out with the King! "Thank you! Thank you very much!"

Beer glasses filled tables; cigarettes lilted between fingers, and conversation flowed. I noticed a fair few British accents in the mix. A well-stocked bar offered a fine selection of British draught ales, including Boddingtons in all its Manchester glory! I squeezed through a couple of tables, receiving welcoming acknowledgements, none of us having previously conversed, but realizing a familiarity all the same. That was the beauty of the Britannia Club; an instant atmosphere of camaraderie. This was my first experience in the normally off-limits bar hidden away at the back of the club. I smiled as I noticed a bright red telephone box, an icon of all that was British, at the far end of the bar. Reggie took one final look over his shoulder, out toward the main hall, then turned, nodded to the barman, and swept the curtains tightly together. I took my pew next to a grand old fella originally from Preston, Lancashire, his unbound enthusiasm for the game rubbing off on me with such infectious pace.

"Should be a cracking game tonight, eh son?"

Naturally, several references to the famous Preston North End soccer player from the 1950's—Tom Finney—were made, along with other stories of a bygone era. As the two of us enjoyed a pint celebrating our Lancashire heritage together, I remember thinking "I hope my enthusiasm for the game is as evident when I reach seventy-five years old."

The match started at an electrifying pace with an early goal from Robbie Fowler for Liverpool. After two quick responses from Newcastle, the half-time scoreline was 2-1 to Newcastle. In the second half, Robbie Fowler pounced once again to tie it all up at 2-2 after some great work from Steve McManaman down Liverpool's right. Newcastle came again, Asprilla sliding in a lovely curled finish with the outside of his right foot to give the lead back to the Geordies. 3-2 Newcastle. I feared the worse. I didn't recall ever hoping for a Liverpool win before, but that night, I got right behind the Anfield Reds, hoping they could turn it around—only to help Manchester United's title aspirations of course!

Liverpool's Stan Collymore suddenly arrived far post and slotted home an equalizer. 3-3! And then, with seconds remaining, all I recall hearing was "Barnes . . . Rush . . . Barnes . . . Collymore closing in . . ." And then "bang," Stan Collymore thumped an emphatic finish into the Newcastle goal at Liverpool's famous Kop end and reeled away in joyous celebration. Final score: Liverpool 4 Newcastle 3!

Manchester United had been handed a huge boost in their quest for the title in the most dramatic of circumstances, courtesy of their arch rivals. Newcastle, it seemed, after dominating all season, had begun to buckle under pressure. Despite the fact that the result helped Manchester United, I could sense that Reggie was over the moon that such a game should grace the club on a Tuesday night, drawing such an enthusiastic crowd, and, of course, winning a small victory in the duel with the women's Bingo Night—confirmation that Reggie truly was king of his empire!

I had witnessed one of the greatest games in English Premier League history, surrounded by an enthusiatic and extremely grateful throng of soccer fanatics, a pint of Boddingtons in my hand, on a Tuesday night in Warren, Michigan. A small world indeed!

18

Double Take

As the 1995–96 English Premier League season wound its way toward an exciting conclusion, my visits to the Britannia Club became a regular occurrence. I had a "mecca" to visit each weekend, centering my soul amid change and adjustment thousands of miles from home. It appeared that the timing of fixtures was increasingly catering to satellite TV demands. The first few times I had visited the club, a blank screen accompanied by elevator muzac would greet me upon my early arrival. Then, with just a few minutes to go before kick-off, the relevant soccer ground would appear, no sound, just picture, and the soccer fanatics present would cheer, realizing that the match was imminent. Several weekends later, snippets of pre- and postmatch interviews with players began to filter into the program package in no small part due to growing the demands from expats. I began to realize clusters of fans throughout the country were gathering to watch early morning weekend satellite presentations in growing numbers. Supply and demand; America is driven by it!

The battle of the two Uniteds—Manchester and Newcastle—was so exciting that fans of all allegiances at the Britannia Club seemed to appreciate the drama of the close race to the Premier League title. Reggie himself appeared to be enjoying the run in. He would emerge from the shadows at the end of each game and turn off the big screen, opting for simpler means to maintain the drama by tuning his sound system to the final moments of the BBC World Service and Sportsworld for the final scores of the day. Was I really thousands of miles away from home in Michigan, or was I back in a social club in the heart of Lancashire, at 4:45 p.m. on a Saturday afternoon, pint in hand and banter full on with mates as the day's matches reached their conclusion, each result read out in a distinct English accent? It appeared that the voice of Stuart Hall was haunting me. That verbal juggler of a reporter, playing over a PA system in suburban Detroit, his flamboyant and poetic descriptions of the most boring of nil-nil draws, drawing bellows of laughter from a gathering of fans from around the world, most of whom were clueless as to who the hell he was.

After trailing Newcastle United by twelve points in late January, Manchester United had managed to overtake their title rivals to lead the league by two points going into the final game of the season. For Newcastle to win their first title since 1927, they had to beat Tottenham and hope that their local rivals Middlesbrough could beat Manchester United. To think that I was about to watch Manchester United win a title "live, as it happened" for the very first time, from more than 3,500 miles away from home, was profound to say the least. I arrived at the Britannia Club early that morning, pinching myself at the opportunity that lay before me. Needless to say, the building was packed with fans from a multitude of teams—everything from a hoard of Liverpool supporters to a solitary West Ham fan, and, yes, even a Middlesbrough devotee!

"Don't even," I told the fella.

"Ah, we're gonna do youz Mank's today!' came his defiant response.

"Good to see you too, mate!" I replied, receiving a pat on the back from the 'Boro fan, confirming our mutual delight at belonging to such a terrific soccer community. Moments like that make you feel right at home. No need for in-depth conversation to acknowledge an acquaintance, just the knowledge that we all understood that unique expat connection through the game that was soccer.

Reggie emerged, the lights dimmed, and there it was: the Riverside Stadium in Middlesbrough. May 5, 1996. "King Eric," larger than life, chest thrust forward, head held high, leading his troops into battle for the final Premier League game of the season.

United began the game on a mission and scored within the first fifteen minutes. I jumped to my feet and the normally reserved Frank bear-hugged me, yelling "Let's go, Gary! Game on!" A sense of destiny filled me, witnessing such a swift start from United. Early in the second half, Andy Cole scored with a sweet, reactive overhead kick within minutes of entering the fray as a substitute. Then, to complete 'Boro's misery and United's ecstasy, a most beautifully executed long drive from Ryan Giggs made it a final score of 3-0! It was a performance worthy of the champions-elect, and there was never a doubt from the first blast of a referee's whistle. The United team rejoiced! Frank and I went nuts. Eddie stood, scarf aloft, his facial expression one of defiance, as if victory had been assured from the get-go. A chant of "United! United! United!" began to echo around the building, countered by the obligatory "Shite! Shite! Shite!" from all of the non-United fans. I took a moment to fully digest what I was watching. Almost a year to the day, I was packed up and ready to leave my homeland, listening with my father to a radio commentary, totally deflated as Blackburn Rovers snatched the Premier League title from United. There was to be no final game letdown this time around. The live broadcast remained on long enough for all present to see the trophy being lifted and the Reds' celebrations.

I pulled away from the throng and made my way over toward the now familiar back room. I entered the iconic red telephone box and dialed a long series of numbers. After a short delay the phone rang just once.

"What a team, eh son? What a team!"

"Dad! We did it, mate! We did it! Superb weren't they?"

"They sure were, lad. And, you know what? It shows — *you can win it with kids*, right son?"

Laughter spewed out into the small confines of the old red telephone box, its unique design cradling our conversation, protecting me from the noisy "goings on" within the building. As I stood sheltered in the authentic piece of British craftsmanship, it seemed to accentuate the importance of my connection, increasing the intensity of the moment. I was in a British social club north of Detroit, far away from home, calling my British father and discussing Manchester United.

United's season wasn't done by a long shot. Without any hesitation, Chicago suddenly came into play. Soul Boy Bill and Big Bob had made it across the Pond and were living "just down the road" in Chicago. I decided on a car rental as a more reliable means of travel along I-94 west, all the way to the Windy City. The T-Bird required a breather.

May 11, 1996: FA Cup final day!

Leaving Dearborn before dawn, I arrived at the Abbey Pub four hours later with an hour to spare before kick-off. The lads had been on a scouting mission to find the best venue. The Abbey had been a renowned Irish Bar in Chicago since the early seventies with a reputation as "the place to be" for all major European sporting events. The boys appeared to have settled well into Windy City life. Such was our zest for life at that time, we were always moving forward to pastures and challenges new, still fluid in our lives, yet constant in our support for each other. As we greeted each other once again, you could have been mistaken for thinking that we had just met up at Henry Boons in Wakefield, West Yorkshire for a cheeky pint! I was the solitary Manchester United fan among our group. Soul Boy Bill predicted that his Scouse Reds would prevail easily and wreck any designs that United had on a second domestic double.

The pub was packed, Liverpool and Manchester United shirts everywhere. I was in my element. I took a moment to reflect on those days as a young lad at home in Lancashire, scarf flung around the T.V. as I lay there on the carpet, watching the three-hour FA Cup build up.

The first half was disappointing with only brief glimpses of both teams' undoubted talent. The second half was not much better as it appeared that we were heading for extra time. With about four minutes to go, United launched an attack towards the Liverpool end and won a corner. I yelled that loudest of yells of encouragement: "Commme on United!" igniting a filthy response from Bill and the boys. The pub's Red Devil contingent renewed their optimism. I loved those moments when a tightly-packed throng in a public house almost raise the roof in support of their team. With time running out, Beckham ran over to take the corner. I surveyed the expressions on the faces of the United fans as the camera zoomed in on the corner flag. You could see the desperate yearning for that elusive United goal. It was no different among us United supporters in the Abbey Pub. The corner kick was swung in and David James flapped. The ball drifted out to the edge of the Liverpool penalty area, out toward King Eric, and with the ball seemingly beating him for pace, already several inches behind his standing left leg, he somehow managed to wrap his right foot around it, and in one glorious flowing motion rocketed the shot towards the Liverpool goal. The penalty area, jammed packed with bodies, surely offered no pathway for the ball. No problem! Goal!

That corner flag contingent of United fans had appeared to have had their prayers answered and the joy on their faces was clearly evident as Cantona raced straight to that same corner of the ground, his teammates in hot pursuit.

United had done it!

The final whistle blew and I headed straight back to find a payphone in order to share the joy with my father. I could hear my mother going crazy in the background. As usual, all my father could hear was a chaotic outburst of joy at the forefront of a bar's wild celebration and noise of a thronging mass, exultant in victory. My father knew the phone would ring. It had become the norm at any moment of United triumph. We had managed to once again share in Manchester United's success.

Needless to say, I thoroughly enjoyed my first night in Chicago. It was great to fall in with familiar company from back "home"—a chance for all of us to take stock having taken the step to travel across the Pond. We initially hit bars around the north part of the city. Did I ever imagine that I would be celebrating a Manchester United FA Cup win, victorious against the old nemesis Liverpool, looking out of a bar window, beer in hand, a clear view of Wrigley Field at dusk and my mates from back home ready to buy the next round?

Walking out into the street to grab a taxi there was a surge of noise as a lit up Wrigley field vibrated within touching distance ahead of us. I thrust an arm aloft as I emerged from the bar on the corner:

"Glory Glory Man United!"

"Take me out to the ball game. . ." the chorus from the stadium.

Sporting cultures collided as I celebrated my Reds' victory only to be drowned out by the sound of baseball fans hailing their beloved Cubs at the traditional seventh inning stretch.

After jumping into a taxi, I marvelled at the kaleidoscope of colors on display as I took in the sights and sounds of Chicago at night. I loved the anticipation of "where next" as our taxi drivers weaved between lanes to the backdrop of the Chicago skyline. The buzz of the Windy City and its pulse were completely invigorating. The Sears and Hancock Towers rose high above us on the fringe of Lake Michigan as we took a brief detour along Lakeshore Drive during one particular bar hop. Toward the end of the night, our compass pointed toward the city's notorious south side. I couldn't believe the line for the club that we'd been recommended and I worked hard not to stare too much at the "playas" around me—always difficult as a young Englishman abroad. Despite being several pints in, I could sense a definite tension in the air. Eventually, after we had all been frisked, we made it inside. The club, resembling an old church, had attention to detail inside that was amazing. High balconies lit up with vibrant color, a light show that pulsed to the rhythm, heavenly yet hedonistic in its suggestion. I was carried away with the wave, tension lifted, consumed with pleasure now that we were among clubbers embedded in a haven in Chicago's south side. The DJ was perched high in the rafters, dressed like a weird combination of Flavor Flav and Boy George, with a frame the size of Biggy Smalls, his ability to influence the clubbers below him clearly evident. Like a revolutionary preacher, both arms making thrusts high into the air above his decks, he rocked his huge body in unison with the pulsating rhythms. Surrounded by supermodel types who were twisting and grinding, oozing sexuality, I could feel the intensity of the moment. I began to sweat. Those same dancers writhing above me were already dripping, soaked in their own perspiration. I stood transfixed, in awe of their controlled gyrations atop six inch heels, tied to the beat. It was an incredible sight. The place was electric and I was engulfed. Nobody seemed to have a care. Obviously not, as a slim white English northerner embedded himself amongst TLC lookalikes, welcoming him into their personal space without any hesitation. It felt unreal. I felt alive.

The lads eventually regrouped at a bar on a floor high inside the building, a welcome reprieve from the non-stop pulsating beats. In one corner of the open mezzanine, several large windows provided us with a terrific view of the nightlife down below. I can only describe it as a Miami Vice-like scene, as I once again pulled on my preconceived images of the U.S. that I had derived from those 1970s and 80s American TV shows projecting through a small television screen into the living room of my rural Lancashire home.

A couple of Camaro convertibles pulled up to the intersection below. The deep bass from their sound systems rattled the windows. Beat met beat; inside to outside, a collision of sound on a Saturday night in Chicago. I had never witnessed anything like it. As the incessant pulse continued, we noticed a couple of the cars' occupants motioning toward us. As soon as we began to respond, a bouncer shot straight over. Yelling above the sound of the music, he told us to move away from the window, informing us that the cars most likely contained gang members and that the motions they were making in our direction were gang signs to test our own allegiance. He warned us that if we considered our lives worthy we would be best advised to move well away from the windows. Keeping our waving hands to ourselves was the best policy, otherwise we could well end up getting our heads blown off before the night was out. Lesson learned. We weren't in Wakefield anymore. Rooftop Gardens this was not!

As daylight approached, a small posse of withered expats crawled back to a small Chicago safe house in the north in order to recover from the exuberance of the city. Later that morning, clinging to any thread of stamina I had left, I pulled away, setting my dial east and a return to Michigan. I smiled as I thought back to a night out with the same lads several thousand miles away on English soil and, just as on that occasion, the common thread was a Manchester United victory.

My first full soccer season in the States had ended and I had witnessed a sensational Premier League and FA Cup double-winning season for my beloved Red Devils. To my great surprise, I had been able to enjoy the victorious ride in venues I never even imagined existed.

Life in America had begun rather well!

19

Quirkyville

Summer rolled around, and with it came a tough choice. I had been apprised of a job opportunity within a local hospital system. I had completed my required year at Jussi's clinic and, after much consideration, handed in my resignation. It was not an easy decision. Jussi had been my passport to the States, supporting me through my initial transition. My time at the clinic had been most rewarding, a terrific place to start my American adventure, but working within a hospital system offered great benefits and a fast track to a green card, and *that* changed everything. I chose to take the new position and stepped into the summer of 1996 full of enthusiasm for another new challenge.

Dearborn's Little Professor bookstore supplied enough soccer transfer gossip and news to keep me going through the soccer-starved summer months. Living at Hotel Hairpiece continued to have its ups and downs. I had found myself a lovely young American girlfriend. Indeed, Julie and I had begun a regular habit of squeezing in a little "afternoon delight" during our days off. One particular "delightful" afternoon, just as things were beginning to get interesting, with romantic music mellowing the scene, curtains drawn, and a definite level of amour in the air, or rather between the sheets, the mood was spoiled by the high-pitched yells from Rhonda calling her pussy! "Mr. Mozart! Misterrr Mozart!" As Julie and I were "fully indulged" by this time, we both tried our best to ignore the shrill shrieks. Then, with no warning whatsoever my door was flung wide open and in burst Rhonda, wig at full tilt, oblivious to our sexual shenanigans. I jumped out of bed stark bollock naked and ushered a rather ashen Mrs. Cloak into the breezeway between my room and the main house. I closed the door behind her and looked over at my girlfriend wrapped in the bed sheets.

"Did that just happen?"

"Unfortunately, yes!"

Rhonda was blissfully unaware when it came to any form of etiquette. Rhonda lived in Rhonda's world. Less than a week after the "afternoon delight" episode, Julie and I were returning from an evening out. We had come across a local live band making a pretty decent job of Radiohead's "High and Dry." There were some excellent local bands and the choice of cover songs was very UK influenced with the rise of the Britpop scene. As we pulled into the driveway around 11:30 p.m., we could see that the garage door was wide open. I was just about to turn off my headlights when I noticed what appeared to be a body slumped on the garage floor, leaning back against a trash bin. I could not believe my eyes. A man covered in blood from a gash on his forehead and looking quite worse for wear.

"Are you OK, sir?" I inquired.

"Sir, are you OK?" Julie repeated as she knelt down close to him.

The poor fellow, obviously the worse for wear, said "Oh? Yes. I believe I am OK." Then, to my surprise, he added "You must be Gary, the English guy?"

"Err, yes, that's right," I replied looking over at Julie somewhat confused.

"Oh, good. Nice to meet you. I'm John. Rhonda's husband. Well, ex-husband to be more precise."

"Oh right. Yes. Of course!" I replied. "The radio man! Nice to meet you."

"What on earth happened, John? How long have you been out here?" said Julie, her compassionate nature coming to the fore.

"Oh? Well? I'm not exactly sure to be honest. Quite some time I believe. I have been here for quite some time."

"Well come on," I said "Let's get you inside, John."

We struggled to get the frail-looking gentleman to his feet. Julie opened the door into Rhonda's back kitchen and I yelled out Mrs. Cloak's name. Rhonda seemed completely unfazed, barely reacting at all as she took her sweet old time to greet us. Since John obviously could use a seat, I decided to take it upon myself to head for the most readily available chair in the small abode.

"No! No! Not that one. That's Mr. Mozart's chair," squawked Rhonda. "Put him over there!" Julie and I looked at each other, our mutual facial expressions more or less along the lines of *are you fucking kidding me?*

"Mrs. Cloak," I said, "it looks like he's been out there for quite some time and that gash on his head needs some attention."

"Oh, he'll be fine!" Rhonda replied, waving her hand nonchalantly.

"He can do as he pleases!"

"Are you going to be OK, John?" I asked, unable to ignore Rhonda's sad and frail ex-husband.

"Oh, I'll be just fine now, buddy. Just fine. You and your lady get outta here now. Thank you for you dragging this old man indoors. On you go now!"

As we began to make our way out, not so much as a word came from Mrs. Cloak. She simply turned away and focused back on her TV. I noticed "Keeping Up Appearances" playing out in the corner of her room. Before exiting the room, the now familiar, piercing shrill of laughter shot forth from Rhonda's lips. It appeared it was business as usual in the Cloak household for another Saturday night with Hyacinth Bucket once again commanding Rhonda's full attention.

Whenever Hotel Hairpiece did receive visitors, it would invariably be Rhonda's son Johnny and his two kids, Sabrina and Myles. Johnny was an "almost retired" (as he liked to repeat whenever I saw him) accountant. He seemed a decent fellow, always thanking me for keeping an eye on his mother. If he only knew the half of it. But then again, I am sure he did. Johnny's appearance suggested one of being stuck in the era of a 60s Woodstocker, far removed from the look of a man who crunched numbers all day. He reminded me of someone and, for a while, I just couldn't pin it. Then one day it hit me: Frank Zappa! The man was indeed the spitting image of the American rock icon.

Johnny's two kids were quiet, not too engaging, but polite enough. Sabrina, his teenage daughter, who appeared to have never had a haircut in her life, would hide behind her locks and hardly ever say a word. Myles, his son, always wore a long dark mac, appearing a tad "Trench Coat Mafia," with hair down to his shoulders and bold, circle rimmed glasses. He did actually tell me one time that he had helped out as a roadie during his summer break from college for a local Detroit hip-hop band known as the Insane Clown Posse. Myles did not strike me as the hip-hop type. I guess looks can be most deceiving. On the occasions where I was unable to avoid a short "meet and greet" in Rhonda's kitchen, I would exit from the gathering, close the door behind me, take a breath, and feel like I had just witnessed the latest casting call for the next Tim Burton movie. I was, indeed, residing at Quirkyville, but for the $200 monthly rent, including amenities and bills, my situation was one that I simply could not turn down.

At one stage it appeared that ex-hubby John was *sort of* back in the fray at the chez Cloak, sort of, as in living in the basement, with a bed about ten feet from the washer and dryer. He had a small TV to keep him company and appeared to be obsessed with either National Geographic shows or Detroit Tigers games. On the odd occasion I took it upon myself to pay John a visit, he would perk right up, offering me one of his Miller Lites. I remember thinking to myself that whatever path this life takes me down, I hope I see the signs before I am resigned to solitary confinement in my ex-wife's basement!

What struck me the most about summertime in Michigan were the heat and humidity. I had never encountered such humidity and two words that I had never had reason before to use suddenly became a staple in my mid-summer conversations: *air conditioning*. This was a Michigan summer necessity. The evening white noise of the "A/C" unit took a lot of getting used to. I also came to understand Michiganders' fixations with the window screens first hand. I had headbutted one at Jussi's house in my rush to get out into the garden, never before having had to contemplate a screen between myself and the gloriously sunny outside world. The look on Diane's face as I stood atop mangled metal and mesh suggested she was indeed just about ready to see me leave.

The prevalance of bugs in summer meant that screens were an absolute necessity to prevent the inside of your home from being overrun by flying critters: mayflys, ladybugs, hornets, and gnats. The king of all Michigan bugs was the godawful mosquito. They would show up in swarms at dusk, ready to dine out on your blood. I learned to use something called Deet, which I had to spray over any exposed skin to fend off the "mozzies." Mozzies sucked!

I was fascinated, though, with the sights and sounds reflecting my presence on another continent. I loved the abundance of blue sky in Michigan, witnessing sunsets west of Dearborn most summer evenings. The early mornings were a delight, often a long, slow dawn greeting me. I found myself enjoying the shade of a tree in the many parks around my neighborhood, just to gain a reprieve from the heat and the sun's constant rays. Southern Michigan was not immune to the weather's ferocity, with May through July a particular period when Michigan could easily succumb to tornado risk. In fact, only a couple of months earlier, I had a small taste of storm cell activity and tornado warnings as the loud warning system rattled our neighborhood one afternoon. A heavy darkness had been building slowly. All of a sudden the air became eerily still. My intrigue had me standing outside surveying the vast, still, and quickly-darkening skyscape, the like of which I had never before experienced. I noted a definite green tinge to the sky—not a good sign according to WWJ 950 weather. I retreated into my pad and within seconds heard the most torrential of downpours accompanied by several repetitive loud bangs and claps of thunderous noise. Trees whipped and branches flew. My landlady knocked on my door and advised me to retire to the basement. Despite that none too enticing request, I decided it a good option. For several long minutes, I suffered Rhonda's explanation of "tornado etiquette," and how seriously these warnings should indeed be taken, during which time I was trying to nail Mr. Mozart with a sneaky back heel as he purred feverishly, excitedly rubbing alongside my leg.

After I was released from my landlady's basement, I could not believe the scene as I ventured out into her back yard. Branches and debris were scattered across the yard and some massive tree limbs were strewn on the main road in front of the house. There was a dramatic drop in temperature compared to the previous fifteen minutes and the winds had totally subsided, leaving a distinct clear blue sky and brilliant sunshine as the storm cell moved on to wreak havoc elsewhere, the calm after a storm for sure.

I was beginning to understand Michigan's obsession with "Weather on the Eights." Surveying the damage outside Hotel Hairpiece that day, it didn't seem quite so crazy after all.

20

Whatever It Takes

Following the prior season's success, United had a summer clear out. Hughes, Kanchelskis, and Ince were sold and Alex Ferguson opted to bring in an unknown Norwegian striker named Ole Gunnar Solskjær. With the Britannia Club and Johnny Cloak's old shortwave radio, I had my bases pretty much covered for a second season following United abroad. My new job complicated matters somewhat, as I was obligated to be on-call some weekends. And, of course, weekend calls had a habit of clashing head on with Manchester United games.

Where there is a will . . .

I tried to ensure that any weekend patients on my shift were up and ready by 7:00 a.m. My live link to England didn't commence until at least 10:00 a.m., allowing a three-hour window for physical therapy appointments and time still to catch the late morning BBC Sportsworld broadcast. Early morning treatments complete, I would leave the hospital and position my car in the parking lot to garner the clearest reception on the shortwave radio—not as easy as it sounds due to those rather temperamental shortwave frequencies. If I was required back on the hospital ward for further treatments, I tried to ensure that they were scheduled for noon, after the conclusion of the day's Premier League matches. I had manufactured a neat little mid-morning English Premier League soccer break, before returning to the hospital ward. Now, should United have secured victory, then the likes of Mrs. Szymanski, recovering from her second knee surgery in four months, would receive my ultimate compassion and care as I remained on a high from the favorable result and in no rush to fly through treatment. She may well have even been afforded a little time for some gentle massage such was my happy frame of mind. Should the result have gone against my Red Devils, however, then, Mr. Jansen "will absolutely get out of bed," despite his hesitancy and resistance. Mrs. Buck "will walk the length of the Hospital corridor" despite "not feeling like it" and "wanting to go for lunch" instead.

United played Tottenham at Old Trafford in late September and the young striker, Solskjær, scored both goals in a 2-0 win. Even Eric Cantona took a back seat as Solskjær—now known as "the baby-faced assassin"—became the player that all Manchester United fans were talking about. A shock defeat at Southampton and humiliation at the hands of Newcastle followed. United did not fare any better in November with a home loss to Chelsea.

December loaded Michigan with considerable amounts of snow and freezing cold winds, making trips to the Britannia Club quite a challenge. Temperatures of minus 15–20 degrees Fahrenheit chilled my skinny British frame to its core. Indeed, just four days before Christmas, I battled a very dangerous and icy drive up to Warren, spinouts evident all along the freeway. I focused hard, maintaining traction as best I could, as drivers weaved back and forth over snow-covered lanes, seemingly oblivious to the treacherous conditions. America never stopped moving, even when "ol' man winter" paid a visit, Michigan style! Unperturbed, I continued my homage and witnessed a 5-0 hammering of Sunderland at Old Trafford. The final goal left me breathless. Eric Cantona receiving the ball on the edge of the Sunderland penalty area. Aware of a defender racing in, the Frenchman arrogantly chipped the ball over the Sunderland keeper and into the top corner of the goal; a French delicacy. It became an iconic moment, not only in United's history, but in Premier League history—our captain, having scored one of his greatest goals, rooted to the spot, slowly rotating full circle to receive full adulation from the Old Trafford faithful, his trademark upturned collar his crown. Frank immediately attempted to mimic the celebration. Rapturous applause broke out as the exultant American completed his impersonation with an inquisitive "Does it get any better than that? Cantona is God!" The arduous trip north that morning had been well worth it.

Early January 1997 and a win against Wimbledon at Old Trafford sent United to the top of the Premier League for the first time in the season. February arrived and the F.A. Cup disappeared. What I remember of that cold winter's night, apart from a humiliating defeat for the Reds, was sitting in a deadly quiet Britannia Club, fully committed to watching a videotaped re-run of the replay from Wimbledon. I sat alone—there were only five or six other people in the entire building—listening to the chants of the "Dons" home crowd echoing around me. I could have sworn that Reggie turned up the volume on purpose to inflict as much suffering as possible on us Manchester United fans. If only he could have shown the same courtesy with the heat as I sat there freezing my bollocks off!

February continued with good results at both Arsenal and Chelsea and then, on March 5, I was able to witness my first taste of live European Champions League action since moving to the U.S. My work schedule for that particular week had allowed me the bonus of a rare Wednesday afternoon off, courtesy of a rather busy on-call shift the weekend prior. The timing was most fortunate since ESPN had chosen Manchester United vs. Porto to be their featured match. Frank had very kindly left a message on my answer machine.

"Hey Gary, you wanker! United Porto on ESPN2! Let's get together over at my place to watch it. Champions League quarter final first leg, dude!"

That Wednesday morning before leaving for work, I received all of the latest news from Des back in Scotland. It served as my prematch fix. My father had the rare opportunity to watch a live broadcast on regular TV in his cozy Scottish cottage, my mother no doubt by his side.

Finishing work early that afternoon I was soon heading toward Ann Arbor. I eventually found Frank's house, parking the T-Bird just a few yards away. It was moments before kick-off, around 2:30 p.m. Michigan time. Perfect timing. I stepped out onto the pavement in front of the Michigander's house. A little rain, surprisingly reminiscent of a little rare drizzle, or "spit," began to fall, rather appropriate considering that the live broadcast was coming from Manchester, England. I immediately became aware of some kind of drawing on the paving stone directly outside Frank's gate. I stopped in my tracks and surveyed the curbside art—a magnificently reproduced Manchester United team crest drawn with colored chalk. The attention to detail was astounding; it must have taken Frank at least half the day to create. I immediately considered that a middle-aged American freelance writer must have a good deal of time on his hands. I also considered that I would never come across such a thing should I be visiting a friend back in the UK to watch a midweek European night match.

"Welcome to Ann Arbor's United Central, my British friend," announced Frank as he opened the front door. "I figured that the artwork would make you feel a little more at home for the match today."

"Superb Frank! Bloody amazing that, mate," I replied, trying to ignore the rain.

"You are bloody well welcome, you wanker!" Frank added. "More than appropriate I'd say, particularly since for the first time ever I have an Englishman, and Man U fanatic at that, entering my home."

"Hey, man!" I felt a firm hand slap my right shoulder as Chinny appeared alongside me.

"I see the car's still going then, man. What the ... you gotta be kidding me?" Chinny's immediate focus was now on Frank's brilliant rendition of the Manchester United team crest.

"Come on mate, pay your respects to the greatest team ever to play soccer, eh?" I teasingly suggested to Chinny.

Needless to say, "Mr. Liverpool" did everything he could to avoid that section of sidewalk, skipping over Frank's lawn as he made it obvious that his allegiance that afternoon was with FC Porto.

As I entered Frank's home, I could immediately hear the Champions League anthem in the background. As I surveyed the rows of books and fine art cradling the walls of the lounge, I became aware of Frank's artistic indulgence. I smiled at the contrast, as I was drawn toward a large flat screen TV, sticking out like a sore thumb on top of a beautiful antique cabinet. Old Trafford, Manchester under the lights was clearly in view.

"Welcome to my Old Trafford, Gary" Frank exclaimed, "take a seat, dude."

I felt comfortable enough to just lay prone on an Indian style rug on the floor, a throwback to my "in home gameday posture," albeit without the 1970s magenta shagpile carpet.

"Come on United!" Frank declared.

"Oh man, what did I sign up for today," Chinny exclaimed as he sat himself down on the sofa. "To be honest, what the hell am I doing here anyway"?

"You're here to hang with your soccer buddies and to watch the greatest team on earth, man" Frank's immediate reply offering his hand to the Korean-American.

"I should have brought my Robbie Fowler tape for half-time," Chinny replied with a large grin as he once again shook Frank's hand.

"Now that's enough of that, mate" I quickly chimed in.

The match started and within minutes United were on the ropes, Chinny springing to his feet, with Porto's Artur denied by Gary Pallister's last-ditch tackle.

Then, on twenty-two minutes, David May, of all players, slammed the ball into the Porto net. He was lying on the ground, inches from the Porto goal line, as the ball came to him and he instinctively reacted.

"Get in thereeee! Yeeeeaaaahhhhh!" Frank exclaimed, leaving no doubt as to his passion for the Red Devils. I remained on the floor, both fists pumping vigorously, receiving a "low five" from the tall Yank as he bent down to acknowledge our mutual support. It seemed we were in for something special. And indeed we were. Porto, overwhelming favorites prior to kick-off, eventually received a 4-0 hammering, leaving Frank and me dancing in delight and Chinny rather nonplussed.

With the game over, the three of us hung for a while and I took the opportunity to ask Frank about the Blind Pig. I couldn't get over how close he lived to Ann Arbor's iconic music venue. I loved my music and, judging by the inside of Frank's home, I could tell that he did, too.

"Yeah, the Pig. Been there many times. Great place."

"I am hoping you have, Frank. Bloody hell, you could fall out of bed and almost be on stage, mate."

"It has a great history, Gary. It's a special place. It was a blues venue originally."

"How did it get that name, Frank?"

"From what I've heard, it's apparently a nod to the days of prohibition when police officers were bribed to ignore illegal speakeasys. It's an awesome name."

Chinny chimed in. "Yeah, Nirvana said the Pig was their all-time favorite venue back in the day. I saw it in an interview on MTV."

"Is that right, mate?"

"Yeah man, REM, Pearl Jam, Sonic Youth, Soundgarden, Smashing Pumpkins, you name it, they've played there. I think even Lennon was there back in the day." Chinny was on a roll.

"Oh yeah, and of course our local boy Iggy rocked the Pig too," Frank added, referring to Ann Arbor's one and only Iggy Pop.

"I am starting to realize that Ann Arbor has a pretty solid musical heritage, eh fella's?"

"A college town always needs a few decent music venues, right? I mean, come on man, you Brits sent it all our way in the early sixties with the British Invasion. Boy, it kicked off for me around that time for sure. I loved all that shit. The Beatles, Stones and the Who. That was awesome stuff, dude. Sill is!"

"Yeah, I guess we did Frank," I replied. "I guess we did mate."

"I was more of a Guess Who man myself," Chinny added, expressing a surprising affection for the Canadian band of the late sixties.

"Yeah, you would be," Frank said rolling his eyes.

"Each to their own, eh lads?" I chimed in.

After our musical banter came to an end, Chinny and I both decided it was time to head out.

"Cheers, Frank! That was brilliant. Really appreciate the hospitality."

"Hey, no problem, Gary. Till the next time, eh? There aren't too many soccer fans around here, particularly any that would understand what's involved here, man."

"Absolutely, mate. Hey, even get to talk a little more music, too."

"And maybe about the absolute greatness of Robbie Fowler huh?" Chinny's cheeky grin preempting our handshake.

"He doesn't give up, does he Frank"?

"No, he certainly doesn't, man."

It was handshakes all around as Chinny and I began to exit the small townhouse, Frank remaining on his porch as we made for our cars.

"Ugh! No way, man," Chinny exclaimed, swiftly changing direction, once again hopping onto the lawn to avoid the chalk-drawn United crest.

Unfortunately, the rain had ruined Franks's prematch artistry. It was now an unrecognizable mess. Nonetheless I pointed down at the sidewalk.

"Hey, Frank! It did the trick, mate! It did the trick!"

"Sure did!" the happy Yank replied.

Then it suddenly hit me.

"You know what Frank? Such commitment to the cause can't go unrecognized. It's simple. From now on mate, there'll be no more Frank."

"What do ya mean, man?" Frank replied, looking confused.

"From now on, mate, I'm going to be calling you Red!"

"Ha! Superb! I love it!"

Our American Manchester United fanatic was seemingly very happy with his new Red moniker.

"Thanks again mate, I mean, Red! Really appreciate it."

"Hey, the pleasure was all mine, my English friend!"

I pulled away from the street waving to Chinny as he headed off in the opposite direction.

"He's not a bad lad for a Liverpool fan," I thought to myself.

I smiled, pumped my car horn and gave a left-hand fist pump out of the window to Red.

Manchester United had one foot in the European Champions League semi-final.

The following Saturday, United lost 1-2 at Sunderland, but with wins over Everton and Sheffield Wednesday, their Premier League aspirations remained on track.

Wednesday March 19, and my schedule at the clinic that particular afternoon was a full one. As kick-off time approached, 2:45 p.m. in Michigan, I could only imagine the scenes in Portugal. As I sped home from work, I made a quick pit stop into the Farmer Jacks supermarket.

"Good evening, sir, and welcome to Farmer Jacks. How are you today?"

"Excited as hell, mate! Manchester United are playing in the second leg of the European Champions League quarter final! How are you, my friend?"

Blank stare from the bemused greeter; huge smile from an Englishman on a mission. Exiting the store, I couldn't help a gentle pat on the shoulder of said greeter as I said "Cheers, mate. Have a good one, alright?" Continued blank stare from the greeter; an even bigger smile on face of the Englishman.

I was totally focused on one thing as I pulled into the driveway of Hotel Hairpiece. I waved my right arm in acknowledgment as I wandered past Rhonda's kitchen window and entered my tiny pad. I immediately shot to the answer machine and hit playback. Messages from Des over in Scotland and Red in Ann Arbor conveyed the news that was fit to print. After a 0-0 return game in Portugal, Manchester United had made it into the semi-final of the European Champions League.

"Get in there!"

April 1997 rushed in and with no conflicting on-call duty at the hospital that first weekend, I was able to make it north for some Britannia comfort, feeling confident that I would see a victory. Derby County, however, proved that no team should be taken for granted in the Premier League. Final result that day: Manchester United 2, Derby County 3.

"Didn't see that one coming, Gary," was Eddie's gruff response at the final whistle. "That's opened the fucking doors a bit, eh?" he added, rounding off his swift and incisive postmatch analysis with a prolonged swig of his Guinness.

"Bollocks!" Red exclaimed as he towered above the two of us, staring blankly at the screen. "Wankers!"

Liverpool and Newcastle had been given a chance to move closer in their pursuit of United. Reggie then hit the BBC World Service Sportsworld radio connect button, a louder-than-usual volume declaring one more time that Manchester United had indeed succumbed to a shock defeat during the title run in. I am sure I saw a smug smile on our lieutenant's face, the significance of the day's result resonating within the room. The Britannia Club United clan was still shell-shocked as a smug Chinny returned to the fore with a later than usual "full English."

"I don't know man, this fried bread tastes even better for some reason today man. Can't imagine why?" he said smiling.

"Fuck off, Chinny!" Eddie replied, never being one to mince his words.

"Hey man, Coventry at Anfield tomorrow. Now this really is getting interesting."

Then, courtesy of the BBC broadcast echoing around inside the building: "Newcastle United 1 Sunderland 1."

"Yes!" came a rapturous round of applause as Manchester United supporters celebrated a draw in the Tyne/Wear derby game, Newcastle only achieving a one point gain on the Red Devils as opposed to a possible three.

"Till tomorrow then guys," Chinny suggested, chewing on his bacon and clenching his knife and fork in battle-ready fashion.

Less than twenty-four hours later we were, indeed, all sat around the very same table. It was Sunday morning in our house of soccer as we settled down to watch Liverpool take on Coventry at Anfield. I delighted in becoming a Coventry fan for a day.

"Fuck that, man!" exclaimed Liverpool's number one Korean American fan, slamming his back against his chair at the final whistle. Not even his hero Robbie Fowler's fifty-second minute strike was enough as Coventry's Whelan and a late, late, finish from Dion Dublin gave the Sky Blues all three points in their fight against relegation. It was no real surprise that Reggie brought proceedings to a more abrupt end than usual that day, ushering one and all out of the Club rather briskly. I drove back to Dearborn enjoying several impromptu thrusts of my forearms and a broad smile to match. I also imagined the grief that a certain Chinny Lee would be receiving from Frank Rock on the ride back to Ann Arbor.

It was the business end of the season and games were coming thick and fast. A mere four days later, United faced Borussia Dortmund in the first leg of the Champions League semi-final. It was a massive game, with

United on the verge of European glory! Once again, the reason I was in the States—work—was a rather inconvenient obligation during a mid-afternoon in Michigan, depriving me of any chance to watch or listen to the big game live. I was certainly on a roll, establishing outlets for my support abroad, more than I could have wished for prior to leaving the UK. It was amazing how that little window that had opened up, that slither of hope that I may well be able to continue my fanatical following of the Red Devils abroad, actually intensified the urgency to connect. I now realized that I wasn't alone when it came to searching for soccer in the United States of America. Yet, for such a monumental fixture as this, I was struggling, really struggling. It was going to have to be a telephone report from Des in Scotland after the work day had ended, and that just didn't seem sufficient given the importance of the match. My mind raced all morning as I committed to somehow finding a better solution.

Then it hit me: Sandy Cabellos!

Sandy was the Occupational Therapist at our hospital-based clinic. A quiet, rather religious lady, she was a dedicated mother to her four children and rather intrigued as to how a young man from England had ended up in her small Midwestern town. I had previously learned that Sandy lived only four miles from my own digs, a point of significance as at that particular time Sandy's neighborhood television cable provider was able to get ESPN2. PBS-loving Rhonda Cloak didn't have the same cable package and watching sports was certainly not part of her DNA. ESPN2 was the channel that would be broadcasting Manchester United's biggest game of the season.

I had chatted with Sandy on several occasions, at one point mentioning my passion for soccer and how thrilled I was to have found the Britannia Club, which incidentally she simply could not believe actually existed in Michigan. That made two of us! She had told me that her daughter was an avid soccer player and was beginning to recognize some of the names of players. Of course, David Beckham was the first name that rolled off her daughter's tongue. I had told Sandy how frustrated I was at not having access to the channel that carried the Champions League games. Sandy's husband, Francisco, was a Mexican native who, on the rare occasions that I saw him, talked only of "The Emperor," Claudio Suarez, Mexico's defender and eventual all-time leader in appearances, playing over a 150 times for Mexico. It seemed that Francisco loved soccer, too. Whenever he popped in to see his wife, our conversations would follow a similar pattern:

"Hey, Francisco! How've you been?"

"Ayee, Garrryy! I am good! Bobby Charlton! Dennis Law!"

"That's good, Francisco! Go Claudio, eh! Go Claudio!"

"Manchester United! Good, eh, Englishman?"

"Indeed Francisco! Look after yourself, my friend."

It was always the same deep and incisive conversation between the two of us.

With a pump of his fist, Francisco would exclaim "Claudio, Claudio," before turning his attention to Sandy to enquire as to how her day was going.

It just so happened that Megan, Sandy's daughter, was off school at that particular time in the afternoon, and, according to Sandy, could "easily record the game" for me.

Problem: Megan had a soccer game herself each Wednesday evening and the whole family went to watch.

Solution: the all-important VHS tape would be left in the Cabellos' mailbox, at the bottom of their garden, ready for me as I drove past after work.

Sorted!

My mission for the rest of the day was to ensure that I remained ignorant of the score at all cost, which, given my surroundings, did not prove too difficult. After work, I pulled up to the Cabellos' household and expectantly slipped my hand into the mailbox. *Yes!* My ticket to Manchester United's most important match in years was lodged inside. I arrived home around 7:00 p.m., avoiding temptation from a flashing answering machine. My newly-acquired 18-inch portable TV with built in VHS instantly transported me to Dortmund, Germany.

United suffered a 1-0 defeat and were very unlucky not to come away with at least a draw. A Nicky Butt drive from the edge of the box rounding off a brilliant counter attack and slamming against the Dortmund post could have given United the lead and that precious away goal. A deflected shot from Dortmund in the second half eventually beat United stand-in keeper, Van de Gouw. United had a tough job on their hands for the return leg at Old Trafford.

Later in April, a victory at Blackburn left United two points clear at the top of the Premier League.

A crunch game awaited United on April 19. Liverpool FC at Anfield.

21

The British Are Coming

The timing could not have been better. I had actually managed to convince my parents to come on over and sample some American hospitality for themselves. Due to their selfless duties of caring for my gran and great aunt—both in their nineties—it had taken several months to convince them that it was a good idea, but with some kind help from my sister and her husband, a U.S. trip became a reality. They arrived in Detroit on April 13, 1997.

"Where the heck have you two been?" The flight in from London Heathrow had filtered through and after what seemed an eternity my parents emerged from customs. They both looked exhausted.

"Bloody ridiculous, Gary," was all my father could muster in response.

"What happened, dad"?

"We've been held up in customs. Two guards. Big bloody guns all over 'em, telling us to stay put."

"What?"

"Oh yeah, apparently they weren't happy with our customs forms, so they had us fill 'em out all over again and then wanted to know more about what the purpose of our trip was," my mother chimed in, looking very tired and irritated.

"I'm not kidding you, Gary. I'm bloody livid. It was totally unnecessary. They were so bloody obnoxious. Like we are a threat to America's national security? For goodness sake, son!"

My father was looking about as disgusted as I had ever seen him.

"Oh yeah," my mother added, "and we don't have our luggage either. Apparently, it's on another flight and won't get here for a couple of days."

"Welcome to America!" I exclaimed wrapping a welcoming arm around each of them. "Come on. Let's get out of here."

"Tell you what, Gary. I could murder a cup of tea" my father commented. Some things never changed.

"A bloody brandy more like," my mother added.

"Ask and you shall receive, mother."

No luggage for two days. The landlady of Hotel Hairpiece, Rhonda Cloak, stepped up, discreetly placing some rather trendy slippers for my mother outside my door; the rather strange looking frilly night gown was kindly declined. My father didn't like the color!

Rhonda also gave us free reign of the washer and dryer so that my parents could wash the clothes that they had arrived in. I made sure to drop a few extra dollar bills in the Folgers tin!

I had purchased a half-decent queen mattress which was flung on the floor in a tight corner of the small pad. No complaints from a very jet lagged mum and dad. Home base was all set. Rhonda seemed somewhat bemused as to how my parents and I could exist in her small bedsit room built for one.

On the first full day of their visit, I took my parents on a guided tour of Henry Ford's home town and surrounding area. They thoroughly enjoyed a walk through American history as they took in Greenfield Village and the Henry Ford Museum. Ford had preserved a large part of America's past all in one central location by purchasing and relocating landmark buildings from all over the country, including Henry Ford's birthplace and the famous Wright Brothers bicycle shop, among many others. Ford's vision had provided the public with a chance to step back in time to experience what an American village may have looked like more than a century earlier.

"More to that man than meets the eye, eh son?" my father said, obviously impressed. I also took them down past the Ford Rouge Complex. The sheer size of the plant blew our minds. I explained to my mother and father that I had been told that the only car continuing to be built there was the famous Ford Mustang and that the factory initially built Eagle Boats to combat the German submarines in WWII, at the request of none other than president Franklin D. Roosevelt.

"Not too bad these Yanks after all then, eh son?" said my father taking it all in. "That must have been quite some operation."

I think he was slowly beginning to forget his first impression of the States and the two grumpy guards in the arrivals lounge at the airport.

Later that evening, a rather disheveled looking suitcase landed on my doorstep courtesy of a local courier service and we decided to celebrate.

I took my parents out to sample some of my yin, this time choosing the New Place Lounge in Dearborn. I could see my mother's eyes light up as a live band began tuning up. Within a few minutes, the opening chords to "Walking in Memphis" filled the bar, and my mother began belting out the lyrics, shouting over to me "Wow, these fellas can't half play, Gary. What a cracking sound."

There then followed a great night tapping our feet to Tom Petty, John Cougar Mellancamp and Aerosmith cover versions, along with other American rock classics. Sawdust beneath our feet, an eclectic mix of characters sat on high top bar stools, pitchers of beer on the table, and a couple of buckets of chicken wings all made for a typical Midwestern bar night for my folks to soak up.

"Saw a bust of Elvis . . . on Rhonda's Avenue . . . followed him up to the gates of Hotel Hairpiece, then I watched him walk right through."

The following morning I took my dad out for a spin in the old black Thunderbird. My mother stayed behind, intrigued with Rhonda as much as Rhonda was with her. I had told my mother not to focus too hard on Rhonda's hair.

"Bloody hell, son! You call these roads? They are bloody awful!"

"Unbelievable isn't it, mate. Welcome to the Motor City, dad!"

"Oh my God, motor madness more like. Haven't they heard of tarmac?" replied my father, grabbing the passenger seat to stabilize himself as drivers weaved in and out of the lanes.

"So what about that then, eh dad?"

"Ouff! That was like bloody Brands Hatch back there, son," my father's description of the English racing circuit not too far off the mark.

"Time for an oil change." I had held off so that I could show my father what it was all about.

I pulled into a local ten-minute oil change location and smiled at his expression as a mechanic waved me into position over his pit just like a ramp agent directing a plane with precision along a runway.

"For goodness sakes, Gary, what is all this about?" my father's surprise continuing.

"Welcome to Pennzoil. How may I help you today, sir?"

"Oil change please."

"Mileage please, sir?"

"102,126."

"Conventional, semi-synthetic or synthetic, sir."

"I'll take a high mileage synthetic, please." I had learned quickly thanks to my Thunderbird's thirst for the black stuff. I had indeed listened to Quincy and Coby that early Saturday morning in Detroit.

"I am probably due an air filter by now too," I added.

"We'll give it a thorough Pennzoil safety check for you, sir."

"Sounds good. Cheers, mate."

"Pleasure sir. Now if you could pop the hood, please."

"This is unreal, Gary!" said my dad, looking very bemused.

We sat and listened as two mechanics worked at a furious pace.

"Power steering fluid."

"Check."

"Belts and hoses."

"Check."

"Battery."

Then a knock on my driver's side window "Sir we would like to check your lights, please."

"No problem. Fire away."

"Front...good! Rear...good! Left indicator...good! Right indicator... good! Full beam...good! "

"Tap your brakes please, sir...good."

"Ok sir, the air filter does look like it needs changing."

"Sure. Go for it!"

For the full ten minutes or so, a father and son sat in an old beat-up Ford Thunderbird, father completely gobsmacked as to the whole process playing out before his eyes. Our chassis was being cranked and the black beast was being fed some delicious new oil, and we hadn't even left our vehicle the whole time.

Another car sat adjacent to ours in a second pit and there was already a line of cars behind us.

The two mechanics had such smooth rhythm to their operation. As the oil was pumped into my engine, my father shouted above the noise: "I have never witnessed anything like this before, son."

"OK, sir. Five quarts of high mileage synthetic 5W30, brand new air filter, tires topped up. Anti-freeze looks good. Windshield fluid topped up. You are good to go. Would there be anything else, sir?"

"No I think that will do it, mate. Oh, how much oil was I down?"

"You were over a good quart down, sir. The pan had a decent amount in it. I recommend you keep on top of it for sure."

"If only you knew," I thought to myself. Then again I'm sure he did, but was just being polite.

"If you'd like to open your door, please sir" said another mechanic looking right at my father in the passenger seat, "and we can lube those hinges there for ya and then you'll be good to go."

"Your total will be $15 and change out the door."

"Cheers, mate. Credit, OK?'

"Absolutely, sir. Be right back!"

"How do you get change Gary when you use a credit card?"

"Nah, dad. He means it's just a little over $15."

"There you go, sir. Thank you for using Pennzoil. Stop back soon."

"That was unbelievable son. Unbelievable!"

And with that, the unit's garage door raised and we were guided carefully forth back into the open air, a subtle nod of the Pennzoil ramp agent's head as we passed him by to the exit.

"A ten-minute oil change. Well, isn't that quite something, eh son?" my father added, shaking his head in disbelief.

We returned to Hotel Hairpiece to rescue my mother from Rhonda and I insisted she take an afternoon spin with dad and me in the newly-lubed T-Bird for a quick look around downtown Detroit.

"Come on, mum. Time to sample your son's wheels."

"Wow, this really is a nice car you know, Gary" my mother said, stroking the cloth on the back seat.

"I tell you what Gary, that Rhonda really is something else. I have just listened to her harp on about assisted suicide and some doctor by the name of Kevarisan or something like that."

"Oh yeah, mum, doctor Jack Kevorkian, mum."

"Bloody hell, Gary. She didn't half go on and on. All sounds a bit dodgy to me, son."

"Yeah, Rhonda is into all that. She's a bit of an activist regarding euthanasia. Been on rallies and everything."

"Come on son, cheer me up. Where are we off to? I need brightening up after that morning. I feel like bloody well topping myself. Anyway what have you two been up too?"

"Gary took me on a death ride and then got his oil changed in ten minutes," my father chimed in.

"Bloody hell, we've all had a hell of a morning, eh." My mother kicked back, winding the window down and as I glimpsed back in my mirror, I noticed her closing her eyes as the Midwestern breeze blew through her dark hair.

"Tell you what, Gary. I can't believe we're actually in America," a gentle smile now settling across her face.

As we left Dearborn and headed east towards Detroit, I turned the radio off and noticed my parents fall silent as building after building looked more and more run down and decrepit. The only sites that appeared to be in operation—glamorous signs pronouncing that they were very much open for business—were strip clubs.

"Bloody hell! They don't half have a lot of strip clubs out here, lad" my father noted.

"Trust you, Jimmy," my mother added.

I decided a quick tour of downtown Detroit would open their eyes even further.

A number of tall buildings stood abandoned, empty, decaying.

"It's an eerie feeling this, son," my father's initial reaction.

"Bloody hell, this all looks a bit dodgy to me. Not what I expected at all," said my mother, her jaw dropping as she tilted her head upwards to check out the skeletons of once vibrant buildings. "You don't come down here do you, son?" a mother's concern most obvious.

"Yeah, I've been down a few times for concerts, but that's down the other side of town. I won't lie, though, it's often a case of a quick in and out."

"We're doing a quick in and out today too, right, son?" my mother's plea.

Empty grass lots running one into another and abandoned homes— once bustling neighborhoods—provided the sad scenery as we turned to head west back to Dearborn. I explained to my parents that the city was once thriving with a population of over two million with many people from the South having come up north looking for work as the motor industry boomed, followed by a slow decline, leaving Detroit hanging on to around 800,000.

"So, with all of those people just up and leaving, the homes they left behind simply fell into decay or were burned down and as a result these grass wastelands dominate the landscape where homes once stood."

"Should we even be driving around here, Gary?" my father added. I could sense the anxiety in his voice.

"Yeah, maybe not. Just a few more minutes though and we'll back on Michigan Avenue and headed back to Rhonda's."

"I can't believe it. I never thought it would look like this," my father said.

The three of us sat in quiet contemplation, a nod to a vibrant past maybe, imagining a city as it was, and not the areas of dead, decaying terrain that now surrounded us. My parents appeared to be reconsidering their prior impressions of Motown—the city of Stevie Wonder, Aretha Franklin, The Supremes, Smokey Robinson, Marvin Gaye and the Detroit Spinners and, of course, their son's current close proximity to it all.

"Well, Detroit, I don't really know what to say," my mother exclaimed as we pulled into the drive of Hotel Hairpiece.

"Come on, heads down. Don't let Rhonda catch us on the way in."

For the rest of the evening, the three of us chatted about the time that had passed since I had left home.

Next up was a trip to the Windy City.

I had decided to rent a Chevy Lumina, to ensure that we arrived in one piece.

"Bloody hell, Gary. I'll tell you what, these seats aren't half comfy." My mother was seemingly on a mission to compliment any American vehicle that she sat in.

We spent a couple of days in downtown Chicago and had a catch up with the lads, enjoying a decent first night in a local restaurant and a chance for my parents and me to see how my British friends were adjusting to life in the Windy City. They were flabbergasted when we stepped off the L-train at Southport, my friends living pretty at the north end of the Southport corridor.

"Well, would you believe it? From Southport England to Southport America, eh son?" My father demanded I take a photo of the two of them outside the "L" station sign.

We ended our first evening with a gentle lakeside walk, my parents astounded at the sheer size of the skyscrapers cradling Lake Michigan. The following day, visits to two of those huge buildings were on our to-do list.

Our first was to the Hancock Tower to sample its famous elevator zooming up ninety-six floors in 9.1 seconds. The rush to the top was a way better option than attempting to walk its 1,600 steps. We read that you could see four states from the viewing lounge at the top: Michigan, Illinois, Wisconsin, and Indiana. We did our best to work out our east, west, north and south as we convinced ourselves that we definitely saw all four states that day.

"Wow! I just can't believe that's a lake, son. It's bloody massive. What an incredible view from up here, eh?" My father stood beside my mother, the two of them simply in awe.

After we made it back to ground level, we all decided that a visit to the Cheesecake Factory—the restaurant at the base of the Hancock Tower— was on the cards.

"Good afternoon. My name is Jenna and I am going to be your server today. We have a selection of specials on offer today...beer specials...on tap we have...and our bottled beers are...now, could I first interest you in any appetizers?" Jenna, our server at the Cheesecake Factory, was certainly making her presence felt. And the range of options was making my mother's and father's heads spin.

"Oh my goodness. Well, I don't really know where to start," said my mother, somewhat flustered by the endless choices. "Jenna, that is quite the choice you have given us, love."

"Why thank you, ma'am. I will take that as a compliment" Jenna replied, adding "I love your accent. It is sooo cute. Are you guys from England?"

"Yes, we are, Jenna. This is my husband Jimmy. We're over here to visit our son here. He works in Michigan."

"That's lovely. I have always wanted to visit England. Well, welcome to Chicago. Enjoy your stay with us."

After ordering an oriental chicken salad and her usual "just a small brandy," my mother sat back soaking in the atmosphere.

My father had plumped for a full rack of ribs. "Never had a rack of ribs before, son. Let's do it, eh?"

"What a lovely girl she is, eh Jimmy? And what a place this is, Gary. Have you seen the size of those plates of food. Oh my goodness!"

"There you go, ma'am. One oriental chicken salad and one small brandy," Jenna said, giving a wink to my mother as she placed the glass down on the table.

"Oh wow! That can't all be for me. I will never be able to eat all that," my mother replied, exasperated at the size of the plate in front of her.

"Bloody hell, Gary! There's enough here for a whole football team" was all my father could say as his "full slab" arrived.

"Is there anything else I can get you guys?"

"You must be joking, Jenna," my mother responded. "This all looks absolutely fantastic, love. I feel like the bloody Queen!"

"Oh, my, gosh. I would love to meet her," Jenna replied, displaying an immediate affection for the British Royal Family.

I didn't even bother to go there.

I smiled as my parents indulged in their meals. Their eyes were everywhere, my mother continuing to emphasize just how large her salad was after each and every mouthful.

"Would you like a box, ma'am?" a perceptive Jenna said, noticing them both stalling, not even half way through their dinners.

"I'm sorry, love? A box? How do you mean?"

I explained the concept of "the box" to my mother and father—and they both immediately requested one, after they had taken a second to get their heads around the fact that they could actually take any food left on their plate away with them.

"Bloody marvelous that is, son. What a place, eh?" said my father, happy at the prospect of finishing up his "full slab" later on in the day.

We returned to our hotel, dropped off the leftovers and relaxed for a while—right after my father had almost been run over attempting to cross the road looking in entirely the wrong direction and stepping out into oncoming traffic.

Time for tower two!

The Sears Tower stood at 1,451 feet high versus the Hancock Tower at 1,127 feet. It was the sky deck on the 103rd floor that will live in our memories for a long time to come. "I can feel the place moving, Gary," said my father, his face a mixture of sheer amazement and complete terror.

"This really is something, Gary! I can't believe it."

"Unbelievable isn't it, dad? What a view!"

As I stood surveying the expanse below me, I had that profound sense of being "in the moment." I was with both of my parents in the City of Chicago looking out over Lake Michigan from the 103rd floor of one of the tallest buildings in the world. I can safely say that none of us could ever have predicted such a moment.

The rest of our stay in the Windy City took in the famous Water Tower and the Magnificent Mile, among other attractions, ironically while sitting atop a British-style double decker bus.

On our journey back to Michigan, my mother, for what had to have been the fifth or sixth time since we left, asked "So what are all these orange barrels about, Gary?"

"Road works are a given over here, mum. Think about the extremes of weather we've got. A hundred degrees in the summer and well below zero in the winter. That coupled with all of the heavy trucks means that you'll see these orange barrels out all the time."

"There aren't half some bloody big bumps on these roads, Gary. It's amazing that any cars can stay in one piece. And it seems much worse the further into Michigan we get" said my father—with a somewhat astute observation.

On our return to Hotel Hairpiece, the three of us decided that a quiet night in was in order.

"Well, that certainly is a tale of two very different cities, isn't it Gary, with Detroit and Chicago" said my father, as he stood leaning against the sink, sipping on a Guinness.

"Bloody hell! What was that?" he said, as he jumped forward spilling the froth off his pint, startled by the noise of the garbage disposal that I had just turned on, as though he was about to be swept into it.

"It's a garbage disposal, dad."

"A what?"

"It grinds up your food waste into small tiny pieces that can then go down the sink."

"Are you serious?" my father said, bending down to investigate the link between sink and trap and how the electrical supply fed the unit.

"What on earth will they think of next, eh son?"

The next morning all roads led to the city of Warren for a very important soccer match. My parents were about to sample the Britannia Club for themselves.

April 19, 1997 and the place was packed for Manchester United vs. Liverpool.

As we wandered in through the darkened corridor, Reggie came into full view, stood on stage, starting proceedings with his usual welcome.

My folks sat down as the Club's newest guest members.

"I can't believe they have a place like this in America, Gary" my mother's response as she surveyed the surroundings.

"Who would have thought it, eh? A home away from home," was my father's repost.

Red, Chinny, and Eddie were the main players at our table.

"Ah, so you're the famous Mr. France then," said Red, smiling as he introduced himself.

"Your son is one mad United fanatic. I will you tell you that."

"You're spot on there son," replied my father. "Tell me something I don't know!"

"He speaks of you every time he is watching a game here, you know," Red responded.

"Yeah, and that phone box over there gets quite a bit of use, too," Chinny chimed in.

"Hey dad," I responded. "Come and have a look at this."

"Ha. That is funny. Queen Victoria," my father said, immediately noticing the regal bust in the backroom bar.

"No, mate. Over here," I replied, motioning toward the big red phone booth.

"Oh bloody hell. You weren't kidding were you?"

"This is it, mate—our United connection. You and I. Go on, get in there just for the hell of it."

My father smiled, stepping into the phone box from where I had made so many transatlantic calls, pre, mid, and postmatch. Those calls home would now have new meaning for sure.

We took up our seats and readied ourselves for kick-off. The atmosphere in the club was brilliant. It was a frenetic first half, as we all had expected. Pallister exposed James' weakness on crosses and bulleted two headers into the Liverpool net. Liverpool's John Barnes split the difference and at half-time, the score was 1-2 in United's favor. Celebrating United's goals personally with Des meant that he would now be able to visualize the scene at my weekend soccer retreat.

The half-time break consisted of Archie and his wife chatting away with my parents. No real surprise there, after discovering the fact that my parents were living in the southwest corner of Scotland.

Andy Cole won the game for us that day with a goal midway through the second half. Liverpool 1, Manchester United 3. The Premier League title had moved a little closer to a place in the trophy room at Old Trafford.

"Well, I believe it's time for a brandy," my mother declared, still applauding the outcome of the match. It was her tendency to take a celebratory tipple should the moment require sufficient recognition. A United victory over Liverpool was certainly sufficient recognition.

As my father stood, about to fulfill his wife's request, Chinny immediately gestured for him to remain seated.

"No, no. Please. Let me get these. What would you like, Mr. France?"

"Are you sure, son?"

"Absolutely, I insist. Sad to say, but I believe your team may well have just clinched the Premier League title. Besides, you can't travel all this way and not sample a little American hospitality, right?"

"Hey, while yer up Chinny, I'll take another Guinness," Eddie chimed in, waving his empty glass in front of America's number one Robbie Fowler fan.

On his return from the bar, Chinny placed a large brandy on the table in front of my mother.

"There you go, Mrs. France."

My mother responded by planting a kiss on the right cheek of the Korean American, his blush instant.

"Yeaaaaah!" we all responded.

"Lovely that, Chinny. Thank you very much, lad." She proceeded to raise her glass.

"To United. Soon to be league champions!"

"United! United! United!" The chorus rang out around our table and into the ears of a solitary Liverpool FC fan.

"Come on, Chinny lad," Eddie cheered, Chinny's still reddened face most evident as he stretched across the table to hand his soccer teammate and United friend a pint of Guinness.

"Well done, you wanker," Red added, patting Chinny on his right shoulder. "Now then. How about we talk a little more about that result?"

"No way, man. You'll be walking home if you carry on with this nonsense!"

I sat back, continuing to enjoy the sight of members from the Britannia Club coming over and greeting my folks and making them feel a part of our unique setup. Des appeared to be in his element in his "home away from home" social club setting.

My parents were terrific during their short time out in the U.S. Despite being in their mid-sixties and dealing with the rigors of jet lag, their energy had been relentless. Their thirst for enjoyment was a joy to behold, particularly after witnessing a Manchester United victory over arch nemesis Liverpool on a big screen in a British-style social club north of Detroit.

It is certainly never easy to wave your folks off, but after our goodbyes, I watched the two of them wander toward the departure gate, my father no doubt keeping an eye out for any guards wrapped in guns. Then, in unison, they turned to wave one final time.

"Keep going, son. Keep on doin' it, lad," my father mouthed.

"Be safe, both of you," I shouted back.

22

Slow Crawl to the Crown

Wednesday, April 23, 1997: No chance to hang with Red over in Ann Arbor for the live ESPN broadcast of the European Champions league semi-final second leg. Trying to take time off as a physical therapist with a full caseload is always tough, and besides, any vacation time that I had accrued had more or less been used up when my folks were over. So the Cabellos family provided me with my only viable connection to the all-important match from Old Trafford. I resisted temptation to call Frank for updates on the match that afternoon and carried on working, counting the hours until I could walk out of the clinic at 6:00 p.m., still clueless as to the score from Manchester. A quick pit stop to pick up the video tape and a swift drive back to Hotel Hairpiece with only one thing on my mind—Old Trafford in retro.

"Go United!" came the shout from behind the kitchen window as Rhonda's eye caught me waving the tape high in the air. I ignored the call of the answering machine, quickly popped the VHS tape into the player and settled back to focus on the tiny TV screen atop the fridge. I detached from my surroundings as I was immediately transported to Manchester.

After only eight minutes United had a mountain to climb as Dortmund scored a vital away goal. United would now have to score three goals before the end of the match to advance to the final. It never happened and the distinctive yellow tribe of Dortmund claimed the night. I sat for a moment trying to comprehend that my team had been beaten by a team whose supporters had been ferociously waving giant blow-up bananas all game high up in the away fans section of the Theatre of Dreams. United had been knocked out of the European Champions League one step away from the final. A German team had "done us"—a German team with a Scottish midfielder. I couldn't believe it. I didn't want to believe it. I was gutted. I reached for the answering machine. My father's voice echoed around the apartment.

"They just weren't quite good enough, lad. Bloody Germans have done us again, eh? Still no European Cup final. Maybe one day, son? Maybe one day? Thanks again for a great trip over. Your mother and I thoroughly enjoyed it. Look after yourself, lad, and go easy on those bloody awful roads, eh."

As my father's voice exited the tape, a second message followed.

"Bollocks!"

The single-word phone message echoed around my tiny apartment. I smiled at the American Midwest pronunciation. Ann Arbor's Manchester United Supporters Club, a membership of one, was also feeling the bitter sting of defeat.

That immediate emptiness of defeat emphasized my circumstance. It had been quite a journey. A challenge trying to piece together sound bites, visuals, reports and venues via which I could enjoy United's European Champions League ride after relocating to the U.S. Everything had seemingly been pointing to a different, more favorable outcome. Domestic double in my first year abroad, and then the "big one"—European Champions—in my second. United's momentum had suggested such. In the end, I knew it was all just wishful thinking.

I pulled on the positive. The Red Devils were now just four games away—possibly even less, depending on other results—from winning the Premier League title once again.

Four games left. Five points required.

May 3, 1997: Leicester City vs. Manchester United was the featured game at the Britannia Club. I had never heard so much noise in the building. With only twenty minutes gone, our Liverpool contingent was going ballistic as United were already 2-0 down: a European hangover, maybe? I then witnessed our new hero, Solskjær, score two goals, the first of which was one of the best counter attacking goals I had ever seen. It began with a great save from Peter Schmeichel. Paul Scholes then picked up the ball and thrust through midfield, offloading to Andy Cole and "bang"—Solskjær. Solskjær then made it a brace in the second half. United had rescued a point. 2-2!

Three games left. Four points required.

Just two days later, on May 5, United had a Monday night match that was not being shown anywhere in Michigan, not even at the Britannia Club. The English Premier League season down to the wire and I was reminded that I was fanatical about a sport that existed primarily for an audience on the other side of the Atlantic. There was no way to see or hear the match. Back to basics once more as I relied upon Des to provide the report late night from his corner of southwest Scotland. United had once again come from behind to claim a vital 3-3 draw at Old Trafford in an apparent thriller of a match with Middlesborough. Solskjær once again scored the vital goal to rescue a point. Des hung on two main points. Firstly, he was astounded to see United's full back, Gary Neville, actually score and, secondly, he had never quite seen a celebration like the one that Middlesborough's Brazilian midfielder Emerson had produced to put them 2-1 up. He also mentioned his blood pressure as possibly being a tad elevated as Boro, at one point, had led 3-1.

United were only managing draws in their slow crawl to the crown.

Two games left. Three points required.

The very next day, on Tuesday May 6, there was the distinct possibility that either West Ham, playing at home to Newcastle, or Wimbledon, playing at home to Liverpool, could inadvertently hand the English Premier League to the Red Devils. As I rushed back to my apartment that evening, I received the two important results from across the Pond. Des had delivered.

"Wimbledon 2, Liverpool 1 and West Ham 0, Newcastle 0! Son we're champions again! The evening news has been showing the scenes from Old Trafford. Fans are out in force celebrating!"

I knew it was late over in Scotland, almost midnight, but I picked up the phone and called Des.

After a few more rings than usual, a sleepy voice answered.

"We did it Gary, son. We did it!"

My father was expecting the transatlantic call.

"Get in there, mate! Championes! Championes!"

"Did you get to see any of the matches over there, Gary?"

"No mate, the Britannia Club didn't have them on. I had to work anyways. So thanks for delivering the brilliant news to my American doorstep."

"My pleasure, son! My pleasure!"

I bid my father a good night and then, just before I walked away from the answering machine, I noticed a second message alert.

"There's only one Man United, you wanker!"

I had to make another phone call, a local one this time. Did I ever think that I would be celebrating a United Premier League title win with an American Manchester United supporter on the day the league was won? The nature of our extended conversation that night reflected on how those "kids"—Fergie's Fledglings—were now looking like "the real deal," as Frank put it.

United had two games remaining, both at Old Trafford. The first, against Newcastle, now destined to be runners up, ended scoreless. And then, the final game of the season and my chance to see United lift the English Premier League trophy.

May 11, 1997: Manchester United vs. West Ham United.

I couldn't wait to get to the Britannia Club that Sunday. The parking lot was packed. El Tico declared "I think you will be here today"—at least that is what it sounded like to me, El Tico's English still not too fluent. He smiled as I handed him my money. That lad still needed a dentist!

All of the usual suspects were present, including, to my surprise, Chinny.

"Well, Frank couldn't have made it without his taxi ride, right, man?" Chinny exclaimed as he reached out to shake my hand.

"You are so full of shit, mate," Eddie declared, nudging the Korean American before wandering off to join the lineup for the "full English" breakfast. I spent the first hour or so mulling around, conversation flowing throughout the building. Archie thought that United were now ready to dominate English soccer for years to come. And who was I to disagree?

11:00 a.m. Michigan time arrived and a proud Eric Cantona once again led his champions out onto the park. A huge round of applause filled the room. Despite our varied allegiances, for a few short seconds, the crowd inside our den realized that our privileged window to soccer from abroad was about to end for the summer. We had been fortunate to see some great games. And that in itself was worthy of a round of applause.

I looked up at the big screen, the sun beaming down on Old Trafford. Red stood tall, head forth, squinting through his thick, circular lenses, and, slowly turning his collar up, exclaimed "All rise for God! We are now in soccer heaven!"

The match began.

An absolute bullet of a shot from Scholes shook the West Ham crossbar, and who else but Solskjær was on hand to head home the rebound. The second half highlight produced a second United goal from Jordi Cruyff, son of the great Johan, United eventually winning the match 2-0.

As I watched the live pictures of the Reds celebrating on the pitch— Alex Ferguson holding another Premier League trophy aloft—my thoughts turned to home. My father had taken a three-mile drive over to

Scotland's most southerly post office. His postmaster friend, Hamish, was one of only a handful of villagers who had Sky satellite TV. I left my soccer gang to head into the small back bar of the Britannia Club. Try as I might, I couldn't seem to connect from the telephone box. Frustrated, and with a frown to match that of the nearby Queen Victoria bust, I eventually gave up trying and returned to the main auditorium to the sound of applause and the sight of Reggie taking the stage.

I later learned that my father's village phone lines were down after a heavy storm. It goes without saying that part of me was in that room above the remote Scottish post office as I am sure Des had thoughts for an expatriate social club that was now familiar to him.

As Reggie stood and tapped the microphone, the room fell silent. It pained Reggie that day. I could sense it, but ever the disciplined and dedicated host, he delivered his final season address.

"First off, let me say congratulations, Manchester United. English Premier League Champions once again."

Rapturous applause filled the room along with whistles and boos from the Newcastle and Liverpool fans as well as the non-United fans present—a chorus unashamedly led by Chinny.

"Thank you also, all of you, for visiting the Britannia Club over this past season. Without your wonderful support and continued patronage there would be no English Premier League soccer in Michigan."

"Reggie! Reggie! Reggie!"

Remaining focused, our leader continued.

"I would like you to thank our cooks and volunteers that also contribute to making these special weekend mornings possible. I wish everyone a terrific summer and hope to see you all back here in August for a preseason screening of the FA Charity Shield. Drive carefully and thanks again."

Everyone present was on their feet, extending their applause as Reggie exited the stage.

As we filed out into the parking lot, I heard Red tease Chinny.

"How about we take the long way home, Chinny?"

"Hey! You'll be walking home in a minute, Frank!"

Handshakes all around, Eddie's vice-like grip matched with a ferocious "Yes! United! Championes! Get in there, son!" Eddie was indeed somewhat of an adrenaline junkie. We all promised to stay in touch and regroup for the following season.

As I pulled away to a chorus of car horns, I reached across to tighten my United scarf in my passenger side window before entering the freeway. As I accelerated toward the mass of traffic, the scarf began to flap wildly in the breeze. I couldn't stop smiling. I was one very happy Englishman abroad.

My second season following United in America had come to an end. The thrill of this Premier League victory felt more intense, knowing just how fortunate I had been to be able to witness it in such an atmosphere — live in a northern suburb of Detroit.

No matter how far away, no matter the time difference, no matter the hurdles, I had continued to find a way to remain forever Red!

23

A British Invasion

The Little Professor bookstore in Dearborn became one of my regular hangouts during the summer, soccer off-season. With no Britannia Club to occupy those Sunday mornings, I continued my English tradition of enjoying a relaxing Sabbath absorbed in the Sunday newspapers with a decent brew in hand. The bookstore was only a mile or so from Hotel Hairpiece, so it made for a decent stroll through Dearborn's old town, Henry Ford's imprint clearly visible with a diverse array of heritage homes and beautifully manicured gardens.

A new publication from the UK—*The Express: A Week in Review*—had caught my eye as it nestled on the shelves next to the *News of the World*, the *Sunday Mirror*, and the *Sunday Telegraph*. It all still seemed rather bizarre to me, and for the uninitiated upon first entering that building, the last thing one would expect to come across would be a well-stocked rack of British tabloids among the likes of the *Detroit Free Press* and *USA Today*. The *Sunday Express* supplement always provided a good overview of news from back in the UK, albeit at least two weeks old. It was all new news to me though, with no other access to the latest happenings from across the Pond. Most of the soccer news was well covered: postseason interviews, reviews, and transfer speculation ahead of the upcoming season. *The Express* was also a great source of information on the latest happenings in the British music scene. I had always maintained a strong interest in music and now that my weekend mornings were, indeed, mostly free, I dared to dream some more, aligning myself with the "can do" American attitude that seemed to surround me. I changed focus somewhat as I began to head into a more musically-inclined direction.

For some time I had considered looking into opportunities that might be available in terms of radio and broadcasting. I discovered a School of Broadcasting not too far from my digs in Dearborn and had gone there for an interview. However, the fees were rather high and I didn't relish evening classes on top of what was already a very busy work schedule, and so I considered a different game plan: a little DIY approach.

Thanks to the Little Professor, I discovered a publication called *World TV and Radio* which provided contact information for radio stations. I compiled a list of radio stations within a two-hour drive of my Dearborn pad and sent each of the thirty-five stations a "Please Hire Gaz the DJ" package containing a cover letter, photo, and an audio tape.

After a mere three replies in the first three weeks—none of which were favorable—I decided to make some follow-up calls. I eventually reached a station in Ann Arbor called Replay 105.1. My call was answered by Replay's sports host, who immediately recognized an English accent, and, after my inquiry, told me that the station's Program Director, a certain Misty Moon, was "just about to call and was excited to chat with me."

"Yeah, right," I thought to myself. I also sensed another "American moment," should the conversation indeed materialize, in that I could well be about to talk to a lady by the name of Misty, a somewhat provocative proposition.

Then, behind the hustle and bustle on the other end of the phone line, I could just about make out the request. "Why don't you come on over to the station, honey? We'll let you know when. OK?" Apparently, Miss Moon was interested in offering me an internship at the station. I put down the receiver. *Yes!* I was beyond excited, producing a "Pearson Pump" with such conviction I almost dislocated my right elbow.

For the next few days, I listened to Replay 105.1 at every opportunity, as I eagerly awaited my invite. The first show I heard was "Misty Moon's Lunchtime Lounge" where Misty would "deliver your requests from the tasty music menu for an entire hour!" During Misty's broadcast, chings and clinks of crockery and cutlery would play along with a vocal montage of imaginary waiters and customers, recreating the hustle and bustle of a busy restaurant. Yes, it was as cheesy as hell, but the punters ate it up!

I finally received my invite to head over to the radio station. They were looking for me to get there late one weekday morning if at all possible. I had to make it work. Luckily, I was able to take off a half day from work after another on call shift the prior weekend.

As I was driving to the station, I got myself pumped up listening to the Misty Moon Show and trying to imagine what she would look like.

"Welcome! You must be Gary," said the secretary.

I was then met by a geeky looking young fellow, full of energy and oozing a positive vibe.

"Love the accent, man! Glad you could make it! My name is Stefan. I'm Misty's assistant. She has just gone on air so come on, follow me."

"Are you kidding me?" I thought to myself, "only two minutes in the building and I will be walking into a radio studio; more to the point, a radio studio with a show being broadcast by none other than Misty Moon!"

"Wow! Sounds brilliant Stefan."

He looked like a Stefan.

We entered a short corridor, the walls of which were adorned with gold and platinum discs. Originals surely not, but they sure looked authentic. I noticed a door up ahead with a light above it.

"Just hang here a second, Gary" said Stefan, continuing forward and peeking through the small window at eye level on the door. I watched him stick his thumb up and then enter the room. A few seconds later, he emerged and whispered "OK, Gary. Misty says that you can enter the studio now. Come and find me when she is done with you OK? Have fun."

"Fantastic, Stefan. Will do. Cheers, mate," I replied, trying to keep my voice down and trying my best to contain my excitement. I gave the lad an impulsive pat on the back. Did I really do that? My excitement was at full pelt—one of those moments in life that you realize you are about to experience something that you have always wanted to do.

I walked through the studio door.

There, in front of me, sat behind the board, was the incredibly sultry Misty Moon, her strawberry blonde hair colliding with the headphones around her neck. Her immaculate lip gloss shone as she smiled. As I stepped in, gingerly proceeding alongside the equipment in order to greet her, Misty stood and offered her hand. She was wearing a pair of jeans that seemed to melt onto her legs.

That first impression of Misty was one of meeting a totally American woman. Go figure, right. But by that I mean that eveything about her was immaculate: her hair, her blouse, her cleavage, her lip gloss and make up, her pearly white pristine American teeth. She would have been right at home in one of those 1980s hair band MTV videos.

"Well hi there, Gary! So pleased to meet you. Welcome to my little world. Come on, sit down over here."

I immediately considered that Misty's world was not at all little.

"Lovely to meet you too, Misty. Thank you so much for giving me this opportunity. I really appreciate it!" I responded in a polite English way, all the while trying not to stare too much at the radio goddess in front of me.

"Now you just sit there and relax. Take it all in!"

Oh I was taking it all in alright. Every single bit of it.

"Thanks Misty. This is fantastic!" sounding every bit the submissive little kid with the candy.

Misty cranked the sound and the Doors' "Light My Fire" reverberated against the walls of our padded cocoon. So apt! I was having an American moment way beyond any other American moment that I had thus far experienced.

As the Doors faded out, Misty shot to a break and then rolled right into a check of the weather. She was in total control of the airwaves and I, of course, was in total awe of her. I was amazed at her calmness and focus. I was also impressed by the amount of British music that she played during her show. Misty's smooth midwest accent seemed to breathe new life into popular British artists that I had taken so much for granted: Rod Stewart, Gerry Rafferty, The Kinks, The Who, Elton John. I quickly developed a newfound appreciation for bands that were on the scene way before I had discovered my own musical passions. The Beatles and Stones featured heavily in the programming, along with songs from T-Rex, Roxy Music, and David Bowie. I began to feel right at home as the captivating Miss Moon and I moved to the musical vibe, enthusiastically discussing the array of British talent that had arrived on American shores over the years. I remained fixated, basking in the moments when Misty made her vocal breaks. She really was poetry in motion, responding to calls and cueing up songs with effortless flow. Her timing was immaculate. She didn't miss a beat.

As we entered the final hour of her show, Misty declared that I would be taught all I needed to know and that, by the time I left Replay 105.1, I would have all the experience necessary to enter any radio station anywhere in the land. Talk about on the job training.

After completing another musical break introducing "Stay with Me" by The Faces, Misty coolly removed her headphones, shook her hair, and then stood offering me her hand.

"Well Gary, welcome to radio! Have you enjoyed yourself so far?"

"Misty, this has been unbelievable. What an experience. Thank you!"

"Why don't you pop out and find Stefan. Work out the best times for you to come on over and help us out. See you around, yeah?"

"Absolutely. Sounds great, Misty. And thanks again."

Sometimes you have to sit back and simply wonder just how on earth you have ended up in a particular moment.

"Well, Gary, how did it go?" Stefan enquired as I walked back into the main office.

"Brilliant, Stefan. Totally loved it, mate."

"Yes, Misty is quite something isn't she? We really can't believe that she is still with us. We're very blessed for sure."

"You sure are, Stefan. You sure are. She was superb."

"Hey, don't get too carried away now, Gary," Stefan seemingly acknowledging what any red-blooded male would when talking about Misty Moon.

As I drove away from Replay 105.1's offices, I once again tuned into the station. Alas, Misty was no longer on air. I listened with intent, though, as a show called "Drive Time" was in full flow. I wanted to educate myself by listening to as many DJs as possible. I couldn't believe that I was now working at an American radio station.

For the next few weeks, I did a whole host of intern duties, mostly during evenings and weekends. On one occasion, I had to climb onto the roof of a bookstore in downtown Ann Arbor to erect a thirty-foot tall balloon penguin—the station's mascot who came out to play at many of our live broadcasts. Did I feel a twat or what? Totally! Particularly on a windy day! But at no time during my internship did I have to make anyone a coffee.

I didn't see too much more of Misty after that first day, as most of my internship during the week was spent in the early evening after my day job had finished. Then, about six weeks into my Replay 105.1 experience, my big break arrived. Misty had been utilizing my accent for local commercial slots, leaving me voice-over assignments and memos to record the odd break for her Lunchtime Lounge show. One day, out of the blue, she requested I meet with her before she left for the day.

"Gary, babe! There is an early Saturday morning slot available. It's a prerecorded show with Scott Studios—but impress me and we may consider making it a live show."

I had been given my chance. One chance to make a good impression!

Scott Studios was the latest software technology when it came to recording and running a complete show log (playlist, commercials and jingles). A DJ could fast forward to the slots which required vocal interludes. It was an ingenious system, enabling a host to record a three-hour show in the space of twenty minutes without even being present in the studio at the time of the show. It prompted the demise of the overnight "jock" of course, as no station wanted to pay for the services of a live DJ if they could get it done in a twenty-minute burst.

Enter part-time weekend DJ, Donny Duggan.

Donny was a great lad, with the ability to smoke more cigarettes in one show than I could ever have imagined. Maybe that was the secret to fueling what was possibly one of the best radio voices I had ever heard. His name had a decent ring to it, too. The two of us immediately hit it off. Donny worked the evening slot and covered most Saturday and Sunday afternoons. He very kindly took me under his wing and coached me on the ins and outs of on-air delivery along with other tips I needed in order to make my radio venture a successful one. We were both enthusiastic and spent hours in the Replay 105.1 production room in the dead of night and dawn of a new morning as we would meet up in order to nail down some precious production time. We would often take a break around 6:00 a.m., sitting on the wall outside the studio as another sunrise announced itself, Donny dragging on his umpteenth cigarette of a still very young Saturday.

I grew to admire the young family man. He was working all hours, doing two other jobs, and giving his all in order to keep a profile in the competitive world of radio. I will always be grateful for the time Donny spent helping a young novice English DJ learn the ropes.

In late June, my break arrived. The Scott Studios recordings for my first Saturday morning slot took me much longer than the requisite twenty minutes ,but the thrill was well worth it. I left the production room around 10:00 p.m. on the Friday. I had booked a hotel room close by just in case I needed extra time with my preparation. My alarm rang around 5:50 a.m. the following morning. My show was due to be broadcast at 6:00 a.m. Rubbing my eyes, I leaned over to switch the hotel clock radio on, my broadcast debut imminent. I knew the last song of the night shift would be "Bennie and the Jets" by Elton John followed by the Replay 105.1 "on the hour" jingle. Then I waited as a short silence—which seemed like a lifetime—was broken to the strains of the theme to "2001: A Space Odyssey" and my voiceover declaration that "Saturday Mornings Will Never Be the Same Again," A quick name check and we were off and running to the sound of "Crossroads" by Cream. I was actually lying in a hotel bed listening to my radio debut on Replay 105.1. Bizarre. And brilliant!

Weeks went by and the prerecorded early Saturday morning show became my own. Then, in late July, Misty suggested it was time for me to present the show live. Not only that, but for a full four hours, from 6:00 a.m. to 10 a.m.

I began to brainstorm how I could personalize my imprint on the station's format. Then a sudden lightning bolt—"The British Invasion." Of course!

Replay 105.1 was an "oldies station," playing music from the 60s and 70s—an integral part of that time in musical history was the Beatles-inspired "British Invasion." The format of show came together quickly.

First up was "The Beatles at Breakfast"—five Beatles tracks and exerpts of Beatles gossip and history. I found a CD of Beatles interviews at Dearborn Music, which I meticulously edited for the show. Next was "The Year in Focus"—five tracks with a request for listeners to name the year in question. This was followed by "The Song Connection"—three songs, with listeners challenged to find the connection. Add to that a few requests and a tad of nostalgia with a British lad at the microphone and . . . Moon loved the idea. The station loved the idea.

As the morning of my first live "British Invasion" show arrived, I stepped into the studio, surveyed the playlist, and watched the clock tick closer to 6:00 a.m. I noticed that someone had pinned a note on the wall above the board. It was a picture of a familiar toddler sat in a dishwasher. The note below read "This is the only way mummy and daddy can wash my hair! Best of luck with your American radio show, Uncle Gary."

It had been sent to the studio by my college roommate, Tom Skinner. I continued to realize how blessed I was to have such great friends.

I sat down, took a deep breath, and opened up the microphone. I felt a massive adrenaline shot as I announced . . . "It's Saturday morning and you're listening to The British Invasion with Gary France live on Replay 105.1!"

24

A Conflict of Interest

"When Saturday comes" an Englishman abroad sits in a radio studio enthusiastically preaching the British music gospel. A dream has come true. Reality still bites though. It is now August and that means one thing—the start of a brand new English Premier League season. Having established a way to watch live Manchester United games in the States, I could not ignore the fact that my new preoccupation, producing and presenting a four-hour Saturday morning radio show, was a definite conflict of interest. There was no time for trips to the Britannia Club. The solution? To get back to basics. I became an FM DJ with a shortwave radio in his bag.

My radio gig required me to remain at the studio until noon to help run the boards. Fall weekends on Replay 105.1 consisted of live remote broadcasts from 10 a.m. until noon and I had been asked to be the in-studio link for the DJ on location. This, of course, clashed with full second half commentary of a Premier League match on the BBC World Service. In order to catch as much of the match commentary as possible, I made sure that I had at least three tracks lined up with the relevant jingles and commercials on Scott Studios. Then, avoiding any listener phone calls, I would dash out into the studio lobby, pull up the antenna, and hunt around to find the clearest possible reception. One minute, I'm listening to Alan Green and his unmistakable Irish drawl as he commentates on the latest Premier League action; the next, I'm introducing a song from Donovan!

I became clinical and methodical in my approach, playing the likes of "Hey Jude" and "Nights in White Satin" — longer songs that would allow for extra time to catch the latest match reports from around the grounds.

It wasn't long before temptation soon got the better of me. OK, so I was in a small town in the American Midwest, but surely there had to be listeners out there familiar with the Red Devils from Manchester. And so, in the land of the evangelist, I decided to preach some soccer gospel!

Hallelujah!

I knew that Chinny would have been on his way to pick up Red. He was always game for a chat and a chance to discuss the day's Premier League fixtures. Heading north to the Britannia Club, the fanatics were well up for some soccer. I took a moment as I had to concentrate on the job at hand a little while longer. As ELO's "Livin' Thing" faded out, I introduced Roxy Music. That sax line over a neat bass run, "Love is the Drug," filled my headphones. As Bryan Ferry's vocals joined the mix, I sat back and took it all in. Moments later I opted for the swift sea change. My brain was running at one hundred miles an hour; nothing new there, to be honest. It was time for a break from the music and to call my mate off air for a short soccer fix. My friend and Liverpool fan was obviously moving into game mode.

"No chance today, Englishman! Your Red Devils are gonna die, man!"

As usual, Chinny had no problem displaying his blatant antipathy toward Manchester United. He did however offer some words of encouragement to a Red Devil and novice DJ, "Sounding good there, man."

At least I was guaranteed one listener that particular morning!

I kept a close eye on the track placement, ensuring that I didn't forget the music while soccer talk between mates continued off air.

The Who's "Magic Bus" was next up and I opted for a prerecorded station ID between songs, allowing the soccer banter to roll on. As I sat in the Replay studios I couldn't help but convey my disappointment at not being able to join my two soccer-loving friends. I was torn, of course, loving my musical indulgence, yet fully aware of what I was also missing: Liverpool versus Manchester United live from the Britannia Club.

"Chinny," I responded, "keep the radio on, mate. I'll be giving you and the tall Yank a shout out in a few!"

"Nice one Gary! We'll miss you up there today. Keep up the good work. Lovin the music man!"

I surmised Chinny was stuck in a musical decade past.

I hung up and decided that it was time for Ann Arbor to sample the build-up to a crucial English Premier League clash.

As the "Magic Bus" drove off into the distance, my musical break went something like this: "Now you may or may not be aware of this, but us British love a good game of soccer. Well, today is a very important day in the English soccer calendar, folks. Today is the day that Manchester

United, the single greatest soccer team on this planet, will be playing their fierce rivals Liverpool, at Liverpool's home ground of Anfield, in the city of the birthplace of the "Fab Four." There will be no trophy at stake—just two teams and two sets of fans *desperate* for their team to win. There aren't many days in sport that offer the atmosphere that will be on display at Anfield today!"

At that point, to my surprise, several phone lines began to light up.

I continued:

"At this very moment, two American soccer fanatics are heading west along I-696 in a blue Pontiac for the hour-long drive to the only venue in this beautiful state of Michigan that shows English Premier League games live. That place is the Britannia Club in the city of Warren. So, a quick hello goes out to Chin-ho Lee and Frank Rock. Oh yeah, and Chinny, I hate to tell you this, but your beloved Liverpool FC are going to get well and truly stuffed today, mate!"

The tones of Gerry and the Pacemakers, troubadours from Liverpool and the adopted Liverpool FC anthem "You'll Never Walk Alone" rang out from the studio. Leaning back in my chair, I could not believe that I was perfectly content to sit and listen to the Liverpool FC anthem!

I reached for the phone lines that were still ringing. "Good morning, you've reached Replay 105.1."

"Waaakeeyy, Wwwaaakeeyy! Is there anybody out there?" came the response in the thickest "Scouse" accent I had heard in a long time. "What's all this crap about Liverpool geddin' beat today by Man U? Have you gone bloody crazy, Gary la? United don't stand a bloody chance in hell, mate!"

"Who's this?" I replied, as raucous laughter filled my headphones.

"It's Mally Mal, mate! I tell ya, yous are doin' a damn good job there, la. This British show of yours is lighting up my Saturday mornings no end, mate. So great to hear a voice from the old country. Just a pity that it looks like I've a lorra work to do in makin' you realize what a half decent football team is, eh mate?!"

Unbelievable!

Early on a Saturday morning in the sleepy town of Ann Arbor, Michigan and the first response I get is from a friggin' Scouser the day that United play Liverpool!

From that morning on, I simply couldn't pass up the opportunity to add further authenticity to that part of the show, utilizing those first words an expat Scouser threw down a phone line to me:

"Waaakeeyy, Wwwaaakeeyy!" followed, of course, by "The Beatles at Breakfast." It worked perfectly.

My weekly call from Mally with his unique Liverpool wit always brightened up my Saturdays. He was the perfect example for all Replay 105.1 listeners of a "Mad Scouser."

As the weeks progressed, I learned more about my new friend's passage to Michigan. After emigrating to the U.S. in 1976, Mally had landed a job at a local private bus company, eventually becoming the owner. An idea soon came to mind and Mally jumped right on board with it. He offered up the use of a bus from his company for a whole day in exchange for some free radio advertising. Donny and I organized a competition for thirty Replay listeners to win a trip to Cleveland, Ohio, home of the Rock and Roll Hall of Fame. Did I ever think that I would end up broadcasting live from the radio station inside Cleveland's music Mecca? Well, as it turned out it, I did, an incredible moment in my radio journey for sure.

The day had started at dawn with everyone gathering outside the Replay 105.1 building. I was at last able to put a face to the fella with that unmistakable Liverpudlian accent who called in regularly with his unique contribution to the British Invasion. True to form, the first words Mally uttered to me when we met that morning were "United are a complete bag o' shite, mate!"

That trip to the Rock n Roll Hall of Fame will live long in the memory — the day that I was driven to Cleveland by a mad Scouser!

And the result of that Liverpool vs. Manchester United game on that sixth day of December 1997?

Liverpool 1, United 3!

Andy Cole scored twice, bringing his tally to twelve goals in his last eight games. Not bad for a player who had been chastised for months by the press, labelling him as not good enough to wear the United shirt, let alone be nominated as their main striker.

Manchester United were still winning, and I, of course, was still supporting, albeit with limited resources and my self-inflicted distraction. Was I about to pay dearly for my lack of "live" support for my beloved Reds at the Britannia Club during their 1997–98 season?

I certainly hoped not!

25

A Touch of Irish

As the 1997–98 English Premier League season began, United fans were still reeling after the shock announcement of the retirement of the enigmatic Frenchman, Eric Cantona, at the age of thirty. In his club statement, Alex Ferguson had made reference to the disappointment that Cantona had felt after losing the European Champions league semi-final to Borussia Dortmund. Cantona, it appeared, had made up his mind rather quickly. He was ready to wrap up his soccer career. He was leaving at the top; as a United legend; as King Eric of Old Trafford!

Red worshiped the Frenchman. And true to form, he had left his take on the matter via a telephone message from his home in Ann Arbor.

"Bollocks, Gary! Utter Bollocks, you wanker!"

Alex Ferguson wasted no time. He completed the signing of a new striker, Teddy Sheringham from Tottenham Hotspur.

I received a report of United's first game of the season from Des back in Scotland. Ironically, Sheringham's United debut was at his previous club Spurs' ground, White Hart Lane. I had to work at the hospital that morning, and so was duly grateful to my father for the postmatch lowdown.

"So how did Teddy do?"

"Poor bugger missed a penalty, son. He hit the post and then blasted the rebound wide."

A baptism of fire apparently for the ex-Spurs man, but United had got off to a winning start with a 2-0 win on the road. Their latest star striker got off the mark at Goodison Park against Everton on August 27, with the help of a deflection, and, by the end of August, United were top of the league, unbeaten after five games,

September started with West Ham at Old Trafford. The Hammers took an early lead, but United scored twice in both halves of the match to win a third match on the trot. Despite being victorious in the Champions League away to Košice of Slovakia the following Wednesday, United couldn't break the deadlock in their subsequent Premier League match away at Bolton.

"That bloody Andy Cole, Gary son. I don't know, he doesn't half seem to miss some chances. Just not sure about him, you know," was my father's transatlantic summation of events at the Reebok Stadium in Bolton. For United's next match, Old Trafford welcomed an old hero for the midweek Premier League fixture. Mark Hughes was now with Chelsea and, of course, he duly scored what looked to be the winning goal. Ole Gunner Solskjær then popped up with four minutes to go to earn a dramatic equalizer. The following weekend, United suffered their first defeat of the season with a one-nil loss away at Elland Road, Leeds. That weekend in Yorkshire suddenly got worse for United as the devastating news surfaced that newly-appointed Captain, Roy Keane, had suffered an ACL tear during the match. Our box-to-box general was to be out for several months. I immediately visualized a certain fan in Cork fueling his "teenage kicks," slamming his beer hard onto the bar!

October's highlight for me, no question about it, was the European Champions League tie that had pitted United against cup holders Juventus. The Rock residence provided the venue and ESPN once again broadcast the event. Ann Arbor's United Central erupted as Red and I went into raptures over a 2-1 win for United. The whole experience of midweek European Champions League broadcasts came with ESPN's unique soccer commentary. A relatively mundane piece of action would be coupled with a Yank voice going ballistic in the background. A throw-in is a throw-in, right? Well, the ESPN commentators would have you believing otherwise.

"Whaaaat a throw-in from Neville!"

There was one particular commentator who immediately stood out from the rest—a co-commentator apparently synonymous with U.S. soccer presentation in various guises for quite some time and, furthermore, he wasn't even from America's shores. His name was Tommy Smyth. If my astonishment at actually being able to watch Manchester United in the European Champions League while living in Michigan wasn't enough, the addition of a voice reminiscent of an Irish steeplechase commentator sucking on helium as the backdrop to the matches definitely made the experience all the more unforgettable.

It didn't take long to figure out that the Irishman had his very own signature call, his verbal delivery building to a crescendo finish as he would describe a goal as "a bulge in the auld onion bag." Imagine

America's finest sports network, the slick ESPN, with all of its technology, innovative in bringing you the Champions League, obsessed with statistics and impressive graphics. Then along comes one-of-a-kind Mr. Smyth with his bulging "auld onion bag!"

Following a short soccer career with his hometown team in County Louth, Ireland, Smyth moved to the States in the early 1960s. He had continued playing soccer for Shamrock Rovers in the German-American League. Smyth became well known in the New York Irish community by commentating on games in Gaelic Park in the Bronx, becoming known as "the voice of New York's Gaelic Park." Indeed, Tommy would use the rather comical remark that he'd "seen better games played at Gaelic Park in Riverdale," during a particularly poor soccer game on ESPN — a homage to his commentating past. According to Red, the Irishman was *the* face of ESPN's soccer coverage, particularly the Champions League.

"Tommy Smyth is *the man* over here, dude. He's the Harry Caray of soccer."

"Harry who?"

"Harry Caray, the voice of baseball."

"Oh right! Yeah! The Chicago Cubs announcer!" My time with Chicago sports mad "Soul Boy Bill" had clued me in on the famous announcer.

Red went on to explain that the icon of American baseball commentary had been around for decades and was synonymous with the game. He told me of how Caray had first started the seventh inning stretch singing "take me out to the ball game."

"I believe he started it at the Chicago White Sox, Gary, but became most famous for his renditions at the Cubs' Wrigley Field, using a hand-held microphone and holding it outside the commentary booth. That break between the top and bottom of the seventh inning is the seventh inning stretch when it happens."

"Yeah I have heard about that, Frank. In fact believe it or not, I may have witnessed it only a couple of months ago."

"Really, you wanker?"

"The night United beat Liverpool in the FA Cup, I was out in Chicago and stepped out of a bar on the corner of Clark and Addison, the lights of Wrigley Field lighting up the sky just north of us."

"You tosser! That is awesome! United beat Liverpool in the Cup and that same night you could well have heard Harry Caray serenading

Wrigley Field. That's awesome, dude!"

It turned out that Harry Caray completed his final broadcast from the Chicago Cub's Wrigley Field in that month of September 1997.

Indeed, I read that his last words from that famous booth went something like: "Well, Harry Caray speaking from Wrigley Field. God willing, hope to see ya' next year. Next year maybe will be the next year we all have been waiting for forever. So long, everybody."

I felt privileged to have heard that most iconic baseball chorus delivered by the man himself.

As for Tommy Smyth "with a y," well he was producing some iconic soccer broadcast comments of his own:

"A peach of a goal!"

"A bulge in the auld onion bag!"

I was enjoying yet another wonderful American moment, but with a definite hint of Irish about it. Tommy's "bulging bag" was often accompanied by a few cheeky statements of the obvious. "It's 1-1. If there are no more goals then it will be a draw!" followed, of course, with "This was Tommy Smyth—with a "y"—as he signified an end to the day's proceedings.

October 1997 finished on a high for United, still top of the league after a 7-0 drubbing of Barnsley. In Europe, a better start would be hard to find. United topped their group, with three wins out of three; several "bulges" of several "auld onion bags," and the resultant scalps of Juventus and Feyenord made the taste even sweeter.

November started brightly with a Sheringham/Solskjær showpiece, as United beat Sheffield Wednesday 6-1. United had also breezed to a 3-1 victory away at Feyenoord in the Champions league. My ability to view United's European games was limited as I had to work and so Des was my match reporter on this occasion. He sounded as irritated as I'd ever heard him when I rushed to get the result from the answering machine. He told of the horrendous tackle Dennis Irwin had received and other blatant attempts that the Dutch team made to maim the United players.

"Bunch of dirty gits, those Dutch are, son. I tell you what though. Maybe I was wrong about Cole. I'm really warming to him. The lad scored a brilliant hat-trick!"

Placing my coat on the rather antiquated coat stand in the corner of my Hotel Hairpiece bedsit, I smiled to myself as my father's message ended. I then took a moment to clench both fists, grit my teeth and put on my game face, fiercely pumping my arms in recognition of my team's result. United were now certain to move on from the group stage in the Champion's League.

Next up: Arsenal at Highbury.

United's previous Premier League win against Sheffield Wednesday had suggested that the season may be a runaway for the Red Devils. A win at Highbury and they would lead their nearest rivals by seven points. Arsenal's manager, Arsene Wenger, admitted that should his Gunners suffer a loss, despite making it very difficult, it would still not be impossible to catch United. Some prematch optimism from the Frenchman, maybe in an attempt to deflate some of the pressure on his players prior to the match.

I continued to be energized early each Saturday morning to get into the studio and do something that I had always wanted to do. It was a total sea change to the weekly grind of physical therapy. However, it came at a price. I was trying to come to terms with the detachment from watching the soccer. Fate had played its hand, providing me with my opportunity in radio but this opportunity happened to coincide with the only couple of hours that I had to remain connected to Manchester United while living in America. I continued to attempt to be in two places at one time, standing on the station forecourt with my shortwave radio tuned to the BBC's "Sportsworld." However, such was the significance of the Arsenal/United match that particular weekend that temptation got the better of me. There was no way I was going to miss it. I had to be "in the moment" watching, supporting my team for such a crucial match. And so, I decided that there was no other way than to play "radio hooky," by taking full advantage of Scott Studios technology. I sneaked over to the radio station the evening before the match and laid down a full-length British Invasion with completed voice breaks and program log, just as I had for my first ever show. Donny was top drawer, kindly offering to step in and cover the board through till the noon hour for me, therefore, ensuring that there would be no requirement for my live presence at all that morning.

It was rather strange listening to my voice fading slowly over the airwaves as I drove out of listening range on my journey north toward to the Britannia Club.

It felt great to be back in the only den in Michigan providing a Premier League match up live that day. El Tico handed me my change as I caught up with him, both of us anticipating a colossal clash.

"Hey! Where you been, man?"

"Here and there, my friend," I replied.

"Yeah, I guess!"

"Good to see you, mate!"

"Good to see you too—*mate!*"

El Tico's English had improved since last I saw him.

"Arsenal are gonna win today, man," El Tico continued.

"Hey, let's just stick to taking the money, mate!"

And with a huge smile, El Tico ushered me in, a dental appointment most obviously still not high on his list of priorities. Then again, who was I to talk. I was sure that my previously reconstructed upper molar placement and propensity for sweets, drinking tea, and supping the odd beer over the years back home could well have me donning the opening pages of the classic book of authentic English smiles! I had been in the USA long enough to realize that "pristine" and "white" were the two best words to use when describing Americans' teeth; "yellowed" and "stained" were much better suited for our English equivalent.

The Club was packed and I was happy to see most of the regular fanatics. I acknowledged Sid and left him to immerse himself in committee matters, his worn-out Everton shirt still clinging tightly to his torso.

In light of my return, I decided to indulge in a Britannia Club breakfast, the smell of the kitchen dragging me across the room. I did happen to notice some of the cook's flakey nasal discharge make its way onto one of the plates of early morning fare and I had to focus wholeheartedly on the particular plate in question to avoid a little extra protein in my own meal! I wandered back to my usual table with a plate of "full English" in hand, surveying each food source closely along the way.

The lights dimmed and Reggie cranked the volume to full throttle. Cheers of encouragement filled the room. With only minutes to kick-off, the atmosphere in our soccer home from home was electric. At that moment, any thoughts of the "Beatles at Breakfast" had faded far from my mind. I did become somewhat concerned as to the whereabouts of my two cohorts, then, with just seconds to go, I was slapped on the back by Chinny and received a firm handshake from Red.

Chinny shot straight over to the breakfast bar for his fried bread fix. Prematch routines are a wonder to behold.

Had we ever seen a better first half of soccer? Arsenal came out all guns blazing, much to the delight of my Liverpool-worshipping friend. Anelka buried a fantastic drive in the United net. Patrick Vierra then let fly with an incredible drive out of nowhere that looped its way over the entire defense, Schmeichel wondering where the hell it had come from. An incredible goal! Arsenal were 2-0 up in no time! What must Reggie have been thinking? A terrific turnout and Manchester United 2-0 down; he must have been well happy.

"There's still plenty of time," I said to Red, trying desperately not to rise to the obvious glee on Chinny's face.

United dug in and Teddy Sheringham managed to breach the seemingly impenetrable Arsenal defense, burying a header past the flailing Seaman.

2-1!

I commented to Red about just how little was being contributed by David Platt. He seemed preoccupied with pulling the shirts off of United players' backs and mistiming tackles all over the park, particularly in the vicinity of Paul Scholes. Platt became the center of our debate as the game went on. All three of us were amazed at his inadequacies that day, as he appeared to struggle with the pace of the game. Meanwhile, right before our half-time pint of "Boddys," Teddy Sheringham did it again, lashing a left-foot drive low into the Arsenal net.

2-2! Half-time.

Our half-time "cream of Manchester" subsequently arrived, each mouthful savored as if we were on strict rations. Momentum seemed to be growing for an appreciation of a decent British ale Stateside. Today the Britannia Club, tomorrow, who knows, maybe "Pucks"?

What was the big talking point with Archie and his wife at half-time? The penalty that never was! Ferguson appeared furious, rightly justified we all felt, as slow motion replays confirmed the referee's mistake. Scholes had been impeded by Winterburn, but it wasn't to be.

"Scholes is at the heart and soul of every move the team makes, Gary son," the Scotsman declared, his lovely wife nodding her approval as always. I really appreciated the subtly placed encouragement from Archie every time I ventured over to his table. Perhaps he was remembering his own days as a young expat and the adjustments he had had to make, moving so many miles from home, trying to find his way in an unfamiliar country.

The second half produced the winner of the titanic conquest. Of all the people to claim it? David-fucking-Platt! Admittedly, it was a brilliant header, but that didn't matter. United were 3-2 down and in the end it was Arsenal's day. Worse still, it was David Platt's day. My return to the Britannia Club and United had lost a crucial game. Arsenal and "David-fucking-Platt" were still right on our heels in the Premier League standings.

For several weeks, I had been trying to push any doubts about my vehicle's ability to provide safe passage to the back of my mind. This, of course, is called denial. But, during my journey back to Dearborn that afternoon, I realized that I could no longer ignore the stalls that occurred pretty much whenever I pulled up at a red light. The next morning I came to the conclusion that the reliability factor of the T-Bird could no longer be ignored. It was, unfortunately, time to act. My first ever set of American wheels had to go. Ours had been a short, tumultuous, yet loving affair. Love at first sight, but, eventually you just have to face reality and simply admit that your relationship has run its course.

It just so happened that a co-worker from the clinic had mentioned that his wife was considering selling her first and only car, a Honda CRX with 130,000 miles on the clock. Yes, it had high mileage, just like my T-Bird, but it was spotless, with one lady owner—and it was a Honda. I sensed that opportunity had knocked and decided that it was meant to be. It was time to let my T-Bird go!

I placed an advertisement in a couple of stores in the Dearborn area. A swift inquiry that very same day from a Chinese bloke eager to adopt the black beast and "make it great again" was simply too much of an opportunity to turn down. The handover was swift. I received $1,300. Not a bad return on a car that could easily have taken its last quart of oil at any moment. It all quickly fell into place. This was, after all, the Motor City, right? I was suddenly the owner of what I hoped would be a far more reliable set of wheels.

Choices, opportunities, I was maximizing every moment I could. America was continuing to push me, to stretch me. Indeed, working long hours at the hospital and dedicating myself to preparing a weekly British Invasion left me with very little free time. I had worked hard to connect and remain connected with Manchester United during my time in the States thus far and to actually be rewarded with live soccer from across the Pond was beyond anything that I could have imagined. Then, all of a sudden, an unbelievable radio adventure presented itself—but was that musical adventure beginning to hinder my unexpected soccer salvation?

26

Highbury Smiles

Planning the weekend Invasion quickly developed into a carefully-crafted routine. Each Friday night, my shift at the hospital complete, I would slip into moonlighting mode and place a call into the station for a quick heads up on last minute logistics. Stefan was often kind enough to spare a little time for my song requests and any new commercial additions for the following morning's show. I always wanted to provide some modicum of difficulty with the phone-in competitions; the listeners didn't want an easy ride, they wanted to work a little for their victory. The prize on offer was usually a ticket for some washed-up band like Foghat or Bad Company. I was never lucky enough to have a trendy Replay 105.1 t-shirt at my disposal; gifts of that magnitude were usually set aside for the more popular, higher rated weekday shows.

I soon realized that the most popular part of the show was "The Beatles at Breakfast." I was enjoying my musical referencing of the icons of British rock 'n' roll—somewhat ironic to me as a countrified "wooly back" from Lancashire delivering my take on Liverpool's favorite sons' rise to "the toppermost of the poppermost." But since I was English, and northern at that, nobody seemed to question my credentials.

As the show lasted four hours, I also decided to put the English newspapers I bought from the Little Professor bookstore to good use by adding some British trivia. Stories of Elton John and his extravagant spending made the cut, as did Mick Jagger with tales of his addiction to fitness. I also included a story about George Martin, the man they called "The Fifth Beatle," marking his retirement from the music industry with an album of Beatles classics performed by top celebrities—among them a version of "A Hard Day's Night" by Goldie Hawn—Mr. Martin noting that this would be the closest he would get to actually spending the night with the blond bombshell.

I still had to pinch myself that I was now regularly producing my own radio show—but I still craved my United fix. The only possible answer, of course, was to compromise. I reverted back to the shortwave radio, to transatlantic telephone calls, and to occasional VHS recordings—old familiar methods to keep up with the Red Devils' progress through the rest of the season.

As the New Year arrived, United were top of the league by five points. 1998 began with a big FA Cup match-up—United having been drawn against Chelsea at Stamford Bridge. Normally, I would have been one of the first punters at the Britannia Club, eagerly awaiting kick-off. Instead, I found myself once again sat in the Replay 105.1 studio, but with my mind firmly on a London suburb. Apparently, I missed a brilliant game that day, with United at one point leading 5-0. Des breathlessly conveyed the details via a late night call, describing how Chelsea had refused to lie down, scoring three themselves, the third goal with seven minutes still left on the clock. United's FA Cup run didn't last long, however. After a replay, Barnsley surprisingly beat the Reds 3-2. Steve Jones was about to leave the South Yorkshire club, unable to get regular first team action. At the last moment, he had been called into the Barnsley side by manager Danny Wilson and scored two goals in a famous FA Cup victory over United. FA Cup history is littered with such wonderful stories.

By the end of February 1998, Manchester United led the Premier League by a huge eleven points over their nearest rivals, Blackburn Rovers. It all looked rather good for United, with Arsenal, Liverpool and Chelsea all well off the pace, three points only separating those teams, along with Rovers in second.

In March, however, United lost 2-0 to Sheffield Wednesday, drew with West Ham, and were dumped out of the Champions League by Monaco. The month had started disastrously and, on Saturday March 14, the Reds needed to respond. I couldn't dodge another radio show and so I utilized the armory that I had at my disposal, trying desperately to tune in to the pivotal United vs. Arsenal match from Old Trafford, at the same time that I was broadcasting the British Invasion show. I was in and out of the studio all morning. The forecourt outside the building was my terrace as I covered every inch of tarmac, avoiding discarded cigarette butts and defying bad reception and fading commentary, in my desperate bid to hear all the action from Old Trafford. It was another strategically planned show of five-minute-plus songs, along with many back to back tracks. The commentary from Alan Green and the BBC provided the usual tension, but I was having real difficulty tuning in. No matter where I pointed the antenna or how loud I turned up the volume, the commentary would completely disappear at random intervals leaving me hanging. Sprinting back and forth in and out of the building, going from "It's Saturday morning and you're listening to the British Invasion," to "come on You Reds," and from "remember, if it's a cool oldie, it's on Replay 105.1!" to "United! United! United!" I clung to any BBC Sportsworld soundbites that I possibly could hear in whatever window of time I had.

The history books will tell you that Arsenal's Mark Overmars ruined my weekend. The truth of the matter was that with that one-nil away victory for the Gunners, Arsenal had a legitimate chance of catching United and stealing the Premier League trophy from the Old Trafford cabinet.

And so, by mid-March, Manchester United were out of Europe, out of the FA Cup, and it was starting to look as though the Premier League could well be slipping away.

Highbury was smiling.

As I pulled out of the business complex that housed Replay 105.1, I decided to tune in. Canada's "The Guess Who" were finishing up their tale of how she had "come undun"—prompting me to consider that United had themselves "come undun" during the month of March.

The very thought of the Gunners being legitimate English Premier League champions-in-waiting prompted the instant necessity for a post-Invasion beer.

27

A Soccer Pub!

The Grizzly Peak Brewing Company was becoming my regular aftershow haunt and that Saturday lunchtime, post-Arsenal trauma, was no exception. I would waltz in each Saturday around noon with a couple of English newspapers tucked under my arm. I enjoyed the friendly atmosphere and interesting conversations with staff and regulars. "The Grizzly" was one of a new breed of pubs in the U.S., known as microbreweries. Bucking the trend of the out-of-the-box U.S. bar, these new brew houses produced their own ales on site, as well as promoting a regular rotation of "guest ales" on a blackboard behind the bar. As an Englishman, I was used to the usual questions pertaining to warm beer and I had developed a stock answer: "You simply can't beat a British style pint!" Having been groomed on the brewers of northern Britain's finest, the prospect of a bottle of gassy American lite ale left me searching for a decent and fulfilling beer to fill the void. At the Grizzly Peak Brewing Company, I found what I was looking for. I would always enjoy listening to the barman describe in great detail each ale that was on offer.

"Good afternoon, sir. My name is Ethan. What can I get you today?"

"Nice to meet you, Ethan. So, what specials do you have on tap today, mate?"

"Oh we have several, sir" Ethan replied, excited to enlighten me on the contents of the guest ales board.

One of those ales happened to be very familiar to me. I waited until he reached it on the list.

"We also have Scottish 80 Shilling. It has a deep amber color with a medium malty sweetness, a fairly low hoppy flavor, somewhat smoky and with a grainy dry finish. "

Having spent time working up in Edinburgh and Leith, the way the beer had been described to me by Ethan that day was a far cry from the flat, heavy taste I had experienced back in the UK. The artwork on the guest ales board made it look like the King of All Ales.

"Good effort Ethan," I thought to myself, but I am going with a steady when-in-Rome number.

"You know what Ethan, I think I'll stick with your Grizzly Peak Pale Ale today, mate"

"Great choice, sir. I will be right back with that for you."

It was never difficult to strike up conversation in a bar in America. The minute I opened my mouth, the fascination always appeared to get the better of the ever-inquisitive local, whose heritage more often than not included a British strain somewhere along the line. An afternoon at the Grizzly Peak Brewing Company was most definitely just what the doctor ordered as I began to unwind from the rigors of a four-hour radio show.

That particular afternoon, as I sat reading a two-week-old copy of the *Daily Express*, a rather well-dressed middle-aged American bloke approached. He had, surprise, surprise, "noticed the accent," having apparently overheard my conversation with Ethan.

The gentleman introduced himself as Dominic Dean. We initially chatted about Dominic's British heritage and he also enquired as to how I had ended up in Michigan.

I began to tell Dominic about my Saturday morning radio gig and how I had met several expats in and around the Detroit area through my love of soccer. Dominic immediately linked soccer with hooliganism and riots. I had a sudden recollection of a day back in 1985 when I stood in the Gladys Street End at Everton's Goodison Park. It was an explosive Manchester United vs. Liverpool FA Cup semi-final and I experienced the "terraced fanaticism" first hand, disguising my allegiance to United, clamoring for cover among a sea of Liverpool Reds as whisky bottles, coins, and flares, flew over our heads.

Dominic was intrigued when I told him of the lengths expats went to keep up with news from Britain, especially the soccer results and latest stories about the English Premier League. He became enthralled as I began to tell him all about the Britannia Club and my current conflict of interest, sacrificing my English Premier League "fix" each weekend morning for an adventure of a more musically-inclined nature.

It wasn't long before Dominic began to tell me about a new downtown Ann Arbor venture—one in which he had played a significant role and one in which he thought I might be interested.

"I tell you what, Gary. What are you up to right now?"

Suddenly, I'm thinking, hold on a minute, this all sounds a bit dodgy. A well-dressed middle-aged fella whose eyes were lighting up with enthusiasm telling me that I was "just the kind of guy he was looking for!" Time for a sharp exit, maybe?

Dodgy, however, could not have been further from the truth. It turned out that Dominic had just sold his store, a well-known local men's outfitters, to two Irish American businessmen.

"Gary, only two blocks from here there are a bunch of Irish guys working hard to put the finishing touches to Ann Arbor's newest and most original pub."

"Are you kidding me, Dominic?" I said, amazed that I had heard nothing about this new and exciting development, amazed that an authentic Irish Bar was about to grace the town of Ann Arbor.

"I'm on my way over now to see how the place is coming along. Why don't you come with me? I think it may be very interesting for a Brit like you to experience," Dominic said as he prepared to settle his bill. "I can introduce you to Tim McMurray, one of the owners. I'm sure he'd like to meet you, especially since you're involved with the radio station. Could be a great chance for some publicity, maybe?"

"Sounds great, Dominic. By the way, what are they going to call this pub?" I inquired as I followed him out. I sensed a kind of "show and tell" moment with Dominic, excited at the prospect of being able to elaborate on the part he had played in the imminent arrival of a new and unique pub in downtown Ann Arbor—and to an actual Brit as well!

"Conor O'Neill's," replied Dominic with a gratifying smile.

The building that was soon to be Conor O'Neill's was only a couple of blocks up the street from the Grizzly Peak. We entered the building from the rear, around the back of one of the alleyways that led from Liberty Street. I remember immediately commenting on the decor of the outside back wall, its shop-like window obvious, with a striking blue border. The display behind the window made for an interesting browse. There was a dusty old photograph of a ship unloading its freight. The title above it read, "Prohibition repeal first shipment of Jameson from Bow Street Dublin," a swift reminder of a very different time in our history. There was also a dated fireplace with several pieces of peat ready for burning. In the midst of our recent Michigan winter, that would have come in very handy.

As I looked closer into the window, the glare from the bright morning sunshine obscuring my view, I noticed several other old photographs and artefacts, all in need of a thorough dusting. I began to imagine how all these items, when eventually organized, would grab the attention of the heritage and history-seeking American punter. It certainly caught my attention that afternoon.

To the right of the window was a set of white steps leading up to the back door, which was once again painted in that most distinctive blue. As I opened the back door and walked into the narrow hallway at the rear of the pub, I was greeted with the haunting distant hum of Celtic music, accompanied by the buzz of all things, interior design. A sound system was obviously being tested, offering a softer ambience and stark contrast to the industry of the workmen. Facing me was a moderately long corridor, the floor of which had a varnished floorboard appearance.

There were two doors on the left-hand sidewall, equally spaced, the first of which I ventured to open, my inquisitive mind getting the better of me. It was the men's "bogs." I remember noticing how spacious the restroom looked, almost as big as my small apartment. I closed the door and decided I would leave the ladies bathroom to my imagination.

Dominic and I then turned the corner, walking further into the building. I looked up and noticed the sign above our heads: "Distillers." There was sawdust everywhere, and the smell of wood was intoxicating. I became fixated on the pub's design. The combination of stone inlays, dark stained wood, and earthy colored tones conducive to a welcoming, relaxing atmosphere.

There was an abundance of Irish twang surrounding me, as each corner appeared to have one or two young men busying themselves with the tasks at hand. All seemed to be intensely involved in their own part of the overall operation. Indeed, if any one of those lads had to maneuvre around us during their work, although very focused on their mission, we were acknowledged with a nod of the head and a few, almost unrecognizable words, due some thick Irish brogue.

Dominic went over to a gentleman who was quite evidently in the thick of things. I listened in as he conveyed to the man how we had just met and that I worked over at the local radio station. He explained how he thought it was a great idea that I came and viewed the pub.

"Gary, I'd like you to meet Tim McMurray."

"Great to meet you, Tim. Gary France."

"My pleasure, Gary. So I hear that you work over at the radio station then, eh?"

"I do Tim, yes. Replay 105.1. The oldies station."

"Oh, yeah, I tune in from time to time," Tim replied, his thick, dark brown hair, pale complexion, and brown eyes emphasizing his Irish heritage.

"I have a small Saturday morning slot, mate. The British Invasion."

"Ah right. So you're the guy who's doing that then. Yeah, come to think of it now, I have listened to you a few times."

Dominic went on to joke with Tim that maybe I could put a word in for Conor O'Neil's during one of my next shows.

"That would be grand, Gary. I plan to get in touch with the advertising folks at the station anyways. It's out there at Domino Farms, right?"

"That's right Tim. Oh yeah, they have a decent set up. They'll be able to run some great ads for you I'm sure."

We continued our chat with Tim enquiring as to how I had ended up in the U.S. Tim then volunteered to show me around.

"Would you like a quick tour of the place, Gary?"

"Absolutely, that would be great."

I let him know how impressed I was with the men's restroom and we both raised a smile.

"Seems I got my priorities right then, Gary, eh," he replied.

"You two go on, I'm going to hang around here for a while," said Dominic stepping away to chat with another man in the thick of things.

Tim started his tour by explaining how "in many parts of Ireland Gary, the pub was viewed as an extension of the living room and it also acted as the local shop in some instances. One corner would serve eggs and the other, foaming glasses of stout."

I told him how I'd had a mini road trip through southern Ireland a few years prior and how I had particularly loved the pubs of Cork, Killarney and as far west as the Ring of Kerry region.

Tim continued, noting how the pub was designed in Sligo, a town in which his own father had once owned a pub. The bar itself was custom made, and had artifacts from all over Ireland.

"The stone we're using is from an island off County Kerry. It has all been gathered by stone masons who lived in the area. Along with the bar, it was all then shipped to Montreal, trucked through Canada, across the U.S. border, eventually landing here in Ann Arbor."

"Bloody hell, Tim, that is amazing. It's definitely come a long way," I responded. The evolution of Ann Arbor's newest pub was already unfolding as a pretty unique story.

Tim then walked me over to the front section. I couldn't help but notice a painting of a young lady on the purple wall immediately to our left. Dressed in the relevant attire to attempt her Irish jig, she looked radiant. A piece of "River Dance" had its place on the walls of Conor O'Neill's.

Tim told me that it was, in fact, a painting of his daughter. He then went on to tell me that having Irish music nights at the pub was very much a part of the game plan. He remained looking up at the picture and, after a short pause, commented: "My daughter passed away Gary, just a couple of years ago. She was only eight years old."

I had only met Tim a couple of minutes previous and a comment like that came at me, as they say in the States, right out of left field.

"Oh goodness me, Tim, mate. I am so sorry."

"Oh thank you. Yes, the wee girl had been suffering from brain cancer. We miss her every single day."

I stood for a second, looking up into the innocent eyes of the young lady on the wall above me. That beautiful painting would undoubtedly keep his young daughter's spirit alive—Tim's eternal pledge of love.

Tim pointed to a portrait of a man further along the same wall.

"Do ya recognize that fella there then, Gary?" he asked, a resolute smile now lighting up his face.

"I have to say I don't, Tim. Who's that then?"

"That, my friend, is the master fiddler Michael Coleman. He is one of County Sligo's very own sons and a true legend. He left for America as a young man, eventually settling in New York where he recorded something like eighty records, influencing a host of Irish musicians."

"Wow, that's amazing," I responded, adding "So what happened to him?"

"Ah, Gary, he passed away. Only fifty-four years old. Buried in a cemetery in the Bronx, I believe."

The picture blended beautifully into the darkly stained walls, and offered up a taste of that fine art familiar with Irish musicians. It was almost as if I could hear the faint surge of Mr. Coleman plying his trade, as a blast of fresh spring air filtered past us, entering the room via the large wooden doors at the front of the pub.

We then strolled over to the opposite corner of the pub, toward a wall with some professionally inscribed notation, depicting the words of James Joyce. It was a brilliant idea, as it lent itself beautifully to quiet contemplation for punters in need of a touch of serenity as they read, or chatted with a friend. Talk about a cozy corner. This "snug" area featured another mixture of dark wood and stone, with warm purple and brown decor. I was already starting to feel right at home in Conor O'Neill's.

As we headed back toward the center, we were entered an area filled with Gaelic football memorabilia. There were old pennants, jerseys, and an array of team photographs. Larger than life, as if guarding all the monuments to the Gaelic calling, was what appeared to have been a hand-painted picture of a player in full flow.

"This, Gary, is a player who was a real sporting hero in his hometown back in Ireland, and it was only right that we had him grace the walls of Conor's own sporting tribute. In fact, I have to tell you son, he is actually my partner in this wonderful venture we have going on here."

"Is that right, Tim? Well mate, I have to say, by the look of that picture up there he won't lack for any determination in making Conor O'Neill's a success. That's a great touch, mate." I looked up once more at the painting hanging above my head. Tim's partner was a bull of a man.

"Oh he's one tough bastard, let me tell you Gary."

As we wandered toward the back of the pub, I noticed what looked like a cubby hole tucked away in a small corner. This would eventually become the Conor O'Neill's "command center" where the pub's satellite TV broadcast equipment would be housed. Tim told me how this area of the pub would include a big screen that could be rolled down to show major sporting events. I immediately thought "well, well, well . . . could we possibly have another Reggie right here in Ann Arbor?" I seized my chance!

"Tim, have you thought about showing English Premier League soccer games? Chicago's bars are really starting to embrace the early morning soccer crowd. The only place I know of in Michigan to show the games is the Britannia Club up in Warren. In fact, there are quite a few folks that travel from Ann Arbor to catch the games up there early each Saturday or Sunday. I'm pretty sure you'd have a ready-made crowd right here, mate."

"Yeah, I have heard of that place. I have to admit though my main goal is to get coverage of the Gaelic football. The rugby internationals are also high on the agenda too. However, I'm sure once we get our act together we could look into getting some of the soccer on."

"Tim, it makes total sense, mate," I continued my push. "It would be great business."

I went on to mention that Ann Arbor even had a specialist soccer store and that "a load of my mates"—I made sure to emphasize that I had acquired many more mates all of a sudden—who played in local soccer leagues were frustrated that none of the European soccer matches were being shown locally.

I continued: "Remember, Tim, the World Cup is only a couple of months away and the U.S. are in it. This would be your perfect chance to get the whole soccer thing off the ground."

I gave it my best sales pitch.

"Ah, you never know, eh, Gary, son. You never know," Tim replied, smiling. "Why don't you continue on and have a good look around, my friend. I'll meet you back here in a few minutes. I have a quick call to make."

I decided to wander further toward the back of the pub, having made it full circle around the main floor. There was a fine piece of woodwork in the middle of the room, creating an opportunity for punters to lean an elbow and chat with a friend, away from the crowd for a while. It read "Shop Front" along with "Stamps for Sale," another heading written into the dark wood. The only thing close to "first class" at this shop front would be a pint. I imagined that dark nectar in my hand, on my first visit to the newly-opened Conor O'Neill's.

There were a couple of men hard at work in the same back corner and both acknowledged Tim as he came back over. Tim explained that this was to be the quieter section of the pub, providing an opportunity for punters to have "a wee blather."

"Gary, I wanted this to depict the cottage wall section of a pub, an area for which, back in Ireland, the barman would open his doors to friends and neighbors alike."

It looked terrific. A mixture of stonewalling and wood, it made me feel more than at any other moment in that building, that I was in the midst of an Irish drinking den.

The main feature of the cozy corner was the warming look of a traditional fireplace, immediately making me think how inviting it would be in the middle of another frozen Michigan winter: a crackling fire along with lively conversation and a pint. What was also noticeable about this area of the pub was the way in which the stone walling blended so readily with the darkly stained wood. As I admired this effect, I noticed a frame containing a map and several lines of notation, leaning on the base of the wall ready for the moment it would take its rightful place on the wall opposite the fireplace.

"Oh what's this all about Tim?" I inquired, bending down to look closer at the frame.

"Ahh, take a look there, Gary. Have a read."

It was titled "The Valentia Slate Quarry" and the print described how the quarry had first been mined in 1816 and how the stone had been used extensively throughout Ireland. It also mentioned that slate from the very same quarry had been used for the roof of the Houses of Parliament, the National Gallery, and the British Museum in London. Conor O'Neill's was most definitely going to be among some prestigious company, as the final pieces of that same stonewalling were being installed.

"That is quite some story, Tim. You've really thought of every angle for this place haven't you?"

"You could say that, Gary. We hope so. Trying to make it special, ya know."

We headed back over to the center of the pub to meet up with Dominic. The sharp-dressed man had obviously visited many times as he busied himself chatting with some of the lads hard at work. I still couldn't get over the fact that his former men's outfitters was well on the way to becoming an incredible Irish pub.

I noticed two or three signposts, typical in their Irish design, lying on their side, all ready to be positioned around the building. I bent down to read them closely: "Dublin 41 miles," "Cahersiveen 2 miles," "Middleton 9 miles."

The three of us admired the "granddaddy" of the place: the bar. It looked magnificent. Either side of the top section of the magnificent structure were the words Jameson's and, of course, Guinness. The centerpiece of the bar was a huge clock. I imagined a barman taking a quick glance upwards before shouting out those famous words "last orders" and "time gentlemen, please."

Tim reminded me once again of how far that "baby" had traveled. It was hard to believe the Atlantic Ocean had cradled it all the way to Ann Arbor without as much as a scratch. As I looked over at it, I considered ordering a quick pint before heading out, traveling on to the vibrant city of Dublin, which according to the signpost lying on the floor next to me was only a mere 41 miles away.

I decided I had taken up enough of Tim's time.

What could I say? I don't think I had ever had an afternoon quite like it. I felt privileged to be able to look in on the place.

"Tim. Thank you so much. What a fascinating tour that was, mate."

Tim shook my hand. "Gary, it has been a pleasure, son. Be sure to come down for a pint as soon as we open now. Look me up and we will chat some more."

"Absolutely, I can't wait, mate. I'll be in touch."

After a quick word from Dominic and a further pat on my shoulder, Tim turned and headed off to the back of the pub, immersing himself in another job that required his input.

I thanked Dominic and told him how he had inadvertently given me a chance to "plant a seed," hopefully bringing English Premier League soccer coverage to an Irish pub in Ann Arbor, Michigan.

Dominic smiled, commenting "What is it about you Brits and your soccer?"

I thought to myself "you'll never understand, mate."

I bid Dominic farewell, and as I walked out toward the back door, I shouted another grateful word to Tim, receiving an enthusiastic wave.

As I emerged from Conor O'Neill's that spring afternoon, the low sunlight immediately hit me in the face, making me realize what a long day it had been. That morning's edition of "The British Invasion" seemed days ago. I had experienced some of the most interesting, impromptu time since my arrival in the land of Uncle Sam. A chance meeting in the Grizzly Peak. A local gent full of optimism, unable to contain his enthusiasm perhaps, regarding events down on Main Street. It had been a "right place, right time" scenario for sure. I remember contemplating how there was truly something about this country and the way in which, quite literally, doors would open and opportunities would present themselves.

I fired up the Honda, adjusted my seat, popped in the cassette of that morning's show—my usual routine, to critique the show on the drive home. As I turned onto Main Street, I glanced over to my right noticing for the first time the shop front of Conor O'Neill's. I loved the contrast having entered via the rear door earlier that afternoon. The building looked almost luminous in its blue and gold, the pub's allure unquestionable.

I remember thinking to myself how good a photograph of another Irish hero, Roy Keane, would look, hanging on the wall next to our Gaelic football friend in that "Sporting Billy" section of the pub, maybe to signify the arrival of English Premier League soccer in downtown Ann Arbor.

Was Southeast Michigan about to get its first "soccer pub?"

My conflict of interest had just become rather more accentuated.

I drove on through town, heading toward the I-94 on ramp east.

"Once again it's Saturday morning and the British Invasion Breakfast show here on Replay 105.1!"

I smiled, still amazed at the fact that I was a DJ on American radio. At that same moment I shot right back down to earth as my mind returned me to the reality of the result at Old Trafford earlier that day.

"Bloody Arsenal again!"

28

Reality Bites

There was still almost a full quarter of the 1997–98 season to go. A win at home against Wimbledon meant that the Red Devils maintained top spot at the end of March with a six-point lead, but Arsenal had three games in hand.

April arrived, and with it, one of United's best performances of the season, a 3-1 victory at Ewood Park, seeing off Blackburn with some terrific attacking football, particularly in the second half. Red called, praising the performance of Andy Cole, insisting he was slowly becoming a convert to the instinctive finishing of United's prolific striker. I was a tad nonplussed, however, as Red went off on a tangent, explaining to me how the camera had picked up one of the Spice Girls in the stand applauding a certain Mr. Beckham's winning goal.

"Looks like he's scoring off the pitch, too, Gary! Man does she look hot!" declared Frank.

The next two results for the Reds were both 1-1 home draws, the first against a Liverpool team ready to spoil any chance Manchester United had of winning a title and the second one against Newcastle. Two crippling outcomes. April 27 and United got back to winning ways, punishing Crystal Palace 3-0 at Selhurst Park. But was it all too late?

Arsenal required just two victories at Highbury to win the coveted English Premier League crown. Derby County and Everton did Manchester United absolutely no favors, whatsoever, and on May 3, 1998, Arsenal football club were installed as the 1997–98 Premier League champions.

No further comment!

No European success for yet another season, and a Premier League title now safely in the hands of the Gunners. I reflected once more on my immersion in radio and how it had diminished my opportunity to sit in front of that big screen at the Britannia Club. My approach to the next campaign would have to be different. For the immediate future, however, I still had unfinished radio business.

The FA Cup final was to be contested between the Gunners and Newcastle United in the spring sunshine at Wembley. Despite that United were not in the final, I figured that the chance to plug the English Football Association trophy was too good to pass up. Mally Mal, the manic Scouser, was "potted up" and sent out to the Replay 105.1 listeners, as he was first to call in and acknowledge the subject matter with his usual enthusiasm.

Between the two of us, Mally and I managed to drum up some interest in that great day in England's soccer calendar, as a modest number of phone calls began to filter through, to the musical backdrop of the sixties and seventies. I sensed that the subject still required a tad more authenticity.

"Hey dad. What do you think about being live on American radio?"

A pause, and then an assured "Alrught! C'mon then, let's do it, son!' echoed back into my headphones. There were only a few minutes to kick-off back in the UK, so the timing was perfect.

As I spoke to Des, I was counting down the seconds to his cue, to the final fade out of "Ride a White Swan" by T-Rex. And then:

"Replay 105.1, your station for good times and great oldies. Gary France here with you once again on this beautiful spring Saturday morning. A very special Saturday morning actually, because across the Pond in England today, it's currently 2:55 p.m., which means that in five minutes time, most soccer fans in England will be sat in front of the telly, watching the FA Cup final between the Arsenal and Newcastle football clubs ... forgive me, my American friends, I mean soccer clubs."

I continued: "Now, if you've been listening to the show over this past year, you may have gathered that I have a passion for the game and so I couldn't resist getting a first-hand report on the build up to today's match back in the homeland, despite, of course, the absence of the only team that really matters: Manchester United! I figured there could be no better call to make in order to offer Ann Arbor a little FA Cup education than to a soccer-mad fella tucked away in a remote corner of Southwest Scotland— none other than my own father!"

"Alright there, mate? How you doing, dad?"

Des launched himself head first into U.S. radio stardom. His composure blew me away. I immediately surmized that he must have been paying very close attention to the BBC Radio Five Live commentary team. He sounded like an absolute natural.

"Too bad it's not United playing today, eh, son?"

"Yeah, they blew their chance many months ago, dad."

"Aye, they did that, son. They did that. Ah well. FA Cup final day, eh? There's nothing like it. Bert Trautman. Stanley Matthews. The memories come flooding back, don't they, lad?" My father often presumed that my FA Cup memories were similar to his own. FA Cup day to me was rather more Pearson and Whiteside than Matthews and Trautman.

I realized that the vast majority of the listeners in Ann Arbor would have no clue as to who he was talking about, but I sensed the novelty of his British accent must have been wooing a few as the dashboard began to light up in the studio. I was about to bid him farewell and play the Animals, as we had established that a song from the Newcastle band fit the bill nicely, but I couldn't shut him up! Off he went again.

"Hey son, Billy Boy Clinton is in Birmingham at the moment, you know. Pint of best bitter in hand, loving every second of his time on British soil."

I perceived a definite sense of pride in my father's voice, perhaps reflecting the fact that a U.S. president had decided to visit a rather less fashionable city in his cherished country.

"He appears to have a taste for it, son, and is using his charm to woo all around him. Tell your listeners he's in Brummy, son. Go on, tell 'em!" my father continued.

"Well I think you already just did that, dad!"

"Aye. Well, take care, son. Look after yourself. We're all looking forward to when you're next home. Those Americans know what's good for them, eh?"

The sentiments were terrific. And it couldn't have worked any better as my father bid farewell to the intro of "The House of the Rising Sun."

The extended air time I had been given that morning couldn't have come at a better time, as I glanced at the clock in between taking the ever-increasing volume of calls. It was almost half-time in the cup final and, bitten by further nostalgia, and a sudden acute burst of home sickness, I moved to the phone lines once again and tried to reach my old college roommate, Tom Skinner. Tom's good luck email still graced the wall of the studio.

"Good lad!" came the unmistakable reply from Hereford, as I said hello to my old mate back in Blighty. Of course, he was home and, of course, he was watching the game. He always did!

I completed my "outro" to the sound of Stealers Wheel, Gerry Rafferty's vocals fading out gently, and explained to the listeners how Tom had been sweating over a bet he had placed on the outcome of the game, hoping that Newcastle United would win. Ann Arbor was about to be introduced to my old college roommate. Tom took his opportunity with aplomb.

"Gary, mate! How are ya, lad?"

"I'm doin' well, mate. How's life back in the homeland, my friend?"

"Well, we have some balmy summer temperatures here in Hereford today, Gary. It's a scorcher and I'm sat out here in the garden sipping a pint of Woodpecker cider."

"What about that bet you had on Newcastle to win, then? Did you pull it off?"

"That hard-earned money went slipping out of my hands, Gaz, as seventy minutes into the match I sank to my knees watching Arsenal score their second. They are actually lifting the cup right now as we speak. Arsenal won it, 2-0 mate!"

"Oh well, there's always the next time, eh pal?"

"Yeah, no worries, mate. Anyway there is some consolation for all those Newcastle fans that may be listening, Gaz. I hear they are going to sign Bill Clinton for next season, due to the fact that they need someone who can regularly score away from home."

There then followed several seconds of two old mates pissing their sides laughing as the Replay 105.1 listeners must have been wondering what the hell was going on. Tom was on a roll. I knew only too well that whenever that was the case, it was not in my best interest, or, indeed, anyone else's, to stop him!

"Hey you better keep an eye on your wife, mate, what with Billy Boy Clinton in town." I dangled the carrot and Tom duly bit.

"Yeah, funny that. She's just gone out, Gaz. Three men arrived at the door and bundled her into a big car. Not sure what that's all about or indeed whenever she will be back."

"Actually Gaz, it's great to see Bill over here, especially in the city of Birmingham. In fact I heard that when he arrived, he was so impressed with the large white Rolls Royce that picked him up, that he asked the chauffeur if he could take it for a spin. The chauffeur duly obliged and sat himself in the back, as Billy Boy took control. Actually, it's a little known story this, mate. Anyway, Bill's beginning to enjoy himself as he starts notching up to speeds of around 90 mph. Of course it didn't take long until a policeman noticed this speeding white Rolls and duly pulls it over. He steps out of his car and walks up to Clinton."

"Do you have any ID, sir?"

"Bill pulls out his ID and hands it to the policeman. The policeman was obviously amazed and called his sergeant back at base to ask what the next step should be."

"Sergeant, I'm a little concerned, as I think I've pulled over someone important. What should I do?"

"How important?" asks the Sergeant back at the station. "A local celebrity?"

"No, I don't think so."

"A well-known sportsman?"

"No, a lot more important than that, I'm sure."

"Well, what makes you think that?" replied the Sergeant.

"Well I don't rightly know, Sarge, but the thing is—Bill Clinton is his bloody chauffeur!"

Tom and I erupted into fits of laughter, our northern English banter infiltrating Ann Arbor's airwaves. I bid my old friend farewell, commenting on the fact that it hopefully wouldn't be long before we would once again share a beer.

All of that aside, the sad reality that day was the fact that Arsenal had now won the coveted domestic double.

Red loaned me his official VHS tape of Manchester United's 1997–98 season in review. Due to my work and life balance, that tape was like gold dust. I felt that there had been a few positives. Andy Cole had played a phenomenal season and Beckham was truly beginning to make his mark in the Premier League. Sheringham appeared to have fitted in nicely after a shaky start and Solskjær, as always, had produced some spectacular moments. All in all, with the injuries sustained, the big one, of course, being to Roy Keane, I felt the team had done enough to shout about. A trophy wasn't always the be all and end all, after all, was it?

Some pride could be had in United's showing that year, right?

Bollocks it could! Was it hell as like enough!

Watching the season review, it became increasingly evident that I had inadvertently reverted back to witnessing United matches long after the final whistle had been blown, scrambling for any taste of what had transpired. I realized that I was short-changing myself, having worked so hard to be present and "in the moment" during those important transatlantic broadcasts. I was neglecting "my" Reds by not being in front of that big screen at 10:00 a.m. each Saturday or Sunday morning. During that crunch time in May when United's destiny was being decided, I was found wanting. As I had donned a pair of radio headphones, "my" team had not put any silverware into the cabinet at Old Trafford.

Then again, there is always a flip side. Could it have been a blessing that I had been musically distracted each weekend? That I was safely detached, hidden from the verbal abuse, protected from having to suffer the undoubted ridicule from rival fans at the Britannia Club and the undoubted torture of watching the Gunners claw their way to another Premier League Championship?

Maybe, just maybe, it had.

29

Perspective

The summer of 1998 was a World Cup summer and France was hosting the tournament. *Magnifique!*

Being a British expatriate in the U.S. during the World Cup seemed to further emphasize my disconnect. Back in Britain, World Cup news and views would have been non-stop. This was not the case in Southeast Michigan—partly through my own doing. Since I did not have cable TV service, I had to rely on phone calls, sound bites from the BBC World Service, and snippets of coverage from American television as and when I could. That having been said, NBC and ESPN were broadcasting matches and so I did manage to watch England, making it out to Frank's in Ann Arbor and catching up with Chinny, Eddie and the lads, as Frank played host each time.

England had clawed their way out of Group G with a win over Columbia, finishing in second place behind Romania. Argentina awaited England in the round of sixteen—a colossal tie by any stretch of the imagination. The match had everything. Two early penalties, Batistuta scoring for Argentina after only six minutes, and Shearer dispatching from the spot just four minutes later. On sixteen minutes, an eighteen-year-old Michael Owen picked up the ball just inside the Argentina half, flew past two players and finished emphatically into the top right hand corner of the net. Zanetti pulled Argentina level in first half stoppage time, scoring a brilliantly worked free kick.

Then, just two minutes into the second half *that* moment occurred. That foolish flick of a right foot followed by that red card. Manchester United's David Beckham was sent off having risen to Diego Simeone's bait. For the remaining hour of the beautifully poised match, extra time included, England dug in with only ten men, eventually making it to penalties. In the end, it all rested on the shoulders of David Batty.

Batty missed the crucial penalty; England always lost on penalties. England crashed out of the World Cup.

The following day after work, I contacted Des for his verdict on the aftermath of the previous night's soccer tragedy.

"It's all over the news here, son. Non-stop. I was tuning into Nicky Campbell on Radio Five Live this morning. It seems like the whole nation is blaming Beckham for England's World Cup defeat."

"He was stupid though mate, wasn't he? Simeone riled him right up didn't he?"

"Yes, he did. But the level of abuse Beckham has been getting today from all over the country, Gary, is just ridiculous."

I, too, was frustrated at the reaction from one of United's, and England's, idols that night. We were matching Argentina. We had a real chance of progressing to the last eight. However, the nastiness, shear hatred, and total preoccupation with Beckham as a scapegoat and focus of blame detracted from what had been a terrific soccer spectacle, albeit a defeat that was tough to stomach.

"Gary, honestly, there were people calling in to say he should be banned from playing for England for life!"

"Bloody hell, dad! That's a bit harsh, eh."

"Oh Gary son, that's nothing, mate. The evening news over here showed burning effigies of him hanging from trees outside homes and pubs all over the country. It's crazy, son. I have never seen anything like it."

"That is bloody crazy, dad," I replied, shocked at what I was hearing.

Our conversation continued for some time and then once we had said our goodbyes, I immediately reflected on what Des and I had discussed. I couldn't believe the postgame reaction from back home.

Beckham's actions were foolish and immature, but the lengths to which the nation was going in order to chastise the man were nothing short of criminal: those Beckham effigies burning outside pubs, denouncing all things United, the Manchester United haters to a man able to shout their corner exultant in their new found cause. Would the same volume of calls have been taken full of such venom, with all due respect, had the player who had been sent off played for any other English Premier League team? I doubt it.

There was no way I was condoning what the lad did that night in St Etienne, but should it really have been a sending off?

What about a booking only?

There have been far worse reactions on a soccer stage and there will be many more. The history of the World Cup itself is evidence to that. Indeed, Simeone's over-reaction didn't cover him in glory either.

I guess perspective was in short supply during the debate that raged among England fans the morning after. It was as if England had amassed a self-elected army of hit men and David Beckham was now on the run. His life would never be the same again. The new soccer season would open the door for abuse the likes of which he may never have witnessed from a soccer stand before. If the reaction to his sending off was anything to go by, then Beckham was going to have to develop a thick skin before pulling on his Manchester United shirt for the upcoming campaign.

As I resided in Michigan, where there was no mention of this in the news, I relied on my father to inform me of the national anti-Beckham outcry. I considered the contrast, a whole nation back home firing opinions left, right, and center in regard to one of its national soccer team player's behavior and subsequent sending off during a crucial World Cup match. Britain's main news programs were apparently dominated by the event, echoing the hue and cry featuring the story high on its agenda and yet, I existed in a state, a nation, in which the news headlines were devoid of such soccer shenanigans.

During that summer, I also began to reflect on life at Replay 105.1. I was loving the ride and throwing all I could into it, initially even a thought toward a possible career change, a different route forward in life. However, I couldn't help but notice the people around me, the dynamics, the behavior of the less enthusiastic diehard deejays beginning to show evident signs of wear and tear, not "making it" in the business, a business in which they had perhaps always dreamed that they would indeed make it. I could sense it was a stressful, somewhat narcissistic, cutthroat industry with little time for sentiment. It was so very competitive out there and you'd be hard pressed to make it in another network, plus that would mean regular upheaval. So many radio jocks were being exploited by the radio company executives who knew that they would prefer to just stick around. Corporate radio was becoming the new industry machine, catering music programming to demographics that offered the biggest revenue returns from advertising. Rumors were rampant at 105.1 that a corporate buyout was in the works. I knew how that would turn out. The little "Saturday morning guy" running his own show would be out of the door in no time. I was sure of that. Was I really going to take this any further, knowing that my full time physical therapy occupation was serving me well? I was so fortunate to have had the opportunity to plan a weekend radio show of my own, but that was the exception rather than the norm. I had been given a wonderful learning curve, on the job training providing me with the tools and experience that I could use, should I consider possibly grabbing a weekend gig in the future.

I began to come to terms with the fact that I had achieved a goal set many years prior. I mean, my own show, styled as I had wanted it; it was beyond anything that I could have imagined. I was feeling good about that. I'd had a decent taste, over a year in the chair, but I began to conclude that it had, indeed, run its course.

And so, with mixed feelings, I concluded that it was time for the British Invasion to come to an end. In late July, I made the difficult call to Misty, explaining that I was so grateful to her for all the confidence she had shown in me right from the off. Misty had truly enabled a dream. Despite her kind encouragement for me to reconsider, my mind was made up. I chose the weekend of September 12, 1998 to be my final weekend at Replay 105.1. This allowed ample time for Misty to reorganize and also for me to fully come to terms with the end of my radio adventure.

"Hey, you gotta to do what you gotta do, babe! It's all good!"

It was nothing more than I would have expected from Misty.

I was good with that.

I wanted my weekends back.

I was going to miss sitting in that studio, but I had come to the realization that I was missing another of my life's passions even more.

30

Au Revoir

August 9, 1998: As was customary for the start of the English soccer season, Wembley Stadium in London was hosting the FA Charity Shield, which pitted the winners of the Premier League against the winners of the FA Cup. Since Arsenal had won both and could not play themselves, then the valiant Premier League losers—Manchester United—were the Gunner's opponents that day. Keano was back; Captain Roy Keane returning to the United side after his long layoff from injury. I was pumped!

I had stayed over in Ann Arbor the evening prior and was up early to cover a Sunday morning show at Replay 105.1. I owed Donny one for helping me out that weekend when I played "hooky" for the Arsenal vs. United match the previous season. After the show was over, I wandered into the center of town and found a quiet corner of the University of Michigan's beautiful central campus. I cast my mind toward a sunny and apparently scorching hot Wembley Stadium. I loved the contrast, as if to emphasize my effort to support from so far away, my small transistor radio pressed tightly to my ear, while watching students drift through the historic grounds of the main central campus of one of America's most prestigious institutions. What I heard was not conducive to easy listening; United were being completely outplayed.

On thirty-eight minutes, Marc Overmars reminded us once again of the thorn he had become in United's side with what sounded like a brilliant shot, lashed into to the top right hand corner of Schmeichel's net. Second half goals from Weah and Anelka completed a 3-0 rout of the Red Devils.

I hung around the campus and pondered yet another defeat at the hands of our enemy. The Gunners' line up that day was formidable. Seaman, Winterburn, Dixon, Adams and Keown forming an experienced and very strong back line. The midfield had pace, power, and skill, consisting of Overmars, Vieira, Petit and Parlour. "Up top" it couldn't get much better than an in-form Anelka and the maestro that was Dennis Bergkamp.

I felt real concern that Manchester United would struggle to overcome the prior season's champions. Arsenal had to be favorites to retain the English Premier League crown for the 1998–99 season. The Gunners were on a roll.

Four days later, United played the Polish side, Lks Lodz, in a Champions League qualifier. This early-season game was crucial, United needing to win the home leg of the home-and-away tie comfortably to stand any chance of Champions League soccer in the season ahead. I imagined a packed Old Trafford back home as I was hard at work at the clinic. I returned home that night to access the reliable Des with a phone report from across the Pond. He explained how Ryan Giggs had stolen the show with a goal, demonstrating his quick first touch and clinical finish, with Andy Cole grabbing the second to give United some breathing room. Final score: 2-0.

"I reckon that's a decent, solid start to the Champions League for us, son." My father sounded content with what he had seen that night on television back home in Britain.

United's first home game of the season against Leicester City went well. I had been discussing with my father earlier in the week just how tricky a side Leicester City could be. Over the past few seasons, they had proven to be one of United's "bogey teams."

I arrived back at Hotel Hairpiece from Ann Arbor after a speedy drive across I-94 in an attempt to make the second half after the show, and grabbed my trusty shortwave radio. It was another beautiful August morning in Michigan, and I decided that a quiet sit and "people watch" in the front yard would be the perfect solution to unwind from the chaos of the previous few hours.

The BBC World Service reception was having one of those days. Intermittent commentary, audio sounding like it was being transmitted inside a goldfish bowl, had me moving the radio every which way I could to nail a clear sentence from Alan Green. The Northern Irishman's delivery and Belfast accent battled admirably with the quagmire of hampered airwaves obstruction and interference.

David Beckham had been harassed, ridiculed, and bombarded with abuse from the media and soccer fans from all over the country since his red card against Argentina. The Charity Shield game at Wembley had clearly shown the response he would be receiving from non-Manchester United fans. He had been loudly booed every time he touched the ball. From what I could gather from the commentary against Leicester City, he was receiving pretty much the same treatment. Then, in the final minute of injury time, the 94th minute, with United trailing 1-2, a free kick! Beckham placed the ball twenty-five yards out from the Leicester goal. I paced the front yard as Rhonda returned home dressed to the nines and took an age to park her brand new Ford Focus in the garage. Her hair looked immaculate, of course. I continued on struggling to decipher Alan Green's words against the backdrop of whistles from the Leicester fans, adding to the cocktail of interference from within that small radio unit held in my left hand. The sound continued to fade in and out, as I desperately tried to listen above the din of lawn mowers, chainsaws, and leaf blowers that echoed around the neighborhood.

Then he hit it!

A sudden roar: that vacuum effect of a roar told me everything as I jumped for delight.

Yes! Beckham had done it.

It was 2-2!

After his summer of torment, he had truly "bent it like Beckham!"

I ran cheering back into my apartment and, before I could close the door, Rhonda appeared from her kitchen.

"Well, Gary, sounds like that United team of yours has won."

"Not quite Rhonda. But they didn't lose!"

"What? That makes no sense," Rhonda muttered, confused, as she retreated back to her section of Hotel Hairpiece. Rhonda had expected either a winner or a loser—the American way, plain and simple.

And so, with that last-second wonder strike from Beckham, "we" were off and running.

A week later, United drew 0-0 at West Ham, a game in which Andy Cole's new strike partner, Dwight Yorke, recently signed from Aston Villa, made his debut. I received a telephone call from my friend and Liverpool fanatic, Chinny, on his return from the Britannia Club. He wasted no time in telling me that, based on his performance in the match, he felt that United had paid way too much for "that Yorke dude."

September 12, 1998: The day had finally arrived. My final show on Replay 105.1 FM.

I had been thinking about how to end my year-long affair with Ann Arbor's listening public. For my choice of penultimate song, I pulled a CD from my bag and cued the track—preparing a surprise for the Replay 105.1 listeners. My sister had always harbored her own dream to record a song. Her husband, Taff, had surprised her one birthday with several hours in a recording studio. Annie recalled it as quite simply one of the best days of her life. She had chosen Elton John's "That's Why They Call It the Blues" as one of the tracks to record.

How on earth could I resist the opportunity that Saturday morning, that final radio show, to put my sister on the airwaves in America? The worst that could happen would be that I got fired. I was leaving anyway, so what the hell? I faded out Genesis, and without further ado briefly added a little sentiment about a sister of mine across the Pond.

"Follow You, Follow Me, by Genesis. It's coming up on ten minutes to ten on this Saturday morning here on Replay 105.1. As we drift closer to the end of the final British Invasion, I can't resist a little sentimentality. Forgive the self-indulgence, but it gives me great pleasure to introduce a young lady from England, a very special young lady. Then, again, I would have to say that. This is my sister Annie with her recording of Sir Elton John's 'That's Why They Call It the Blues' here on Replay 105.1 FM, your station for good times, great oldies, and, the odd British cover version!"

Then came the surreal moment as the walls of the Replay 105.1 studio echoed with the sound of my sister's voice. I couldn't get my head around it. I made sure I was recording the moment so as to be able to send Annie her very own piece of radio history. She still finds it hard to believe that she was on the radio in the U.S., sandwiched between Genesis and The Beatles! During the last few minutes of that final show, I received phone calls from listeners wishing me well and saying how much they enjoyed my sister's effort.

"Gary, la! I'm gonna miss that accent, you United bastard. Great job, son. Great job. Thanks for putting a smile on this old bugger's face each Saturday morning. Good luck to you, son." I also wanted Mally to know how grateful I was for his own unique contribution and support during the Invasion. Compliments flying back and forth between a United fan and Liverpool fan—hope indeed springs eternal!

Ten o'clock duly arrived and so, for the final time, I said: "Have a great week ahead. This is the Englishman France saying tara, au revoir—and whatever you do in life always remember to Follow the Sun"— the Beatles track bringing the British Invasion to a close.

As I left the studio, I remembered the nervous excitement I had felt the morning of my first live broadcast. It had been an unforgettable year. I had come out of it with a demo tape and ample on-air experience. It had been an absolute blast producing and presenting my own show, and that will stay with me forever.

There was one other thing that stood out that morning. Something that had caught my eye as I had been sat with my friend Donny in the studio for that final hour. It was the commercial log for his show that followed mine.

"Hey Donny, wait a minute. What's that there?" I asked my friend as I spotted a familiar name slotted in on the programmed log on the computer screen.

We both listened closely as an Irish lady talked over a backdrop of tin whistles and the clink of glasses, advertising a pub by the name of Conor O'Neill's.

Immediate memories of sawdust and stone walling from that visit back in April filled my head and signified what may well lie ahead.

I smiled to myself. I wonder. I just wonder?

31

Going Postal

United secured qualification into the Champions League "proper" with a 0-0 draw against Lks Lodz out in Poland. As September rolled in, the Reds rolled on with a Premier League win at home to Charlton Athletic, with two goals apiece from Ole Gunnar Solskjær and Dwight Yorke. I have to say that the consensus from Red, Des, and myself was one of an underwhelming nature when it came to the Yorke addition. Chinny's analysis was rather more harsh. "He's totally crap, man!" Were United still trying to fill the void left by a magnificent Frenchman? Yorke had to be given a chance.

I was able to see highlights of the match from Red who had managed to record the game at 1:00 a.m. on a Tuesday morning. From time to time, ESPN2, seemingly on a whim, would drop their scheduled programming—maybe the fifth or sixth rerun of a local bass fishing competition—and broadcast highlights of an English Premier League game. Soccer enthusiasts were able to get their fix once in a while, even if they had absolutely no idea when the games would be available. It remained clearly evident where the priorities of North America's sports program directors lay. English Premier League soccer was tucked away in a dark cupboard and only pulled out whenever there was a complete lull in programing, it seemed.

Relying on infrequent taped highlights was at times frustrating. With Mrs. Cloak not having opted for cable, I wasn't about to fork out for the whole household package. I was hardly home, and soccer coverage was so sparse. I appreciated my "supplier" from Ann Arbor, even though most of the time, courtesy of Des, I would already know the scores of games I was not able to watch live. It wasn't long before Tommy Smyth began cutting himself a larger niche for his "auld onion bag" with a weekly show covering Premier League highlights—another valuable lifeline for the soccer following fraternity in the US.

There was also a growing optimism that ESPN2 was going to make its live coverage of midweek Champions League games more regular. With kick-off times at 2:45 p.m. in Michigan, I had to figure out a way to grasp that midweek soccer nettle; not easy with a full time job.

Having provided me with the occasional VHS-recorded midweeker, Sandy dropped the bombshell that no more video recordings of Champions League games would be winging my way from Chez el Cabellos.

"We hardly watch the television these days, Gary. There really isn't anything worth paying for on cable. It's getting so expensive too."

A few seconds passed as I contemplated what appeared to be the abrupt end to my midweek Manchester United connection. I had been spoiled rightly enough, but the thought still stung.

"Hey, Sandy, no worries. I get it. I really do. It's a lot to fork out, particularly when you're not watching it."

Sandy's wheels were spinning, I could tell.

"You know what, Gary? I have an idea. Let me call my friend."

"Okay?" came my somewhat perplexed response.

"Hello, Dorothy!" Sandy's voice was considerably louder than normal and managing to turn several heads in our busy physical therapy department, "I wondered if you could do me a favor, honey? A favor. A favor, hon! Dorothy, let me call you back in two minutes."

Sandy made her way toward the conference room to continue her conversation, adding "I'll be right back Gary. I think I might have a solution for you."

Within minutes, Sandy reappeared. She had come up with a brilliant Plan B. Seventy-eight year old Dorothy Bottle had apparently stepped up to the plate, becoming my new European Champions League silent partner.

Such was my excitement at the possibility of once again being able to watch United's Champions League games, I decided to go all out and upgrade to a premium quality, extended-play VHS tape which I handed over to Sandy.

This is how it would all go down.

The evening before an all-important Champions League game involving United, Sandy would place a call to Dorothy, providing the covert operator with the kick-off time, the names of the two teams involved, and the proposed length of the broadcast.

Dorothy had indicated to Sandy that immediately upon completion of the game, she would venture outside and place the video into the mailbox at the foot of her driveway. Under no circumstances was I to contemplate knocking on her door or even approaching the house. Sandy was also under strict instructions to tell me NOT to arrive to pick up the tape before dusk.

Sandy went on to explain that Mrs. Bottle was a very private person—more so in her old age—and rather ornery at times.

"Dorothy never wants to be bothered in person by anyone, Gary. We used to see her at church, but she hasn't attended in a long time. She has become very reclusive. I think her hearing has a lot to do with it. Our family has always kept an eye on her though."

"So why in the world would she do something like this, Sandy?"

"I really don't have an answer for you, Gary. I do know one thing though. She would often talk about her British heritage and she certainly seemed to know what I was talking about when I mentioned the soccer, so maybe that has something to do with it?"

"Blimey! Well, I'm certainly feeling very honored then, Sandy."

"As well you should, Gary! As well you should," Sandy replied, smiling, adding "Blimey? I love that word, Gary. Sooo cute!"

And so, thanks to a completely out-of-character gesture from a reclusive elderly lady, Mrs. Dorothy Bottle was to become my new "soccer angel."

September 16, 1998: The very first "Operation Dearborn Dorothy."

I left work around 7:00 p.m., anticipation in full tilt, having resisted any temptation to call Red or my father. I followed Sandy's directions carefully and spotted a secluded bungalow on the edge of town, set back from the other homes. It had a fairly lengthy driveway, at the foot of which stood an all-American mailbox, reminiscent of a British bread bin atop a rather grand wooden platform. I spun around and pulled up alongside, making sure to be close enough to reach out of my driver's side window. It took a decent tug to get the mailbox lid open. I eagerly reached inside. *Yes!* All had gone according to plan. I paused for a moment, considering my usual instinct to thank my new benefactor: a polite knock on the door perhaps. However, given the terms of our prematch contract, I did not want to jeopardize my Champions League connection. I quietly pulled away from the mailbox, looking back at a house shrouded in darkness.

My attention switched to the tape in my hand. I couldn't get home quickly enough. Flinging the door open, I immediately noticed the flashing red light of the answering machine. Resisting, I adjusted my already-in-place United scarf and slotted the tape into the built-in VHS slot.

I was ready for ninety minutes of Champions League soccer, Manchester United against Barcelona, a solitary United fan following his team thousands of miles from home, millions of people across the Pond having already seen the match now tucked up in bed and fast asleep. The two teams were about to go head to head in the Champions League "Group of Death," a sellout and rapturous crowd packed into Old Trafford on a perfect autumn evening, and, for me, it was all thanks to the mysterious Dorothy Bottle.

United made their intentions clear right from the get go with an all-out assault on the Barcelona goal. Beckham flew past a Barcelona defender. I shuffled to the edge of my chair as his cross fired its way into the Barcelona penalty area, beckoning for someone to connect. Someone did, and that someone was Ryan Giggs.

I leapt into the air! What a goal!

Thank you, Giggsy! And thank you Dorothy Bottle!

And then Paul Scholes lit up Old Trafford once again. 2-0!

My tiny portable TV atop my fridge shuddered at the force of my celebration.

Barcelona pulled a goal back early in the second half, the ovation, as expected, non-existent, as the Catalonians hurried the ball back to the halfway line to resume play as quickly as possible. Disaster then struck as Jaap Stam continued his shaky start to life at Old Trafford, fouling Rivaldo in the United box.

Giovanni stepped up to take the penalty. 2-2!

After that second goal, Barcelona began to grow in confidence. Then, a free kick for United on the left-hand edge of the Barcelona penalty area, about ten yards out.

I hoped! Beckham delivered! Goooooooalll!

I floated around the room in absolute ecstasy, yearning to be with the fans inside Old Trafford.

A crazy ten seconds followed with Barcelona pummeling United's goal until the hand of Nicky Butt popped up, preventing a certain goal. Butt was subsequently sent off and Louis Enrique converted the penalty.

Final score: 3-3!

It had been an incredible start to the group stages of United's Champions League campaign.

My Champions League lifeline remained intact, thanks to Dearborn Dorothy—whoever she was!

32

Windy City Weekend

The British Invasion was over and a radio-free weekend had arrived. But with it came an immediate conflict of options. My mate "Soul Boy" Bill had decided that it was time to leave Chicago and head back to Britain, and so the friends he had made in the Windy City had arranged a leaving do on the Saturday night to give him a decent send off. I decided to go for a quick "in and out" of Illinois to maximize the short weekend window. There was also a small matter of United vs Arsenal in the Premier League on the Sunday.

I was working late Friday and so this time I opted for an early Saturday morning flight across Lake Michigan, having established a very personal airport "park and ride" service. Cue Celia Bertram, my wonderful co-worker, alias "Fluffy," so called for reasons I am hesitant to mention. Let's just say that being a Southern belle, she was rather partial to her refried beans. I guess it was her honesty and down to earth demeanor that drew me to her. I recall early on in my tenure at the hospital, I was working with Fluffy and we had to treat a client up on one of the orthopedic wards. As we stood in the elevator, she insisted that we make a quick detour before we got to our assigned client. Fluffy knew everyone it seemed.

"Come on Garr, we have to go say goodbye," Fluffy insisted.

"Why who's leaving, Fluffs?" I enquired.

"Nobody," she noted. "Follow me." Fluffy lead me down one of the ward corridors, her distinctive swift, shuffling gait making it difficult to keep up with her. She slowed in front of a room and tapped gently on the door while inching it open, quietly announcing her arrival.

"Hey Clint. It's me, Fluffs, and my friend Gary from Britain. We've just come to check that you're OK." Fluffy moved close to the gentleman's bedside, continuing with her softly spoken words. The patient's tired eyes opened. He was obviously a gravely ill man. I stood next to Fluffy's side as I witnessed her generous act, the palm of her right hand gently wrapping over the patient's forearm. Fluffy then turned to me after gently placing the man's hand under the sheets for warmth.

"OK, Garr. Come on. Time to go."

And with that we exited the room and headed for our scheduled client. We learned later that the patient we had visited passed away that same afternoon.

"Well, Garr," Fluffy said "at least we got to say goodbye."

There are certain people you meet in your life that make you a better person for knowing them. Fluffy was one of those people. Despite our very different backgrounds and age difference, ours became a close and valued friendship.

Fluffy lived a mile away from the clinic and only two miles from Detroit Metro airport. That Saturday morning, I left my old Honda in her driveway and was then driven at snail's pace to the departure gate, although still in plenty of time to make my flight to Chicago. I thanked Fluffy and bid her farewell, as her scrawny white poodle huddled for warmth on her knee. As I made my way toward the entrance, I heard Fluffy call out. "Garr! Call me as soon as you land back Sunday night. Doesn't matter what time, ya hear me?" Hearing a toot from a car horn, I turned back and noticed Fluffy pulling away, still waving enthusiastically.

I arrived in Chicago one whole minute earlier than the time that I had left Detroit, having moved from Eastern Standard Time to Central Standard Time in the blink of an eye.

The venue for the night was a new Chicago "safe house" in the northern suburbs. The house had been recently purchased by "Big Bob," my Geordie mate, a further sign that he was taking life in the U.S. very seriously. Soul Boy, the lads, and myself, were all, of course, very glad about this since it meant another excellent pad was available in which to kip. It was a huge place and Soul Boy, because of his imminent return to the UK, had rented one of the many rooms in the new Geordie palace. We resisted a Chicago South side stint this time around, settling for local bar time and an extended house party into the early hours of Sunday.

I awoke early with the usual grogginess associated with minimal sleep and a raucous party night prior, the Arsenal and Manchester United game being my subconscious alarm clock. I had "made friends" with a Canadian girl the previous night, the two of us deciding to sneak away, claim a room in Big Bob's B&B, and "unite our Commonwealth ties" after the party. *"Oh, Oh, Oh Canada!"* She made an early exit that morning to get back across the city to her girlfriend's home before jetting back to Toronto later in the day. We both seemed set on a Toronto/Detroit liaison in the not too distant future.

There was such a cultural mix of young professionals in the healthcare systems of America's Midwest, indeed many areas of the States I am sure, and the party that night in Chicago had emphasized the fact. It was always fun to meet and greet with such interesting people from many different countries. It was such great energy, most of the folks excited at the challenge of living abroad and bringing their own perspective on life in America.

Big Bob wanted nothing to do with Manchester United or Arsenal, particularly the morning after a late one. He slept like a bear; no surprise after drinking Chicago dry of its whisky the previous night. Judging by the smirk on the girl's face that I saw exiting his room, I sensed that Big Bob may well require rest and repair for the remainder of the morning anyway.

I quietly wandered back into the kitchen after saying goodbye to my own Miss Canada.

"Oh hey," Big Bob's conqueror, confidently acknowledging me as she was still fixing her jacket

"Hi there," I replied, unable to resist a wry smile. "Here, let me help you with that."

"Oh, no need. I'm good. Thanks though."

"Great party last night, eh?"

"Oh, yeah, for sure!"

A short sharp silent moment, before…

"Well have a good one" the girl said, turning to open the door.

"Yep, you too," I replied, just about squeezing my response in before my mate's latest fling went skipping nonchalantly down the outside steps and off into the Chicago dawn.

Soul Boy, on the other, hand hadn't even stayed at the "safe house," sneaking off into the early hours, obviously having decided to say goodbye to Chicago in his own inimitable way. He had been receiving quite a bit of attention from a work colleague, an Occupational Therapist nicknamed "The Kink," not only because of her renowned erotic tendencies, but more for her reputation for having such apparent sexual stamina that she would keep going "all day and all of the night!" Soul Boy, it seemed, may well not be making it back to the safe house for quite some time.

And so I was to plough a lone furrow that morning. I wandered out to the closest main street from the safe house to hail a taxi. It took a little while, but I nailed it.

"Abbey Pub, please, mate. I believe it's on Grace?"

"Yeah man, I know that place" the driver exclaimed, "I'll have you there in twenty minutes or so, man. Not much traffic at this time on a Sunday. Church aint out yet."

"I guess you could say I'm off to my own church."

"Yeah, right man. I get it, brother. Twelve noon somewhere in the world, right?"

My driver must have continued nodding his head for at least another couple of minutes after his comment, trying to grab my attention through his rear view mirror.

I finally gave in.

"Well mate, it's not really about the beer for me this morning. It's more about the soccer."

"Right! Right man! I guess so with that accent, dude. Where you from man?"

"Where do you think, mate?" I replied, initiating my favorite name-where-I'm-from game.

"Oh man, I don't know, you gotta be from Australia. Some place like that, dude."

At least he didn't say Spain, so I threw him some slack. But Australia and soccer?

"Close. I get that a lot, mate. Probably because I say mate a lot. Actually, I'm from England"

"God damn! I should a got that right away, man" the driver replied, slapping his steering wheel hard with both hands as if he had just lost the chance to win a week's holiday in Aruba.

"Yeah you English sure love your soccer don't ya man? You're all crazy. All that fighting 'n' all, huh?"

Here we go I thought. I didn't even go there.

"Yeah, we love it, mate. That's why I'm up after a late one last night."

"I know that's right man. What's the game today?"

"Manchester United against Arsenal. A big match and early in the season." I extended my answer, sensing the man's genuine intrigue.

"Oh, yeah, man. Manchester United, I've heard of them. Aren't they like the Yankees of soccer?"

"Except that they kick the ball, right?" I couldn't resist.

"Yeah, man! You know what I'm saying though. They're like a big, rich team, huh?"

"I guess they are, yeah. Been my team though for as long as I can remember. Since the mid-70s."

"Yeah, I get that. I get that. You gotta know my pain then, huh? I love the Cubs, man."

"Oh boy, I really don't know what to say about that, mate, except, hang in there, buddy!"

"Yeah. Like you say, man, that's my team. Always will be, man. That's the way it is, right, brother?"

"Hey, hold on there. Whoa. Whoa." The driver swerved sharply and pulled over to the side of the road.

"Man, what's going on here?" he exclaimed.

I sat in amazement as he placed his vehicle in park, left the hazard lights on and stepped out to go to the assistance of a gentleman who appeared to have a problem with his own vehicle.

My own instincts took over.

"You guys need a hand?" I enquired, as I stood clinging to the back door of the taxi, half in, half out, the stranded driver with an ear to his bright red phone and chattering away as he kicked the bumper on the rear of his vehicle several times.

"Naw man. It's all good. Hey, can you move over though? This guy needs a ride." I couldn't believe it as the taxi driver was lugging a suitcase for the man in distress, placing it in the trunk of the taxi. The man with the broken down car then slipped his mobile phone into the inside pocket of his smart jacket, took a last glance into his car through the passenger side window before taking the driver's lead and heading to the back seat of the taxi. I slide along to let the guy in, placing my bag between my feet on the floor behind the passenger seat.

"Oh man. Thanks. Thanks a lot, dude."

"Rough morning, eh" I engaged immediately.

"Hey! Always remember, we always gotta help each other out in this life, right?" the taxi driver declared.

"Sure do, mate" I chimed in.

"Too many people in too much of a rush to go nowhere, man. We gotta take our time. Be a brother. Ya know what I'm saying?"

Our taxi driver was rolling out the philosophy.

"Absolutely, mate" I made sure I recognized the man's compassion.

"Well brother, you won't get any argument from me" our man in distress said, acknowledging the driver. "Thanks so much for stopping. That was so kind of you."

"What happened mate?" I enquired.

"I was driving along, quiet Sunday morning, and then I see this goddamn muffler in the road and couldn't avoid it. Took my tire right out, man."

"Ouff! Nasty."

"Yeah, I don't have time for this shit, man. I gotta get to O'Hare."

"You managed to get her parked up on the curb pretty good though, mate."

"What's that? Oh yeah, yeah seemed a safe place to park up."

"Never a dull moment, eh mate? My names Gary," I added, offering my hand to an understandably Mr. Stressed.

"Oh hey, sorry man. Kyle. Kyle McLoud."

"It's all gonna work out, man. I'll get ya there, my friend. I'll get ya there," another piece of brotherly positivity from the driver's seat.

"Yeah, my wife is on her way over along with the tow truck. They'll sort it all out. I gotta get out of town."

"Nice one. Good to meet you Kyle."

"Good to meet you. Gary, right?"

"Yeah that's right. You must have some Scottish roots with a name like that, eh?"

"Yeah, somewhere down the line, I guess. Man, I gotta get over there. I'd love to play St Andrew's someday."

"Into your golf then, eh?"

"Oh yeah. I would have been out there this morning if I didn't have to shoot out to New York. What about you?"

"More of a soccer man myself, Kyle."

"Go figure with an accent like that. Where are you from anyway?"

Here we go again.

"England."

"Well I gathered that. But whereabouts though?" Kyle replied, convincing me that his grasp of geography was slightly better than the taxi driver.

"Close to Manchester," giving my usual explanation in order to make things somewhat easier for an inquiring Yank.

"Ah, gotta be Man U then, right?"

"Absolutely, mate," I replied, smiling at Kyle's astute observation.

"Actually trying to get over to watch a game right now, mate."

"Really? Wow, where's that then?" I wasn't really sure whether Kyle meant actual venue or my intended destination.

"The Abbey on Grace. They should hopefully have the live feed from London. United are playing a team called Arsenal today and I am trying to catch it."

"Oh man that's awesome. Didn't realize you could catch those games out here. Hey, hope I haven't made things difficult for you. What time does it kick?" I smiled, hearing "kick" and not "kick-off."

"About five minutes ago." I couldn't help myself.

"Oh, shit man. Sorry to have held you up, Gary."

"Oh it's all good. I am sure we aren't too far away."

Then right on cue.

"Hey brother," our zen master taxi driver chimed in "the Abbey is here on the right! Here ya go man."

"Superb. Cheers, mate" I noted reaching forward. "So what's the damage then?"

"What's the what, now man?" a confused driver responded.

"Oh yeah, I mean how much do I owe you, mate?"

"Right man! Right! Sixteen bucks should do it."

"Here ya go, keep the change, mate. Really appreciate it."

"Thank you, man. You have a good day and enjoy your soccer game."

I grabbed my bag and shook Kyle's hand.

"Good luck with your trip, mate. Great to meet you"

"Thanks, man. Good luck with the game. Go United, I guess, huh!"

"Oh I'll get him there, man," our driver added, continuing on his mission.

I was feeling a decent vibe from the taxi cab.

I slammed the door, tapped the roof of the cab and gave a thumbs up as I stepped away. I stepped onto the curb and heard "We gotta all look out for each other, man! Remember that! Look out for each other."

"If only there were more people like that in the world," I thought to myself.

I gave a wave and as I did so I contemplated the fact that a cab ride in Chicago on an early Sunday morning had resulted in two random Americans actually aware of who Manchester United were.

As I turned and stood looking at the Abbey Pub, I had a sudden flashback to that FA Cup final weekend when Cantona won the cup for United against Liverpool. It had been a lucky venue that day. I hoped for the same again. Upon opening the door I heard the immediate, comforting echo of Martyn Tyler's voice. There were only a handful of people inside, craning necks, leaning back against chairs or standing, fixed on the scene at Highbury displayed on screens dotted around the bar.

I opted for a solitary spot intent on full absorption into the match. I placed my bag on the floor beside me and sat down on a high top chair close to the far corner of the bar. I gave a nod to the lad behind the bar and glanced up at the TV screen. I had joined the match several minutes in, but I had made it. My head throbbed like a mamba, the moment that the effect of a short kip, a long night, and a "Canadian connection" all kicked in at once. But I had still made it to the match!

It looked like a pretty open game. Andy Gray began making a comment and then, just moments after I had walked into the building, Martin Tyler makes a call.

"The ball swings in towards Adams and Arsenal have the lead they thoroughly deserve!"

"Look at Stam!" I said to myself, out of frustration. "What have we done?"

The new United defender was rooted to the ground as Adams displayed his heading prowess, burying the ball into the United net.

1-0 Arsenal!

Only fourteen minutes gone in the game. It looked ominous for my team.

And one minute before half-time, it went from bad to worse.

"Static Stam" once more looked inept as Anelka gratefully accepted his second stab at goal after a marvelous initial save from Peter Schmeichel.

2-0 Arsenal!

Early in the second half, Nicky Butt mistimed a tackle, and was given a straight red card.

United's defensive frailties continued, Stam's below par performance continued, and five minutes after entering the field of play, Freddie Ljungberg nipped in to lob Schmeichel.

3-0 Arsenal!

My misery was complete. Arsenal had "done us" yet again.

As soon as the final whistle blew, I acknowledged the barman and gave a nod to one or two obvious, and dejected looking, Red Devils. I swung open the exit and, lugging my bag over my right shoulder, emerged back out into the light of day.

I had time to kill before grabbing the 'L' and so I took a late morning, post hangover, postmatch stroll around the neighborhood. I was fascinated by Chicago's architecture in those suburbs. An abundance of very distinctive "two flats" were a staple. Apparently built in the early nineteen hundreds, they resembled a small house atop another. The owner would often live on the bottom and rent out the above one. They littered Chicago's lanes. The lads had rented one when first over in Chicago from the UK, and their owner lived above them. Taking in the surroundings that Sunday morning had provided another "American moment" for this Englishman abroad.

Alas, my Sunday morning stroll did little to avert me from the fact that United had been well beaten at Highbury.

I eventually caught the train and headed south on Chicago's elevated line, the magnificence of the metropolis aside Lake Michigan was a sight to behold. The journey was deceivingly long, a couple of line changes and around an hour and a half before eventually reaching Midway airport.

As my flight was readying for touchdown into Detroit Metro Airport that evening, I considered the impact such a result would have on the rest of our season. It didn't bode well, but it was still early days; only September. I pulled on my optimism. It had been a terrific weekend and a great send off for my old mate Bill, wherever he was, but my head was filled with the frustrations of the game. Jaap Stam was poor. I remembered that Red had called me during the World Cup, having just watched Holland, his analysis apparently spot on: "What have we done, you tosser?"

I then considered how long it had taken Schmeichel to adjust to life in the English Premier League. He hadn't turned out so bad in the end. The statistics didn't lie though. United had conceded six goals in two games. Ferguson, it appeared, had some defensive issues to address at the start of the new campaign.

Back in Detroit, I began the long walk out of the arrivals lounge. It wasn't long before I had made it to the exit doors of the airport, walking over to the call box to contact "Fluffy's Taxis."

"I'm on my way, Garr!" Fluffy said, without even allowing a full ring of the telephone. Within minutes, there she was, waving, energetic as ever, animated in her greeting, her nightgown most evident in the early evening of autumn. Among the sleek black Detroit Airport limos, yellow cabs and hotel buses emblazoned with brand names, Fluffy stuck out like a sore thumb, her best friend, the manic poodle, high on its hind legs atop her lap. I trotted over and jumped into the car, Fluffy flicking and playing with her 70s Streisand style frizzy perm. What do they say about pets and their owners? Her devoted companion was looking about ready to piss itself, paws now resting on the steering wheel, apparently ecstatic that I had arrived back safely in one piece.

"So, how was it then, Garr?"

I hesitated for a moment, looking up to the evening sky, noticing a plane making its descent right above us. My mind wandered for a moment back to that quiet bar on Grace Street. I chose the positive response, not wanting to bore my friend with the rudiments of another Manchester United defeat and how it had somewhat dampened what had been a tremendous Windy City weekend.

"A top time as always, Fluffs."

"Oh, to be a fly on the wall when you British boys get together, Garr."

"So glad you weren't, Fluffs. So glad you weren't."

"Spoilsport you are, Garr. Let's go and get that car of yours."

After a swift car switch and my gratitude to Fluffy once again, I left her small sub division and sped off east along US-12 heading for Dearborn, roughly twelve miles away. A couple of miles into the journey, I passed through the town of Inkster. I called it "the meat in the sandwich": more urban blight, and empty lots, this time between the cities of Dearborn and Wayne. I had to pass through it every day going to work. I noticed a wasted-looking elderly looking gentleman leaning against a half-cocked bus stop sign as a middle-aged lady pushed an empty shopping cart along the sidewalk, no supermarket in proximity, as she wandered around in a pair of beat-up training shoes, a total mismatch for the black ankle length coat she was wearing. It was around eighty degrees outside; one of those humid autumn nights in Michigan. I also noticed a young skinny man sat crossed-legged on the curb in front of an abandoned Coney Island restaurant, a cigarette dangling from the corner of his mouth, his eyes heavy, hair bedraggled. Further east, I pulled up to a red light. A man stood holding a cardboard sign: "will work for food." I did all I could not to stare, but our eyes met. The man looked empty, sadness radiating from his being as cars sped by heading north and south at the intersection, causing him to grip his written plea even tighter. A picture speaks a thousand words. I considered his story. It could have had so many permutations.

"Always remember, we always gotta help each other in this life, right? We gotta help each other out, man." The Chicago taxi driver's words echoed in my head. I reached into my wallet and grabbed a twenty dollar bill.

"Hey, God bless ya, man. God bless ya, my friend!"

Only minutes earlier I had left the hustle and bustle of a cosmopolitan airport, driven through bustling neighborhoods—families and tenants, all trying to grasp that little slice of the American dream. I had passed a hospital and then the Mile High Club, its neon sign leaving nothing to the imagination—its close proximity to Metro Airport validating its monstrous size and well-stocked parking lot, suggesting affluent punters with time to kill during a "lay" over! And yet, within a few minutes, I had wandered into a different world. I still struggled to get my northern English head around the stark contrasts that America throws at you in just a couple of miles of separation.

I entered Dearborn city limits and within moments I was pulling into the driveway of Hotel Hairpiece. All appeared quiet on the Rhonda front. She was, no doubt, preoccupied with her PBS Sunday night television and the latest episode of some British period drama. Detroit Public Television loved them. And Rhonda Cloak loved them. As I walked into my bedsit apartment, I placed my bag down on the floor and instinctively wandered over to the answering machine. I flicked the switch and slid the volume button high.

"Bollocks, you tosser!"

Yeah—cheers for reminding me, Red!

33

New Dawn Rising

September 24, 1998. The Premier League fixture list had pitted United against arch rivals, Liverpool, at Old Trafford. It was a midweek league fixture and my physical therapy duties kept me late, just as well really because there was to be no tape delay presentation at the Britannia Club that particular night.

Liverpool vs. United and all I had to rely on was a Des recap.

"Fergie rang the changes, Gary. He brought Yorke back in and put Gary Neville in the center of defense next to Stam. Irwin grabbed a penalty early on. Scholesy was the one though. From a Liverpool corner we counter attacked so quickly. Yorke passed it out wide to Cole on the halfway line and Cole did brilliantly, outpacing Liverpool's defense and then sweeping in a cross with his left foot. It reached the edge of the box and out of nowhere Scholesy hammered a superb left foot shot which flew into the top left-hand corner. It was a brilliant goal son. A brilliant goal!"

I listened to my father's enthusiasm. It was reminiscent of a report from BBC Sports World. He had to wait, himself, to watch the highlights that evening and yet I "felt it," that move for the second goal, passionately described over a telephone line over 3,500 miles away.

United had beaten Liverpool 2-0, a much-needed response after the debacle at Highbury.

September 30, 1998: United were over in Germany for their next Champions League tie. The Red Devils had a battle on their hands against Bayern Munich, the two sides hoping to go through from a very tough European Champions League "Group of Death." Dearborn Dorothy was to be my match provider.

As I entered my apartment after work, the answering machine light blinking, I resisted any temptation to listen to my messages. I flicked back the recliner and fast forwarded the VHS tape. Kick-off time.

Munich took the lead after only eleven minutes with a dubious offside goal from Elber.

1-0, Bayern Munich.

United hit back with a first European goal from Dwight Yorke. 1-1.

The second half arrived, and with it, two huge talking points:

Scholes appeared to have used a sneaky hand in controlling the ball. It wasn't spotted by the ref.

2-1, United.

Then, with seconds remaining, a catastrophic error from Schmeichel allowed Elber to claim a lucky goal.

2-2.

Barcelona had beaten Brondby to go top of the "Group of Death" ahead of United and Bayern. Only two of the four teams could progress in the competition. Dearborn Dorothy had brought an American "hump day" to a satisfying close. In just three days' time a new dawn was about to rise on my soccer watching abroad.

Saturday October 3, 1998: The early morning excitement was back with a vengance, recollections of being up at the crack of dawn to venture to the Britannia Club. This time, however, the destination was different. The open road lined with a mass of red, yellow, orange, and gold, announcing the fact that the fall colors had arrived in Michigan. I was an expatriate "soccer pioneer," cruising along to Blur, Verve, Oasis, and, of course, New Order, totally pumped and ready to experience a brand new venue. I left the freeway at the Ann Arbor exit and travelled the two miles or so to Main Street.

Within moments, she came into view: Conor O'Neill's, 318 South Main, Ann Arbor, Michigan.

As I approached the parking lot, temptation got the better of me and I tuned my radio to Replay 105.1 FM. The instantly recognizable sound of Tears for Fears and "Everybody Wants to Rule the World" came on, a subtle British reverberation from a different decade to the one in which I had absorbed myself during my short tenure at the station. It seemed to emphasize my radio days as done. Replay 105.1 had moved on. I had moved on. No more British Invasion. No more Beatles. No more Stones. No more Who. No more The Guess Who! And most definitely no more Gerry and the Pacemakers. I was back to live Saturday morning English Premier League soccer broadcasts. Life was good.

It was around 9:20 a.m. and there were only two cars in the large municipal parking lot. Approaching the pub's rear entrance, I noticed that the window display of all things Irish was now fully furnished, looking resplendent as the last hint of an early morning frost clung to its glass. I walked up the back steps and popped my head into the doorway, the instant hollow echo of music from inside suggesting an empty pub. I was immediately approached by an industrious looking fella who greeted me with a smile, placing his broom on one side as I caught his attention.

"Sorry to bother you, mate. I'm here to watch the soccer. What time are you opening?"

"Oh? Right. There's nobody here yet. I am just clearing up from last night, man, but you're more than welcome to come on in and take a seat if you don't mind the mess."

"Cheers. No problem. That's grand, mate. What's your name?"

"Charles," he replied, offering his hand. "I'm Charles, the cook."

"Charles, thanks mate. I'm Gary. Great to meet you."

Charles had the happiest of grins, immediately offering me a coffee as he led me into the main area of the pub. I thanked him and said I'd take a look around if that was OK. With that, Charles disappeared around the corner towards the back door, mop firmly in hand.

As I stood surveying the scene, I was amazed at just how much had been done since that afternoon back in the spring when I had had my own private tour with the owner, Tim. The place looked fantastic!

The stale smell of a Friday night of drinking, blending with bleach, filled my nostrils. I figured that business must have started off rather well. There was a definite "morning after the night before" air to the place.

My initial feeling, as I sat alone, was one of being somewhat surplus to requirements, as if I had turned up and missed the wedding, but the cook had some leftover dinner just to make me feel my journey hadn't been wasted. I surveyed my surroundings. It was a far cry from the start to soccer watching at Conor O'Neill's that I had imagined. The fact that I was soon about to enjoy a Manchester United match live from England seemed quite unfathomable.

"Build it and they will come."

Well, they did. And I had.

But, apparently, nobody else had been given the message.

A couple of other workers appeared. They looked South American. A nod was all I got, and I was sure that they must have been wondering who I was and what I was doing there. I headed over toward the Sporting Billy section of the pub where the pull-down big screen was located, the stickiness of the floor emphasizing the need for further janitorial services.

Chairs were still atop tables and the screen was not yet rolled down. I grabbed a stool, sat, pulled out my British newspaper and positioned myself for an ideal view of the screen.

Several minutes later a disheveled-looking young lad waltzed in, seemingly surprised to see me in the building.

"Morning, mate," I exclaimed, "how's it going?"

"Knackered, mate Last night was a late one. I only left this fucking place six hours ago. I suppose you are here for the game, right?" replied the young barman.

"Yes, mate. My name's Gary," I replied, offering my hand.

"Oh yeah. Sorry man," he replied shaking my hand. "I'm Johnny. Nice to meet you. Can I get you a coffee?"

"Thanks a lot, Johnny," I replied "but I'm OK, mate. So are you expecting many folk this morning then?" I said, hopefully.

"Well, if last week was anything to go by, we should have a few in soon. Kick-off is at ten, right?"

"Yep, mate. Manchester United today, right?"

"Yes. Manchester United and Southampton, or so I was told. Hopefully, a few will turn out to watch Manchester, eh?"

With that, Johnny and I continued chatting. He told me that Conor's was packing in the college crowd from the University of Michigan, with some very favorable women to men ratios—a cheeky grin accompanying his comment. According to Johnny, the ladies had taken great delight in the sanctity of Conor's environment, compared to the meat markets of the other campus watering holes, possibly the cultural draw.

From vibrant fun-filled evenings in a pub filled with beautiful women to the early morning drag of middle-aged soccer-loving blokes requiring nothing more than a stool, a hot cuppa, and some good craic with the lads. I sensed the young American before me was not so pleased to have "gotten" the early-morning nod.

I delved back into my newspaper and felt the excitement building as the large clock above the bar read 9:45 a.m.

I reflected back to the days when I used to arrive at Old Trafford, taking up my usual position in the paddock at least two hours before kick-off, the echo of the tannoy keeping me and the other early diehards company. I had that same feeling as I sat in a new Irish bar in an American Midwest town—a feeling that was somewhat more accentuated with the realization that on first arriving in the States three years prior, I presumed I would have no chance of seeing any Reds games live again.

The all-important time of 3:00 p.m. on a Saturday afternoon in England was about to have relevance in Ann Arbor, Michigan.

After messing for a while in the Conor O'Neill's "command center"—aka, cupboard full of wires—Johnny reappeared, turned on several TV's and ventured over to unlock the front doors. Only then did I realize that I truly had "sneaked in the back door."

A group of around ten lads ambled in and began vying for the best seat for a view of the game. I instantly spotted my United cohort. All of the lads looked half dead, but a certain glint filled their eyes, their passion for soccer and their team leading them to the doors of an Irish pub early on a Saturday morning.

"Mate!" I shouted over to Red.

Red's bespectacled face frowned in my direction as he tried to make out who was calling him, a frown that instantly turned into a huge grin upon recognition.

"Hey, how's it going, you bloody tosser, you wanker, you?!"

I smiled, proud to have received such a verbally gratifying barrage from the gangly Yank so early in the morning,

Having spoken earlier in the week, we had arranged to meet up, knowing the game was featuring United. It was just like old times and the two of us immediately began focusing on our good fortune, realizing how lucky we had been to find a place like Conor's.

Red pulled up a stool.

Within a matter of seconds, our South Korean Liverpool-loving comrade made his own appearance.

"United. Fucking shit, man!"

Chinny had arrived. Red and I smiled.

All week, the Liverpool diehard had been saying there was no way he was going to come down to watch Manchester United. However, a reunion of the Britannia Crew was long overdue, and too hard to resist, even for our professional United-hater.

Game time approached, and, with it, an increasingly-frustrated looking Johnny continued with his attempts to make connection with the satellite feed. Johnny had called for help from a stern-looking, shaven-headed Irish barman, Danny. The two busied themselves, popping their heads in and out of the cubby hole, at times appearing clueless but fully focused on the task at hand, a few "fucks," "shites," and "fuckin' shites" thrown in for good measure as they continued to stare up at the blank blue screen in desperation. Kick-off time had come and gone.

Nothing!

Red, Chinny, and I looked at each other and Chinny commented on how Reggie—the "Britannia guru"—would have had it all under control, even finding time for a prematch raffle.

And then, without warning—after a loud crack, pop, and a fizzle— there it was, a vibrant Dell in full color accompanied by a full-blooded burst of volume from the pub's surround sound speaker system. Danny nodded to Johnny and trudged slowly back over toward the bar to resume his prior tasks.

10:10 a.m. October 3, 1998.

Our Conor O'Neill's soccer-watching experience had begun!

Get in there!

There was an immediate cheer from the assembled throng, giving the impression that the room was filled with around three hundred people and not the devoted ten or so soccer fans who had gathered to pay homage, several of whom were still taking off their jackets with a yawn. I reflected on how far we had come—the comfort of a pub, sitting, relaxing, watching a soccer match beamed live from England via satellite. The moment felt significant. We were home!

Commentator Martin Tyler's voice was instantly recognizable and the picture was an absolute beauty, instantly commanding the attention of everyone in the pub.

The game picked up a decent pace, but the volume went sadly in the opposite direction until it became non-existent. Still, we didn't care, our eyes totally fixed on the screen above us.

United had started well. Red pointed out that Fergie had gone with Blomqvist, and we were already talking about how Cole and Yorke were beginning to click. Right on cue, Cole burst down United's left flank driving in a low cross for none other than Dwight Yorke.

Southampton 0 Manchester United 1!

Chinny sarcastically pointed out that United had wisely decided to go for an all-black kit this time, a far cry from their fateful visit to England's south coast two years earlier when the Reds that day had become the "Speckled Greys," prompting their infamous shirt change at half-time— the resulting score a 3-1 defeat for United. Most of the United players had apparently struggled to see each other throughout the first half. They then came out second half in an even more hideous blue and white vertical striped number. The United marketing department for a short time there seemed to have lost the plot. I am sure Fergie would have reverted to type and simply seen red with the players after that defeat.

As the first half came to a close, United held onto their one goal lead.

During half-time, I reflected on the evident willingness to please. Waiters and waitresses arriving for their shifts immediately busied themselves, providing free coffee and tea, ferrying between the soccer fans until the bar opened. I began chatting with a lady who had wandered in just after the match started. She appeared to be in charge that morning. She was an Irish lass named Connie. I learned how Connie had been in the States for quite some time, having worked for a couple of other Irish brew companies. She was also the apparent go-to person when it came to social events at the venue. Needless to say, I spent a good chunk of the chat promoting the need for regular weekend English Premier League soccer.

"Och, Gary son. We're giving it a wee go right now for sure."

On visiting the "bogs" at half-time, I noticed a decent feed of the commentary present in there. Why was that significant? Well, the only downside to the show that morning was the muffled delivery of Martin Tyler as we all struggled to hear his voice through the speaker system in the main bar. On the other hand, in the men's bathroom it was loud and clear and I listened intently to the segments playing during half-time, smiling at what I heard.

The satellite provider had decided to visit Newcastle in the northeast of England to solicit the opinions of some of the local factory workers as to the following week's Premier League fixtures. I returned to the main paddock area with most of the early morning soccer goers in stitches as various Geordies had been filmed while indulging in their occupational tasks up in Newcastle. The camera would zoom in at trendy angles, postures emphasized even more with the lack of sound. Then, at the very last moment, a metal worker would pop his head up out from under his welding mask and hit us with his verdict for a particular fixture that weekend. We had been spared the thick Tyneside dialect, unless your bladder had directed you into the men's bogs!

It appeared that the Premier League coverage had started to sell one of its strongest assets: the sheer ingrained passion of the homeland supporters, their working class backgrounds, and what their team meant to them. Newcastle was a city that portrayed that for sure. The league's marketing machine wanted the world to know that, too. The marketing gurus wanted to sell the English game to a global audience that would align itself with their "product"—a product with a history and heritage; teams with legacies and followings that were second to none.

Sell the English game to the world. Go global.

As I looked up at the screen, I felt a definite pull for home.

As I settled myself back into our paddock for the second half, a new punter arrived, taking a stool next to me. We acknowledged each other and he enquired as to the game and the score. Well-spoken with a distinctive southern English accent, I noticed how quickly he became fixated with the match. He reminded me of an English country gent.

The game picked up its pace in the second half and the player that Red had mentioned several times—Jesper Blomqvist—soon began to play a prominent role. He reminded us all very much of Giggs in his style of play. It appeared he would give Giggs a run for his money during the season, knowing how injury prone the "Welsh Wizard" had become. A beautifully weighted flick with the outside of his left foot released Cole on the edge of the box and the United striker finished exquisitely, floating the ball over the Southampton keeper into the right hand corner.

2-0 United!

An instinctive volley from Jordi Cruyff late on in the match completed victory.

3-0 United!

And that was that.

My first morning at Conor O'Neill's couldn't have gone any better.

When the final whistle blew, a swift mass exodus began from the bar out into the midday autumn sun. Red and Chinny bid me farewell, Red apparently having family commitments and Chinny continuing his study that afternoon at the University of Michigan. All three of us agreed — Chinny somewhat begrudgingly of course—that we had seen a pretty good first match and were very happy to consider Conor O'Neill's our new home for English Premier League soccer.

Throughout that second half, I had continued to chat with the English gent, and I accepted his offer to stay at Conor's for lunch and some postmatch banter. It didn't take long to warm to a man like Alfred Montague.

"Now that is one regal name, fella," was my instant reaction as he introduced himself.

"Please, just call me Fred," the gentleman responded, warmly.

We pulled up a table just under the now hidden screen and decided a pint of Guinness and some Irish fare was the order of the day. "Maureen's Irish Stew" seemed rather appropriate.

Fred enquired as to my business out in the States, and I obliged with all the relevant details. His face lit up with my British Invasion tale, commenting how his wife Alexia had mentioned to him that she had been listening to "an English chap" on the radio one Saturday morning.

I was intrigued to hear Fred's own story.

Fred explained that he had left England in the mid-60s, and after an initial spell in Canada, had eventually settled in the States. His business was finance. He had his own office in downtown Ann Arbor and lived about five miles out of town. I was taken aback when he revealed that he was sixty-six years old. I would have sworn that he was mid-fifties at most, his tracksuit bottoms, running shoes, and smart sweatshirt a testament to his obvious dedication to fitness.

I asked Fred how he had kept in touch with the game before he had found our new Irish den.

"Well, you know Gary, there has been very little opportunity to follow the game out here. I guess you could say I have been in the soccer wilderness for almost forty years, my friend."

Fred continued. "I was able to see the odd game or two, particularly when the CBC in Canada showed the FA Cup final. In recent years, coverage of the World Cup made its way onto the cable networks and gave me a lifeline every four years at least. Other than that, I have had very little in the way of options."

I began to fill Fred in on the outstanding coverage we had found at the Britannia Club and he seemed perplexed, having never heard about Reggie's establishment. A broad smile filled his face as I told him all about Reggie and his one-of-a-kind presentation style.

"So how did you find out about Conor O'Neill's showing English Premier League games then, Fred?"

"Well Gary, almost every lunch time I frequent local restaurants for a beer and a spot of lunch. Just a few days ago, I passed Conor's and saw a sign on the door stating that Premier League soccer would be shown this Saturday morning. So here I am!"

Fred and I continued to chat for another couple of hours sinking a couple of pints of Guinness each. We both smiled as I toasted the arrival of our "medication" as another round arrived. Our conversation had been so enjoyable that we agreed there and then that "medication time" should become our postmatch ritual.

There I was, a "young fella" of thirty-four, and Fred, a zestful sixty-six years young—two English expats brought together through our love of soccer. It had been a perfect first Saturday watching my beloved Reds in the comfort of Conor O'Neill's. The result and the company had been "spot on."

34

Short Back 'n' Sides

October was proving to be a good month for Manchester United supporters. That emphatic win at the Dell—my first game at Conor O'Neill's—was hopefully a sign of things to come. United's next Premier League fixture was a home game for United against the usually tricky Wimbledon. The founding members of Wimbledon's "Crazy Gang" were no longer playing, but the "Dons" were still a very combative side. This time, however, goals from Giggs, Beckham, Yorke and two from Cole ensured a Red rout: 5-1 to United. The following Wednesday, United demolished Brondby away in Denmark 6-2 in the European Champions League. Des provided fuel for my imagination with his postmatch report, particularly raving about goals from Keane and Solskjær. I smiled to myself as I listened, imagining my father punching the air for each of the United goals.

I couldn't wait to get back to Conor O'Neill's to watch more soccer games, but, as fate would have it, my weekend commitments at work suddenly ramped up, closing that door for a while, just as an Irish pub had opened it's own.

Due to my unfortunate near-term work scenario, I reconsidered all of my otherwise available United supporting alternatives. Nothing was off the table. I reverted back to newspapers from Little Professor, postmatch calls to my father and, of course, some shortwave satisfaction in the form of the BBC's Sportsworld broadcast via the World Service. Then, out of the blue, I mustered a rather unorthodox game plan. It was a stretch, but needs must.

There are certain things an Englishman abroad relies upon, and a decent cup of tea will almost always be close to the top of that list. I realized that America loved its coffee and I was finding a good cuppa hard to come by in Michigan.

Soon after my arrival into the States, my mother had taken it upon herself to provide me with a "tea top-up" direct from the homeland. Two-hundred tea bags were meticulously placed into a Royal Mail jiffy bag, perfectly designed to cushion the contents, and the fresh-smelling brew would arrive safely at my doorstep.

Earlier that same week I had received my latest parcel. Subsequently, a lovely brew was helping me get through some patient note dictations that were keeping me late at work one night. As the drink began stimulating my senses, I hit upon my most ambitious, albeit, rather pathetic attempt yet to maintain my United connection. And so, of all things, a Dictaphone became the central player in my latest quest to receive soccer news from across the Pond.

I purchased an additional small recorder—I would utilize my one from work Stateside—complete with several lengthy audio tapes and shipped them back to Blighty.

I instructed my father how next to proceed.

Initially dumbfounded, most members of my family responded rather predictably.

"What the bloody hell has he sent us this for?"

Then, with some gentle prompting, the fun and games from three generations began. It was great to hear familiar voices, talking about the latest happenings back home, narrowing that Atlantic divide. I would reciprocate, sending heartfelt messages from America's Midwest, a tiny voice recorder slipped into my pocket to capture local accents, interactions and dialogue in and around the neighborhood.

It wasn't long, though, before the equipment soon found its true worth, as my father began recording excerpts from the BBC's flagship Saturday soccer morning show "Football Focus" and mailing the tapes back to Michigan in double quick time. It took me right back to my childhood. On occasion, I would receive a back-to-back special; two weekend shows, one after the other. My father had gladly slipped into roving reporter mode often competing with a West Highland terrier along with my mother screaming at him to "turn that bloody TV down" or "fancy another cuppa, Jimmy?"

The quality wasn't great, but I cared not. I had manufactured another soccer fix, able to listen to more snippets of United news. Tea bags and tiny audio tapes were bundled into a padded parcel for delivery into Dearborn. U.S. Customs and Border Protection had a rather unique combo to deal with. I, on the other hand, had a sneaky slice of British soccer contraband along with a good cuppa.

The weekend of October 24. 1998 arrived and I was able to time manage my on-call shift to commence Saturday lunchtime. Not enough of a window to squeeze in a visit to Conor O'Neill's, but allowing me to revert back to my trusty shortwave radio.

Also that Saturday I figured that I would be able to squeeze in a much needed haircut at Gino's—the no-frills barbershop owned by an Italian American who pulled no punches when it came to his views on the world according to Gino. Conveniently placed about a half mile from where I lived, the conflict of long work days in the week, a soccer season, and on-call duty meant a very short weekend window for the chop. Gino was only open from 9:00 a.m.-ish until 12:30 p.m.-ish each Saturday. I say "-ish"as the doors would open for business depending on the man's mood that particular day. If first in, I could get my ears lowered, and still make it home for 10 a.m. (3 p.m. in England)—i.e., kick-off.

That particular October Saturday, as Gino's came into view, I was pleased to see no cars were parked outside and upped my stride to secure my position as first in line for the swift in and out.

A car soon pulled up right in front of the store. Seconds later, another and then another. I glimpsed at the clock inside, the sun making it hard to read the hands on the face. It appeared to read 9:10 a.m. and there was still no sign of Gino.

The first car that had arrived was sitting right in front of me, a large Crown Victoria, often described as an "old man's bus." Moments later, the passenger door swung open and a husky voice beckoned me over.

"Come on there, boy, get yourself in. It's too cold to be standing out there on a morning like this." Indeed, it was another very chilly fall morning in Michigan.

"Cheers mate, that's very kind of you," I gladly replied.

"The name's Victor Neuman. Nice to meet you, boy," the introduction followed by a shaky, but deliberate, handshake.

"Gary France, Victor. This is great, mate. That heater is most welcome. Bit nippy out there, eh?'

"Never doubt this old motor's ability to deliver, boy."

I was amazed to discover that Victor was all of ninety-four years young. He was in incredible shape. He proudly told me that he was a great grandad several times over and the reason he was out for a haircut was to "look sharp" for his great granddaughter's birthday party. As we continued to put the world to rights for several more minutes, I developed a swift admiration for the gentleman next to me, his self-preservation obvious. I kindly accepted the encouragement Victor gave after I had briefly explained my reason for being out in the States.

"Man, you've come a long ways to end up sittin' next to an old dude, waitin' for a haircut at Gino's, eh son!"

As Victor spoke, the lights came on inside the shop. Victor turned off the engine and reached for his cane before shuffling out of the car. I strode across to the shop door, allowing Victor through to be greeted by a smiling Gino—a little unusual for the normally slow to warm proprietor—as he opened his shop for another day.

"Morning, doc. Victor."

"Morning, Gino," we both responded.

The Italian maestro ambled over to his till, depositing his float for another day at the office. Before Victor took a seat, I told him that I felt like saluting him, noticing his army-like appearance that morning, his perfectly ironed beige colors making him look like a four-star general. Victor smiled and pointed above Gino's chair with his weathered looking waking cane, his other arm in full salute, and there in front of us was a painting of what was obviously the ship and general for whom our master barber had served during his seafaring military past.

"All I need is the cap, Gary, and I'm all set!"

Victor was indeed the spitting image of the man in the painting and the three of us burst out laughing, Gino and I offering our own staunch salute of respect for the old man as I let him go ahead of me to take his position as Gino's first victim.

Gino came out all guns blazing, leaving nothing to the imagination in regard to his opinion on "that lot downtown." That particular October morning, he had all the ammunition he could possibly have wished for as another customer asked him what his thoughts were regarding the imminent implosion of one of Detroit's finest buildings—Hudson's—the huge, one-time bustling department store building which now lay empty and vandalized. Hudson's had been a symbol of Detroit's heyday, but the building had been abandonded for over a decade. Its pending demolition was part of the so-called reformation of Detroit. The media had been all over the story for the last week, and Gino needed no encouragement.

"I tell you what," he said, as he began to chop away at what little hair was left on Victor's head, the old warhorse nervously looking on as the intensity of Gino's chopping increased in tandem with his indignation.

"If we're lucky and those explosives experts have done their job, the whole fucking place might end up blown to the ground, leaving the Detroit River to flood in and swallow the whole fucking place right up!"

I sat quietly, amazed at the response in the shop, as fits of laughter surrounded me. It didn't take a brain surgeon to realize the allegiance of my locals. Victor's hair was getting shorter and shorter as Gino continued with his tirade.

"I tell you, I remember living down there as a kid until those rats drove us all out. Those things were like small dogs. We used to climb onto the roofs of the houses down the back alleyways. On a cold winter's day, we'd pull the icicles off of the gutters and throw our homemade spears down to try and kill those fuckers as they rummaged through the trash. You see, that's what happens when you treat your neighborhood like a landfill, leaving all your shit around for vermin to have a field day with."

I was completely taken aback at the forthright nature of Gino's opinions, along with the collective laughter that surrounded me. The interactions left nothing to the imagination.

On my initial visit to Gino's, I had told him that I was working at the local hospital and Gino had immediately assumed that I was a doctor, despite my initial best efforts to put him straight. He bombarded me with stories of his newborn granddaughter and the excellent treatment his daughter had received at the very same hospital. I decided to play along. My elevated medical status became irresistible. Gino would fire his opinions on everything and anything to all customers present as he worked away on a client's hair. The opinions would fly back thick and fast from all corners. Most of the time, I would just sit in silence. Then, after his usual predictable pause and a dip of his clippers, he would look for me.

"Hey, so what do you think, doc?"

I would just smile, offering little in the way of a reply, happy to play sidekick, the whole shop staring at me wondering who the hell I was, before returning their gaze to Gino as he rattled on. I was his "silent partner," consulted on everything from the effects of a local landfill to the ever-increasing Arabic population in the area.

"Hey, so what do you think, doc?"

On every visit to Gino's, such was the passion of his diatribe, I could never get a word in. On the rare occasion that I did have the chance to reply, I would take every opportunity to play up my newly-promoted medical status, happy to play my role of doctor in the world according to Gino. I would return many times to that barbershop always to be greeted with the same three words: "Good morning, doc!"

My ten-minute walk home passed quickly as the chill wind nipped at my freshly-shaven head. I shot into the apartment and quickly tuned into the BBC World Service's Sportsworld in anticipation of the day's fixtures. Second half commentary imminent, I heard a report from Pride Park, Derby. United were being held 0-0.

I eagerly awaited any news flash from the match. Then, with a quarter of an hour remaining, "There's been a goal at Pride Park!"

The commentator's voice began to pick up as I listened closely: "Powell whips it in and there's Burton. Derby County take the lead. And I must say, a deserved lead it is, too." United equalized near the death, demonstrating their resilience, leaving Derbyshire with a point. One week later, it was Everton and yet another away victory for the Red Devils, destroying the Toffees with an energetic 4-1 win. The commentary roundup that day out of London describing a good display from Blomqvist yet again, the Swede showing persistence as he scored the fourth with his head at the second attempt. It was a relevant goal because the next day I received a phone message that was unmistakable.

"Great save, but it is not enough. It's four for Manchester United and they are *rampant!*" It was a recorded snippet of commentary courtesy of Red, one that had the American declaring his obsession with his new favorite English adjective. Although he did state that he was still very much enamored by "wanker, tosser and bollocks," *rampant* was to become Frank's word of choice whenever United took control of a match.

November rolled in and, with it, the news that Peter Schmeichel, United's brilliant Danish goalkeeper, was to retire at the end of the season. Des dropped the bombshell as we talked early one morning. We both agreed that so much had been written about Cantona and his influence on the Manchester United title-winning teams of the recent past, but that surely Schmeichel had had as much influence himself. The season we had chased Keegan's Newcastle, so many 1-0 wins had been possible only thanks to the Great Dane.

On November 4, United were "rampant" against Brondby at Old Trafford, with a 5-0 win. That same evening, Barcelona had been beaten by Bayern Munich, leaving the Reds nicely poised to progress to the latter stages of the European Champions League.

On November 14, it was time for another visit to Conor O'Neill's, this time to watch United take on Blackburn Rovers. I arrived in Ann Arbor around 9:30 a.m. and was pleased to see my new friend, "Regal" Fred Montague, standing outside the pub in anticipation of the game ahead. Charlie the cook played savior, relieving us from a possible soaking, offering us a place inside whilst he finished cleaning up.

Fred and I walked over to a small penned-in area right in front of the screen, made unique by the inclined wheelchair-friendly ramp enabling alternative access. There was a decent amount of chairs around and I took it upon myself to begin shuffling several into place, ready for Red and Chinny's arrival. I suppose I was instinctively preparing our stand, our forum in which we could come together as a unique band of soccer brothers.

Several minutes later, the lads began to filter in. Along with Red and Chinny was the familiar face of Jacob, the Liverpool fan I had last seen way back in the days of the Britannia Club. His faithful, now somewhat tighter, bright yellow Liverpool shirt emblazoned with its Crown Paints logo still his favored match day attire.

As usual, there was a slight panic as a tired-looking Johnny tried to catch the satellite reception. At precisely ten minutes after ten we were blessed with Old Trafford in full view. The pitch looked a mess, but the soccer from United was spot on, with Scholes and Yorke scoring two crackers to give United a 2-0 half-time lead.

During the half-time interval I managed to get over and chat with a lad who was wearing a United shirt.

"Hey, mate. My name's Gary. They're playing well again, eh?"

"Yeah man! I'm Ahmed. That pitch looks like shit though doesn't it?"

I discovered that Ahmed originated from Jordan and was studying at the University of Michigan. I went on to ask him how he had become a United fan.

"I have an uncle who went to university in Manchester and many years ago he sent me a United goalie shirt."

I smiled as Ahmed joked about how he wouldn't have enjoyed the last few years as much if that shirt had been from Liverpool.

"No kidding, man!"

The young Jordanian was a welcome addition to the crew as he settled in with the lads in our newly-named "Conor's Paddock" for the second half.

The next forty-five minutes had everything, with Beckham's histrionics getting under the skin of Tim Sherwood, the Blackburn captain, the latter eventually receiving a red card. After a terrific finish from Scholes, United were coasting at 3-0—or so we thought. In the blink of an eye, Blackburn's ten men made it 3-2. After another shaky defensive performance, United managed to hang on for the three points.

Medication time.

Regal Fred ordered our pints of Guinness and we were joined by our new Middle Eastern friend Ahmed, as well as Chinny, who opted for his prescription of Newcastle Brown. A South Korean American Liverpool fanatic drinking Newcastle Brown and a Jordanian with a liking for Guinness and Manchester United. I reveled in the diversity surrounding me that day.

Fred began the proceedings by telling us of his latest venture—opening a soccer school in Costa Rica. "As you do," Ahmed jokingly remarked, taking his first sip of stout.

"I invested in a property by the sea over there four years ago, which happens to have a substantial area of land adjacent to it—ideal for a soccer pitch or two. We have goalposts, kits and the pitch is beginning to resemble a decent playing surface. Some of the local kids there are already showing real potential. The school has begun to develop a real reputation, so much so that there has even been contact from the Italian side Perugia who recently purchased second division Costa Rican side Guanacaste with a view to developing it as a farm team. Isn't that amazing?"

Our newly-elected soccer patriarch had brought some photographs along with him. It was a beautiful property with incredible seascapes, a bright blue-sky blending with the rolling water. Practicing in those surroundings would have had me turning up for training every day eager to put on my boots and play.

Fred became most animated as he showed off photographs of the young soccer players, ranging between the ages of seven and thirteen.

"You can teach kids anything if you get them young enough. The focal point is becoming totally acquainted with that soccer ball. We want it to become second nature." The smiling faces on the photographs were a testament to the opportunity the school would provide to the kids to develop their soccer skills.

The three of us wished Fred every success with his venture, reminding him, not that we needed to, that a certain fella called Paulo Wanchope had originated from those same shores.

"Oh my goodness, the kids there idolize him," Fred added.

As time approached 2:00 p.m., everyone shook hands, wishing each other well for the week ahead, looking forward to the next time Conor O'Neill's dished up another Premier League game. A Jordanian, a Korean American, and two Englishmen had thoroughly enjoyed each other's company and an outstanding morning of soccer coverage.

As I exited the back door of Conor's, I was blinded by the afternoon sunshine as I was once again cast into the reality of the outside world. As I made my way toward my car, I smiled to myself. Our clan of socer fanatics at Conor O'Neill's was beginning to take shape.

35

Play of the Day

"Gary, I'll take it, mate!"

All said and done, United were second in the league behind Aston Villa and well-placed in the Champions League. Who was I to disagree?

Red and I were chatting early Monday morning to review the weekend's results. It seemed Americans were constantly on the phone during worktime, so I decided "when in Rome." The center of our conversation that morning was the match that coming Wednesday against Barcelona at the Camp Nou. Red immediately offered to record the game and resist watching any of it allowing me to get over there later that evening. No need for Dearborn Dorothy this time.

I thanked Red for his consideration.

"Absolutely, you tosser!" came the warm repost from my United friend and American wordsmith.

Wednesday, November 25, duly arrived, and, along with it, a classic European Champions League encounter.

I bolted from work, bidding a good evening to our receptionist Hannah as she blurted out "Go United!" By this point, my work colleagues were well aware of my love of Manchester United, despite having no clue as to what on earth a European Champions League was. The sentiments were appreciated all the same.

Red was not your typical American. He had ducked out of the rat race, opting for quiet family life in a bohemian corner of town. He loved his culture; a knowledgeable art, music, and film critic, he spent most days at home working as a freelance writer. He enjoyed talking about what life in Europe must be like. I sensed his connection to its more laid back culture. "You British appear to have the right balance when it comes to life man," he would say. "Corporate America" were swear words to the Rocks. Red's wife Nina's involvement in all things environmental was testament to that. She worked tirelessly in the Ann Arbor community supporting as many green policies as she could. Obviously besotted with his lovely wife and their son, Red was terrific company for those big United nights.

We took up our positions that evening in front of Red's television, a whole continent away from the match. The fervor and deafening roar of both sets of supporters in the Camp Nou, baying for each other's blood, came across surprisingly well on the American coverage.

"C'mon lads," I bellowed from my gut as the referee blew his whistle to start the encounter. Only seconds into the game, the American commentator provided us with the commentary neither one of us wanted to hear. "It's a disastrous start for Manchester United. Sonny Anderson makes it 1-0 to Barcelona."

A great finish and how well he celebrated it too, firing his imitation bullets in a fast tirade into the crowd as he sprinted back to the halfway line. The Spanish crowd rose to their feet in unison and you would have been forgiven for thinking that United were about to be gunned down with consummate ease.

Red reminded me of the many occasions United had fallen behind to an early goal. It wasn't long before Blomqvist once again justified his place, playing a simple, but effective, pass into the path of Dwight Yorke as the rest of the Barcelona defense were caught napping. Yorke let the ball do all the work, one-touch from his right foot and, then, bang!

1-1!

The second half got even better. As six Barcelona defenders stood between Keane and the two United strikers, the Irishman swiftly drilled a ball into Yorke's feet. The scorer of United's first goal nonchalantly dummied the pass, fully aware of the position of his strike partner. Andy Cole returned the favor, Yorke obliged again, and Cole cooly finished one of the best goals you will see in any corner of the soccer world. It was a one-two of the highest quality on one of the greatest stages in the world.

The game continued at an incredible pace, and soon the Spanish side responded.

A shot from Rivaldo deflected off the United wall, and I witnessed the intent and determination on the face of the Brazilian as he marshalled his troops, beckoning them to find that higher gear in order to finish off Manchester United. It was an ominous sight as the Spanish side sprinted back and the home crowd's celebrations erupted.

2-2!

Red turned to me. "Gary, this is the moment for United to show us what they got, right?" My American friend had nailed the situation.

David Beckham was beginning to get the better of the Spanish left full back and Red and I met in the middle of the room in mid air as Yorke came close with a clinical header, once again the cross reaching him from the foot of the Englishman. Moments later, same combination, but a much better result, as Beckham's first-time cross was met by Yorke's diving header catching the whole Spanish defense napping.

Yes! United were back in front. 2-3 to United.

The defiant celebratory scenes on the Manchester United bench said it all. The team wanted to come away from this one with the rest of Europe totally aware of their European aspirations.

As the two of us willed United on to a famous victory, Rivaldo took the game by the horns. Barcelona moved into their most dominating phase of the game. A cross from Sergi dissected two United defenders and landed onto the chest of the Brazilian who brilliantly controlled it and produced an overhead kick that left the Great Dane standing still and wondering where the hell it had come from. A truly magnificent strike!

3-3!

Rivaldo continued to take the game to the Reds. An incredible shot from all of twenty-five yards rocketed against the bar. The Spanish Giants smelled blood. There were back heels, swift off the ball movement, and Schmeichel had to earn his money in those last few minutes. However, in the end, United held on. Red and I knew we had witnessed a very special match.

"Wow Gary! Wow! That, my friend, was a soccer match!"

I was persuaded to hang with the family for dinner as Nina returned home from work. Nina prepared a vegan meal—a rather tasty mix of soy-based sausage and veggie burgers, surrounded by an array of crisp vegetables and organic potato chips. I imagined the contrast to how my aftermatch antics would have been back in Blighty. Probably stood with a pint, nibbling at a bag of pork scratchings, ready to round it all off with a meat pie and chips or "batter bits 'n' gravy" on the walk home from the pub. The alternative brand of match hospitality from my Ann Arbor friends that night was a most enjoyable substitute.

As we were finishing up our meal, the TV in the background, sound muted, was displaying the main ESPN channel and its round up from the world of sports. ESPN aired a daily segment called "Play of the Day," a quick, exciting piece conveying the most skillfully executed or poignant play from the world of baseball, basketball, NFL football, or ice hockey.

"Pass me the remote, please honey," Red requested of Nina as he bit the top off a carrot—organic of course.

"Hey Gary, you wanker, look at this!"

We stared at the screen, the picture portraying the Camp Nou and the unmistakable American accents from ESPN's studio screamed the name "Rivaldooooo!" as we were reminded once again of the nature of that brilliant overhead kick by the Brazilian.

"See that, Englishman? ESPN excited about a *soccer* play! Now that is quite something!"

Could soccer possibly be nudging itself a little further into U.S. mainstream sports culture?

With that, I bid Red and the "Family Rock" a good night and thanked my hosts for providing me the opportunity to savor such a titanic Champions League battle . . . and a half decent tofu sausage!

36

Filling Up the Ranks

Saturday November 28: A dull morning, the damp air reminiscent of northern English drizzle—or as we like to say in Lancashire, spit— making me feel right at home as I hit the freeway for Ann Arbor.

Arriving around 9:30 a.m., I was pleased to see that a small posse was already assembled on the pavement outside Conor O'Neill's. Jacob and Chinny couldn't believe that I had turned up for a game that didn't feature Manchester United; Chelsea and Sheffield Wednesday the two teams landing on the screen at Conor's that day.

"Just wanted to see how the other half lives, fellas," I immediately replied.

10:00 a.m. arrived and there was still no sign of life inside our haven. A tall fella who I hadn't seen before started to get irate, banging on the windows and making the point that his beloved Chelsea were playing. He wanted in pronto. His noisy protest reverberated, echoing around Main Street. Within seconds, Charlie the cook emerged, declaring that Johnny was on his way. One by one, our band of soccer diehards slipped past Charlie and into the inviting warmth of the pub. "About bloody time," I couldn't help hearing, as the tall bloke passed by Charlie. Sure enough, Johnny soon appeared and immediately slid into the cubby hole to rapturous, if yet most sarcastic, applause. He looked knackered.

The rather impatient Chelsea fan couldn't seem to let it go, continuing his rant, letting Johnny know that he was none too happy with how his early Saturday morning had started. The Conor O'Neill's Manager for that day was having none of it, not even rising to the jibes, as he continued fiddling away with the satellite system. A flicker of the screen, accompanied by a deafening fizz on the audio sound system, and Stamford Bridge appeared, baked in autumnal sunshine. We all shot to our self-styled Conor O'Neill's paddock.

Chelsea had started well and it wasn't long before they had taken the lead with a goal from Zola. The writing was on the wall for a rout. However, Sheffield Wednesday made it through to half-time without conceding further, the Blues holding on to that one goal lead in a game that was fast deteriorating, much to the disdain of our Chelsea fan.

I wandered over to introduce myself.

"Chelsea letting it slip a bit, eh mate?"

"Fuck me! I don't know what's going on. They come out all guns blazing and now it looks like they can't be fucking arsed."

"Let's hope for a better second half, eh mate? My name's Gary!"

"Yeah, mate. Peter Cavendish. Nice to meet you. Shit, what about this place getting their fucking act together, eh? Five past ten and still no sign of the fucking staff. I've had it mate, I'm telling ya. They don't give a shit. We come in here at night, spending all our money and they can't be arsed when it comes to arranging the soccer. I am not happy, mate! Not happy at all!"

I soon realized that Peter, with his obvious Type A tendencies, was none too happy with life in general at that moment in time: angst and negativity enveloped his persona.

"Come on, mate," I responded. "How privileged are we. We're thousands of miles away from home here."

"No fucking excuse, mate!" "Blue Peter" was having none of it!

The second half of the match basically came and went. Sheffield Wednesday scored a deserved equalizer and the game ended 1-1. Despite it being an "uninspiring bag of shite," according to Peter, for most everyone else present, the match had provided another much-needed top up of expat soccer fans' comradery.

Postmatch "medication" was provided courtesy of Regal Fred as we awaited the final scores on the big screen in front of us. The pub had begun to leave the satellite feed on for ten minutes or so after the match to allow the punters the chance to see how the other teams in the Premier League had fared that day. Muffled acknowledgements matched subtly-clenched fists as supporters recognized their own team's result, much to the intrigue of the general public arriving for lunch.

As the postmatch Guinness went down, our new friend, Blue, made his way over. I discovered that the Chelsea fan, originally from Croydon in south west London, was currently in between jobs, as he had been helping his wife of several years establish herself within the ranks of General Motors. He told me that she was dealing with the recent spate of strikes in and around Michigan and was very involved, noting that his third marriage was currently on the rocks and that he'd hoped for a "pick me up" from his beloved Blues that day.

Soccer as a tonic for marital woes? A far stretch maybe. I sensed the genuine anguish in Blue's voice as he continued.

"I reckon I'm totally heading for a divorce, mate. My wife is all about the career thing and doesn't seem to understand the word compromise if you know what I mean."

It's funny how people just "spill it all out" sometimes even though you have only just met them. I was beginning to notice a definite sense of getting straight to the point when conversing with expats. Maybe it was simply due to that instant connection with a fellow countryman amid the unfamiliar?

It appeared that the ladies had certainly given our Blue a run for his money over the years. I joked as to the secret of his youthful appearance, immediately thinking that after three marriages, a couple of daughters in their twenties, and with him also being a Chelsea fan, he had every right to be a bedraggled, wrinkled mess.

"Yeah, very funny, mate. It's my genes, Gary. My dad died at ninety-four and he had me when he was fifty-four."

My parting words for the Chelsea fan later that afternoon: "Try and remember all the names on the Chelsea teamsheet by the next time we all meet at the bar," a reference to Chelsea's unique "league of nations" of players. Blue laughed and, shaking my hand, wished me all the best, expressing how he had enjoyed our chat. He told me that it might be a while before he next hit Conor's, due to his present circumstances, but once things were more settled on the domestic front, he would be in for a much needed tonic with the lads.

The following day presented Manchester United with a tough game at home to Leeds United. The "Des Hotline" came to my rescue. Radio Five had provided my father's own connection to the game back in Scotland and he gladly passed on the news of a 3-2 Manchester United victory. As November came to a close, United remained second, a solitary point behind Aston Villa.

December arrived, and, with it, United secured a 1-1 draw at Aston Villa, who had been holding top spot for several weeks. This was followed by more midweek European Champions League action when United played host to Bayern Munich. Time once again for Operation Dearborn Dorothy.

Six o'clock that evening, after an uneventful work day, I fumbled around in the now familiar mailbox and grabbed my VHS lifeline. The prospect of a place in the European Champions League quarter finals was at stake.

"It may get a tad noisy, Rhonda," I said, waving my videotape in the air as I acknowledged my landlady on my way toward my apartment.

"Go United!" she replied, her mad smile barely visible through a steamed up kitchen window.

Tape in. Game on! With just two minutes of the first half remaining, Beckham swept a long ball across field to Giggs who controlled the pass, weaved his magic, and delivered a beautifully placed pass to the edge of the Bayern box where Roy Keane rifled a shot low into the back of the net. Tommy Smyth "with a Y" time, the ESPN commentator, declaring the "auld onion bag" to be well and truly bulging, his Irish accent appropriate for the wonder strike from United's Republic of Ireland captain.

The half-time broadcast remained unbearable, with the same four or five infomercials on heavy rotation. The airspace was filled with pitches to flog anything, despite the demographic being that of soccer fans: some quirky engineering masterpiece designed to make chopping carrots and onions quicker; some cheeky bloke with a cockney accent trying to flog us a psychedelic colored multipurpose rag and mop. There was even a psychic inviting calls and promising to enlighten prospective clients on what path in life may well lay ahead of them. The only ad close to being at all relevant for a majority male audience was a five-minute men's hair replacement infomercial with its laughable side profiles of tubby middle-aged men surrounded by women half their age who wouldn't normally look twice, seductively running their fingers through the hair of the male studs, attempting to entice the audience to rid themselves of those frustrating years of baldness. Thank God for fast forward!

Fifteen minutes into the second half, Bayern equalized. The game eventually petered out to a draw, which meant that both teams would qualify for the knockout stages of the European Champions League.

United had done it! Once the Champions League recommenced in February 1999, United would be back in the hunt for that elusive European crown.

In the lead up to Christmas, United earned a 2-2 away at Tottenham followed by another draw at Old Trafford, this time with Chelsea.

December 19: My alarm went off. To be honest I'd been awake a while, the anticipation of another soccer escape on my mind. It was still dark outside, no surprise as it was just two days shy of the calendar's shortest day. Once I was dressed and ready, I quietly stepped out into the driveway of Hotel Hairpiece. I started the car and slowly reversed out. I couldn't ignore the closed curtains of the homestead. Rhonda must still have been two sheets to the wind. Minutes later I was heading onto I-94, destination Conor O'Neill's. Daylight began to break as I blazed my trail west. I eventually reached downtown Ann Arbor and smiled at the mass of Christmas lights adorning the trees lining the sidewalks on either side of Main Street. I considered that it may be a good idea to turn them back on as a way of illuminating the dank and dreary early morning sky above me. It was the final Saturday before Christmas and yet hardly a soul was out. I swung left around the back of Main Street and into the parking lot. I got out of my vehicle and contemplated the silence as I took a quick stretch. Moments later, I sauntered over towards Conor O'Neill's, only to discover that the back doors were locked. As I turned around, I practically bumped into two blokes, looking like Tweedledee and Tweedledum. They must have wandered up through the alleyway. Both had big grins, their bodies tightly wrapped in the authentic red Sharp-sponsored shirts of Manchester United, each wearing a United scarf.

"Morning lads. No guesses as to who you're following, then?"

"Too right! So what time do they normally open? Isn't the game at ten?"

"Well, knowing this place, mate, we might make it in by half-time. Listen, my name's Gary. Good to meet you."

With that I offered my hand and as I shook the first bloke's hand, I felt like I had seen him before. Then it dawned on me.

"Did you guys used to go to the Britannia Club?"

"Yeah! Sure did! Never missed a Man U game. What a place. My name's Den and this is Don."

"Couldn't make that up really could you, fellas."

"Yeah, I guess not," Den replied, looking somewhat confused.

"The United double," I added, thankful my comment was met with a mutual hearty laugh.

"We're totally good with that!' replied Don.

As we stood and chatted for a few more minutes, Red and Regal Fred appeared. I introduced them to Michigan's own Manchester United double act and it wasn't long before a smiling Connie, on duty that day, opened the doors to another Saturday morning of soccer.

As we walked into our haven once again, Den began to tell me how he had recently heard that Conor O'Neill's was showing live Premier League games, prompting him to call his old mate Don to come along. Their hour-or-so journey from Michigan's capital city, Lansing, was made even sweeter once they found out that there was no cover charge. Den and Don excitedly prepared themselves for their first Conor O'Neill's experience to watch United take on Middlesborough.

Middlesborough had started the game well, capitalizing on a poor defensive display from United and were two goals to the good by half-time. During the break, I chatted more with the United double act, intrigued as to how their passion for all things Manchester United had come to be. Den filled me in.

"I started playing soccer when I was about eight. Pele was the hero of just about every young soccer fan in the U.S., mainly because we hadn't really heard of any others! It wasn't until several years later, when I started to appreciate the finer aspects of the game, that I began to look toward the professional leagues for inspiration."

At that point, Regal Fred joined us and became captivated, asking Den whether he could recall the first ever game he had watched.

"I faintly remember watching the '86 World Cup final. After that I started picking up issues of *Soccer America* to read about the European teams, since there was no regular soccer on American TV. That changed in 1990 when TNT started to show World Cup games."

It was during the late 1980's that Den had, in his own words, become drawn towards Manchester United.

"I had a good friend whose grandfather was from England. He was a Liverpool fan so I had to support Manchester United, just to irritate him right? Trying to keep up with United with little or no access though was tough. I would check the scores in *Soccer America*, which were usually a week or two behind. I do remember being very excited to watch the FA Cup final in 1994, even though that presentation was a week old!"

Den said that the first live game he ever saw United play was the first leg of a 1994 European Champions League tie with Barcelona at Old Trafford. ESPN was broadcasting Champions League games that year. He remembered the match in detail, even the fact that United had not lost a game in European competition on their own patch for forty years. He took great delight in describing the cheeky back heel by Lee Sharpe, leveling things up against Barcelona that night.

"Yeah, well let's not mention the return leg at the Camp Nou," I replied.

"How did you meet Don, Den?" I asked, untwisting my tongue after the question.

"We met at Michigan State. We quickly became friends, our passion for the game obviously helping. It was Don that introduced me to the Britannia Club, where he would often go to see weekend satellite broadcasts of the games. We'd have to get up before dawn for those early games, but we loved it. My first trip to the Britannia was for a game between United and Sheffield Wednesday, late in the 94–95 season. We won that game 1-0 with a goal from David May in the fifth minute. Believe it or not, though, due to satellite difficulties, we didn't even get to see the goal."

I always found it such a fascinating side script to the soccer experience abroad, learning how various supporters had come to follow their teams and how they had come to connect with the beautiful game in the first place.

"For the next few seasons, we visited the Britannia Club whenever possible, despite the two-hour drive from Lansing," Den commented.

At this point, Red joined us and I explained that Den and Don were two of the United clan across the room from us at the Britannia Club. They both received a high five.

"Mate, Reggie was the best, wasn't he?" as I made reference to the King of the Britannia.

"For sure, man! I loved the way he used to announce the cars that were illegally parked and warn us all what would happen if they weren't moved. He was a pretty serious dude. I have to tell ya, the one thing I loved the most was that English steak pie and chips. I had it every time I went there, along with a pint of Boddingtons, of course."

"Lads, what would be your greatest memory from the Britannia Club then?" I offered, sounding like a TV correspondent by this time.

Don responded immediately: "Oh man, it's gotta be the one where King Eric scored the winner with only five minutes to go to beat Liverpool. The place was packed. Standing room only. The United fans went absolutely berserk!"

As the big screen at Conor O'Neill's indicated United's imminent return for the second half, Don quickly finished off his story.

"I have to tell you guys quickly before the game restarts. I actually made it to Old Trafford in May '97. It was with the USA United Supporters Club. The match was the season finale against West Ham. We'd already clinched the Premier League title by the time the game took place and it made for an incredible party atmosphere. Just being there, seeing United lift the trophy for the fourth time in five years was truly amazing, but of course it was tinged with a hint of sadness, with it being King Eric's final game for United."

"Hey, not too shabby a game to get over for when you look back in years to come, eh?" I commented.

With that, we drifted back to our seats, hoping that United would oblige with a "comeback of comebacks" in the next forty-five minutes.

As Nicky Butt powered a header into the net and Paul Scholes rifled in a second for the Reds, I had an immediate flashback to the Britannia Club, as Den and Don indulged in their own boisterous display of Red celebration. Red and I couldn't help but to join in. United's late surge wasn't enough though as Middlesborough held on to win it.

Final score: 2-3.

Despite the final score, it had been a cracker of a first game for the "new lads" at Conor O'Neill's. Slowly, but surely, we were filling up the ranks inside our new soccer den.

37

An American "Gooner"

It wasn't even Christmas and with over half of the season remaining, the holy prophet, Mr. Arsene Wenger, had already announced that the English Premier League title was out of reach for his Arsenal team. The mind games had begun in earnest.

December 20, 1998: It was Arsenal's turn to face a youthful Leeds United. I wanted to form my own opinion on the reemergence of the Whites among the Premier League high-flyers and, so, headed for Conor O'Neill's. Unseasonably warm for late December, with the temperature a crazy 70 degrees Fahrenheit, I wound down my driver's side window as I shot along I-94 at 8-30 a.m. A scorching sun on my face was not what I would ever have expected five days before Christmas in Michigan. As they say "If you don't like the weather in Michigan, wait five minutes and it will change." Well that particular day it didn't, and it remained positively balmy for the entire weekend.

Reaching Ann Arbor, I was greeted by the sight of early morning joggers and a bustling hive of activity indicative of a community more than happy with winter's delay. So what did I decide to do with the gift of a gloriously resplendent sunny day in late December? Sit in a dimly-lit Irish bar for pretty much all of the daylight hours!

Most of the lads were there that morning, appearing to have made the same decision. I passed a sarcastic comment that because Manchester United were not playing, the staff appeared to have made an extra effort to get up on time to set up the satellite well before the start of the game. Johnny just smiled and tuned us in to Highbury, north London.

Regal Fred had brought a friend whose allegiance was most apparent, given the brightly-colored Gunners scarf around his neck. He introduced us all to Cliff Miller, the Arsenal obsessive. Cliff attempted to shake everyone's hand while hardly taking his eyes off the screen, as Arsenal took to the field.

"C'mon Arsenal! Let's go you Gunners. Yeah!"

Having heard that our Saturday morning crew contained a number of Manchester United supporters, Cliff appeared ready for war. He was vehement in his vocal support for the Gunners, chastising Fergie's men, as the referee blew his whistle for the start of the game.

Cliff had a definite air of authority about him. He appeared focused and intense. His piercing glare at the television screen provided claear evidence as to his passion for the team from North London. Without averting his eyes from the scenes over at Highbury, he reminded us that: "You lot couldn't even beat Middlesborough yesterday. Come on you Gunners!" declaring Middlesborough his current second favorite team. The early morning serenity of our Premier League experience was being sabotaged by none other than an American Gooner. I loved it!

As the game got underway, Arsenal struggled, with Leeds hounding them at every attempt. The first twenty minutes were not a pretty sight for our newest crew member. However, after twenty-six minutes we were given our first chance to experience the bizarre vocal celebrations of one Mr. Clifford Miller, Bergkamp's brilliant finish finding the top corner of the Leeds net.

"Whey hey! Whey hey! Come ooon you Arsssse! Whey hey! Let's go, let's go, let's go!"

"What the hell was all that about?" I motioned to Red, both us a tad disturbed by our new recruit's rather strange reaction. I rolled my eyes at Fred in search of an explanation of the Gooner's antics. Fred just shrugged his shoulders and smiled.

Seven minutes into the second half and Vieira, beating two Leeds defenders, slipped the ball past the Leeds keeper to give the Gunners a 2-0 lead.

"Whey hey! Whey hey! Come ooon you Arsssse!"

He was off again, his outburst this time accompanied by some very loud applause that ricocheted off the pub's four walls.

Hasselbaink pulled one back for Leeds and Cliff's head bowed briefly as he scowled at the Arsenal defense. Then it was all over. Petit hammered one into the far corner, making it 3-1 Arsenal. Or rather I should say:

"Whey Hey 3, Leeds 1!"

As the game came to an end, a couple more "Whey hey's" and a "Come ooon you Arsssse's!" later, I managed to grab a little of the Gooner disciple's time. I was fast realizing that behind most of the fans that met in our newly titled "soccer pub," there was always an interesting back story.

This was very much the case with Cliff Miller.

The Arsenal fan was born in England and was most certainly articulate, radiating an air of importance. He told me that he had moved to the U.S. when he was twelve years old. Cliff went on to describe, with vigor, his love of the game and how he became a founding member of the Ann Arbor Soccer Association.

"I was the first person to give Ann Arbor a soccer club, which, of course, I named Ann Arbor Arsenal!"

Fred interjected. "Gary, you remember when we were talking about how Michigan Stadium would have been ideal for hosting the World Cup in '94? Well, Cliff was a part of the Michigan World Cup Committee that was was instrumental in the city's attempt to bring it here. Boy, how he tried, but the U of M just didn't want to know. If it wasn't for the U's strong allegiance to American football, Ann Arbor may well have played a part that year."

Cliff continued. "I got to know most of the people on the U.S. Soccer World Cup Committee. I fought tooth and nail for the Ann Arbor cause."

Cliff felt that the University had truly missed out on a golden opportunity by stubbornly sticking to its football principles.

"We all agreed that it would have been a terrific venue. 110,000 seats crammed tightly together making for a brilliant atmosphere. The stadium is less than a mile from downtown with tons of vendors ready and willing to accept the boost in trade. In the end, our influence did pay off somewhat and we were able to secure three World Cup matches to be played in Michigan, but up in Pontiac at the Silverdome. It wasn't the Big House, but World Cup soccer had made it to Michigan. We were very proud of that. The Silverdome had artificial turf and so thousands of green sods had to be flown in. We were then able to turn the pitch into a World Cup standard playing field."

Cliff, Fred, and I continued to chat.

"Gary, did you know that Cliff's father actually died at the Battle of El Alamein, fighting alongside Montgomery no less. That final hurdle of the WWII desert campaign."

"Wow! I have no words," I responded. "Oh wait a minute, yeah I do . . . no wonder you decided to support a soccer team called the Gunners, eh Cliff?"

"That's one way of summing it up, Gary," Cliff replied, the three of us smiling before sipping our beer in unison, three soccer fanatics killing time postmatch in our very own soccer pub. I had thoroughly enjoyed meeting such an interesting and devout soccer fan that morning. A man whom it appeared had done so much to try to promote the beautiful game in the USA, both locally and nationally.

Four days later and Christmas Eve rolled in and, with it, the obvious pull of home, family, and friends. In Michigan, Christmas Eve seemed to have a totally different feel than in the UK. Ann Arbor resembled a ghost town with most establishments closed by early afternoon. There was a strong emphasis on family time, with most people beginning their festive celebrations in a more sedate manner at home, as opposed to the packed and raucous pubs back "home."

The Premier League, with its jam-packed festive program, helped to maintain a true sense of Christmas for an English expat. Courtesy of my shortwave radio, I received the gift of a Manchester United home win against Nottingham Forest.

Five days later, on my return home from work, Des told me that the crunch game between United and Chelsea had ended in a 0-0 draw, with Schmeichel saving our skin with a brilliant save from the ever-dangerous Zola. And so, as 1998 came to a close, the top of the English Premier League read as follows:

1. Aston Villa	39 points
2. Chelsea	37 points
3. Manchester United	35 points
4. Arsenal	35 points

With twenty games played, the "big guns" were taking aim for the Premier League title. I was pretty sure that we would be seeing Mr. Cliff Miller—our American Gooner—at Conor O'Neill's a tad more often.

38

A Trip to Rome— but No Treble

I made the phone call to Connie late in the day on January 2, 1999. The Conor O'Neill's manager confirmed that they would be showing the Manchester United vs. Middlesborough game the following morning. The two teams had been drawn together for the third round of the FA Cup just weeks after Boro's shock win at Old Trafford.

The usual suspects were camped outside the front door of Conor's by 9:20 a.m. The FA Cup excitement had inspired the early risers. It was bitterly cold. Our soccer faithful were unwavering, though, battle-hardened in their dedication to the cause. Fred was spotted jogging up the road, putting us all to shame with his rhythmic pace, his breath clearly visible in the cold winter morning air.

As the clock closed in on 10:00 a.m., we began to grow anxious and several of the lads began banging on the door. Out popped Charlie as always, teasing us that we would have to wait until they had finished cleaning up from the night before. Even he knew today was a special day on the soccer calendar as he announced "FA Cup day, right?"

"Too right! Come on Charlie boy, let's be gettin' in mate!"

"How about getting the kettle on, fella? It's bloody freezing out there," I suggested, as we hustled in and headed for the paddock.

The screen had been pulled down and Danny the barman was attempting to nail a picture. "Ah, this fucking bastard has been playin' up. Come on, fer fucks sake!" Danny was a man of few words, most of them swear words, all in his thick Irish drawl. As he continued to struggle, we all took the piss. "Hey, shut the fuck up, will yuz," was all that could be heard from inside the cubbyhole below the screen. We had to wait until five minutes into the game before Old Tafford appeared. It was a gloriously sunny January afternoon in Manchester.

Red gave me a high five. Chinny, predictably, bellowed "Come on Middlesborough!" Another morning's entertainment was set to begin.

We then noticed a familiar face over to our far right. It was none other than Eddie, the United fan from the Britannia Club. We hadn't seen him in ages. Eddie introduced his friend Jack, who, by the look of the latest United home shirt he was wearing, was another Red Devil to swell the ranks at Conor's. Such was everyone's focus on the game about to commence, it was only a swift hello before Eddie and Jack bid a hasty retreat to a free table behind us, eyes already fixated on the big screen above us.

United had begun well with their usual attacking mindset when at home, laying down a marker in the opposition's half. With a short break in play, commentator Martin Tyler made the point that it had been ten years since Andy Townsend had popped one in during an FA Cup game when, of course, fate duly responded. Completely against the run of play, Boro won a free kick which was lofted high towards the edge of the United box. Letting the ball do all the work, Townsend, right on cue, slipped it agonizingly across Schmeichel and into the United goal.

Middlesborough had the lead, as Danny howled from behind the bar, his cries of joy met with equal enthusiasm by all of the other non-United fans scattered around the bar. Surely lightning couldn't strike twice for Boro at Old Trafford?

Half-time arrived and I headed over to chat with Eddie and his mate, my chance to reacquaint myself with a Britannia comrade. I hadn't seen him at all in Conor's since the Irish bar had opened its door to the early Premier League and FA Cup soccer traffic.

"Not too good at the mo, eh lads?"

"Gary, mate! How ya doin'? Here, meet my mate Jack."

Alright, Jack? Great to meet you mate. How's it going?"

"Good to meet you Gary. Another Red Devil, eh," Eddie's friend added. I instantly recognized his North West English accent.

"Absolutely, mate. Seems like we have safety in numbers now, eh."

"No doubt, mate. No doubt," Jack agreed.

"What about this then, eh? No more long drives to Warren," Eddie exclaimed, adding "I couldn't believe it when I first heard about it. So close to home. I've been so fuckin' busy with the family and work, but gotta free up the schedule for the weekend fix now, right?"

"Yeah, life can get in the way, eh fellas. This is me now most Saturdays and Sundays for the matches that matter, as long as I can dodge the on-call at the hospital."

"I think we'll be doin' the same, mate. I am sure my wife will be glad to see the back of me for a couple of hours" said Jack.

"So what do you reckon second half?" I asked

"Long way to go yet" Eddie smiled.

"Oh, we'll do 'em, no problem," responded Jack with a confidence in the Reds I would come to recognize every time I was to hang with the lad.

Eddie commented on how he was missing the early morning editions of the British Invasion on Replay 105.1, recalling our chats over the radio request line as he was about to finish the night shift at the bakery. He always offered genuine encouragement, telling me how well the show was sounding, which I really appreciated, especially in those nerve-racking early days.

"Oh, so that was you then, eh? The British Invasion. Yeah, I tuned in quite a bit." Jack chimed in, adding "Nice one."

"Yeah, I loved doing it, Jack. It was a great escape for a few hours. Something I'd always wanted to do ya know," I replied.

"Oh mate, that was some good stuff. It was brilliant to hear a Lancashire accent early doors on a Saturday morning," Jack added.

As we squeezed in a little more half-time chat, the two British expat Ann Arborites switched gears, filling me in on how their soccer team had just won the local league in their first season. Apparently, it was quite an eclectic bunch of lads from all over the world, Chinny's appearances continuing to add a little South Korean flair by all accounts.

At the start of the season, Jack went to register the team and was asked for a team name. This happened to be one small detail that they had all overlooked. Since he needed to register that day, the first name he came up with was Bienvenu United—a nod to Lionel Bienvenu, presenter of a Sunday evening soccer highlights show on the Fox Sports Network. A far cry from the reserved and measured British commentators that we were all used to, Lionel was very in-your-face and extremely confident in that all-American ex-frat boy way, and looked as though he would be more at home presenting a wrestling or American football show. Over time, however, it became evident that Lionel relished the job and knew what he was talking about. He took delight in the names of players, such as Nicky Butt and Muzzy Izzet, which he would make sure to repeat over and over—again, a far cry from anything you'd see on British TV. He also liked to throw in abbreviations such as "PK" for a penalty kick and the "EPL" for the English Premier League.

"You know what, lads? I would call that sheer visionary. Look how

EPL is now on the tip of everyone's tongue," I offered.

Initially, the name Bienvenu United was a bit tongue in cheek, but in his own way, Lionel Bienvenu was ahead of his time—a missionary, spreading the soccer word in Yankee land.

Jack continued: "We decided to contact Lionel personally. I sent him a photo of our Bienvenu United championship-winning team, and, to our amazement, we actually got a mention on his show—a national show—along with a graphic showing the Ann Arbor league standings with Bienvenu United at the top. All a bit surreal, really. Lionel even said that he wanted us to continue sending the results of our games each week so that he could keep track of his namesake team, saying how proud he was to be associated with the league winners. He even sent us a signed photo. So, yeah, he's like our cult hero now."

A ripple of applause filtered through Conor O'Neill's, signifying the start of the second half. I shook Eddie's and Jack's hands and wandered back to my seat in the paddock, happy that a United cohort from the Britannia days was back in town, along with another Red Devil to swell the ranks.

As I was heading back, I passed by a fella who looked really familiar. It suddenly dawned on me.

"Didn't you used to go to the Britannia Club, mate?"

"That's right, yeah! I thought I recognized you too, mate," a clear Scouse accent punctuating the air.

"Me name's Carl, mate."

"Nice to meet you, Carl. I'm Gary," I replied, realizing I was shaking the hand of yet another Liverpool fan.

"I recognized a few of yous sat there this morning. Only problem is, most of you lot appear to have that Man United disease."

"So says the completely unbiased Koppite?" I fired back.

"The one and only, mate. The one and only!"

"Yeah you'll get over it, pal! Hey, why don't you come and join us?"

And with that Carl headed over to join the lads in the paddock.

Handshakes all around and, at the same time, Crown Paints Jacob put in a late showing, his ever-present, tighter-by-each-appearance Liverpool shirt catching the eye of the latest addition to our gang.

Carl was quick to realize that he had several sympathizers when it came to Liverpool—Jacob and Chinny, of course, being the two most vocal. No surprise that he immediately positioned himself among the

Scouse fans for the rest of the morning.

The second half began with no sound and an ever-worsening picture as, once again, the Reds took to the turf of Old Trafford, a ripple of applause filtering through the room.

"What's going on, mate?" Scouse Carl wasted no time in letting Danny know that the Conor's paddock was none too happy with how bad the reception was becoming.

"Hey, der's fuck all I can do about it, fellas. I believe it's dat big fucking tower at the University blocking any chance of good reception," replied the Irishman, reluctantly walking over from behind the bar to check the coordinates on the screen.

Red looked at me. "That what?"

"I believe he said it's dat big fucking tower at the University, mate."

"Hey, put the dime in the slot, dude!" some wise guy shouted from somewhere in the darkness.

"I reckon it must be raining in Manchester!" an obviously northern English accent belted out behind me.

Minutes later, we were up and running again. United were in full view and once again bearing down on the Middlesborough goal. A beautiful reverse-pass from Giggs into Andy Cole's path and "bang"! Superb finish. And just like that, it was 1-1.

The United clan rose as one, Red's hand held up for a high-five.

Fred got his usual shaking from me as I sat behind him proclaiming the "absolute class" of my beloved United. I recognized a worryingly "Americanization" in my celebration. In all my years of sitting in the paddock of Old Trafford, I'm pretty sure that I never high-fived anyone.

United continued to attack and it wasn't long before the inevitable occurred. "Penalty, ref!" Red roared, his usually reserved demeanor non existent.

The referee agreed with Red.

Mr. Steady, Dennis Irwin, stepped up.

2-1!

And then, all of a sudden, it was 3-1 and game over.

Ryan Giggs had put the seal on it. The final whistle blew and with it a moment that often emphasizes my expat status, as I am sat in a dimly-lit bar on the stroke of midday when an impromptu round of applause graciously commences in acknowledgement of our early-morning soccer fix from across the Pond. The response from everyone seemed the right thing to do realizing how privileged we were to have a lifeline to our religion.

That afternoon's postmatch medication time soon got under way with Fred ordering two pints of Beamish, a dark alternative to Guinness this time around. The results of the other games flashed up on the big screen, confirming that several of the big guns had made it through to the next round of the FA Cup. Medication time that afternoon took on the theme of FA Cup memories past, Fred making us all aware of his age, describing days of hard, wet leather footballs and players immune to concussion. The conversation flowed as usual and Carl soon made his mark with a wonderful story demonstrating his love of the beautiful game.

It all began as I jokingly taunted our newest member about the demise of his beloved Liverpool, and the current reign in the domestic game of Manchester United. We both exchanged verbal jabs: a Manchester United fan and a Liverpool fan expressing polite niceties, but both of us fully aware that it was never going to be a friendship made in heaven.

It wasn't long before the conversation converged on the famous FA Cup final encounter of 1977. The men from Merseyside, had they beaten United that day at Wembley, would have gone to Rome for the European Cup final the following Wednesday, just one win away from the unprecedented achievement of the three major trophies in one season: the English championship, the FA Cup, and the European Cup. The Treble. No team had managed such a feat in all of British soccer history.

Of course, my own delight in the outcome of that game as a United fan was mentioned earlier, but it was certainly worthwhile acknowledging Carl's Liverpool perspective. Liverpool FC dominated the domestic game throughout the mid- to late-1970s and would continue to do so for a good number of years. Carl and I both enjoyed taking digs at each other until he began the tale of his postmatch trauma from that day back in May 1977.

It had been at the final whistle of that FA Cup final defeat at the hands of Manchester United that the then 19-year old Scouser made himself a pledge. "One way or another, I knew that I had to get to Rome for the European Cup Final."

"It was a kind of spur of the moment thing. Well, not completely. You see, my mate and I took our passports with us to London because we did talk ahead of time about the general idea of going. I still wonder if we had beaten United in the FA Cup final whether we would have been content with just heading home and celebrating, considering the Rome trip not really necessary. "

In the end, after the FA Cup final defeat, Scouse Carl had indeed decided to don his backpack and set the compass for Italy's capital.

We all listened intently as Carl relived his pilgrimage. Chinny and Jacob were clearly in awe of someone in their presence actually having made it to one of the most famous games in Liverpool's history. Even Red was captivated as Carl's tale of his trip to Rome exemplified all that he loved about the passionate devotion of Britain's soccer fanatics.

Carl continued. "Our ticket search was not too bad as it turned out. We heard that there were English touts near the main bridge to the ground. We went with two other fans we had met and sure enough we found one. I think we paid twenty quid which was pretty much all we had. I remember being concerned because the tickets were weird looking and did not show a price."

Carl reminded us that on that night in Rome back in 1977, Liverpool were playing their sixty-first game of the season. He told of how, as he entered the stadium early that Wednesday afternoon, he could not believe the amount of scousers who had already made it across Europe to be there. "It felt like a home game. The noise was incredible and I remember surviving on adrenaline as the trip across Europe had taken a couple of days and, needless to say, I barely got any sleep. Then the lads came out onto the pitch and I realized how much I had wanted to be there."

The smile on Carl's face as he remembered that day was lighting up our Irish den. He continued.

"It was a close-fought game with Liverpool taking the lead with a goal from Terry McDermott. We went bloody crazy! I was in a sea of red, just grabbing and pushing anyone and everyone. It wasn't long though before Borussia equalized. That seemed to spark the Germans as they took control of the game for a while and almost took the lead if it hadn't been for Ray Clemence playing a blinder in goal."

"The intensity of the vibe all around me and the importance of the occasion almost became too much—actually being there in Rome and the effort that I had made to get there. The sleepless nights in train stations. The hours hitching and riding trains across Europe for four days were so worth it at that moment. I have to say it was really getting to me, though. I was emotionally spent, totally engulfed with events out there on the pitch. Then we get that corner. Playing in his six hundredth game for Liverpool, Tommy Smith rises above everyone else and pops one in. We all rose as one. I couldn't believe Tommy had got the goal. The most unlikely of match winners. I truly believed from that moment that it was our destiny to go on and win that biggest prize. I felt like a king. Being there, witnessing one of our greatest soccer moments, live, as it happened."

Despite my devotion to the Red Devils, I had nothing but respect for Carl's allegiance. I understood it. I felt it. It was total fanaticism.

The emotional Scouser continued. "Phil Neal went on to seal it with a penalty after Vogts had fouled Kevin Keegan. Keegan was playing out of his skin, knowing that this was his last game before venturing off to Hamburg later that summer. And he did us proud that night!"

"How did you get back, Carl?" Chinny inquired

"Oh my god," Carl laughed, "the trip home was a big part of the fun. The Italian cops marched us all back to town. We stayed with the main group getting on trains and nobody was checking for tickets. Pretty lucky really, 'cos we had no money to get home. Hadn't even thought about that! I figured that they all just wanted us to get the hell out of there. It was pretty much the same story when it came to the channel ferry and then train back up to Liverpool. There was definitely safety in numbers that night for sure."

Our newest member of the Conor's paddock had captivated us with his story as the memories of that famous night came flooding back. *Walk on, Carl.* Chinny and Jacob were still in awe as Carl wrapped up his tale of Rome. Liverpool FC had a unique supporters club brewing inside the walls of Conor O'Neill's.

It had been another great morning in our Irish soccer den. I smiled at the fact that United fan chatted with Liverpool fan, Arsenal fan mingled with Chelsea fan. The rivalries lived on, but there was something that united us all, something for which we all were grateful, that common thread of knowing the privilege we felt having found our haven for access to soccer live from the homeland. It brought us out, together, each of us excited for that weekend morning buzz. It was the foundation of our new, growing community at Conor O'Neill's.

As everyone wished each other well for the week, we began to exit the pub as one; fifteen to twenty soccer diehards full of their fix, at least until the next time. Several Premier League team shirts lit up Main Street, causing a few heads to turn. It was Sunday, of course, and we were leaving our own place of worship, an Irish pub and establishment that was now ready to return to business as usual, ready to welcome punters looking to watch some NFL football perhaps.

On my return to my Dearborn pad, my answering machine was once again bursting at the seams with transatlantic messages: Des, my old mate

Pete Monk, and even my mate Chicago Bill, now safely back in Blighty, were all singing from the same hymn sheet. United had been drawn against a team from close to Stanley Park, Liverpool, in the fourth round of the FA Cup—and it wasn't Sid Stone's Everton.

I could not believe it. We would definitely be seeing more of Scouse Carl again very soon!

39

It's Our Day!

A relatively small crowd had gathered at Conor's on a cold January morning in Ann Arbor to see the Reds gain three more crucial Premier League points with a 4-1 win over West Ham United.

I learned later from Des, that Peter Schmeichel had slipped off to Barbados, ordered by Fergie to take a rest. We both commented on the hard life soccer players appeared to lead. My father was digging up all he could muster to keep me connected to the Reds.

That rest for Mr. Schmeichel had appeared to do the trick, with United running out 6-2 winners in their next game, away at Leicester on January 16. Three more vital league points with a hat-trick from Yorke, two from Andy Cole and a late goal from Jaap Stam.

The following week brought with it the monumental FA Cup tie.

Liverpool weren't having the greatest of seasons—they hadn't for some time now—but this was their chance to put a big dent in United's campaign with a victory in the fourth round tie.

Needless to say, the prematch talk between Des and I focused on the outcome of the impending game. The FA Cup conversation appeared to stimulate his memory banks, as he recounted the greatest FA Cup final he had ever seen.

"The Wizard of Dribble, son! The one and only Stanley Matthews. It's a game I can recall as if it was yesterday. The 1953 final between the two Lancashire giants of the time, Bolton Wanderers and Matthews' team, Blackpool. It also happened to be the day that your grandad brought home our first ever television: black and white with a fourteen-inch screen. He'd bought it at Turner and Boothe's, the electrical retailers in Southport where I'd just started work as an eighteen-year-old apprentice. I couldn't believe it when the set was placed on a table in the corner of our room. I was actually going to be able to watch the game live from Wembley Stadium! Stanley Matthews in the flesh inside our very own TV."

My father was on a roll.

"The game itself was also memorable because it seemed like it could well be the last chance for the great Matthews to win a coveted FA Cup winners medal. Gary, I still, to this day, get a shiver talking about it. With less than half an hour to go, Blackpool, after two dreadful mistakes by their goalkeeper, were down 3-1. Then Matthews, at thirty-eight years old, passed to Mortenson to score. Mortenson then got another with a hell of a free kick. The game was suddenly level at 3-3. It was amazing to see all of this unfold live on TV right there in our living room. Then, with only a minute remaining, Matthews again beat the Bolton full back that he had given a torrid time to all afternoon and crossed the ball for Perry to put the ball into the Bolton net for the winner. Blackpool 4 Bolton 3! I still remember the emotion as we all sat huddled around the screen watching Matthews receive his winner's medal. Even Aunty Kitty had a lump in her throat. That is one memory that will stay with me forever, son."

As I put the phone down, I felt like I had just watched the game in its entirety, such was the passion with which Des had described the action. His FA Cup blast from the past had fueled me for an early morning jaunt to Conor O'Neill's. Not only that, but I had just found out that I had a great aunt named "Kitty"!

I lingered for a second, thinking about the contrast of my father's experience back in the early fifties; a televised match on the family's first ever black and white TV set versus my own imminent visit to an Irish pub in Michigan to watch a game live via satellite feed from more than three thousand miles away.

Father and son predictions for Sunday, January 24? We both felt it would be a close affair, with United having to be very wary of the dynamic young Liverpool star, Michael Owen.

Throughout the week, I had been contacting Conor O'Neill's as I had heard from Des that the game was kicking off early. We prayed that our soccer pub would pull through.

"The thing is, Connie, it's an 11:30 a.m. kick-off in England, which means 6:30 a.m. here. Do you think there is any way you can show it at Conor's? It's pretty early, I know, but you'd make a lot of lads very happy."

"Well, 'tis very early, darlin'," Connie's Irish drawl unmistakable via the telephone line. "But listen. If you's can round up enough people to guarantee covering the cost of us putting it on, then we will try our best to make it happen, OK? It will be around fifteen dollars a person cover charge."

"You beauty! I'm on it, Connie."

A grapevine is an amazing thing when it swings into action, with all of the regulars from Conor's helping to spread the word on hearing that Connie had given the green light to show the game. The reaction of our own paddock to that fantastic news was top drawer. Calls were made to ensure we would all be setting our alarm clocks very early for Sunday morning.

I awoke the morning of the match at around 5:00 a.m.—way before my alarm, prematch expectancy masking my tiredness, the deathly quiet of my surroundings accentuating my solitary quest. It was a bitterly cold morning, my outside thermometer registering an insane minus eight degrees Farenheit (minus twenty-two degrees Centigrade). Rising from bed, I immediately put on several layers to fend off the bitter cold (did I ever imagine that I would be wearing a United shirt over thermals?) and tiptoed out into the yard, the stillness of winter evident as the cloudy breath escaped my mouth. Starting the car engine, I glanced at the long icicles hanging down from my front bumper, frozen solid to the ground—quite a sight to an Englishman used to a more moderate winter clime. The old Honda heater was then left to do its work early so I wouldn't freeze my bollocks off all the way to Ann Arbor.

I had been placed under strict instruction to call Chinny as I left Dearborn—my early departure time ensuring that he would be nudged into action and able to make it to the game on time. Chinny did not do mornings. I smiled as I put the phone down, having spoken only to an answering machine, my rather contained low-decibel thrust of "Glory Glory Man United" his wake up call before I wandered out to my now cozy warm oven of a Honda CRX.

Headlights occasionally dazzled me in the midst of a dark mid-winter's morning as I sped along I-94. There was a complete absence of prematch build up on the radio as I blazed a solitary trail, my excitement at full tilt regardless. My quiet journey through the darkness gave me pause to reflect. Conor O'Neill's had pulled out all the stops to acquire soccer broadcast rights and now here they were, about to open up on a frigid winter's morning for a gang of soccer fans standing on the pub's doorstep at 6:15 a.m. while the majority of the town slept. Surely, this was some kind of notable first.

As I reached Conor's, I noticed a small group of lads huddled outside the building, wrapped up and in constant motion in their attempts to fend off the bitter morning cold, a single street light illuminating the group in the dark, sunrise still another hour away. There wasn't another soul to be seen.

"Good lads!" I chattered, my usual greeting extending from my very cold lips.

"Gazza!" Blue exclaimed, looking knackered and I'm sure thinking to himself "what the fuck am I doing here?" — a testament to his enthusiasm for the game and his expat allegiance.

A tired and frozen looking Red appeared, wrapped up in his usual combo mac, his gangly silhouette instantly recognizable through the dark. Red lived about a mile away from Conor's — a long, cold walk through a piercing winter chill. There was no doubt as to the American's total conviction to the Manchester United cause that morning.

A few minutes later, Chinny appeared, crossing over the road with one eye still closed and looking half dead, his obvious disgust for the ridiculously early kick-off time of 6:30 a.m. on full display. The Liverpool ranks were well represented with Chinny, Scouse Carl, and Crown Paints Jacob all there.

We had our own squad of United fans, including Red, Eddie, Jack, Den, and Don. Fred sat on the fence, saying that he "just wanted to see a wonderful game of soccer."

As kick-off time approached, doubt began to creep into my mind. Would there be anyone at Conor's to open up? I reached up to the window with the help of sixty-six-year-old Fred's cupped hands and perched on the precarious ledge. I banged that desperate bang to elicit a reaction from anyone within, frost on the window flickering down. Several others followed suit, desperation beginning to filter into every shudder of the windows, the volley of knocks echoing down Main Street and disturbing a couple of pigeons as they flew from their perch atop the canopy of our Irish den.

Several minutes later, looking way more tired than usual, Charlie appeared. "Good morning, gentlemen. Wow, are we in a rush today?"

Nobody seemed interested in a rebuff, as the crowd shuffled past Charlie in silence, desperate for warmth. I glanced over my shoulder as I moved closer to the door and noticed a police car slowing down outside the pub, the cops obviously intrigued as to why the pub was opening its doors at 6:30 a.m. on a Sunday morning. Intrigue was all, however, as there was to be no intrusion from the fuzz that morning.

Inside, the screens showed their usual blank blue, indicative of no satellite feed. There was no game and no Johnny.

Just as we were about to take matters into our hands, Chinny declaring that he could handle the logistics of the TV set up, Johnny arrived, looking rather shocked at the size of the crowd at such an early hour.

Blue, no surprise, was mouthing off.

"This just gets fuckin' better and better. You think they'd have it sorted by now, wouldn't ya, eh? There's no way I am paying for this game, I'll tell ya that!"

"Hey, c'mon Pete, mate. Chill, brother."

There was no convincing our Chelsea man, though, and as his remonstrations built, he gave a nod to a fella who had just waltzed in.

Enter Robbie who, in his instantly recognizable Manchester accent, exclaimed "What the fuck? Where's the game?"

"Another Red Devil", Blue emphasized as he formally introduced me to the swift mover.

Welcome, Robbie, alias Twinkle Toes.

Floating on air and all Lightfoot Lil, his slight figure glided past the throng that was gathered around the paddock.

"I thought the fucking game was meant to be on?"

The lad's head was bobbling back and forth in such quick fashion I thought it was going to come off.

"Morning mate", I calmly interjected, shaking Robbie's slender hand, "I think Johnny's getting there. A couple of technical glitches by all accounts it seems."

"They always have technical glitches at this dive," Blue noted as he glared in Johnny's direction.

Robbie's cheeks were blood red from the cold of the chilly January morning. He couldn't stand still, darting around, on his toes of course. His swift, nimble, high-stepping gait reminded me of Lionel Blair or Fred Astaire on speed.

Blue explained that Robbie was a professional dancer and had just bought a dance studio in Lansing.

That explained everything.

"Nice one," I replied. "That was a bit of drive for you this morning then, eh Robbie?"

"Hell no, stayed over last night after tying one on in here, mate. I might as well have crashed under that table to be honest. I'm feeling a bit delicate this morning."

"You should be, mate. She looked like she could have eaten you up for breakfast!" Blue was straight in regarding Robbie's antics the previous night.

"She bloody well did. She tied me in knots mate. She was gaggin' fer it. She didn't even give me chance to take me Salfords off. I can hardly walk this morning. Getting up to come here for the footy was tough."

No wonder the lad's cheeks were red.

"She was dead into it though. I'm bloody well knackered!"

A vision of this Robbie in nothing but his socks was a little much for me at that time in the morning, so I swiftly changed the subject, wishing Twinkle Toes all the best with his new venture.

"Cheers, mate. Don't have much time on my hands right now to be honest, so I won't be down here too often. Needed last night though to be honest!"

"Sounds more like she did, mate" I added.

"Ouufff!" I don't know mate. I don't know!"

"What do you reckon today then, Robbie?" I asked

"What, you mean when they actually get this fucking game going?"

"Yeah, bloody ridiculous this. What the fuck are they up to?" Twinkle Toes and Blue, the none-too-happy-chappys were complaining in unison.

"Alright lads. Well, enjoy the match."

"Yeah, whenever it starts" said Blue, still on a rant.

"Oi," Robbie yelled over toward Jacob and Carl, "United are gonna stuff 'em. 3-0! No problem."

Float on, Robbie. Float on.

By this time it was 6:45 a.m.—fifteen minutes into the match—and there was still no sign of Old Trafford on the screen. The natives were getting restless; none more so than Blue and Robbie.

Johnny had been running back and forth and using the phone to get a hold of any help he could. His prayers had obviously been answered as there, through the front doors, entered our savior, Connie.

She looked worn out, hair all over the place, no make-up, but she certainly looked like a lady with a little more purpose than our young stand in. It struck me that Connie always knew what she was about. She immediately called for order.

"Fellas, fellas, 'tis the Sabbath, so just watch yer tongues, will yous?"

The Conor's staff huddle grew under the big screen as the chants began to fly. "You don't know what your doin! You don't know what your doin!" A bad choice I felt as it certainly wouldn't endear us to the early risers among the Conor's staff.

"Don't bite the hand that feeds" were my only thoughts.

And then, at 6:50 a.m.—bam! A satellite picture as clear as a bell. Old Trafford looking resplendent. The noise from the ground instantly deafening, mixing in with a big cheer from everyone inside Conor's. I looked across to Blue who simply shook his head in disgust.

Connie rose up smiling and as she walked towards me and placed her hand gently on my left shoulder. I received a wink that pronounced that Irish cheekiness, confirming her achievement pulling the early morning event off. As if I ever had any doubts?

Everyone was intently focused on the game. The pace was frenetic. There was just one thing missing—there was no indication of the score. Seconds later that all changed.

"You fucking beauty!"

"Yesss!!"

"Get in there!"

"Fuck!"

The scoreline had appeared in the top left-hand corner of the screen, clear for all to see.

Manchester United 0, Liverpool 1.

I could not believe my eyes as Carl, Chinny, Jacob, and every other Liverpool fan present began a volley of high fives and shouts of exhilaration. Jacob's trusted Crown Paints shirt almost burst open at the seams at the force of his celebration.

"You're not singing, you're not singing, you're not singing anymore. You're not singing anymore!!"

Conor O'Neill's had woken up.

Chinny had most definitely woken up!

"Plenty of time, mate," I defiantly murmured to Red.

"Oh yeah, plenty, you wanker!" Red replied, the quiet calmness in both our voices hiding the shock and turmoil within.

Some fantastic interplay down the right flank by United resulted in a swerving cross from Yorke that Brad Friedel palmed to the edge of the box, but the ever-alert Roy Keane swiftly attempted a fierce header goalward. It clipped the goalpost, flew across the line and of all people, it was Paul Ince making a last-ditch effort on the goal line, preventing an equalizer. All eyes looked to the referee, and there was no response. The action replay confirmed a great decision had been made and Scouse Carl and his Liverpool brigade echoed their pleasure.

"It's going to be our day lads! It's going to be our day!" Carl bellowed, the smile on his face matching that of Paul Ince.

Could it be that after the humiliation of the last few Saturdays down at Conor's, our Liverpudlian friend finally had something to cheer about?

Chinny and Jacob certainly felt so.

"Go 'ed, lads! Go 'ed!" a loud Liverpudlian voice chimed in from behind us, one that had me turning around to see who it was.

"Good lad!" I shouted across to the fella and immediately received a big grin, along with clenched fist. He was stood, coffee in one hand and cigarette in the other, looking well up for the rest of the titanic battle ahead, certainly not hiding the fact that he was emphatically Liverpool through and through. The strongest of Scouse accents and cheekiest of grins backed it up but there was no stereotypical Liverpool perm or track suit, just a balding head atop his non-descript attire.

The half-time whistle blew and we all applauded. I stood up and stretched, feeling the after effects of that frenetic first half. Blue came over, still adamant he was in no way going to pay for the game as the late start was occurring too many times. I didn't bother to debate him and left him to stew, deciding instead to introduce myself to the bald headed, loud-mouthed Scouser who had caught my eye during the first half.

"Cracking game, eh mate? Liverpool are giving our lads a run for their money today. My name's Gary."

"Oh no, not another fucking United fan! You're all over the place, you lot. Ah, it's nice to meet you, la. The name's Gerry. Gerry George!"

With a sip of his coffee and a drag of his cigarette, Gerry began what I have now become fully accustomed to as a non-stop-gob-attack.

Gerry told me that he had only that week been rushed into hospital after suffering an angina attack, coming out Thursday after refusing to take a stress test. And here he was—absorbed in the game that was hardly quiet and uneventful.

"Bloody hell, Gerry! What the fuck are you doing here so soon after that, mate?" I asked.

"Well Gary, la, as I said to my missus as she tried to stop me coming down here—if I am going to cop it, then I may as well cop it watching

Liverpool rather than sitting at home eating fucking bran flakes! You know what I mean, mate?"

Gerry noted that his coffee and cigarette combo was still very much a part of his regimen, while acknowledging that he was undoubtedly going to have to change his ways if he wanted to continue to watch his beloved Liverpool.

"No argument from me there, mate," I replied.

Gerry and I continued our half-time chat and I listened intently as to how he had come to find Conor O'Neill's and his soccer fix abroad.

"I work for Ford, mate, for their electrical and fuel handling division, and I came to the States from Hungary several years ago."

"Bloody hell, mate. You get about, don't you?"

"Gary, mate, that's half the problem, lad. I'm sent all over the bloody world and this body of mine gets torn in half with all the time changes. Don't get me wrong, lad, the money's good, but it can't half get bloody stressful."

"So how did you find out about Conor's then, Gerry?"

"An old mate of mine from Ford's who actually played for Norwich City at one time. His name's Dave Head. Have you heard of him? Anyway, Gary, he told me about how good the craic was down here. So, here I am!"

We continued to chat and Gerry told me about how he first started to watch his beloved 'pool.

"My earliest memory was of being taken to Anfield when I was about eight. My dad had me on his shoulders in the Kop. I remember that they were playing Bolton, but I haven't got a clue what the final score was. What I do remember is a fight breaking out between one of the Liverpool players and the Bolton goalie. I had a great view and loved every second of it. Those were the days when Anfield held 61,000 people! Brilliant, it was."

Gerry would have gone on all day if I had let him, but it was time for the second half to start. He was obviously a Liverpool FC nut, but none of us are perfect. I could live with that. I was just glad that he had found refuge among the underground ranks of the soccer crew at Conor O'Neill's. I was busy shaking the hand of my new friend when Connie stepped in and asked if I would kindly take a cap around to ask for the cash to help pay for the broadcast.

"Sure! No problem, Connie."

"Ah, yer a darlin' Gary," Connie responded actually slapping an old cap into my hand.

As the second half started, I decided to collect the cash as soon as possible so that I could relax for the remainder of the game. There wasn't any hassle from anyone in regard to the fifteen dollar cover charge, especially with a second match on the menu at 10:00 a.m.

Then I reached Blue.

As I passed the cap under his chin he stared at me.

"No fuckin' way, mate! You have got to be joking!"

Blue's mate Robbie also refused. "They took a fuck load of money off me in here last night. I'm not giving 'em anymore, mate. Fuck that!"

"C'mon, lads. You know they opened up especially early for us."

"Don't give a fuck, mate. They need to get their act together. I'm not paying for a game when we miss half of it."

Blue was so adamant that I decided not to take it any further and just thought "what a dick." I couldn't help but feel that Peter and Robbie had been left to feel like the odd men out as the rest of the lads willingly coughed up, with grateful smiles at that.

There's always one, I guess. Well, sometimes two!

Chores over with, I focused on the action once again.

Giggs slipped the ball to Keane who let fly with a strong shot, a deflection leaving Friedel laying prostrate as he watched it whistle past the post and out for a corner.

"I'm telling ya, it's gonna be our day!"

Carl was relentless!

My new Scouse mate Gerry added his voice to the chorus.

"Hey there Gary, la! Hey Gary! How you feeling there, fella?"

Little did I know that this "Hey Gary, la!" was the first of many that would haunt me whenever we were both present at Conor O'Neill's. The man was to become relentless in his barrage.

"Hey Gary, la? Did you see that, mate?"

"Yes, Gerry," I would think to myself, "of course I fucking saw it. I am in the same fucking pub as you, aren't I, watching the same fucking game?"

Minutes later, it was Gary Neville's turn to surge forward with a neat pass into Cole. Terrific interplay between Cole and Yorke before Keano connected with a thunderous drive which rattled the upright as it shook to its foundation in the turf. The rebound found its way to Giggs, and Jamie Carragher threw his body at the ball forcing yet another corner. It was desperate stuff from the Liverpool defense.

I sat motionless as Den looked across and bellowed "what the fuck have we gotta do man? What have we gotta fuckin' do?!"

Time was running out.

"Hey Gary, la. Hey, Gary. How you feelin' there, fella?"

This time, Gerry seemed even more assured, knowing that we were close to full time. Seconds later Andy Gray, Martin Tyler's partner in the Sky TV commentary box, took a leaf from "the book of Scouse Carl," exclaiming, "Looks like this is Liverpool's day!"

The pub exploded with laughter!

Carl raised his arms in triumph.

I sat there, concentrating, focused, urging the Reds forward as they tried desperately to even the score and force a replay. Den and Don were going ballistic and it was quite a sight as they beat on their bellies, contorting their faces, urging on "their" United. It was not yet 8:00 a.m. and the noise in our den had the occasional onlooker peering through the windows to see what was going on inside.

Then, finally, it happened.

With two minutes remaining, Giggs and Beckham stood over the ball on the edge of the Liverpool penalty box. Beckham floated the ball in, almost as if in slow motion as it bypassed everyone until it reached the head of Andy Cole. Falling backwards, Cole managed to channel his header across the goalmouth and standing just inches from the line was Dwight Yorke who swiftly turned the ball into the Liverpool net.

Pandomonium!

I chose to sit rooted to my seat, drinking in the moment I had been waiting for all game. Red dived across and high-fived me. Den and Don were bouncing off each other, their United regalia barely still intact and Eddie and Jack were going nuts, Jack grabbing hold of Eddie's ponytail almost yanking the thing off with his bare hands.

I immediately thought of the reaction back home. How wild must it have been? I was at Conor O'Neill's in Ann Arbor, Michigan in the American Midwest and I couldn't have asked for a better atmosphere. It felt brilliant. Absolutely brilliant!

United 1 Liverpool 1!

The chaos settled into a nervous hum as the game resumed with barely any time left on the clock. Any complacency from either team would surely lose them the tie.

"I love this team man they never give up! They don't know how to." Red was in awe of "his" Reds from Manchester and loving his addiction to English soccer.

"Hey Gary, la. You're a right bunch of jammy Mank bastards. That's what you are, mate! Jammy fucking bastards!"

Gerry proceeded to throw his cigarette onto the floor in front of him, stamping it into the freshly-varnished wood. He did not need to be anywhere near to a stress test at that moment in time, let alone have his blood pressure taken. I was seriously recounting my abilities at CPR as it looked like they may well be required. Let's face it, Gerry, like most of us, was not about to change any time soon.

"Liverpool's resistance is finally broken and there is still time for more," declared Martin Tyler.

All of the lads were shouting for their respective team. The United lads were sensing the kill, while Carl, Jacob, Chinny, and Gerry had more of a look of desperation about them, willing their Liverpool team to simply hold on and make it back to Anfield for another crack of the whip.

The commentary was in review mode as Andy Gray pontificated while Martin Tyler took a back seat to listen and recharge.

Not for long though.

The ball was pumped into the Liverpool box where it reached Paul Scholes.

Tyler took over.

"Scholessss!"

In quick succession, the name of Norway's "Baby Faced Assassin" rolled off Tyler's tongue and the volume of his delivery almost shattered the sound system.

"Solskjærrrrr!"

2-1 United!

Conor's went nuts!

The impossible had happened, and as I high-fived all of my United crew, I took a split second to look across to my new mate Gerry. Gerry's expression was one of devastation, his face blood red and contorted, his expression of glee and expectation now replaced by a sarcastic smile of disbelief, matched only by the look on Scouse Carl's and the other Liverpool lads faces.

It wasn't going to be their day after all!

That's what makes soccer the great game that it is.

That Sunday morning seemed to propel Conor O'Neill's and it's motley band of soccer fanatics to a new level of soccer watching abroad. The highs and lows; the "It's our day! It's not our day!" It had been an astounding game of soccer, bonding a bunch of fellas together in such a unique setting.

As the excitement died down and reality once again beckoned, and as several of the lads began to venture outside into the early morning cold, Blue and Twinkle Toes Robbie came over.

"Hey Gary, mate. Here's that money. Pass it on to Connie, will ya?"

"Nice one, lads! It's the least we could all do after all the effort to open up so early, eh?"

"For sure, Gary mate. Got to admit I've mellowed a little after that win. To be honest mate, I was hungover as fuck when I first walked in this morning" Robbie added.

"No worries, mate. No worries!"

I learned later that Peter was still in the middle of his acrimonious divorce and was in none too happy a place, which went some way to explaining his mindset earlier that morning.

Due to Michigan's alcohol laws preventing the sale of any alcohol on a Sunday morning, there would be no "medication" for sale for another four hours.

Fred suggested that to kill some time, we take a stroll down Main Street to stretch our legs. Most of our immediate paddock was up for it, even though the temperatures hadn't budged much since 6:00 a.m. Amid the warmth of a local coffee house, the soccer banter quickly resumed and we began to reminisce about our FA Cup memories down the years. Fred spoke of a game from 1948. He painted the picture well as we sat and listened, the coffee house's steamed window panes sheltering us from the blistering cold. Red, still wearing his combo mack, hands grasping a cup of Columbian brew, pricked his ears up, smiling as he could begin to envisage even more, the historic past of a country he had become very fond of through his appreciation for the game of soccer.

Fred, our elder statesman began.

"London in April 1948 was a dreary city. Three years after the end of the war, most of the bomb damage was still evident and there were many shortages. Britain was in the throes of significant social changes

IT'S OUR DAY : 273

under a Labour government reflecting the disillusionment of its people with decades of unsympathetic conservative politics. However, none of this mattered to me at the time. I was a teenager on my way to watch Manchester United play Blackpool in the Cup. My father had got me a ticket and for some reason I went alone. Did he not want to go or could he not get another ticket? I knew he was excited about it. But like a good parent, he didn't discourage his son and there I was on that sunny April day walking towards Wembley with thousands of others. The crowd was orderly with none of the raucous behavior of later years about which I have only read, having lived in the States for over thirty years now."

I smiled, at that contrast to the present day, and remained fully engrossed in Fred's story.

"I remember the green of the grass and the sounds of the crowd. I remember Matthews and Mortenson playing for Blackpool and Charlie Mitten for United. I remember the magic fifteen-minute period in the second half when United scored three times during an awesome display of passing to come from 2-1 behind and win 4-2! At the time one of papers described those few minutes as a purple patch."

It seemed rather poignant that Fred would continue with a reference to his early admiration for Manchester United, particularly on a day that the current United team had achieved such a memorable comeback.

"It seems strange to me now that I had such a reverence for Manchester United because I had never seen them play. There was no TV so my feelings had to have come entirely from newspaper reports and radio. Apparently it seemed the reporting press regarded the qualities of this team highly. Anyway, I was not disappointed. My only regret is that I cannot remember all the details of the game or who the other players were. It's no doubt buried inside me, available through deep hypnosis only."

I took another slow sip of my warming English brew, and commented on the fact that Fred was in danger of becoming a closet Manchester United fan—a statement he vehemently denied, making it clear that he had no favorite team.

We all remained riveted as he rounded off his tale.

"I was in Wembley Stadium one other time in my life. It was the same year. I was lucky to go and watch one day of the 1948 Olympic Games. I saw Gaston Reiff of Belgium win the 5000 meters against the great Emile Zatopek. Fanny Blankers Koen won the the women's 100 meter hurdles and American Mal Whitfield beat Jamaica's Arthur Wint in the 800 meters."

Red commented on how impressive Fred was remembering the names of those respective athletes, and that it may have been his addiction to running that had enabled him to recall them more easily than several of the soccer players of the Wembley Final that same year.

Fred simply replied, "Races are easier to recall, my friend. A time. A winner. Perhaps even a record. It's all facts, you see."

After our coffee shop interlude, we all wandered back over to Conor O'Neill's, the warmth of the pub cradling us as we entered its walls. A second FA Cup installment of fourth round FA Cup action was being beamed live. We had the chance to experience our first double-header live from England. I still, to this day, though, cannot remember the match.

Why would I? The unforgettable game we had witnessed earlier that day had had it all. As I returned home that afternoon, phone messages were lined up on the answering machine. I even received one from my longtime friend Pete Monk, with whom I had witnessed an emotional day on the terraces of Goodison Park, in the Liverpool end; he a Liverpool supporter and me, a United fan, at the 1985 FA Cup semi-final. After all those years, the significance of a game such as that one must have resonated with my old Lancashire friend, prompting his phone call across the Pond.

Pete made his remarks in his all too familiar slow and calculated manner. I imagined his mouth slowly circling around each word in that unmistakable Pete Monk verbal delivery: "You jammy bunch of United bastards!" It is nice to know that old friends rarely change. And it was another moment that I realized that in the scheme of things I really wasn't that far from home.

40

Getting to Know You

An away victory at Charlton Athletic took Manchester United to the top of the Premier League at the end of January 1999. The top four clubs were:

Manchester United	*pld 23*	*pts 44*
Chelsea	*pld 23*	*pts 43*
Aston Villa	*pld 23*	*pts 43*
Arsenal	*pld 23*	*pts 42*

Michigan was now in deep freeze. I was glad to have my Saturday morning distraction. The warm glow of an Irish pub early on a weekend morning certainly helped to ease the winter blues. Conor O'Neill's complete with its open log fire and warm hospitality provided a terrific alternative to my early arrivals into a cold and lonely Replay 105.1 studio.

In early February 1999, Steve McClaren arrived at Old Trafford from Derby County as United's new assistant manager, Alex Ferguson astutely acquiring the services of an emerging and well-respected English coaching talent.

Ironically, United played Derby at the Theatre of Dreams the following Saturday. An excellent strike from Yorke, who was beginning to hit an even richer vein of form, pinched a 1-0 home win for the Reds.

A couple of days later, I hit a road block. An occupational hazard stopping me in my tracks.

I had been working with a somewhat difficult, and, in my mind, psychosomatic patient. In the middle of the second week of February, "Dana Drama" trudged into our department, hell bent on showing all present just how pissed off she was at the world. Weighing in at a whopping 280lbs, she had a supposedly serious back problem.

Dana's negativity strained my positive energy every single time I treated her. I put my game face on and greeted her in my professionally upbeat manner. The upcoming Academy Awards ceremony would have applauded her acting abilities. She would, without doubt, have been in Oscar contention for best performance in transitioning to an upright position from a waiting room chair. She was totally unaware of the fact that, minutes earlier, I had watched her emerge from her car without a hint of difficulty.

I ushered Dana into the treatment area. She was a big lady alright. It was a definite struggle, as she became more and more dependent on me. Then, with a loud and full-throttled scream, she beautifully choreographed her attempted collapse in the middle of our hallway. It was performed in such a way as to maximize viewing potential and had the opportunity for many witnesses to see just how well the next few seconds were dealt with. To put it frankly, she had given herself the best chance of trying to extract a clinical mistake from the staff actually taking care of her. Fortunately, we had a great team when it came to dealing with such situations. That still didn't hide the fact that I had to attempt to stop this very heavy lady from hitting the floor and injuring herself, all 280lbs plus. It was instant dead weight, and had caught my somewhat skinny 170lb frame completely off guard.

The next few days I continued to work and ignored the advice of my peers to take some time off and recover from what was developing into my own frustrating back problem.

As the weekend approached, I decided to forego my Saturday visit to Conor's. I could hardly move. I finished work early Friday and decided to rest up all day Saturday. The scheduled game at Conor's was Blackburn Rovers against Aston Villa, so at least I wasn't missing a Manchester United game. Fred called to check on me, concerned by my absence from Conor's that morning. He twisted my arm to meet up with him the next day for the Sunday morning game between Derby County and Everton. After all, he insisted, a medication time may just be the tonic. It was a kind gesture and reason enough to meet up with my friend. My decision was also influenced by the fact that I had learned via radio of the amazing feats of one Ole Gunnar Solskjær scoring four goals in a matter of minutes that same Saturday against Nottingham Forest at the City Ground. Yes, my back was an issue, but it isn't very often a scoreline of 8-1 occurs, so I had to make it to Conor O'Neill's to catch the highlights.

Needless to say, I didn't alert the local speed cops as my chariot limped its way west on I-94. Mine was a gentle passage that Sunday amid some of the most hazardous winter weather of the year to date. As I attempted to maintain a decent posture while driving, I began to realize that I had made a bad decision, the snow layering inch upon inch on the surface of the freeway.

I meandered into Ann Arbor at a safe, slow pace, ploughing a lone furrow. Being a Sunday, of course, the county road commission had been in no rush to clear roads, particularly for an English soccer fan making the crazy decision to get up early and drive. I eventually made it, a tad unsure of where curb met tarmac, due to the now several inches of snow blanketing the town.

Gingerly walking, or rather slipping, toward the pub's back doors and up the back steps, I entered the building. Straight away, I spotted a lone figure, focused on the big blue screen in front of him.

I stood behind Fred for a second and smiled to myself as he remained totally focused on the picture—or lack thereof—ready for any sight of Pride Park, Derby. The poor audio feed also made Martin Tyler sound more like a vintage Norman Collier, the stuttering comedian, famous for his unique staccato broken English.

Fred sat center stage, concentration total, a solitary man previously deprived of more than thirty years of live soccer action from Britain. The harsh winter morning had not dampened his enthusiasm.

I wandered up to him and gently tapped him on the shoulder.

"My friend," he declared and proceeded to shake my hand. "How are you feeling?"

"Oh, I've felt better, I must say, Fred. But I made it! Looks like they're really packing 'em in this morning, eh mate?"

"Gary, I was almost considering leaving. This game is terrible and the reception is even worse. Still, it's a game of soccer so who knows what will happen, right?"

After a kind thought regarding the progress of my back, Fred offered me an insight into the proceedings of what was obviously proving to be a dour affair between two teams at the foot of a Premier League table, embroiled in a fight for survival. Fred was touting the talents of the young prodigy, Francis Jeffers, who had made the starting lineup for Everton alongside the mouthful that was Ibrahima Bakayoko.

"He's been a delight to watch so far, Gary. The only bright spark in this dreadful game."

As though on cue, Jeffers dabbled in some trickery and released Barmby to score the opener.

"What was I telling you Gary? He's a great little player!"

Fred was happy to watch any game of soccer, no matter the level. He went on to tell me that he had become engrossed in an international under-21 tournament being held in France. He had received the package by chance from his pay-per-view channel and had watched most of the tournament, assessing several young players for the future.

Half-time arrived and I focused on the screen. It was the moment I had made the journey for: the previous day's soccer highlights.

Fred and I leaned further forward and were joined by most of the skeleton crew from behind the bar and from the kitchen. All the talk focused on Solskjær's four-goal burst at the City Ground, Nottingham. My anticipation was at full tilt as I watched the first goal from Dwight Yorke fly into the Forest net—his sixth in as many matches. Knowing the final score, it surprised me that Forest were level after only six minutes. The lead then returned to United with a Cole strike before half-time.

As the highlights of the second half began, the screen once again began to flicker. I saw Cole's second and United's third goal. The picture then stuttered through the skills of Blomqvist as he set Yorke up for his second, United's fourth.

And then the inevitable. More interference.

As the picture returned, the clock in the corner read 80 minutes with the score still 4-1 to Manchester United. We were all aghast as to how late it had been for the "Baby Faced Assassin" to make his mark. Brian Clough, the famous manager of Nottingham Forest once made the famous soccer statement "it only takes a second to score a goal."

I rubbed my hands together at the mouthwatering prospect of the Solskjær goals. I looked up at the screen and saw Beckham running the show, another beautifully weighted pass into the path of Neville. And then the screen went blank. A sarcastic cheer rang out from the seven or eight of us in the building. The picture returned seconds later to the sight of Ole's celebration. Another splutter and off it went again. This time the pause was longer and when it returned a second time, with it came the sight of a smiling Ole Gunnar and a scoreline that read Forest 1 United 8.

We had missed all four of the Norwegians goals!

"What the hell!" I exclaimed, exasperated.

"Would you believe it? Now that is a shame, Gary."

"Ah, poor piece of luck that, Gary son. Poor piece of luck, so it is," added Danny, our Irish waiter.

Brian Clough's words resonated, now with a little more irony.

As the second half of the Everton and Derby game commenced, the reception difficulties continued. Such was the annoyance of our attempts to keep our eyes focused on the game, Fred and I instead decided to indulge in further conversation. That morning, I got to learn a good deal more about Regal Fred.

Fred appeared to be a compassionate man, with an ardor for life that drew you in. He wasn't loud and he wasn't pushy, but he possessed the aura of a man who had lead life on his own terms. What I appreciated most about him was the fact that although he was moving toward his twilight years, he continued to pursue new challenges. There I was, thirty-two years his junior and yet both of us sat deep in conversation.

At that moment, I remembered Stenny, a friend from back home who was a good number of years older than me. We had been sat sharing a beer together after Wiggy, our dear and close friend from those village soccer matches, had been laid to rest after a tragic accident. With an unmistakable Lancashire accent punctuating the sentence Stenny had noted that "friendship has no age barriers does it, eh lad?"

As Fred and I spoke of our past and hopes for the future, it didn't seem to matter that Everton were blowing a one goal lead and would leave Pride Park empty handed and even further in the quagmire of a Premier League relegation battle. It didn't matter that the blue screen above us had just about given up on any attempt to deliver the Solskjær goal fest from the previous day. What did matter was that I was spending time with my new friend, Alfred Montague.

One of the most gratifying aspects of being a soccer fan miles from home is meeting other expat soccer fans and becoming immediately connected by that shared love of the game. Long-lasting friendships arose out of those get togethers at ungodly hours.

Fred had noticed how I would always call my father after any United win. He had recalled my jubilation the day that United made their incredible late comeback to beat Liverpool in the FA Cup, smiling as I ran to the payphone to make the quick call to Scotland to share in that memorable victory with my father. Immediately after that call, it was Fred who had enquired, amid the mayhem of the celebrations, whether or not I had got through—his reaction perhaps a reflection of the bond with his own father in years past.

We continued to chat and Fred spoke of how he admired my evident positivity in life. "For one so young, you certainly seem to be in touch with what you want out of life. Don't ever change, Gary. Keep with that frame of mind and you will do alright." There are certain sentences that resonate.

I learned that Fred had been a successful businessman and that he had gone through some midlife difficulties following a divorce. Yet there he was, mid-sixties, fit as a fiddle, having rebooted and started from scratch. He had remarried and was father to a beautiful twenty-year-old daughter.

We continued our conversation, and after some time, Fred enquired as to how I had originally come to be in the States. After filling him in on the process, Fred then enquired about my family.

"Any brothers or sisters, Gary?"

"Just the one sister, Fred. I lost my younger sister. She died when she was six. I was eleven at the time."

"I am so sorry to hear that. If you don't mind may I ask what happened?" the compassion in his voice as clear as day.

I felt comfortable enough to open up and tell Fred about my sister's struggle throughout her short life. I spoke of the community and the support our family had been given during that most difficult of times. I spoke of my parents' sacrifices and how my father had left his job, starting his own business as a self-employed electrician to free up time to take my sister to the many hospital visits her condition had required. I couldn't help but notice Fred's total focus on my story and felt encouraged to continue. I told Fred about how my sister had to battle the doubters as she developed, managing to attend school, using calipers to walk freely over short distances.

"So, do you think that's why you became involved in the health profession?" Fred asked.

"Oh, without a doubt, Fred. It had a major influence. I have often thought about that. I was humbled at such an early age, not only by my sister, but by all the other kids. They were such an inspiration. Also, experiencing first hand the kind support we received from health professionals and groups within our Lancashire community."

"And your little sister eventually passed away, Gary?" Fred remarked, his tone inquisitive, denoting genuine interest in my story.

"Unfortunately, yes, she did Fred," I replied, explaining to him how our family was hit head on with the grief of a child taken so young.

"You know Fred, I guess looking back and having gone through emotions like that at such an early stage in my own life, I couldn't help but have to grow up quickly, right?"

Fred went quiet. He tightened his lips, closed his eyes and began gently shaking his head side to side.

"Sorry, Gary. Just a moment, please" Fred's eyes opening, appearing to well up as he proceeded to slowly bow his head.

The man's empathy was immediate. His compassion obvious.

It was a quite remarkable moment for me and I will never forget the response I received from my friend that day.

After composing himself, Fred began to tell me more about his own father. He had briefly mentioned him in a prior conversation. All I really knew was that he had at one time worn the colors of Sheffield United — "a strong athletic center forward," I had remembered Fred proudly remark.

"Gary, my father once sat me down and told me of a cup semi-final in which he had played at his usual position of center forward for Sheffield United. Sheffield United were losing 1-0. I think the game was at Villa Park but have never confirmed the location. I was reminded of the story he had told one day while I was idly looking through a publication of all of the league tables and semi and final cup results from the inceptions of the competitions through 1996."

By this time the two of us were digging into some Maureen's Irish stew, complemented perfectly by a pint of the black stuff.

"I saw that in 1923 Sheffield United lost 1-0 to Bolton Wanderers. Dad had told me a tale from that game that no chronicle had ever registered. He told me of how he had had an opportunity to score an equalizer during a goalmouth melee. The ball had run loose to him in front of the goal. As he went for it the goalkeeper dived down and he sensed immediately that if he kicked the ball he would probably also kick the face of the goalkeeper!"

Fred then paused for a second as if to reflect a little further, a proud smile emerging on his face.

"As my father told me the story, he said that he just couldn't do it and stopped short, allowing the ball to be safely gathered by the keeper. He also told me how he was later booed off the field by his own fans. The moral, of course, was not lost on an eleven year old, and I have never forgotten the story or the images it evoked. My father had demonstrated a noble streak. I admired him so much for that one simple decision on the field of play that day. Not many players in that position would have done the same."

A thoughtful gaze appeared on Fred's face. His reflective smile said everything.

The clock above the Conor's bar was fast approaching one o'clock and we both decided it was time to escape into the mid-afternoon air. The morning had flown by and even though it had been a disaster as far as any attempt to see a hatful of Premiership goals, specifically four goals from the boot of a talented Norwegian named Ole Gunnar Solskjær, I would remember that morning for a very long time.

I had fallen upon good company. A kindred spirit if you like. Despite our generational divide, our connection was immediate. My experience of watching soccer as an Englishman abroad was made all the more enjoyable alongside such a soccer addict and respected English gentleman.

Oh yes, and the final score that day?

Derby County 2, Everton 1.

Fred and I had not seen either of Derby's goals.

But that was OK.

41

"By the Shorts and Curlies"

After securing victories against Derby County and Nottingham Forest, next up for United was a fifth round FA Cup tie against Fulham. Conor O'Neill's featured the game and I watched a gutsy Fulham performance, United eventually coming out on top courtesy of an Andy Cole strike. Den and Don—Michigan's United double act—provided the usual high-fives, bear hugs, and chest bump rallying cries after the goal went in. I was beginning to warm to such exuberant displays.

February 17, 1999 and a midweek clash.

Arsenal FC were the visitors to Old Trafford.

The Gunners had escaped with a Marc Overmars winner the previous season. I hoped that this time the outcome would be different. Having to work, once again detached from the actual moment, I cast my eye at the clock on the department wall at 2:30 p.m. Eastern Standard Time (7:30 p.m. in Manchester). Old Trafford resonated in my brain as I continued with the treatment of my clients, focused on the job at hand, yet at the same time consciously willing United to victory. At the end of my work day, I flew into my apartment and flipped on the answering machine for the all-important match report from Des.

"Honestly Gary, you can't get any of the big games now on BBC or ITV. It's all about that bloody Sky dish thing! I am not paying that much, I can tell you right now! Anyway, son, I listened to the Radio Five commentary. Good old BBC! The match was close and could have gone either way. Here's the run down mate." My father was sounding like a true professional, his on-air delivery via phone from Scotland as reliable as ever. I clung to his every word. I'd yet to take my coat off and stood in anticipation, desperate for news of a United win.

"It was a miserable bloody night, Gary. Heavy rain pounding down. The commentators continually made reference to it. A typical winter's evening in Manchester. Both teams had their chances early on it seemed but I would say that Arsenal's Seaman was the busier of the two keepers.

Then United got a penalty. No Dennis Irwin tonight so the duty fell to ..." There followed a teasing pause from my father, playing the role beautifully, leaving me poised and ready for the outcome before he said "Dwight Yorke ... and he bloody well blasted it wide!"

"Nil-nil at half-time, son. United came out with real purpose in the second half and sounded the more threatening of the two sides. Then, against the run of play Kanu shot down the middle and entered the United box. The ball broke to Anelka and the French lad blasted it high into the net. Gary, after that, Arsenal stopped everything that was thrown at them, son. The weather worsened and the game appeared to be slipping out of United's reach once again."

Bloody hell. Not again, I thought. Surely not.

"Beckham then hit a cross field ball to Phil Neville on the left and his cross was met by Andy Cole who headed it past Seaman. Apparently, that was the first goal Arsenal had conceded all year. More importantly for us of course, was that we had equalized! Anyway, the game ended at 1-1, so we're still top of the league, son. Still top of the league. Hope you're doing well over there, Gary. Keep goin' son. Keep goin'!"

High Glen Cottage's transatlantic postmatch wrap had done me proud.

A few days later, the Reds played Coventry City.

Conor O'Neill's had the match.

The morning began with the usual antics of our beloved Arsenal fanatic, Cliff Miller, bursting through the door and straining his neck to see what was on the screen above him. Upon realizing there was no sign of his beloved Arsenal, worse still, that it was the Manchester United match, he immediately turned and left.

"I just don't understand Cliff. He's in his own world isn't he?" Fred declared. "Unless it is his Arsenal, he simply will not stay. Doesn't even stop to say hello!"

"Yep, that is one focused dude," declared Chinny.

Conor O'Neill's had a fairly good crowd that day and United ended up beating the Sky Blues 1-0. Most of the lads decided to hang around for the postmatch medication time.

Fred kicked us off, commenting on how much United really were beginning to look like a team who just knew each other's instincts, so evident during the move that resulted in the goal against Coventry that day. Even Chinny and Crown Paints Jacob, Liverpool's representatives for the day, reluctantly agreed. Red went on to kindly inquire about the progress of my niggly back, taking the piss, stating that a physical therapist should have been well on the mend by now.

"Yeah very funny, Red," I responded.

"Didn't you once work for a rugby club, Gary? I seem to remember you mentioning that once before over at my place while we were watching a match. Come on, tell us more about trying to get those players fit, you tosser" said Red insisting I produce a medication time story of my own.

Red had brought it out to play, so why not. I took the bait.

"Well, it's about seven or eight years ago now, but yeah I did actually work as a team physio for a Premier Rugby League Club back in the UK. The players in our squad at the time were a mix of British, Australian and New Zealand International players. Some really great players to be honest and a lot of them loved a postmatch beer or ten, and being sponsored by one of the local breweries certainly fueled that desire. After any away game the back of the team bus was always filled with at least three twenty-four pack crates of bitter, most of them empty by the time we made it back to the ground.

"Yeah, I saw one of those rugby games once on TV over here. Damn, those guys go at it for sure," said Crown Paints, adding his two pennies worth.

"No pads or anything. Those boys hit hard, man. Don't they all end up with those funny ears?" Chinny added.

"Chinny, you're spot on there, mate. Cauliflower ears!"

"Isn't that like what wrestlers get?" Fred added.

"Yeah mate, all that cartilage around the ear gets hammered and over time it causes that familiar deformity."

"Damn, Gary, you've suddenly gone all cruciferous on us, man," Jacob quipped.

"Gone all bloody what?" Eddie chimed in.

"Cruciferous. Cauliflower. A member of the cruciferous family."

"Only you would make a comment like that, Jake," Chinny replied.

"Well, of course, it's a great source of antioxidants and has amazing anti-inflammatory powers as well, Chinny," Jacob replied, simply unable to help himself.

"Bloody hell, Jake, that's enough, mate! This is turning into a bloody Whole Foods commercial," said Eddie. "Let's just get back to the footy, eh?"

"Well, rugby right?" added Red, bringing me back in from the cold.

"Where the hell was I? Oh yeah, back to that half-time dressing room. A dressing room that often depicted a war zone. Players slumped with their ears half bitten off, mostly of your cruciferous cauliflower variety of course, Jacob. They could well have used some of those anti-inflammatory powers for sure."

"Nice one, man," Jacob acknowledged

"I tell you what lads, those players were animals. They'd come in with bites in the groin."

"Bites in the groin? What the . . ." Eddie stated somewhat perplexed, almost choking on his beer.

"Yeah, bites in the groin, mate. Those scrums can't half hide some right shenanigans let me tell you."

"Oh right. Now I get it, mate. Now I get it," Eddie seemingly a tad more comfortable with the bite in the groin scenario.

"Oh yeah, black eyes, bleeding skulls, dislocated fingers, dead legs, and all the time my skinny frame would be buzzing around the injured, trying to patch up who I could, while our manager was barking his instructions, laying into players, firing them up prior to the team stepping out onto the field for the second half."

"Sounds pretty damn intense," Den observed.

"Adrenaline in full flow mate," I replied.

"Anyway, you get the picture. Now, one particular night, during training, I was working at full tilt, injuries piling up mid season. A heavy loss the weekend prior had left us in shambles to be honest. I remember being fully engrossed in my treatment of one particular player's shoulder injury, up in the tiny physio room inside the stadium. Suddenly I hear this screeching holler from downstairs, under the main stand, close to the home team changing rooms."

"Gary! Gary! Where the fuck are ya, mate? Get your fucking arrrrse down here now, son!"

"It sounded like the manager, and he appeared to be in some considerable distress. I dropped everything and pelted it down the stairs. Had there been a severe head injury? Had someone been knocked out? God forbid swallowed their tongue? It sounded serious. It was all going through my head."

"Gary! Get down here, pronto!" the manager was not letting up.

"I reached the changing rooms only to find them empty. I swiftly moved into the back shower area. There, cutting an isolated figure, stood our team manager, stark bollock naked, towel in hand, scratching his 'arrrrse' with an obvious grimace."

"What's up, boss? I mean what else do you say with that vision in front of you? I was still gasping from the pace at which I had cut and run to his aid."

"With a completely serious face—I can still see it to this day—the manager of one of Britain's most prestigious Rugby League clubs looked me straight in the eye and replied, Gary you've got to give me some of that fuckin' Anusol cream for these fuckin' hemorrhoids, son? My arse is fuckin' killing me! I have had enough of this shit, son!"

"No pun intended right" quipped Jacob once again.

"You are on fire today, mate" Chinny lauded Jacob.

"Well, more like your manager's backside was, right Gary" replied Fred, running with it beautifully, as we all rattled out another laugh.

"Man, that coach had you . . . what is it you English say? Oh yeah, by the shorts and the curlies," said Red, our small soccer clan immediately bursting into fits of laughter.

"No, no mate, you mean short and curlies, right?" replied Fred.

"Short and curlies? Oh, okay, you wanker. I got it! Singular not plural. I love that. Short and curlies. Love it!" Red was always keen to ensure his British slang stayed up to scratch, adding the phrase to his ever-growing list.

As the laughter died down, Den quietly asked "Hey, Gary, how long were you at that club for then?"

"You know what, Den, I was there for just over a year or so. I received a job offer to work in the beautiful city of York, jumped at the chance and ended up relocating for a new and challenging hospital post there. I handed in my notice at Hemorrhoid RLFC. Collecting my final pay packet—the usual nineteen pounds for the week (three nights and a weekend game)—I felt that I had earned the respect of the manager and players. It had been a terrific learning curve early on in my career and a job that had certainly given me the confidence to work with professional athletes should the opportunity arise in the future."

"Nineteen pounds, Gary? Nineteen pounds?! And for all that responsibility. That's crazy!" exclaimed Fred.

"Oh, how times have changed, eh friend," I replied.

"Yeah, I'm sure that would still buy you a few short and curly cauliflowers though, right, you wanker?" added Red.

"Certainly would, Red. Certainly would. You kill me mate! You kill me!"

"Wonderful that, Gary. A little rugby flavor to our Saturday morning medication time, eh," exclaimed Fred.

And with that, Fred stood, smiled, and shook each of our hands.

"Same time next week then lads?"

Demonstrating a fit athletic stride, the grand old gentleman of our paddock walked towards the exit, another Saturday of soccer at Conor O'Neill's in the books.

42

A Fleeting Friendship

When you have a friend like Norfolk Nobby, a friend who is unapologetic about his total disdain for all things United, a friend who thinks that Ryan Giggs has no ability whatsoever, and a friend who scoffs at any United success ever achieved—then you have a friend who sucks you into the wonderful to and fro of transatlantic soccer punting between two United polar opposites.

Yes, Nobby is, indeed, a staunch United fan, but Nobby's allegiance is to a different United.

My Norfolk pal is adamant that he never supported a team until he hit twenty-three years old. That was his age when he moved into a rented house in Sheffield, a mere two-hundred yards from Bramall Lane, home of Sheffield United FC, aka The Blades.

Nobby once told me that during his very first weekend in Sheffield, he was sat in the lounge of the terraced dwelling clearly able to make out a song coming from the ground across the street:

"Brian Deane and Tony Agana, wibbly wobbly woo. Put 'em together and what do you get? Top of Division Two."

"It was like a wave washing over me," said Nobby, "and then after hearing the famous chip butty song sung to the tune of John Denver's "Annie's Song" for about the seventeenth time in a row that same afternoon, I realized that I may as well support the team because it felt like I was anyway."

"You fill up my senses,

Like a gallon of Magnet,

Like a packet of Woodbines,

Like a good pinch of snuff,

Like a night out in Sheffield,

Like a greasy chip butty,

Like Sheffield United,

Come fill me again."

And so, as the chorus washed over my friend, as if to hypnotize him, he instantly became a committed "Blades" fan. After attending four home matches in quick succession, Nobby put it to me like this:

"I was teamless and so I guess I simply became a supporter by default. That song from the terraces had a pretty decent ring to it, too!"

After my own beloved United had received that infamous 5-0 drubbing at the hands of Newcastle United back in 1996, I received a "congratulatory" telephone message from Nobby. I had expected nothing less. It was one of many that day to be honest. Nobby's piss take was extended further as a second barrage arrived in the form of a letter a week or so later, as if to prolong the agony of what was indeed a dark day for the lads from Old Trafford.

It read as follows: "Don't you dare think you are getting off lightly with a quick, dear, oh dear!" referring to my telephone message that had attempted to beat him to the punch.

Nobby is never beaten to the punch.

"Five star, Famous Five, five alive, high five, five o'clock shadow and any other five I can fucking well think of! Yes, five is such a beautiful number. But the best five of all is the one that is followed by a big fat nil!"

On the morning of February 26, 1999, the day before United's next game against Southampton, I received yet another Nobby Special courtesy of the Royal Mail, this time listing Nobby's top ten reasons for loathing Manchester United. The man was on a roll. It was excellent timing to be honest and really fired up my own United spirit.

Here are some excerpts that my friend had listed in his latest transatlantic attempt to rile me:

"Reason No. 2: United! Their fans call them United and yet there are at least fifteen other Uniteds at last count. How did the United of Manchester gain exclusive rights to that name? Maybe it's because they have united the country in its loathing of them?"

"Reason No. 3: Success! OK, I will admit my own personal dislike also stems from United's continued success, however, this would not be such a factor if it didn't get rammed down my throat at the end of each season."

Nobby also continued to harp on about a certain young Welshman.

"Giggs, Gary, is crap! He has the crossing ability of a hedgehog. Decidedly poor. Drop him. He suffers from prodigal son syndrome."

I continued to write as often as I could to my old mates back home. Never forget your friends and family, right? Those letters were such an important line of communication. I made an immediate note to remember to send Nobby a Manchester United Christmas card later that year, one with Ryan Giggs on the front!

United's league campaign continued with that final game for February—a 2-1 win over Southampton.

There was a late scare from LeTissier, but earlier goals from Roy Keane and Dwight Yorke secured the points.

How did I know? Courtesy of Nobby of course!

The lad called and left a message declaring United's sheer luck at achieving the valuable three points.

"You jammy bunch of Manky Bastards." More often than not that was indeed the chosen, endearing turn of phrase from friends back home, should United have persevered in a tight match. "It took you eighty minutes to break down that Southampton defense mate, and even then Le Tissier almost pulled it out of the fire."

That win over Southampton had United still sitting pretty at the top of the Premier League at the end of February. Only four points separated the Red Devils from the chasing pack lead by Chelsea. If Arsenal were to win their two games in hand, then they would be only two points behind United.

March 1999 was about to usher in a seemingly non-stop run of Premier League, FA Cup, and Champions League matches. First up, United played host to Inter Milan in the Champions League quarter final first leg.

With some good pre-planning, I was able to leave work early that afternoon. Dorothy's Champions League Lifeline would not be required. A long drive to Ann Arbor was out of the question since Red was out of town and so I decided to stay local. ESPN2 was broadcasting the match live. Dearborn's cable network had its limitations and at times had not shown the games. It was also a non-descript Wednesday afternoon as far as restaurants and bars were concerned.

Northeast Dearborn had a restaurant known as Chili's, priding itself on a variety of burgers amid contemporary southwestern decor, with restaurants in all fifty states. I had visited Chili's a couple of times prior to my Britannia Club days, when I was resigned to watching the Detroit Lions play for my weekend sporting fix. I didn't foresee any problem with the restaurant sacrificing one of its many screens in order to make a

Manchester United fan very happy. A prior phone call had linked me to a manager, who it turned out, actually originated from South Korea and who immediately understood my request.

Game on!

The greeter—it was still a strange feeling to have the door held open for me and a smiling happy face welcome me in—escorted me to the manager, a very friendly young man who immediately recalled our telephone conversation. Enthusiastically grabbing a remote control, he lead me to a TV in a quiet corner. I settled in, and with the volume at just the right level for my personal enjoyment, up popped Old Trafford, floodlit and looking resplendent on a night of such importance. I'm sure that every soccer fan living as an expat in America can relate to the excitement I felt as the stadium came into view; the joy at finding a source that is broadcasting a match of such importance, immediately transported me back "home."

I knew the prematch talk would have focused on Beckham and Simeone and their clash at the World Cup the previous summer. I also knew that Manchester United had to take the initiative and nudge ahead in the first leg of what was going to be a tough tie against the Italians. A win was required and no away goals could be afforded.

United started brightly and I began to draw attention from other corners of the bar as my cheers and reactions became increasingly animated. An occasional punter would walk by, intrigued and inquiring if it was soccer that I was watching. I imagined how different the atmosphere would have been at any pub in Lancashire, where I would most likely be clamoring for a view of the TV. I was a world away for sure.

Beckham picked up the ball on the edge of the Inter Milan box and whipped in a cross first time which was met majestically by Dwight Yorke as he dived and headed the ball into the net. A beauty of a goal! With only six minutes on the clock, United led 1-0!

I was alone in my celebration, inside a restaurant whose clientele were more concerned with the flavor of a juicy chicken wing or the size of their glass of chilled Bud Lite. In a strange way, that simply heightened my connection, isolated in my support for my team.

As my encouragement grew louder, a man from around the corner from where I was stood came over and joined me. Initially, not too forthcoming, he eventually introduced himself as Larry. His distinct Irish accent was a dead giveaway, and, at around fifty years of age, he appeared rather portly with a ruddy face. I imagined that he may have made close friends with a few "wee drams" over the years.

"Son is that Manchester United playing on that there screen there?"

"Yeah, mate, it is!"

"Well, what the hell?" the Irishman responded in disbelief.

"They're playing Inter Milan in the Champions League quarters."

"You're kidding me." His gentle Irish tone melded with a Detroit American twang. "Ah, now. Fantastic."

A broad grin appeared on Larry's face as he pulled up a chair. Looking a little more comfortable and willing to offer a little more in the way of conversation, Larry spoke again.

"Son, it's been ages since I've seen a game of football. So long. This is bloody marvelous. Manchester United, eh? Well I'll be damned. Oh, I am up for this so I am. I never knew the television carried the games now."

After Larry's initial introduction, we hardly spoke another word as we both became engrossed in the match.

I later learned that Larry had grown up in Cork and that he had been in the U.S. for more than twenty years, employed by the Ford Motor Company. Perceiving his thrill at watching the game, I told him about Conor O'Neill's and he immediately scribbled the address down on a napkin, enthusiastic about the opportunity "to drink a decent pint as well," as he put it.

The tempo of the game picked up and the ball once again found itself at the feet of David Beckham and his beautifully-flighted cross appeared to have a homing device on it as it once again collided with the head of Dwight Yorke and beat the Italian keeper all ends up.

2-0! United were in command.

"Yes!"

ESPN commentator Tommy Smyth was a little more ecstatic in his description of another ball hitting the "auld onion bag" and as I watched the goal celebration, I was nudged by Larry.

"Hey, is that a fucking Irishman commentating?"

"Yep, certainly is mate. And he always brings his auld onion bag along with him, too."

"Well, would you believe that?" The comment once again drawing a broad grin from Larry, now even happier because not only was he seeing his first soccer match in many a year, but the commentary was being provided by an unmistakable accent from his home country. Larry began to settle in as he lit up his cigarette, placing it between the end of middle finger and thumb of his left hand, the dark nicotine stains on his fingers affirming his habit, as he held a glass of "the black stuff" in his right hand. I considered Larry had drifted back to a bygone era and was stood in his local pub somewhere on the Emerald Isle.

Half-time came and went. I made my usual phone call to High Glen Cottage to get the view of the game from Des. Once again, the miles just melted away as we both concluded it was a question of making no mistakes from here on out. Don't concede an away goal.

Returning to my spot, I noticed Larry was deep in conversation with a very attractive, rather exotic looking woman, obviously several years younger than him. The conversation looked a wee bit intense, so I turned away and focused on the second half.

Not surprisingly, Inter Milan began to come into the game more and more. Tommy Smyth brought out his usual phrases.

"2-0 is the hardest lead to defend."

"The most dangerous score in football is 2-0."

"This game is far from over yet!"

"Inter Milan need a goal!"

Larry wandered back over and stood beside me once again. You can take the man from the game, but you can't take the game from the man. I could sense a definite tension and couldn't help feeling that the conversation with his lady friend had not been the best. A quick look to where she was sat bore evidence, as her facial expression told all.

As I returned my gaze toward the screen, I was stopped in my tracks as I witnessed one of the greatest saves I have ever seen from Peter Schmeichel. My reactions afterwards were lost on everyone, except for the Irishman stood next to me.

"What a save! Did you see that? He is bloody incredible, mate!"

"Son, I did see that. One hell of a save. Truly it was!"

Schmeichel had leapt into the air like a tiger, arms and legs astride, as the huge left hand of the brilliant goalkeeper batted the ball away. The Inter Milan striker remained prostrate on the floor in disbelief at what he had witnessed. Following the save of the season, Inter Milan's Simeone had a header disallowed. The Inter Milan defender, Colonesse, then dummied Schmeichel and hammered his shot goalward. Standing dead center of the goal line was Henning Berg, making the clearance of his life.

The game ended United 2, Inter Milan 0.

Mission accomplished.

The Irishman next to me offered his hand. I shook it gladly, reminding him of the Saturday mornings at Conor O'Neill's. He had obviously enjoyed his impromptu helping of European soccer. He sighed, gave me a nod, and then shot over to the corner in which his lady sat. I watched the cold reception he received. I had enjoyed Larry's quiet presence. I hadn't been alone in cheering the Reds on.

I walked over to the bar and shook the manager's hand, thanking him for my lifeline to the game. As I turned to exit the restaurant, I noticed that the interrogation from Larry's lady friend was continuing. In an attempt no doubt to grasp some relief, the Irishman offered me an enthusiastic wave. I returned the compliment. Rather you than me, mate!

Larry never did make it down to Conor O'Neill's—at least not when I was there. In fact, I never did see the fella again.

43

A Finn's Take

Just three days after the crucial home win over Inter Milan, United were back in action with a much-anticipated FA Cup tie against Chelsea at Old Trafford. Both teams were riding high at the top of the Premier League and the big game was scheduled as the live match at Conor O'Neill's.

Fred left me a phone message the night before the game.

"I'm really looking forward to resuming my medication with you and the lads tomorrow. I trust your back is feeling better, my friend. Get a good night's rest. I just spent the evening discussing the meaning of life with my wife and after a lengthy debate, the only conclusion I could come to was a one-word answer—*soccer!* Look forward to seeing you in the morning, Gary!"

The large crowd gathered at Conor O'Neill's that Saturday morning witnessed a combative affair with Paul Scholes and Roberto Di Matteo both receiving red cards. The game itself gave all the Manchester United lads plenty of opportunity to pit our support against Blue Peter, our resident Chelsea fan. The loudest cheer of the day was the moment when Gary Neville, of all people, having connected with a Beckham cross, hit the post early in the first half with a diving header. Miracles do indeed happen! In the end the spoils were shared and the game ended 0-0. This meant yet another game for United in an already-congested fixture list

Blue was content, stating, as he swaggered out of the bar and into the Ann Arbor morning sunlight, that Chelsea would easily be victorious in the replay at Stamford Bridge. I remained behind with other members of our Saturday morning soccer club. It was medication time.

I had invited a work colleague from the hospital to join us. Originally from Finland, Jari and his young family had also made the trek across the Pond to Michigan in search of a little more opportunity for themselves. We had spent many a lunch break discussing soccer and his knowledge of the English game was impressive.

Jari and I normally met up for beer and wings at a bar in Detroit every couple of weeks—"wings" referring both to the tasty, edible kind and, of course, the Detroit Red Wings. Being a Finn, Jari loved his ice hockey. It was rather reminiscent of my midweek outings to Pucks with Jussi.

Jari accepted my long overdue invitation to head down to Conor O'Neill's to catch a game. Apparently the English game had wide coverage in Finland and it had been a permanent fixture for Jari and his father each Saturday.

Our medication Guinness soon arrived and Red, Chinny, Den, Don, Jack and, of course, Fred and I settled in for a tale of Finnish soccer fanaticism. With a determined swig of his beer and an acknowledging smile that affirmed his choice of beverage, Jari began to tell his story.

"Every Saturday afternoon, my father and I would go for a long ski, returning home by five to get ready to watch an English First Division match together. I was about twelve when I first started watching. Of course the games were broadcast in the Finnish winter when it was very dark and cold with the temperatures often well below minus twenty."

"Jari, that sounds like Michigan to me" exclaimed Red. "We could have skied down here to Conor's the day United played Liverpool in the FA Cup. It was minus twenty-two early that morning."

With a wry smile Jari took another sip of the black stuff and continued.

"One of the things that I remember was the commentator. His name was Aulis Virtanen. Hell, I don't even know if he is still alive or not. He would always be over in England for the broadcasts and he had his very own style when it came to calling the matches. Overall, he was quite calm in his delivery. He was always fairly neutral and not very explosive at all. Actually, he was really quite boring come to think of it."

Finns aren't exactly renowned for their explosive verbal delivery, I quietly contemplated. Jari continued.

"Virtanen did have his own phrases for certain game situations though. A good example of this was when somebody missed a goal, he would always describe this situation with the same word every time— 'Rahtusen!' It meant 'just a little bit.'"

"Somehow I can't quite imagine Martyn Tyler coming out with 'Ooh, just a little bit!' and a nation of soccer addicts acknowledging the close call," I commented.

Jari just smiled and carried on with his tale in his inimitable modest Finnish manner.

"My father and I were very familiar with the English teams. We always got the weekly newspaper, which specialized in English and Finnish soccer. In fact, I remember for a short while the focus on the TV and in the newspapers actually changed to the German league, the Bundesliga. This was a huge disappointment to everyone and soon the TV networks realized it, quickly returning to broadcasting English matches. My father and I were happy once again and it wasn't long after that that I started to follow West Ham. I had chosen a team that was doing well at the time, but more so I liked their attacking style of play."

"The West Ham way is what they call it, Jari," Chinny interjected.

"Chinny should know!" Red added, confident in his American friend's soccer nouse.

"Yes. I think I heard that. I remember the player Trevor Brooking, and I remember going crazy when he scored the winning goal against Arsenal in the FA Cup final. He often played for England too, right?"

"Yes, he sure did my friend," replied Jack. "Good player he was, too," an assuring smile filling the face of my United cohort.

"Yes, but I think the main reason why I liked Brooking the most was that he had married a Finnish lady. When I found that out, then, of course, I had to support West Ham!"

"Good lad," the communal response.

"I remember following the English national team, too. Watching those games on a Saturday kept me very familiar with their players. It was so exciting whenever they played Finland. I think they played them one time at Wembley, right?"

Of course, none of us had a bloody clue, but we all nodded in agreement, pretending to remember that classic encounter!

"In fact, I remember," my Finnish buddy continued, "on two occasions having the chance to see Liverpool play in our home town of Oulu. This was in the European Cup. Very exciting! I think Liverpool were the best team in soccer at the time."

"When weren't they?" uttered a defiant Chinny.

"Well, err, like, right now," smirked Don, his Manchester United shirt just inches from the face of the Korean-American Liverpool fanatic.

Jari continued.

"Yes, but they were in the seventies and eighties. They actually did play our hometown team, Oulun Palloseura. Well, the team was from my father's original home town and we called them OPS. I grew up in

Pudasjarvi, but I was born in Oulu, though, so I guess I can, after all, call it my hometown too, right? We saw lots of games there."

"Steady on mate. I am on Finnish town overload here" I swiftly added, jokingly.

Once again, unperturbed, Jari continued.

"Oulun Palloseura won the Finnish championship two years in a row 1979 and 1980 and, as a consequence, played in the European Cup twice. On both of those occasions we played Liverpool. I remember the 1980–81 match well. We all traveled to the match by bus. A huge group of us. The atmosphere in a Finnish stadium was very different to what it must have been like in England. The crowds were much smaller, around 2,000, but I believe we managed around 10,000 for that particular match against Liverpool. I couldn't get over all the singing and chanting from the English supporters. It made for a terrific atmosphere. I had never witnessed anything like it. It was so exciting to see Liverpool play in Finland. I will never forget it. We actually managed a 1-1 draw. This, of course, drew great excitement from our fans. My father and I loved it. For the return leg at Anfield it was sadly a very different story. We did score, but Liverpool unfortunately scored ten! Indeed, the following year we didn't fare much better, losing 0-1 in Finland and 7-0 at Anfield."

"Liverpool had your number, eh Jari?" Jack commented.

"Yes, they sure did, I guess. And one time that number was sadly ten!"

Laughter filled the air and we all awaited more on the Finn's take on soccer.

"Of course, whenever I watched any games on television with my father, we would always keep up a true Finnish tradition at half-time."

"What did that involve?" asked a curious Don, "out for another ski? A ride on a reindeer maybe?"

"Well, my friend," replied Jari, "you are not too far from the truth"

"After taking a sauna we would emerge from the heat and run around outside in the snow before jumping into an ice-cold pool."

"Wow," said Jack. "How did you avoid getting a heart attack? That sounds like a pretty hardcore half-time ritual to me."

"Well, we Finns are built with solid steel," replied Jari, smiling. "We would then watch the second half with a table full of food prepared by my mother. Our supper would consist of bread, fruit and sausages—lenkki-makkara, grillimakkara, mustamakkara, and my favorite, siskonmakkara.

Oh, yes, and that reindeer you were talking about, Don, actually ended up on our table! My father would always make sure he had his favorite beer. Lapin Kulta! That beer was very famous. It still is. It is brewed in Lapland. You do realize just how much we Finnish people love our beer, don't you?"

And with that, Jari smiled, raised his glass and said "Kippis!" before downing the rest of his Guinness, licking his lips, and placing his empty glass back down on the table in front of him.

"Fascinating. Absolutely fascinating!" exclaimed Fred "I would never have imagined the English league games being so popular in Finland. This game truly has its appeal all around the world, doesn't it?"

Medication time over with, we wished each other well and wandered out into the early afternoon sunshine, all feeling a tad more enlightened about a small region in northern Finland.

Three days later, I was at work mobilizing an elderly patient's injured ankle, around 2:30 p.m. My mind was on a game taking place three thousand miles away—the FA Cup replay against Chelsea at Stamford Bridge in London. As soon as I got home, I shot straight to the phone and dialed High Glen Cottage. It rang just one time before Des answered.

"That Dwight Yorke is quite some player, Gary! I tell you what!"

"Yes! They did it! They did it, right?!"

"2-0, mate! Both goals from Yorke. They all played a blinder, but Yorke was especially outstanding."

"Brilliant! That's it, mate. We're in the semis! Yes!"

"Yes, we are! But now for the bad news, son" replied my father.

"Oh no, so who's injured now then, dad?"

There then followed several seconds of silence before my father uttered the words, "no, it's nothing like that, son. It's that United have been drawn against Arsenal!"

44

Fat Lady Not Yet Singing

Despite Manchester United's unbelievable run of success over the past few years, the 1998–99 season, with the possibility of an unprecedented Treble on the horizon, was gearing up to be a season like no other. I continued to do whatever I could to keep up with it all despite living in an area where pretty much nobody had any knowledge of, nor cared about, the Red Devil's run back across the Pond.

I was fortunate to be a part of a small, tight network of soccer fanatics at Conor O'Neill's. However, once out of that circle, I immediately stepped back into a United void. Apart from transatlantic Des, Sandy the occupational therapist, and Dearborn Dorothy, I appeared to have little else around me to punctuate the United journey during my day-to-day existence. Why would I?

Most of the people with whom I interacted were all about how the Detroit Lions were doing, how the Tigers spring training was going, along with the Detroit Pistons and Red Wings progress in the post-season basketball and hockey playoffs.

Manchester United? Forget it!

I needed to work harder to create a vibe; my own vibe. I had to develop an atmosphere, something to detract from the lack of United stimulus during my workday. I wanted to feel it more as my team began their monumental assault on all three fronts. I didn't want to miss out on the joy of the ride.

Then it hit me. The solution was right there in front of me. I just had to open my eyes a little wider. My prospective fellow supporters of the cause were the very same people who had not yet signed on to soccer, let alone offered their allegiance to any team. My patients!

Little did they know it, but my regular clientele were ripe for influencing, ready to be educated in all things Manchester United, to be given the opportunity to stand up for the one team that matters and to understand what being a United fan was all about. It was a win-win.

My patients become the lucky ones with a chance to jump in on United's incredible charge and, in return, they could provide me with somewhat of a United buzz during work hours.

I decided that best policy was to target my most affable patients. It would take a little time, but I reckoned I could get one or two on board. I started by talking about Old Trafford and how it held over 70,000 fans. I emphasized the stadium's incredible atmosphere and its historic past.

"Yeah, but Michigan Stadium holds over a 100,000 fans, and that's for college football."

Ok, so it seemed that I may have more of a battle on my hands than I had bargained for.

Several of my patients appeared to be genuinely interested—or were good at feigning interest—or maybe they were just intrigued by the wacky English guy treating them, "you know, the one who's crazy about soccer."

Undaunted, I continued in my crusade, explaining just how momentous a year it could be for my team.

I told seventy-five-year-old lifelong Detroit Tigers fan, Jerry Freeman, about how United were moving ever closer to winning the English Premier League, the FA Cup, and the European Champions League all in one season. I explained how this had never been done before and the enormous effort it would take for one team to win all three trophies in one season. He took it all in. He had to—my enthusiasm wouldn't allow him any other choice.

"That's pretty cool, Gary. So does that mean Manchester can then go on to the World Cup?"

I still had my work cut out.

I began to use props.

I shared stories from my three-week old copy of "Four Four Two" magazine from across the Pond. It was a monthly publication so some of the stories were still quite current: essential reading for the uninformed American. I went for product placement. A carefully selected patient sat killing time with an ice pack strapped to his or her knee, for instance. One or two took an immediate shine to the journal.

"Wow, Gary. So it seems like this United is pretty good, huh?"

"I love these names, dude. Hotspurs! Lie-ses-ter City! There's even a team with Wednesday in its name? That's awesome!"

It was a promising start to my game plan.

I even began to utilize my old United scarf, taking it into work on the day of a midweek game and on most Fridays prior to a big game the ensuing weekend. Again, having chosen the right patient, I would have them hold the scarf aloft and give me a blast of "United! United! United!" It was always funny hearing that Midwestern accent pronouncing my team. Mrs. Klus, full of surprises, went all in, almost falling off the treatment plinth in the main gym area, her center of gravity getting all screwed up, forgetting about the four-pound ankle weights still wrapped around her shins. I was relieved to be in close proximity to provide the eighty-nine-year-old with the relevant assistance required before she added a fractured hip to her list of ailments.

Back in Britain, it would have been a complete contrast. My father told me that United's run was gaining more and more traction in the news. Analysts, pundits, and supporters were all beginning to talk about the inconceivable—a treble of trophies!

Could it really happen?!

If United were able to overcome Inter Milan in Milan—a far from easy task—they would be through to the semi-final of the European Champions League, as well as being top of the Premier League, and in the semi-final of the FA Cup.

I continued to tune in to the first hour of BBC World Service coverage before leaving to watch live games at Conor O'Neill's, and would listen intently as the pundits began to talk more and more about "the T word" during prematch discussions. The subject of United's treble chances began dominating early weekend morning conversations in our soccer sanctum. There was inevitable pushback from the likes of Chinny, Blue and Cliff—the latter, of course, only gracing us with his presence should his beloved Arsenal have been the featured match—but all in all those conversations provided us United fans with the opportunity to indulge in the unfolding saga. I relished the banter of our gang.

Medication time on Saturday, March 13 consisted of that one topic only—the possibility of the Treble landing in Manchester by May 26, the date of the 1999 Champions League final, to be played at the Camp Nou stadium in Barcelona.

Before our soccer townhall commenced, we all sat through an entertaining match between one of United's Premier League title rivals, Chelsea, and a resilient West Ham United. "Gooner" Cliff did pop his head in early on, only to scowl, swiftly turn away and head for the exit. Conor O'Neill's was beginning to develop its own weekend morning routine.

I enjoyed another entertaining few hours, wandering around the pub and chatting with one or two regulars, adding more names to faces. It always amazed me how many people from all over Britain turned up each weekend. That morning alone, I had chats with fellas from Barnsley, Liverpool, and Sunderland. The majority of the English fans were on placement in Michigan with the Ford Motor Company. Everybody looked knackered after getting up early on the back of a long work week and a possible late Friday night, but, nonetheless, they would always show up, maintaining that important connection to the game. Opting for an early-morning beer or two, medication in hand, each one of them added further novelty to watching English Premier League soccer in the USA.

Our very own "soccer pub" was continuing to evolve before our very eyes. It felt as though we were pioneers, crusaders if you like, defying the odds, building momentum for an underground sport in the hope that one day it may well become a part of mainstream America sporting culture.

The referee blew his whistle for full time. West Ham United had managed to beat Chelsea 1-0 — a very welcome scoreline for all Manchester United fans. It went without saying that Blue was far from happy with the result, but he did concede that Chelsea only had themselves to blame. After giving him the obligatory piss take that he was due, we made sure he joined us for medication time.

The Guinness duly arrived and Fred chimed up.

"I hate to say this lads, but I have a funny feeling that United are going to end up with nothing. The fixtures are going to mount up and it may well just all blow up in their faces. I can't help feeling that they are too stretched."

The non-United clan immediately jumped on the bandwagon to agree with Fred. It didn't take much for scouser Gerry George, to chime in.

"Hey Gary, la," bombarding me head on as always. "You're going to be lucky to win anything, mate. I tell ya, lad, Fred is spot on there, mate. It's going to be too much. United are gonna end up with fuck all!" he said with a broad smile.

Blue graciously predicted that United would win the Premier League, but felt that the two cups may well be a bridge too far.

Chinny confidently and categorically predicted that the Old Trafford cupboard would be bare. No surprise there.

All the lads in the Manchester United corner — Den, Don, Jack, Eddie, Red and I — remained quietly optimistic.

Fred was adamant.

"I honestly do feel it will be way too much my friends!"

As the scores appeared on the screen, I clenched my fist and looked at Fred.

"Hey, there's no fat lady singing just yet, mate!"

United had beaten Newcastle United 2-1.

The Red Devils were slowly beginning to pull away from Chelsea. There was, however, an enormous threat waiting in the wings:

Arsenal FC!

Prior to leaving the pub that Saturday, we all arranged to meet four days later at 2:30 p.m., Michigan time, to watch the crucial second leg of the Champions League quarter-final against Inter Milan. ESPN, complete with Tommy Smyth and his "auld onion bag," had scheduled it as the featured game and Conor O'Neill's had promised to show it on the big screen.

Bring it on!

45

Bellissimo!

After arriving home from work on the evening of Tuesday, March 16, I listened to a message from my father. Des indicated that the Brazilian superstar, Ronaldo—arguably the world's best player—was in contention for a return to the Inter Milan side for the crucial Champions League quarter-final second leg against United in Milan.

"It's going to be one hell of an atmosphere inside the San Siro. But if we can make it through this one, we're going to be on our way, son!" Des had spoken, further fueling my excitement at the upcoming big game.

Wednesday, March 17 duly arrived, and with it, a packed caseload of recuperating patients. There was simply no way that I would be able to leave work early. That afternoon, I ignored the urge to call Conor's. I also resisted the urge to call High Glen Cottage for a live progress report. Even though the suspense was killing me, expat soccer fan discipline had to be demonstrated. My work colleague, Sandy, had already contacted Dearborn Dorothy, and there would be a VHS tape of the game waiting for me in her mailbox for pickup after work.

Despite my patients having no idea what I was talking about, I still attempted to build a little excitement by describing the importance of a certain soccer match in Italy that was happening right at that moment. I kept my eye on the department clock all the while between 2:45 p.m. and 4:45 p.m., contemplating events over in Milan. At 6:30 p.m., Michigan time, I completed my patient documentation, locked up the department, and headed out to my car. Pulling out of the hospital parking lot, I couldn't get to Dearborn quickly enough.

Arriving at Dorothy's, I noted that her curtains were closed as the dimly lit streetlights reflected on her house. I reached into her mailbox and, sure enough, there it was—the coveted prize. Merging with traffic on Outer Drive and Pelham Road, I thought to myself how it was highly unlikely that anybody else on those roads had a VHS recording of a European Champions League quarter final on their passenger seat.

As I walked into my apartment, the flashing LED light of my answering machine lit up the darkened room. I resisted all temptation, turning off the volume for incoming calls, a sense of self-satisfaction at having avoided any information on the match. Of course, one benefit of being in Michigan was that nobody was going to inadvertently blurt out the scoreline anyway!

I popped the tape in, sat back, and a flood of excitement hit me as the magnificent San Siro stadium appeared on the screen, the Italian "ultras" as vibrant as ever bouncing up and down as one.

I let out my solitary roar. "Commme Onnnnn You Reds!"

Less than ten seconds later, there was a knock on my door.

"Gary are you OK?"

The recently less intrusive Mrs. Cloak, her wig well positioned, was voicing her concern over the outburst from the bedsit at the back of her home. Her inquisitive "force" — or rather, nosiness — remained strong. She simply couldn't help herself.

"No worries Rhonda," I replied. "I'm getting set to watch a very important soccer match from Europe."

Mrs. Cloak tilted her head back.

"Oh right, right. United?"

"Of course!"

"Then I guess it's Go United, huh?"

"Perfectly put, Rhonda. Perfectly put! And I will apologize now for the ensuing cheers and expletives!"

"Hey, you do what you gotta do, Gary. I'll leave you and your crazy game alone," Mrs. Cloak replied, waving her arm high behind her as if to signal "whatever" as she headed back toward her kitchen.

"I'll be watching an excellent new documentary about Death Row."

"Oh. Right. Sounds very uplifting. Good luck with that, Rhonda!"

As I closed the door behind me, I smiled, momentarily reflecting on my presence in Quirkyville. Then, my focus on the San Siro became absolute. Victory, or the right result on the night, would leave Manchester United sitting proudly in the final four of European football.

The ESPN coverage prior to the match seemed to center around Inter Milan's Brazilian superstar striker. Despite lingering questions as to his fitness, the mere presence of Ronaldo in the starting lineup had the Italian fans whipped into a frenzy. I looked closely at the United players' faces. To a man they appeared ready for the battle ahead.

The referee blew his whistle.

Game on!

From the start, Inter Milan had only one purpose and attacked, wave after wave. Schmeichel escaped a penalty call against him and moments later made a magnificent save from Zamorano. Zanetti then hit the post with a superb effort. It took United almost the entire half before they got a sniff; even then Cole blasted it high and wide. How United reached half-time without the Italians scoring I will never know. Tommy "auld onion bag" Smyth was having kittens.

I still believed. I always did—particularly as I watched Diego Simeone leave the field having twisted his ankle. I am sure I saw a Beckham smile.

I paused for breath as I fast-forwarded through the usual artificial theatre that was American infomercials, thinking just how everyone would have been reacting in the pubs back home in Britain and how the lads at Conor's would have chewed over that first forty-five minutes.

The second half brought more of the same. Ronaldo got free in the United box, but once again Schmeichel stood firm. I was glad to see the Brazilian superstar's day done around the sixtieth minute as he gave way for young prodigy, Nicola Ventola. Sometimes, however, you have to be careful what you wish for.

"Ventola picked his spot and his shot flew over Schmeichel and into the auld onion bag. Manchester United have it all to do now!" Tommy's words echoed from my tiny television screen. Just three minutes after entering the field of play, Ventola had given Inter the lead.

It was still 1-2 overall in United's favor, but the Italians could smell blood. If they grabbed one more goal then we were heading for extra time. Chance after chance went begging. United were riding their luck.

Then, with only eight minutes remaining, Dennis Irwin whipped in a terrific cross, Andy Cole nodded down beautifully and Scholes did the rest, burying the ball into the back of the net. I bowed my head, eyes closed tightly, gritted teeth, clenched fists pumping back and forth, repeating to myself "yes!, yes! yes! yes! YES!"

"Paul Scholes pops up in the penalty box at exactly the right time and places his shot beautifully into the auld onion bag! United must surely be in the semi-finals now!"

Tommy was right. 1-1 on the night. 3-1 on aggregate. We had made it to the semi-final of the European Champions League!

Thank you Dearborn Dorothy! Thank You!

I was dancing with every Manchester United supporter in Britain that night, even though most of them would now be asleep. I had waited for the moment. The answering machine was no longer off limits. Time to share in the joy. My refusal to succumb to prior temptation, discipline rewarded. United victorious.

Red sounded ecstatic as he declared how the crowd at Conor's had been behind United all the way. He said that there had been a surprising amount of the regular weekend morning clan there, and considering that it was a 2:30 p.m. kick-off on a work day afternoon, there were obviously a few who had managed a rather lengthier lunch break than anticipated.

My father came across a little more measured, but very happy, calmly noting a professional Manchester United performance, and adding "but by god son, they weren't half lucky in that first half!"

Manchester United were now just two games away from what would be their first appearance since 1968 in the final of Europe's premier cup competition!

The following Sunday, United earned three more crucial Premier League points with a 3-1 win over Everton. On the same day, we watched a Chelsea side still fighting for the Premier League crown, duly demolish Aston Villa 3-0. The crowd at Conor's was small, but, of course, it contained Blue Peter, who, despite his earlier proclamation, let it be known that his boys in blue were not done yet. Blue didn't seem quite as miserable these days. It's funny how a decent string of results for your team can change your outlook for the better.

The month of March 1999 had come and gone and the Premier League top four were as follows:

Manchester United	*played 30*	*points 63*
Arsenal	*played 30*	*points 59*
Chelsea	*played 29*	*points 56*
Leeds United	*played 30*	*points 54*

With eight weeks of the season left, United were sitting pretty at the top of the Premier League.

In the European Champions League semi-final, they had been drawn against Juventus.

In the FA Cup semi-final, they were to play Arsenal.

And I was about to move with the times in pursuit of "my" United.

46

Saturday Morning Drill

Saturday April 3, 1999: Time for United to visit Selhurst Park to play Wimbledon. And time for another visit to my rather unique Italian barber. With no on-call duty at the hospital, I figured that I could fit in a quick trim at Gino's and still make it over to Conor O'Neill's for kick-off. Needless to say, however, I had figured wrong. Why did I insist on my choice of barber? Simple really. At only $8 a cut, the price was right, not to mention the inadvertent, yet unashamedly un-PC entertainment. I planted myself outside the door to Gino's at 8:45 a.m. aiming to be first in line for the chop.

As ever, the man made his appearance from the back door of the shop, slowly ambling his way across the shop floor, coffee and donut in hand, *Detroit Free Press* tucked under his arm and mumbling "mornin'" as he opened the front door to his business. He wandered over to the window to open the blinds to the world outside. Still yawning and making it plainly obvious he wasn't too convinced about being inside those four walls, he stood for a few moments and paused to read the newspaper headlines.

Dressed in his usual Seventies silk shirt, large pointed collar, top three buttons open with gold medallion on full display, he wasted no time letting fly with his first barrage.

"Jesus! Look at that, another one gets a bullet downtown. I'm tellin ya man, they should just blow that fucking place up and start again."

Taking another gulp of his brew, his eyes closed, he flicked his head and hand in unison to beckon me over to his center of operations, flinging the newspaper down on the seat beside him. Like a bullfighter teasing his prey, he threw the barber's sheet high in the air, his years' of experience timing its landing to perfection as it settled gently on my shoulders.

"So how you doin', doc?"

"Doing well, Gino. How about yourself, my friend?"

"Can't complain. Another day closer to retirement, right? What's not to like about that?"

"Good lad! Now how about getting me out of here quickly Gino, so I can catch up with my soccer, eh?"

"No problem, doc. Boy, you English sure love your soccer. In fact, I thought about you the other day. I had two guys in from England."

"Really?" I responded, surprised.

"Yeah, sure did. They had just arrived to work at Ford. I told them about that place you go to watch your soccer. Ann Arbor right?"

"Yeah mate, that's right. How the hell did they find out about your place, Gino?"

"Get this! Apparently they had gone on that internet and looked up a barbershop in Dearborn. Mine came up with five scissors after it!" Gino said, proudly.

"Five scissors, eh, Gino! That sounds pretty good!"

"Yeah man. Can you believe that? I'm on the fucking internet. This world is fucking crazy man! Five scissors! Are you fucking kidding me?"

Gino's dry smile appeared as the buzz of the shears hit second gear and the shaky hand of the Italian barber leaned ever closer to deliver his first sweep.

Of course, I should have known better. After only one majestic swipe of Gino's clippers, they were swiftly turned off and my barber was once again up on his soapbox.

"Check this out, doc! Have a look at that!"

"A look at what, Gino?"

Three shaggy-haired customers sitting along the far wall of the barbershop raised their heads in unison.

"A politically correct road crew! Right outside. Look! Look at 'em!"

Gino pointed with his shears to the six individuals directly across from his shop, all busy trying to improve one of Michigan's busted up road surfaces.

"They've been here all week. Check 'em out! You have your small, hard-working Asian guy. An Arab, of course. Two blacks. An elderly white dude, and, go figure, a woman in charge of the lot! God damn, man. Clinton would be proud of that crew, I'm tellin ya! Hey and you should see that woman. She loves that road drill man. Look! Look! Here she goes! She'll be on it all day if she has her way. Look! Watch her just tuck that fuckin thing right up in there and . . . oh yeah, you know she loves that! Look at her she doesn't want to let that sucker go, does she? Look! She's lovin' it man! Lovin' it! Nobody else is gonna get near that thing for a while, I'm tellin ya! Here, let me give her wave. Hold on a minute there, doc."

"Hey there, honey! Yep, you, boss! How's it goin'?"

Gino waved his clippers above his head in the shopfront window. The man simply had no shame whatsoever. By this time, everyone in the shop was peering forward to get a view of the "Fixing the Road Show." Gino's already shaky hand is doing the mamba and I am still eagerly awaiting the second sweep of his shears, hoping it will actually hit my head.

My openly-opinionated barber came out with some crazy, shocking, shit at times. His in-your-face political agenda, did, however, make the normally mundane task of a haircut pretty memorable.

"Hey, come on Gino. The game's going to be over by the time I get out of here, mate."

"Alright! Alright! Chill out, man. Damn, you English are pushy!" Gino refocused and was on a roll as he must have gone at least a full minute without stopping to make any further comments. That didn't last long though. Clippers off and Gino was "off on one" again.

"Gotta tell ya, doc. I had a guy in here yesterday. Runs a security firm downtown at the Opera House. Ya know what he was telling me? What he does before every show down there? He gets down there with his guys an hour early to clear away all the bums and panhandlers littering the streets, waiting to beg for green backs off the show goers as they arrive. He tells me they have to do that because it's the only way to get the place looking first class as all the opera lovers arrive. Ya know what? Those same people then stand there and comment about how fantastic the city is looking, about how Detroit is really making a comeback. Bullshit is what I say! If they had seen the place just minutes before. Hell, the security guys said that in the past there have been situations where they've been spat at and had to go to hospital for a goddamn AIDS test. I tell ya, you wouldn't get me down there. No fuckin' way, man!"

I did not comment. How could I? That was a fire that needed no more fuel. I simply waited in silence for Gino's diatribe to end. I needed my haircut. And fast.

Several minutes later, my prayers were answered as Gino brushed me down.

"Alright! There you go, doc. You have yourself a good day now, doc. Enjoy your soccer. What is it I'm supposed to say? Go Man U or something?"

"Hey, you're catching on, Gino! I'm impressed!" I replied, smiling. "See you in a couple of weeks, eh?"

"Get outta here, doc!"

Honking my horn, I pulled out from in front of the store. A wave of the old man's clippers above the head of a rather nervous looking client returned the gesture, Gino, all the while, pointing to the hardworking road crew that I was about to drive past before I reached the I-94 freeway.

I had departed "the world according to Gino."

It was 9:30 a.m. and I had a half hour to make it to Ann Arbor before the start of the game. This particular Saturday morning at the beginning of April, however, appeared to have brought out the orange road barrels in full force, signifying the spring onslaught of road repairs. Only happens when you're in a rush, right?

"You're a little late today, aren't you?" the new parking lot attendant at the back of Conor O'Neill's rather astutely noted. It appeared she had already familiarized herself with the comings and goings of her patrons.

I quickly made for the back of the pub, weaving my way through the corridor leading to the main area and over toward our paddock. All of the United lads were present; even Ahmed had made an appearance. Indeed he was the first to turn and notice me. I had a lot of respect for the big man from Jordan. His knowledge of the history of Manchester United was most evident whenever we chatted.

"Gary, my friend!" the big fella announced, his handshake backing up his larger than life verbal greeting with equal effect.

"Good to see you mate. How are they doing?" I replied as I edged my way around the lads to say my hellos.

"1-0 down already, for fuck's sake. Only five minutes gone."

"You're kidding me! It's always the same bloody story with Wimbledon."

"Yeah, but it's been all United since then, Gary," Red chimed in.

I settled into the chair that Fred had kindly saved.

"Guess who walked in ten minutes ago, looked at the screen and swiftly walked out?"

Clifford Miller's Saturday morning had been ruined once again.

"Amazing, Gary! Just amazing!"

I repositioned my chair and was immediately transported to Selhurst Park in London.

On the stroke of half-time, after a non-stop bombardment of attacks from United, Beckham struck, hammering the ball into the net. His forward roll after the shot came from his sheer determination to make it to the ball before anyone else. The United crew roared and high fives flew back and forth.

I loved those moments: a multicultural Red congregation celebrating together as one—along with the inevitable Scouse interruption.

"Hey Gary, la! Bunch of jammy bastards, mate! You've done absolutely fuck all so far! You don't deserve that goal. Jammy beggars!"

Good old Gerry George.

United had thrown everything at Wimbledon's defense and he calls it "doing fuck all"? The Conor O'Neill's experience was made all the better by Gerry's smiling red face and sarcastic comments.

The second half was more of the same. Attack after attack and even after Ole Gunnar's arrival had been greeted by all the United fans with a huge cheer, the Dons defense stood firm.

Final Score: 1-1. Two vital points dropped.

"Yes! Thank god for that!" screamed Den, his eyes fixed on the big screen above our heads. Arsenal had only managed a draw with Southampton, leaving United four points clear at the top of the table.

Medication time was rather apt that morning; our chosen topic for discussion being, of all things, prostate issues. Fred had been tripping back and forth to the bathroom rather frequently lately and had become rather frustrated with the whole affair.

"Honestly Gary, this getting old lark doesn't half have its fair share of inconveniences. I've had the urge to pass water a lot more lately and it just isn't seeming to get any better. I'm up and down the second I have a drink. I've made an appointment to see a doctor at the U of M hospital next week to have some tests done."

I tipped a glass for the sprightly fellow, sending a good wish for his appointment, promising that I wouldn't "take the piss."

"Well, for that I will be rather grateful, Gary," replied Fred

One by one, the lads began to drift away, early morning worship over. It would be another week before our congregation returned, a unique flock, ready to assemble in our very own House of Premier League soccer.

I considered that there was one thing on the minds of all our United clan; a collective mindset, as we exited the back doors of the dark pub into the brilliant sunlight. A certain team called Juventus. The Italian giants were set to arrive at Old Trafford the following Wednesday for the first leg of the European Champions League semifinal. With a midfield consisting of Zidane, Deschamps, Davids, and Conte, their dynamo of a captain, United would be up against it for sure.

I handed my parking lot ticket to the smiling attendant.

"Have yourself a great week, okay, honey?"

I acknowledged her kind wishes, wound up the car window, and with Juventus on the horizon, thought to myself "I bloody well hope so!"

47

Hangin' on the Telephone

At approximately 2:00 p.m. on Monday, April 5—it arrived. A large, white box was plonked on my desk at work by our inquisitive secretary. I was now the proud owner of a laptop computer. The lads down at Conor's had been baffling me with their recent conversations about e-mail, www this and that, soccernet.com, football 365.com, and official team websites. I was now going to join the ranks as a net-connected soccer fan. My following Manchester United abroad experience had suddenly reached new heights. I still had John Cloak's small and battered shortwave radio in my armory for the times I was unable to make it over to Conor O'Neill's, but now I had daily access to soccer news instead of having to wait for two-week-old British tabloids for insight and analysis on United's "Treble Assault."

Many of my friends back in Britain weren't online yet—certainly not family—but a phone call, letter, and even the occasional Dictaphone tape would continue to link us as they had done since my arrival on American soil.

April 7, 1999: Dearborn Dorothy to the rescue once again.

Work had me tied. My patients had me tied, as once again I had no escape route from my commitment at the hospital. I created the required banter in the treatment room and gym and watched the clock tick closer to 6:00 p.m. Within minutes I was back home, comfortably positioned in my shabby old recliner. It was 6:30 p.m. in Michigan and, once again, I had been able to avoid the result of a huge Champions League tie, the semi-final first leg no less, live from Old Trafford, Manchester. I paid no attention to my new toy atop my table, nor the answering machine. I sat alone in my Red Devil den, focused, the unmistakable voice of Tommy Smyth my only company. I was ready.

"Tonight Manchester United must, above all else, not concede a precious away goal to Juventus!"

There was only one team in it for the first forty-five minutes. And that team was not United! Davids, Zidane, Inzhagi, Deschamps and Conte were bossing the Red Devils. Eventually the pressure told and Conte pounced onto a cheeky nutmeg on Paul Scholes, courtesy of Egdar Davids, and snatched that all-precious away goal.

"United have it all to do now!"

"The Italians are certainly in the driving seat now!"

"That was the last thing Manchester United wanted so early into the game!"

Yeah, thanks for pointing that out, Tommy! But how could I chastise the Irishman and his most obvious of responses? He was, after all, my salvation, my European voice of soccer on U.S. TV.

Half-time arrived and I flicked through the analysis without even blinking, heading straight to the second half. There were no two ways about it; United had simply been outclassed.

The Italians held strong for the entire second half. Then, in stoppage time, Gary Neville launched his trademark long throw into the Juventus box. After several seconds of "keepy uppy" between defense and attack, the ball fell to Beckham and he propelled an overhead pass toward the goal. After another goalmouth scramble, the ball landed at the left foot of a certain Welshman. Ryan Giggs did not need a second invitation as he hammered the ball home. Bone-tingling shivers engulfed my torso once again. I ran with the players, sharing in their celebrations. I imagined as best I could the reactions back home as that ball hit the back of the net. United had used their "get out of jail free" card at the very end of the game.

I heard footsteps outside the apartment. Mrs. Cloak was coming up the stairs from the basement. She must have heard my joyous celebrations as I heard her shout out "Go United!" before the sliding door at the side of the house was closed.

I replayed that goal over and over and over again. In the scheme of things it was an absolutely crucial strike! We could now head to Turin in two weeks' time with a real chance of European glory.

The games kept coming. Four days later I was smack bang in the midst of another soccer soap opera. I couldn't believe my eyes as I wandered up toward Conor O'Neill's on April 11. It was by far the largest line I had seen, reaching all the way around to the end of the block. Everyone was there. At the front of the line, and stood with his face peering through the window, was our very own Gooner, Clifford Miller. There was no doubt this time as to whether he would be able to see his beloved Arsenal. Gunners scarf draped around his neck, Cliff appeared confident and ready for battle.

A passerby carrying what appeared to be his packed lunch could not let his intrigue go unanswered. He walked up to the line and enquired as to why on earth we were all queuing outside the pub so early on a Saturday morning.

"It's the FA Cup semi-final, mate. We're here to watch the soccer from England," exclaimed a young man, clearly another Arsenal fan, whom I had not seen before. Our passerby raised his eyebrows, nodded his head, and wandered away, looking completely none the wiser.

Five minutes before kick-off, the doors were opened. I noticed Red and Chinny make a beeline for the paddock and, along with the other lads, they managed to save me a seat.

A huge cheer filled the pub as Johnny emerged, remote control in hand. One click of a button this time and there, before us, appeared Villa Park, a sea of red and white.

The anticipation was total. I was in my element!

"Come on Arsenal!"

It was like a completely foreign noise. Our American Gooner, whose appearances throughout that year had been so sporadic, was making his presence felt, cheering on his beloved Gunners. He was up for it and there when it mattered. A volley of noise was returned from the United faithful.

Game on!

I watched the first few exchanges closely, sizing up the opposition and getting a feel for the teams. I came to a quick conclusion that each team pretty much mirrored the other. Each had their warrior at the back, United's being a now more settled Jaap Stam and Arsenal with their warhorse, Tony Adams. United had their combative midfielder Roy Keane and Arsenal had Patrick Vieira. Marc Overmars was Arsenal's tricky winger as was Ryan Giggs for United.

United appeared to hold the edge early on and raised the roof on a couple of occasions with near misses. I smiled on each occasion as our dear friend Mr. Miller waited until the chorus died down before chanting loudly "Coooome on you Arsssssssenal!"

After fifteen minutes, one of the Conor's waiters came around to collect our ten-dollar cover charge. Everyone reached quickly for their money, hardly paying attention to the lad they were handing it to, totally focused on the screen above them. On several occasions, the poor lad only just escaped being clobbered as arms flailed in response to a flowing attack by their team.

On thirty-eight minutes, Ryan Giggs left Lee Dixon for dead and sent in a curling cross that had Yorke at full stretch to head it on to the waiting Keane who hammered a sweetly-timed half volley into the roof of the Arsenal net.

"Yes! Get in there!" The United clan went nuts!

1-0 United!

Or was it?

Gooner Clifford Miller's voice rose above everyone else's.

"Offside! Look. It was offside!"

"What the fuck?" exclaimed Jack.

"You have got to be kidding me!" shrieked Den.

"Oh no, no way, you tosser" declared Red as the replay was shown. Dwight Yorke was the player adjudged to be offside. To say it was a close call was a definite understatement.

Danny, the Conor's barman and fanatical Liverpool supporter could be heard along with Gerry George the Scouser, the two of them in a fit of thunderous laughter.

Half-time arrived and I wandered over to chat with Gerry George, who, as usual, stood alone at his corner of the bar.

"Hey Gary, la. Tough break that, eh?" he said smiling. "You still haven't won fuck all yet lad, 'ave yas?"

Gerry had showed genuine interest in my well-being and I never forgot that, as each week I would wander over for a few minutes for a catch-up with a fella who grew up not a million miles from my own home. With a flick of his cigarette, gulp of his coffee, and the odd heart arrhythmia no doubt, he proclaimed that United were "gonna get stuffed in the second half." With that, I patted him on the shoulder and made my way to the back corridor for my half-time ritual.

"That was a perfectly good goal there, dad. We should be 1-0 up right now," I exclaimed, barely giving my father chance to answer the phone.

"Oh, they're all debating it here, son. All the punters on Radio Five are feeling the same way. Shame really. I mean it sounded like a cracker of a goal."

We had a few more brief words, both hoping for a positive outcome for United in the second half before hanging up. I smiled to myself after sharing another important United moment with my father.

United had most of the play in the second-half, but couldn't seem to put the Gunners away.

Four minutes into extra time and Arsenal's Vivas was gone; sent off!

Clifford Miller ripped his scarf from his neck and threw it down onto the table in front of him. The United clan applauded loudly. Eddie, fresh from a morning away from the baker's dough, reached forward and offered a high five, in his usual calm and collected manner. We grinned at each other as we sensed a United victory.

The sending off, however, seemed to galvanize the Arsenal players, who were now pushing forward more and more in the closing moments. Schmeichel made a brilliant save with his legs from Ljunberg and Gary Neville's last-ditch saving tackle denied Bergkamp, following a run that had seen him almost take on the whole of the United team single-handedly. The sounds emerging from Clifford Miller's mouth on both occasions had me seriously considering his sanity.

"Way to go Arrsssssarghehhh!"

As Red so aptly put it, "our Clifford is one quirky dude!"

At the final whistle, the American Gooner slumped back in his chair looking exhausted.

What a game! What a morning!

The aftermatch ambience had a definite air of gratitude as, despite our allegiances, we all realized how fortunate we had been to witness such a thrilling game live and as it happened.

Medication time was, of course, centered on the outcome of the replay that would follow in four days' time.

Wednesday, April 14, 1999: One particular American "hump day" that I will never forget.

Conor O'Neill's had agreed to broadcast the replay, once again demonstrating its commitment to soccer, given the cost involved for that one-time FA Cup satellite relay. And once again, with it being midweek, I was faced with a full patient caseload and no way to make it to Conors for the crucial game. Even more frustrating was the fact that because it was the FA Cup, no cable television channel carried the match in the USA. I couldn't even call upon Dearborn Dorothy to provide me with video evidence after the fact.

The usual prematch call from High Glen Headquarters back home in Scotland started my day off nicely as my father and I chatted around 6:00 a.m. (11:00 a.m. UK time). Des was well up for it and told me that Sandy, the Postmaster of Drummore, was to play host, providing Drummore's only Sky TV option.

"United are going to Wembley. No question about it, son!"

All day, all I could think of was the game. My Manchester United shirt was laid out on my desk, the team badge evident for all to see.

"So, is Manchester in a big game today then, Gary?" asked my patient, Detective Simpson, a Type A personality if ever there was one.

"Massive game, Steve. I wish I was at the pub with the lads watching it. Some of us have to work though, right?"

"Couldn't you play hooky?"

"Now who would be treating you right now then, mate?"

"Yeah, you got a point. Glad you didn't go, man. 'preciate that!"

"I'm sure hoping my shirt will do the trick, mate"

"Hey, do what you gotta do, English guy! I'm glad you're here, man." And with that, Detective Simpson turned and slammed a six-pound plyoball into the trampette, his face full of intensity.

"Arrgghhh!" The man was pumped, as if ready to bodyslam a wanted felon. The gym always knew when Detective Simpson was in the house.

As the clock reached noon, I decided to call Red. His voice was full of prematch excitement.

"I'm meeting Fred and the lads at Conor's around 2:15p.m. United are going to Wembley, man. The Treble is alive and well, you wanker! You could still meet us. Come on man! Do it!"

"Frank, I would love to, mate, but there's just no way whatsoever."

At that moment in time, I wished that I was a freelance writer working from home just a mile from Conors. I thanked Red and told him to give my best to all of those lucky enough to get a few hours off work.

"Rest assured mate, I am paying my own homage to the day here at work. I've got my United shirt draped over the back of my chair and am making very sure that all and sundry know why."

With an honest regret that I couldn't be there, Red bid me farewell.

The early part of the afternoon seemed to drag as kick-off time approached. I tried to build some prematch excitement with my patients, although trying to convince eighty-year-old Mrs. Kaslowski, recovering from a knee replacement, of the significance of a soccer game in England had its challenges. Any reference to Manchester United appeared at first to go in one ailing ear drum and out the other, her face contorting in reaction to my "physical terrorism" manually stretching her stubborn knee joint. However, undeterred, I likened the situation to her beloved

Red Wings in their pursuit of The Stanley Cup. She then seemed a little more receptive, even commenting that the colors of the United shirt were "simply gorgeous."

With the department full, another patient of mine waited in line for his torture. A young baseball protégé, Dave, was a great lad and we hit it off well each time he came in for treatment to his fractured patella. Dave was sports mad and, by now, well aware of the United challenge. In fact, he had brought in printouts from soccer websites to demonstrate just how clued in he was. His girlfriend was also a keen soccer player.

For April 14, 1999, as the clock hit 3:00 p.m., my United cohort comprised of Detective Simpson, Mrs. Kaslowski, and Dave.

I first called Conor O'Neill's around 3:20 p.m. and waited with baited breath as the phone rang. One of the bartenders answered.

"Conor O'Neill's. This is Ewan." The background noise was deafening. I could hear ooh's and ah's from the assembled fans.

"Ewan! It's Gary, lad. What's the score my friend?"

"Oh, Man U has the lead. Beckham just scored a cracker!'

"Get in there! You beauty! Brilliant! Thanks so much, Ewan mate."

"I tell you what," Ewan continued "there's a grand turnout today for this one. The atmosphere over there at Villa Park looks incredible!"

"Cheers, mate. I have to fly. Some of us have to work you know! I may give you a call later, okay?"

"No worries, buddy. Right you are, Gary!"

With that, I regretfully put the phone down, albeit it with a big smile on my face, and returned to Mrs. Kaslowski and her stubborn knee.

"Well?" she inquired. "Is your team winning?"

"They sure are, Elly. But there's a long way to go yet." Mrs. Kaslowski's gentle smile quickly turned into a grimace as I continued to persuade her prosthetic knee joint to do the job it had been inserted to do.

Dave shouted across the gym as he pounded the treadmill.

"United are up then?"

"Yes, mate. 1-0. Beckham!"

Detective Type A shouted "Way to go United," increasing his pace on the static cycle, beads of sweat now dripping from his furrowed brow.

I had my supporters for the cause.

I continued to follow the clock.

Ewan played his part with each phone call I made. He told me that

Dennis Bergkamp had equalized and that Arsenal were beginning to take control of the game.

With what must have been my fourth or fifth call to Conor's, I heard the news that turned my stomach.

"Keano's gone, Gary! Red carded!"

The phone hadn't even completed a full ring and Ewan hadn't bothered to announce Conor O'Neill's, now certain of who it was, and hitting me with the bad news straight away.

"Second bookable offence, Gary. He chopped down Overmars in his tracks. United are hanging on now. Arsenal have even had a goal disallowed for offside."

I put the phone down once again and spent the next fifteen minutes wandering around in a daze, attempting to treat patients, but with my heart in a stand at Villa Park. I called Conor's again at full time.

"Bejesus, Gary. It's some fucking game, this is!"

"What's the score, mate? The score?!"

By now, pretty much the entire clinic, co-workers and patients alike, looked on in a mixture of bemusement and amusement. They had all been drawn into the emotion of an FA Cup semi-final that was being played out thousands of miles away in Birmingham, England. I had to admit, it was a totally bizarre moment, in a setting that was so "un-soccer."

"Gary! It's not over! Schmeichel has just saved a penalty from Bergkamp, two minutes into extra time! I tell ya, it's fuckin' unbelievable, man! Un-fucking-believable! It's going into extra time!" The noise level in the background was ear splitting.

With that, I hung up once again, immediately conveying the news to Dave, well, to most of the clinic to be honest, ensuring everyone latched onto the energy from across the Pond, even if many of them had no clue as to what I was talking about. And if they didn't, Mrs. Kaslowski could fill them in once she was settled in with an ice pack on her knee.

That following thirty minutes was pure torture.

I attempted two more calls, both to no avail. I dialed again, anxiously waiting for the Irish voice that had been my lifeline all afternoon.

"Sit down, Gary!"

"Ewan, mate. Come on. Lay it on me, pal!"

After a playful pause, the young Irishman, his voice clearly hoarse, probably from answering the telephone a million times in the last two hours or so, continued. He sounded exhausted.

"Gary, I have never seen a fuckin' game like it! Unbelievable! United down to ten men in extra time . . ."

"Yeah, yeah," I urged him on.

"Ryan Giggs . . ."

"Come on! Come on, pal!"

I began to yell down the phone as he mentioned the Welsh wizard's name, anticipating one of those BBC World Service broadcast moments when they flipped around the grounds for a latest score and you knew that your team must have the goal, as commentary starts with them.

"Ryan Giggs scored the most unbelievable fuckin' goal I've ever seen in my life!"

"Yeah, yeah . . . and . . ."

"United won it! 2-1 in extra time!"

"AAARRRGGGHHHHHH! YYYEEESSSS! GET IN THERE!! Thank you! Thank you, Ewan mate!"

Momentarily oblivious to my surroundings, I slammed the phone down. I think I heard Ewan's laughter at my impassioned response prior to my swift disconnect. I kissed the badge. I held my shirt to the sky. I fist pumped into the heavens, legs astride, firmly fixated to the spot in sheer delight.

Dave leaned over, almost falling off the treadmill, slamming me a high five. "Way to go Man U! That means that the Treble is still on, right Gary?"

Dave was right. The Treble most certainly was still on!

Mrs. Kaslowski reached for my hand. Impulsively, we began a gentle jig. Manchester United had just beaten Arsenal in one of the most compelling FA Cup semi-final matches and I was dancing with an eighty-year old Polish lady who had undertaken her first knee replacement. She was loving it. I was loving it.

Moments, sometimes you just have to grab them!

I threw my shirt on, thrust my arms aloft, and a round of applause instantly broke out, echoing around the clinic.

Here I was in the American Midwest, wearing my United shirt, at my place of work, as a bunch of patients cheered a Manchester United victory.

Adrenaline sure is a wonderful thing!

It wasn't until later that night after speaking to Red that I realized just how close United had come to crashing out of the FA Cup. Red was ecstatic, and repeated over and over his disbelief at Ryan Giggs' "wonder goal." He said that Eddie had his coat in hand ready to leave and was hiding his head in his hands as Bergkamp stepped up to take the penalty. He had pissed his sides at Clifford Miller's reaction when Schmeichel thwarted the big Dutchman—an Arsenal scarf once again launched across the room—this time landing perfectly on Den's United head!

Red continued. "Gary, the poor dude was just distraught, man"

"I bet he was, mate."

"He was inconsolable. I watched him take himself off to a corner of the pub. He just sat there, head in his hands, unmoved as one or two of the lads provided a consolatory pat on the back. I did genuinely feel for the guy."

"Tough pill to swallow that one mate, for sure!" I responded.

"But hey, you tosser! The Reds go marching on, on, on!"

"Get in there, Red! Get in there!"

Red wrapped up his call by telling me that he couldn't help but notice that the phone behind the bar had been ringing off the hook.

"Gary, it never stopped ringing. The young barman was up and down all the time."

After a short pause, I laughed.

"Red, mate. That was me! How the hell could I work without knowing what was going on at Villa Park?"

My fellow Red paused, laughed, and replied:

"Good lad! Bollocks to you, you wanker!"

That night I rejoiced in the new buzz of the internet, reading from all of the sources now available at the click of a mouse. I realized that the lucky fans at Villa Park had witnessed something very special, something very special indeed. I opened my emails and took great delight in the abundance of messages from my friends back home.

Norfolk Nobby, the Sheffield United nut from back home, had bundled a message through. I smiled as I read his regretful admission that the man he had chastised, Ryan Giggs, had scored a goal that would "deffo keep 'em talking for some time to come," although, true to form, he concluded that Arsenal's defense "really should have had him."

Despite the connections, I could not escape from the realization that I had yet to see *the* goal that everyone was talking about. All I had to go on were descriptions of how amazing it was. Two days after the game, however, I arrived home to find an e-mail message from Jack. I opened his message and saw the words "Ryan Giggs Wonder Goal." I had to click a link to a video download; all new to me. After what seemed an eternity, I could not believe my eyes as there in front of me was an actual video clip. Jack had done it! He had sent me a video of Ryan Giggs' "wonder goal" via the wonders of modern technology.

It really was one of *the* greatest goals that I had ever seen. Giggs had picked the ball up in the United half, a wayward, tired giveaway pass from Arsenal's Patrick Vieira. Without hesitating, Giggs latched onto it and burst forward hitting the space ahead of him. He entered the opposition half, four Arsenal players blocking his path down the right. Such was the juncture of the match and with United down to ten men, had I been watching it live I would have been screaming for the Welshman to release the ball to Dwight Yorke, who was making a run wide. Yorke could then have headed straight for the corner flag. The ten men of United could have run down the clock and hung on for penalties. Giggs, however, had other ideas. He began his dribble at full pelt, taking on each and every defender ahead of him, even beating Lee Dixon twice, before instinctively hammering a finish high into the roof of the Arsenal net. The Arsenal keeper David Seaman had no chance, his right arm flapping-backward flop combo was a total contrast to Giggsy's sublime strike.

I played it over and over. As a certain Irish barman had described United's winning goal that night: "un-fucking-believable!"

After watching the goal for about the tenth time, I replied:

"Cheers for putting me out of my misery. Next time though, someone better tell Giggsy to keep his shirt on!"

The dream of the Treble was very much alive!

We had reached the FA Cup final.

I was just about to close my e-mail in box when I noticed another message entitled "Without a Doubt."

I opened the message.

"Without a doubt, my friend, that was the greatest game I have ever been to." I eagerly clicked open the attachment and could not believe my eyes as a scanned copy of a ticket to the FA Cup semi-final replay popped up. Such irony: my college roommate Stanley Armitage, the avid Leeds United fan, had actually been at one of the most memorable games in Manchester United's history.

I shut down my computer and smiled.

48

Full Steam Ahead

Saturday, April 17, and United continued their winning ways with goals from Solskjær, Sheringham, and Scholes securing three more crucial Premier League points with a 3-0 win over Sheffield Wednesday at Old Trafford.

What was the topic for our postmatch medication time that morning? The outcome and significance of events from Villa Park three days earlier. The conclusion that most of us reached was why the hell hadn't anyone thought about asking the management of Conor O'Neill's to record the bloody game?

Fred and I remained behind after the rest of the crew had departed. I noticed he was looking a little tired and toasted to a healthy week ahead for my friend, wishing him the best of luck with the investigation into his personal plumbing.

"Oh, it will all be fine Gary if I could just stop peeing almost every hour that God sends me."

Forty-eight hours after United's victory against Sheffield Wednesday, Arsenal hammered Wimbledon 5-1. Just six Premier League games remained for United. Arsenal and Chelsea, right on their tail, each had five games remaining.

The top of the Premier League read as follows:

Manchester United	*played 32*	*points 67*
Arsenal	*played 33*	*points 66*
Chelsea	*played 33*	*points 64*

On Wednesday, April 21, it was time for The Big One—the massive winner-takes-all second leg of the European Champions League semi-final against Juventus in Turin. Should United make it past Juventus, they would be in the final of the biggest club competition in Europe for the first time since 1968! I felt it. I wanted it. When you are a diehard fan of a club, it doesn't matter what the circumstance. Whenever, wherever, right? On American soil or not, I remained fully invested, emotionally and spiritually. When a day like this comes along, it is *the* only thing that occupies one's mind.

And, of course . . . once again, I had no way to leave work. Thankfully, Dearborn Dorothy came through again.

Another lunchtime call to Red built the fever even more. It was just an hour or so before kick-off. Thirty miles west of my workplace, Red and most of our paddock would be making their way to Conor O'Neill's. I simply couldn't get away to join them.

"I'll have my tape in hand, mate. I will give you a call after the game to break it all down. Go United!"

"We'll be thinking of you, Englishman. For the glory, glory, of Man United, you wanker!"

"Right back at ya, Red."

I am sure soccer fans will tell you, watching a match with a crowd of fellow fanatics adds so much to the moment: the vibe, the banter, the thrill of willing your team on. However, I am sure fans will also attest to the fact that sometimes it's about the solitary, enforced on occasion, other times by choice. Alone, sat watching your team, fully focused on every single second of the game is sometimes just how it has to be. No distractions, fully concentrated, totally in the moment.

Stuck at work, unable to hang with the lads for some of those important midweek European matches due to the nature of my job, I had to continue with my own Plan B. I had no problem, though, pulling away into my soccer bunker, just United and I. Dearborn Dorothy would once again kindly provide me with my Red connection. I was completely okay with that, ready to once again slip into my own United zen. My team and I were still on the journey, a journey that we were hoping would take us all the way to Barcelona.

"Go Manchester!" my landlady yelled through her kitchen window as I walked by once again, waving a VHS tape high in the air above my head.

If only you knew, Rhonda, I thought to myself as I scurried into my apartment. *If only you knew.* I immediately sank into a world many miles removed from the breeze that filtered through my window that spring evening in Michigan.

I fast forwarded the tape, ready for the entry of the teams, accompanied by commentary from Tommy "auld onion bag" Smyth and the ESPN crew.

The commentators were full of it.

"United arrive in Italy clinging to a Champions league lifeline."

"United have to score."

"Juventus score and this tie is as good as over."

"United must not concede an early goal."

With the match about to kick off, I paused the tape. I had the liberty, thanks to the elusive Dorothy. I sat and stared at the screen. The small television atop the rattling fridge, my scarf draped around the screen's perimeter. Despite the match having already been played, I felt present, in the moment, ready for the referee to blow his whistle and the second leg of a Champions League semi-final to commence.

Again, the answering machine flashed and again I ignored its plea.

"Come on United!"

Game on!

With six minutes on the clock, Zidane whipped the ball into the United penalty area. Filippo Inzaghi got goal side of Gary Neville at the far post and nudged it home.

1-0 Juventus.

Disaster.

Five minutes later, after a wicked deflection off Stam, I watched the ball loop agonizingly over a flailing Schmeichel. Inzhagi again.

2-0 Juventus.

What the?

So much for my positive thinking.

Stop!

I paused the tape once again.

Surely this was not happening.

United, already 3-1 down on aggregate.

A moment of thought.

The bright side. I always tried to look on it. Only eleven minutes had gone, that meant we had at least seventy-nine minutes left to play. Bags of time—and not forgetting a little "Fergie time," too.

Cole, Yorke, Beckham, Keane, Scholes. They hadn't even got going yet. They were all having the season of their lives. They had it in them. United had it in them.

I was defiant. I still believed.

I stared intently at the screen and pressed the remote. The room was immediately filled with deafening noise. The crowd inside the Stadio delle Alpi was going nuts.

"Juventus have one foot firmly in the Champions League final!"

"United have it all to do now!"

"Come on United!" I roared once again.

It was a simple scenario as far as I was concerned. A goal, just one goal for United, and we were right back in it.

I still believed. I had to!

United dug in. And, then, on thirty-four minutes, my optimism was rewarded. Through sheer determination, Roy Keane got his head onto a David Beckham corner.

Yes! Get in there! 1-2! 2-3 on aggregate.

I stood, arms aloft, wide smile, in awe of the action on slow motion replay. Keane sensed it, immediately sprinting back to the halfway line. There was still work to do, but it was definitely "game back on!" Tommy Smyth's words sounded like poetry: "Oh, I tell ya's, we have ourselves a game now. A brilliant header from Keane gives Manchester United a lifeline." I rewound the tape again and again. The header was sublime.

A few minutes later, Zidane played in a wonderful cross and Conte connected. Schmeichel was flapping, nowhere near the ball. I watched it's trajectory. It was about to loop into United's net and, without careful monitoring from Jaap Stam, it indeed would have. Zidane continued to be a menace. Minutes later, after giving United a fighting chance, Keane received the ball short. Zidane intercepted the pass and sensed a chance to break. With a desperate lunge Keane caught the Frenchman.

Yellow card! Should United make it through, Keano, our captain, would now miss the final. I focused on Keane. He was playing on the edge, driven, committed. He was playing for his team, continuing to lead, yet all the time fully aware that this game was where the European journey ended for him. He was playing for his team, continuing to lead, to try and take United on to the Camp Nou.

And then, around ten minutes after Keane's goal, with Juventus starting to look a tad rattled, Beckham found Andy Cole in an uncustomary right wing position. Cole's quick touch and looping cross into the Juventus box found Dwight Yorke whose powerful diving header sailed into the Juventus net.

2-2! Unbelievable!

I leapt into the air. I dived with Dwight, fists clenched, with only an auld onion bag for company!

An incredible turn around. Back from the abyss, United now had the upper hand. If the score remained the same, the Reds would be on their way to Barcelona for the European Champions League final! Yorke and Cole were beginning to run the show. Moments later, Yorke rifled a low drive across the Juventus goal, rattling the bottom of the upright. Juventus were suddenly hanging on for half-time.

Half-time arrived. Juventus 2, Manchester United 2! 3-3 overall!

There was no chance of a half-time call to my father. It was over and done with back "home." Des, of course, would already know whether United had reached the final and was most likely tucked up in bed. I still had a full second half of nerve-jangling soccer ahead of me. United now had those two crucial away goals. I settled myself in for the forty-five minutes that would determine whether the Reds would make it to Barcelona.

Juventus started the second half well and, within minutes, I held my head in my hands.

"Goal!"

Inzaghi was swiftly adjudged to be offside. The replay confirmed the referee's great call.

Ouuufff!

The Juventus manager, Carlo Ancelotti, went for broke, playing three up top and his gamble almost paid off. Jaap Stam, however, was immense, holding the United line.

I could see Juventus were becoming more stretched.

Then, an instinctive Scholes reaction, as he lunged into a Juventus player. He knew. The referee immediately brandished a yellow card. United's diminutive midfielder would also now miss the Final should United hang on. I noticed Keane rub the back of Scholes' head as the young Englishman walked away. A captain's reaction. The Irishman was the only player on the park that could truly empathize with how Scholes was feeling at that very moment.

The game became wide open, Juventus having to go for it, United responding on the counter. Chances fell to both teams.

Then, Peter Schmeichel took a long goal kick, the ball eventually landing at the foot of Dwight Yorke. He controlled it and showed real poise, sucking in the two defenders, immediately dissecting them like a knife through butter.

Here we go. I could sense it. Striker's instinct.

I was on my feet once more. The Italian keeper came to meet Yorke and in doing so brought him crashing down.

"Penalty!"

Time stood still for a second. I watched the ball roll to the feet of Andy Cole. A tight angle was not going to defy the striker the chance to book United a place in the Champions League final.

Juventus 2 Manchester United 3!

"Full steam ahead Barcelona!" the commentator exclaimed.

I watched the clock, now willing the game to finish; that tense countdown with your team on the brink of victory.

The referee blew. Game over! United had done it!

The Camp Nou was now reality. United were heading for the European Champions League Final!

I stood rooted to the spot in the small apartment and watched the looks on the faces: the players, the manager, the coaching staff, and of course, the crowd. I saw Schmeichel lift Beckham with one adrenaline-pumped right arm, the two of them jubilant, acknowledging the the traveling United fans.

Yes, it was a taped event, but for me it was "the moment!" I continued pumping my fists as I replayed the Cole goal over and over. I thought of the wild celebrations that would be happening back in the old country that night.

Pausing the celebrations my attention then turned to the answering machine. It's incessant blinking made that a given. I shot over and hit the playback button. Des sounded exhausted and hoarse as he spoke straight after the game and I could even hear my mother screaming in the background as he attempted to leave the message. At moments like this, you would have to be completely devoid of emotion to not feel homesick. Of course I did. But I had been able to see the game, and that, along with all the sentiments received from home, had created a very short distance between England and the USA. ESPN did not feature any postmatch interviews as their programming immediately switched to baseball. But none of that mattered. All that did matter was that Manchester United now had plans for the evening of May 26, 1999.

The final message on the answering machine was from Regal Fred. "Well, I have to hand it to that team from Manchester, Gary. They played their hearts out. What a game! I was thinking of you as I watched the match with the lads at Conor's. In fact, you know what? Afterwards, I listened very intently, but try as I might, I, too, could not hear any fat lady attempting to sing."

The following Saturday we were once more graced with the presence of Clifford Miller, with the featured game at Conor O'Neill's being Arsenal against a struggling Middlesborough side.

Cliff was unrelenting in his celebration of what I have to admit was a ferocious assault by the Gunners that day. Goal after goal went in, Arsenal eventually putting six past Boro. The Gooner's smile grew wider and wider and his taunts more frequent as he stole the show in the pub that morning. Arsenal had taken their chance to go top of the Premier League. It was a phenomenal performance and United fans recognized the massive battle that still lay ahead in the fight for the Premier League title.

The top of the Premier League table on Saturday April 24 read:

Arsenal	*played 34*	*points 69*
Manchester United	*played 32*	*points 67*
Chelsea	*played 33*	*points 64*

Medication time that morning consisted of who else but Clifford Miller center stage. He couldn't pass up the opportunity to gloat and taunt all the United boys present as best he could, sipping away at his Guinness, Arsenal scarf proudly resting across his shoulders, proclaiming his Gunners ready to win "their sweetest Premier League title in years" — the one that would ruin Manchester United's unprecedented Treble!

"Well, it is certainly so very nice of you to join us today, Cliff," I remarked. The jibe went unnoticed, simply rolling off the American lawyer's back as he refused to allow anything to deflect from his moment. Cliff and Fred chose to stay; two old friends enjoying a catch up. I had other fish to fry and as I wandered toward the exit, I heard one last cry from their corner.

"United have no chance now! Come on the Arrrsssse!"

Without looking back, I raised my hand to dismiss the comment, a huge grin on my face and wondered when I would see Cliff again. Probably not until the final day of the Premier League season!

Sunday, April 25 and United managed a 1-1 draw away to Leeds United, the Yorkshire team themselves sitting fourth in the English Premier League. Chelsea drew 0-0 at Sheffield Wednesday that same day, keeping their own title hopes alive, too.

Arsenal and Chelsea each had four games remaining; United had five. The top of table on Sunday April 25 told the story. All still very much to play for:

Arsenal	*played 34*	*points 69*
Manchester United	*played 33*	*points 68*
Chelsea	*played 34*	*points 65*

An old school friend of mine called me from Lancashire after the Leeds United vs. Manchester United game that day. Doddy and I had been friends for years and he was a devoted Leeds fan, often visiting Elland Road with his father. We were both proud of the fact that we had maintained our friendship for so long, and whenever there was a significant game between our two sides, either one of us would often make the call.

Doddy told me that he had been at the game and was impressed with Manchester United's resilience, but, of course, still felt that Leeds should have come away with the points. I returned the phone receiver to its rightful resting place, smiling at how the game of soccer can continue to keep two old buddies in touch after so many years.

It was later that year that Doddy would welcome his second child; a boy. It goes without saying that I was honored when he called to ask me to be his son's godfather. I gladly accepted, honored to have the opportunity to steadily influence the young man to favor the United of Manchester before his father could damage him for life!

49

Taxi Please!

Certain things are destined to remain with you throughout your lifetime. My red machine, the Honda CRX, was not one of them! As the night sky was drawing in on the evening of April 28, I left Farmer Jacks supermarket, my car loaded with groceries. It had been a long, busy day at work—they all seemed that way in America. I was listening to Garbage on Detroit's Alternative 89X, finally letting go of the day, when, all of a sudden . . . bam!

Out of nowhere, a huge Chevrolet Lumina ran a stop sign and slammed into my passenger side. I had seen the oncoming vehicle a split second before impact and had tried to swerve away. However, the actual collision was brutal. I was travelling at almost fifty miles an hour. I hit the grass verge in the middle of the intersection, instantly anticipating the car rolling. The next thing I remember was sitting lurched over my steering wheel, surrounded by the wreck of what was once my car. I managed to lean back and noticed that my vehicle was still upright. I was surrounded by a mangled mess of colorful fruits, vegetables, eggs, and other assorted groceries, all topped off with the fresh, crisp aroma of Clean Fresh Burst laundry detergent.

I quickly removed the keys from the ignition—an episode of the hospital drama Casualty back in Britain had taught me something—as I released the seatbelt. Emerging from the remnants of my vehicle, the first thing I noticed was a young lad who was talking on his cellphone and was visibly shaken. I stood and stared at him.

"What the fuck were you thinking, mate?"

These were the only words that I spoke to him for the next forty-five minutes. Mr. Lumina's repost was continual, apologizing profusely, whimpering on in an incessantly-annoying high-pitched tone, still attempting to continue a conversation on his mobile phone.

In next to no time, the place was swarming with people, witnesses confirming to the two policemen that Mr. Lumina had indeed run a stop sign and was at fault. There were flares all over the road diverting traffic and gawkers—"gawker slowdown" was a common turn of phrase on news radio WWJ 950—were having a field day.

The emergency services arrived quickly, adamant about checking me out. I wasn't being clever when I insisted all was fine, but I knew the pain in my chest was more from the seatbelt's protection and that some ice and rest that night would suffice. After watching the sad sight of my car being towed away en route to its final resting place, I reflected on the final song blaring from its sound system at the moment of impact that evening. I smiled. It was rather apt that the band on 89X had been none other than Garbage. Looking at my vehicle as it left the scene, heading for the car heaven, it looked every bit a pile of metallic junk.

I was offered a ride home by a State Trooper. The theory that the highest percentage of car crashes happen five minutes from your own home had certainly held true. As I exited the police car, I thanked the State Trooper for his help and trudged up the path to my apartment. I wrapped myself in ice and reflected on what the hell had just happened.

I had no car. In America that translates as being "up the creek without a paddle."

I had no way of getting to work.

Fluffy to the rescue! Taxi Number One.

"Reliable" was Fluffy's middle name. Okay, so she tended to arrive a full hour before pick up, insisting on staying in her car to wait for me, regardless of the weather. The aroma of her Macdonald's breakfast sandwich patties mingled with potpourri overpowered me as I entered my ride, but that's Fluffy for you. I wouldn't have it any other way. She had saved my skin on several occasions, and was doing the same again.

Taxi Number Two was none other than Frank "Red" Rock.

In just three days' time United were due to play Aston Villa at Old Trafford. I had to somehow get to Conor O'Neill's. Due to his phobia of highway driving, Red had always relied on Chinny for his ride to the Britannia Club. And, so, when I received a call from Red the evening before the game, offering to travel the thirty miles or so to pick me up, I cannot begin to tell you how grateful I was. I also cannot begin to tell you how much I was shitting my pants!

The American was adamant.

"Bollocks, Gary! We've gotta get ya to Conor's for this one, dude! Us Reds have got to stick together, man!"

The morning of Saturday, May 1 arrived, and with it, the most torrential rain I had seen in a long time. At 8:30 a.m., as agreed, I spotted an aging Chevy Celebrity, its windscreen wipers working double overtime. Hunched over the steering wheel, with an expression that suggested a most treacherous passage, Red pulled into my driveway.

Looking pale and exhausted and struggling to make himself heard over the noise of the rain, Red motioned to me.

"Dude! Get in! Quick!"

"Mate, you're a total savior!"

"Gary, I know you would have done it for me, so don't even think about it. Fasten your seatbelt. You're gonna need it for this ride, Englishman."

"Good lad!"

With the heater on full blast and the windows still steaming up constantly, Red struggling to see, his nose practically touching the windshield, we headed west toward Ann Arbor and Conor O'Neill's. Let's just say that it wasn't the fastest journey I had ever encountered and certainly not the most reassuring. We must have been overtaken by just about every car on the road, but thanks to my mate, my fellow Red, we made it in time for kick-off.

That beautiful embracing wall of sound warmed our hearts as we wandered through to the Conor's paddock and met up with all the lads for what was another terrific turn out.

"Bloody hell! You both look like you've seen a ghost!" Eddie exclaimed as we settled in. A further nod from all the lads and then everyone's eyes wandered up toward the TV screen and Old Trafford, Manchester. Game on! Manchester, the "rainy city," was basking in glorious spring sunshine and the atmosphere in the ground appeared to be one of celebration.

A soft own goal from Aston Villa's Steve Watson midway through the first half opened the scoring for United. Villa, to their credit, were not overawed and ten minutes later they were back on level terms.

1-1 at half-time.

Just as we were settling in at the start of the second half, David Beckham sent a swerving shot into the top left-hand corner of the Villa net. My chauffeur for the day stood tall for a high-five.

"Maybe you should come and pick me up every week United are on, eh Red?"

The game ended up 2-1 with United securing three more vital Premier League points. Chelsea beat Everton 3-1 at Stamford Bridge. Arsenal's game against Derby County was to be played the very next day. Prior to the Gunners match, the top of the Premier League table now read:

Manchester United	played 34	points 71
Arsenal	played 34	points 69
Chelsea	played 35	points 68

United had leapfrogged Arsenal to go top!

Medication time consisted of a piss take about my CRX's long overdue passage to the afterworld and we all raised our glasses in a toast to my deceased Japanese friend. I was gutted that she hadn't quite made it to the 200,000 mile mark. As I left that day, bracing myself for the ride home, I considered how to get new wheels, and fast.

The ride home with Red was pretty much a repeat of our outbound journey: the tall American, scrunched over the dashboard, intensely focused for most of the passage. I remained quiet so as not to unnecessarily distract my nervous chauffeur.

"There ya go, Gary. We made it huh?"

"Red, I cannot thank you enough, mate" I replied, shaking my friend's hand as I leaned to release the seatbelt.

"No problem, Englishman. Now just wish me luck for the journey home, will ya?"

"Fancy a stretch of the legs before you head back," I offered, a chance maybe for Red to gather his thoughts before facing another I-94 crush.

"No way, man. If I get out of this car, I may not want to get back in!"

"Got it, Red! Got it! Safe passage then, mate. Again, thanks so much. Truly appreciate what you did today."

"Till the next time, Gary. United top of the league man! Top of the league! The unimaginable Treble is alive and well!"

And with that I watched Red attempt to reverse out of the Hotel Hairpiece driveway. After what seemed an age, I waved him off. Of course, I don't think he even saw me.

The very next day, Sunday May 2, Arsenal did indeed beat Derby County to once more move above United at the top:

Arsenal	played 35	points 72
Manchester United	played 34	points 71
Chelsea	played 35	points 68

The following week started with a touch of good fortune. A local garage owner that Fluffy knew happened to have "just the thing for me."

"It ain't the best lookin' motor but I reckon it will get you around safely for a while, man," said the local neighborhood garage owner, Big Al. There was nothing big about Al. Standing at all of five feet, his skinny frame couldn't have weighed more than 140 pounds, soaking wet. His friends and family obviously had a terrific sense of humor. Fluffy had apparently known him for years.

"Al is a great guy. He'd give you the shirt off his back," she had told me.

My wardrobe was full enough, thank you; all I required was a decent motor from his lot.

"Fluffs, if I can just find a cheap, reliable motor I'll be dead chuffed."

"Dead what?"

"Chuffed, Fluffy. Dead chuffed."

"Doesn't sound too good to me, that, Gary"

"Dead chuffed? It means well happy. Very glad. You know what I'm saying, Fluffs" attempting to educate her in some northern English banter.

"How can you have *dead* and *happy* in the same sentence? That's pretty messed up."

"Just like your daughter would probably say something is *pretty wicked*, right?"

"You have a point there Gary. You do have a point."

Two days later, I became the proud new owner of an "old but reliable," according to not-so Big Al, 1988 Pontiac 6000 with 186,000 miles on the clock.

I handed Al a cheque for $1,000 and thanked him for getting me back on the road. I refrained from telling him I was dead chuffed, let alone even just chuffed. A straightforward thank you seemed quite sufficient and a lot less complicated.

Fluffy had helped me out again. I had new wheels; well, pretty old ones to be honest, but it meant that I was independently mobile once more.

Without a vehicle in the States, you are truly screwed. I was always amazed by the sight of drivers who looked to be in their nineties, hunched over steering wheels, driving at least fifteen miles an hour below the posted speed limit—such was the case due to the lack of public transport in most areas.

On my arrival home in my new chariot, I went straight to the laptop to get the result of United's crucial Premier League clash with Liverpool at Anfield, the distractions of my car troubles having thrown me a tad off kilter. With the laptop, I now had United games "on demand" along with prematch build up and insight from United greats such as Paddy Crerand, Frank Stapleton, and Mickey Thomas. I listened closely to the replayed commentary—a wonderful option for those of us unable to catch the match in real time. With only minutes to play, United were hanging on for what would be a crucial 2-1 win.

And then—"Di Matteo to McManaman. McManaman drills it through to Riedle. There's trouble here for Manchester United. Out comes Schmeichel. The ball is loose in the box. It falls to Ince . . . and it's 2-2! Paul Ince has equalized for Liverpool and looks to have stolen two points from the hands of his previous club."

Fuck!

On the same night, Arsenal achieved a rare win at Tottenham, beating their north London rivals 3-1. I was sure that I could hear Cliff's cheers all the way from Ann Arbor. In addition, Chelsea secured a 1-0 win at Leeds.

Double fuck!

The Premier League top three after the May 5 midweek fixtures read:

Arsenal	*played 36*	*points 75*
Manchester United	*played 35*	*points 72*
Chelsea	*played 36*	*points 71*

Arsenal were now three points clear at the top. Had Paul Ince, of all players, derailed United's chance of winning the Premier League title—and the Treble? There were a couple of messages on my answering machine. The first was from my father expressing his dismay over the sending off of United's Dennis Irwin and then one from Fred commenting that he felt that it was going to be simply too much for United to win all three trophies.

I typed seven words in an e-mail to Fred,

"There is no fat lady singing yet!"

50

Game Plan

May 9, 1999: The featured game at Conor O'Neill's was Middlesborough versus Manchester United. Ann Arbor's #1 Gooner was a no show, not even a late visit to gloat after Arsenal's 3-1 midweek win over Tottenham which had propelled Wenger's team into pole position in the Premier League.

The significance of the day's game on Wearside was clear. United had to win to tie it all up on 75 points at the top of the Premier League.

All of our United clan were there.

Red had reverted back to walking down to Conor's. "It'll be a while before I take the car for a spin again I think, Gary!"

I burst out laughing, giving an impulsive slap on his right shoulder.

"Steadier on two legs then, Frank?" Eddie said, confirming the tall American's choice of transport that morning.

Tim, the manager at Conor O'Neill's, and Connie, had put in an "early doors" appearance. Both came over for some prematch banter.

"Pretty amazing soccer season this is turning out to be then, Gary?" said Tim, shaking my hand.

"Hiya, mate! Thanks again for this, eh. Being able to watch these games here, Tim, it's absolutely brilliant!"

"Oh no problem, Gary. You guys have been with us since the beginning. Its great seeing all the familiar faces. I love this early morning crowd."

"Auch, we love puttin' the games on for you fellas. No bother at all. You're our early morning crew. A pretty special bunch," Connie kindly added.

"Bless ya, Connie" I replied, wrapping my right arm around her shoulder, and then, turned toward Tim.

"Yeah, Tim, just think mate, Gaelic football. I dunno mate, not quite the same vibe, eh?"

"You know what, Gary son, I have to admit, soccer has been the way to go. Gaelic footy is my game though. Always will be."

I took a look over at the picture on the wall—the one of his friend and business partner, the Gaelic ball player in full flow.

"For sure mate. That's how it all started for both of you, eh."

"Aye. 'tis. Listen, enjoy the game, Gary. Enjoy the match, lads" Tim announced, the gathered crowd returning a thankful gesture.

"Anyone for tea or coffee, lads?" Connie asked.

"Bar will be open in an hour or so, fellas. Enjoy yourselves now, eh."

I took my seat and smiled, seeing Den and Don decked out in their glorious red, white and black.

"New hat there, Don?" I inquired, noticing the unmistakable cap he was wearing.

"Yes sir! eBay, Gary! Gotta love it!"

A sign of the times for sure.

Jack was there, as was Blue along with Twinkle Toes Robbie who was back in town for the day.

"Hey, we aren't out of this yet, mate," said Blue, reminding me that his Chelsea blues were still chasing United and Arsenal.

"For sure, mate. The way this season is going, who bloody knows?"

"Not a frickin' chance, mate," Robbie chimed in. "You must still be half pissed from last night, Pete."

The lights were dimmed. We were ready for the off.

Middlesborough started off with purpose.

"Ouuff! That was close, mate." I nudged Fred as a Boro shot grazed United's post.

"How did that not go in, Fred?"

"Unbelievable! It sure is tense isn't it, Gary."

Then, right on the stroke of half-time, a measured "up and under" from Nicky Butt sent a high ball into the Boro box and, with a move seemingly born out of tomfoolery on the training ground, Sheringham connected, lofting a simple header over to Dwight Yorke, unmarked at the opposite post. Yorke sprung high and scored.

"Yes!" I yelled, jumping to my feet and giving it a manic Pearson fist pump.

Red countered, doing some kind of seizure-like full body shake screaming "Yes! Yes! Goal! Goal!"—the American always his own man.

Den and Don, as per usual, were tubthumping after the United goal and Twinkle Toes, the dancing Manc, appeared to slip into a smooth hip hop groove to annoy Blue—our resident Chelsea fan showing his obvious disgust at events on Wearside.

Eddie and Jack stood applauding, smiles like Chesire cats, Eddie remaining on his feet for several minutes post goal, his right arm aloft in salute, fist clenched and a defiant grit of his teeth clear for all to see. Eddie could feel it. All of our United clan could feel it!

In the end, Dwight Yorke's goal ended up being the winner. Three more huge Premier League points for Manchester United. With two games to go, the Premier League title race remained wide open.

After the win at Boro, United moved back to the top of the Premier League merely by the number of goals scored. In other words, it could not be any closer.

Manchester United	played 36	points 75	goal diff +42
Arsenal	played 36	points 75	goal diff +42
Chelsea	played 36	points 71	goal diff +26

As most of the lads slid away that morning to resume normal transmission, Fred and I remained. A bowl of Maureen's Irish Stew and a pint of Guinness had become our familiar fare for medication time.

"They really do just find a way to win Gary, don't they?" Fred commented.

"Hey, no argument from me, mate."

Fred gave me an update on his health situation.

"I have an appointment with the surgeon on Tuesday the 18th, Gary. I'm considering getting rid of this bloody prostate. Hopefully, that will mean an end to this dreadful situation. It really is becoming a frightful nuisance, peeing all the time. When I am up and down all the time, I can't concentrate on the games. Something has to be done."

"Wow, that has all happened rather quickly. You do know that's only four days before the FA Cup final, don't you, mate?"

"You better believe it, Gary. I'm not going to miss the FA Cup final."

After a slow, deliberate swig of his half empty glass of Guinness, Fred laid out his game plan.

"The doctor said that if surgery is required, he will just go ahead and do it. He assured me that I'd be back home a couple of days later."

"Yeah, but mate, that'll only give you a couple of days before the big game."

"Gary, I have it all under control. I'll rest easy from the moment I come around and have requested the surgeon reassess me as early as possible after the operation. I made sure that he knew all about a rather important soccer game at Wembley, London and I gave him strict instruction to ensure that I am released in sufficient time to recuperate and get over to watch the match."

Fred's conviction was commendable, ensuring me that he would not miss the game under any circumstances, not even for a "rusted old prostate gland" as he put it. I went on to assure him that we would save the most comfortable pew in Conor's for his delicate posterior.

"Well, make sure you remind that surgeon to set his alarm early and get you out on time, eh?"

We raised our glasses to toast a speedy recovery after which Fred, as if on cue, made a beeline for the bathroom for about the tenth time that morning.

Just two days later, on May 11—a day after Chelsea had drawn 2-2 with Tottenham—Stan, my old college roommate, sent me an e-mail about his conflicted feelings:

"Bastardddddd!"

Stan's e-mail headline was in reference to his beloved Leeds United's massive 1-0 victory over Arsenal—a win that handed Manchester United a huge leg up in the race for the league title, the Premier League top three now reading:

Manchester United	*played 36*	*points 75*	*goal difference +42*
Arsenal	*played 37*	*points 75*	*goal difference +41*
Chelsea	*played 37*	*points 72*	*goal difference +26*

The games kept coming thick and fast.

Wednesday, May 12, 1999: The day after Arsenal's loss to Leeds, Manchester United played Blackburn Rovers at Ewood Park. The Rovers team was managed by Brian Kidd, one of the Manchester United heroes from their night of European glory back in 1968. This was United's chance to put one firm hand on the Premier League Trophy. I called my father for the match report.

"Blackburn nil, United nil, son. And apparently Blackburn almost sneaked one in near the end, but all said and done the draw gives us the edge for Sunday, eh? That result means that Blackburn are relegated. I can't see Kidd lasting too long there now. Most of the pundits over here are saying United can win the Premier League and FA Cup, but that the

Champions League may be too much. I reckon they have every chance son, every chance."

And so, on Wednesday, May 12, 1999, with only one game left to play in the 1998–99 Premier League season, the race for the title came down to this:

Manchester United	*played 37*	*points 76*	*goal difference +42*
Arsenal	*played 37*	*points 75*	*goal difference +41*
Chelsea	*played 37*	*points 72*	*goal difference +26*

Chelsea's title challenge was over.

It was now a two-horse race.

Sunday, May 16—the final day of the season.

It was going down to the wire.

51

Ted

I wandered into work the next morning, my mind consumed with events 3,500 miles away. My patient, Dave, the young baseball player, had zoned right in on United's title challenge and greeted me with more printouts from ESPN's soccer website with reports of the Arsenal vs. Leeds and United vs. Blackburn games.

"It looks like Man U has a real chance for the first part of that Treble now, man. I was reading this article online last night and it sounds like it was a shock that Leeds pulled out that win against Arsenal, right?"

"Dave! Just ask me how happy I am this morning, mate," I replied smiling.

I continued to put Dave through his paces on the treadmill to a return to full fitness. I was enjoying witnessing the young American's enthusiasm for the game while he worked hard on his rehabilitation. Dave's girlfriend, Sandy, was alongside him, enjoying the soccer chat. The conversation that morning was all about the Treble. I could never have imagined that I would be discussing such a potential feat at all, let alone with patients in a hospital clinic in Dearborn, Michigan.

As Dave and Sandy prepared to leave the clinic, Dave mentioned that they may well head along to Conor O'Neill's for Sunday's broadcast of the final day of the Premier League season. Enticed by my description of the atmosphere, they felt it would be the perfect time to hit our soccer pub.

My next patient, Ted, had immigrated to America from his native Ireland in the early 1970s. We had connected well in the few weeks he had been coming in for treatment and it hadn't taken me long to realize that Ted loved his soccer. With the snippets of news from the cable channels and his newly-installed internet service at home, he was enjoying a larger taste of soccer news from Europe.

Ted was a terrific fella. I marveled at his determination to succeed with his rehabilitation after the trauma of losing his left leg to diabetes. It was a humbling experience, watching him struggle in his wheelchair and attempting his walks in the supporting parallel bars we had set up in the department. Getting used to a prosthetic limb in his mid-70s must have been incredibly tough, but Ted was determined, a real fighter and such a positive force every time he entered our department.

Our discussion that morning centered on the history of soccer in America. Soccer had almost taken off in America with the advent of the North American Soccer League, a professional league which ran between the late 1960's through to the mid 1980's. Ted told me about how the matches were regularly broadcast on network television in the mid- to late-70s.

"The most prominent team, son, and the one team I kept my eye on was the New York Cosmos with the likes of Pele, Beckenbauer and Carlos Alberto. My personal favorite was the Italian striker, Giorgio Chinaglia. Phenomenal player he was, Gary. Would you believe that his career started in Wales? His family moved there after the war. One hell of a striker he was, son. Scored goals for fun."

I had to confess to Ted that I only vaguely remembered Chinaglia from the 1974 Italian World Cup side, my focus having been so much on the Dutch, with Neeskens and Cruyff commanding most of my ten-year-old headspace that summer.

Ted recalled the buzz when Pele arrived at the Cosmos.

"Gary, son, that fella's arrival seemed to transform soccer in the States. The crowds for Cosmos games went through the roof and something like ten million people watched his first game! Can you believe that, son? Ten million people in America tuning in to watch a soccer game?"

"Pretty impressive, that is, Ted. Hard to imagine really."

I stooped closely over Ted's wheelchair as we took one of the many breaks in a strengthening regimen required for a man of his age. I ignored the overhead communication system echoing around our department as I listenined intently.

"I bet you didn't know that George Best came over here too, did you, son? Followed by yer man, Cruyff he was. Pretty amazing if you think about it."

"Yeah, Ted, I vaguely remember all the big names hitting America. So how come the league didn't last?"

Ted continued.

"Well, I reckon it all came down to overspending in the end, Gary son. The Cosmos spent millions and the other clubs just couldn't keep up.

348 : LIFE, LIBERTY, AND THE PURSUIT OF UNITED

There was no real competition and I think the audiences kind of dried up after a while. Shame really."

"They've got the MLS now though, right, Ted?"

"Aye, son. Just a couple of years ago. But who knows how long that will last? Trying to break the massive television audiences for the NFL and for the baseball, basketball and hockey will be really tough. Good luck to 'em, but I really can't see that having much of a future over here."

"They're going to have to compete against the English Premier League as well, right Ted? Maybe that will take off over here, too?"

"Oh, I dunno about that, son. But wouldn't that be grand, eh? Premier League games on regular TV over here. Maybe some day, eh?"

Before Ted left the clinic that morning, we chatted about the upcoming final day of the Premier League season. I suggested he come and watch it with us all at Conor O'Neill's.

"Oh, Gary, I don't know about that, son. I don't travel too far these days, you know. It's a hell of a hassle going anywhere with crowds, you know?"

"Ted! Let me spell it out for you, mate. On Sunday, the first part of an unprecedented Treble for Manchester United could happen. You can't miss it, mate! It's history in the making. We have a great set of lads at Conor O'Neill's and I know you'd love it down there. Come on Ted!"

"Ah, I just don't know about it, son," Ted replied looking uncertain. "What about access to the place?"

"Look, Ted. There's a parking space right outside the front door. And there's a ramp. I've noticed it many times. I am a physical therapist after all, right Ted? Tell you what; I'll get there early and park my car there. I'll wait until I see you coming up Main Street and then I'll flag you down. The game starts at eleven, so if you come by at ten, that'll give us plenty of time. Keep an eye out for an old maroon Pontiac 6000. You can't miss it mate. It'll be the most unstylish motor on the block! I'll move my car and you can move yours into that same space. Within seconds you'll be out of the car, into your wheelchair, and sliding on in to Conor's with me. Easy, mate! There's another ramp in the bar right up to our paddock area. You can meet all the lads and you'll have a grandstand view of the match."

The Irish eyes of the elderly fella smiled at me.

Ted offered me his hand, now appearing thrilled at the prospect.

"You know what, Gary? I will. I'll do that. Thanks, son! Thanks so much! I'll be up bright and early and looking for that old Pontiac of yours.

It's been a long time since I've watched a game in a pub with a bunch of the lads, ya know."

"Brilliant! I am so glad, Ted. Fantastic, mate!"

As Ted made for the exit of the department, struggling to propel his wheelchair after a rather lengthy physical therapy session, I turned to him and waved.

"Sunday, Ted! See you Sunday, my friend!"

"That you will, son," Ted replied, smiling. "I'll be there! I'll be there! Look for a bright green Chevy Cavalier the color of the green in the Irish tricolor. That'll be me, son."

52

Just the Job, Son

Sunday, May 16, 1999: It was a beautiful spring morning in Michigan as I hit the road shortly before 9:00 a.m. The tranquility of my journey to Ann Arbor provided stark contrast to the events about to unfold in Manchester and North London. So quiet was the highway, I felt like a Sunday driver gently meandering toward the "Thou Shall be Blessed Full Gospel Outreach Ministries" church. And, yes, that truly is the name of a church en route to my own Church of Soccer — an "American moment" if ever there was one.

As I left the metronomic sound of tire to concrete slab, I pulled off the freeway and onto Main Street's smoother tarmac that cradled me toward downtown Ann Arbor. Stillness persisted, as if suggesting one and all within the city were taking a well-earned pause for breath before fueling their determination to go again in that truly American all-or-nothing way at some stage later in the day.

I saw the parking spot, right outside the front doors of Conor O'Neill's, and immediately slipped my Pontiac into place, awaiting the arrival of the one-legged Irishman. Right on the stroke of ten, Ted's Chevy Cavalier approached. I stepped out into the road and waved him down. A quick maneuver and I had vacated pole position for him. I put the hazard lights on and shot across to wish the fella a good morning.

"How's it going there with you, Gary son?" an invigorated looking Ted greeted me.

"Not bad, mate. So are you all ready for the big game then Ted?"

"Ah son, this is spot on so it is," Ted replied, enthusiastically shaking my hand.

I shot around the block to the back of the pub and parked my own vehicle. The stillness of the air and the chill of the early spring morning filtered through my body as I walked the familiar few yards to the back door of Conor O'Neill's. The only noise evident that morning was an occasional car as it drove by, carefully obeying the speed limit as if in acknowledgement of the Sabbath. The stillness continued up until the moment I opened the back door. As soon as I stepped into the familiar dimly-lit corridor, my pulse began to race as my ears attuned to the sounds from within. A sudden blast of noise lifted me as I walked closer to the main arena. I bid good morning to one of the waitresses as I passed the kitchen at the back and then, on entering the bar, I could not believe my eyes—a pregame show in full flow, courtesy of Sky Sports. Our expat soccer world was slowly, but surely, continuing to develop with extended offerings as the demand warranted.

I walked the few yards into the center of the den and received an enthusiastic welcome from the posse sat ready and waiting in our paddock.

Ahmed was already tucking into a Donegal Fry.

"Gary, how are you? Can't wait for this game to get going."

"You and me both, Ahmed. Looks like the cooks got you squared away early, mate. Tad hungry, eh?"

"Friends in high places, Gary. It's my prematch meal. Always of vital importance!"

"I can see that, mate!" I replied, shaking the lad's hand after witnessing the precision with which he had placed his fork down on his napkin.

"Good luck today, Gary!"

"Right back at ya, Ahmed," I replied, receiving a huge grin from the big Jordanian, brown sauce lining the outer edges of his mouth, his red United home shirt with the name Giggs arched across his shoulders.

We were two soccer fans, far from our home countries, both clearly understanding the significance of the moment that lay ahead, a moment we hoped would provide a faultless satellite feed: boy, were we now getting picky!

Chinny and Crown Paints Jacob had also put in an appearance and Scouse Carl wandered in right behind me.

"For the love of the game, eh lads," I quipped.

"Hey, listen mate" Chinny responded "you can't beat this. Even as a Liverpool fan, I'm really looking forward to it."

"Robbie Fowler or no Robbie Fowler?" I teased my mate.

"Robbie Fowler or no Robbie Fowler, my friend."

Scouse Carl stood among his Kop clan. "Last day of season and all that" he said, validating his presence at a United match early on a Sunday morning.

"Good lad!" I responded.

"Hey, Gary" Crown Paints chimed in, "This should be very interesting. How are you feeling?"

"Well-pumped, Jake! Hey, I see the shirt is still going strong there, mate." I couldn't help but make reference to Jacob's now bursting-at-the-seams faded old faithful Liverpool away shirt.

"I love this shirt! It's my out watching soccer go-to fashion garb!"

We all burst out laughing.

"I think we get that, Jakey lad!"

"Hey, I don't think they've had a better one since, man" Chinny added.

"No, I'm right with you there, Chinny" Carl added, "best 'pool shirt for years mate."

"That's why I hang with it, guys. I love this shirt!" Jake confirmed.

"I got it, mate. I got it!" I replied, shaking the Liverpool fan's hand.

On a day of such significance for all Manchester United fans, Jacob seemed stuck in a Liverpool FC time warp and was loving every second of it. It was great to see the Koppites out for the last game of the season. There was never any doubt, to be honest.

All in all, there appeared to be a fantastic early gathering. Connie had sneaked the lads in from the back of the pub prior to opening time, Ahmed's early breakfast testament to that.

Nice touch!

"Hey, Red, save a space for us there will you, mate? There's a buddy of mine who may need a little room for his wheelchair."

"No problem, you wanker. Got it."

I placed my jacket down on a chair next to Fred, receiving the usual calm and collected "Morning, Gary" from our elder statesman.

"How's it going, my friend?" I acknowledged.

After more high fives and handshakes, I made my way over to the front door. Connie, one step ahead of me, was opening up for business.

"Hey! What about ya's there, Gary?" her soft Dublin tones most soothing. "I reckon you must be pretty excited, eh, fella?"

"Hey Connie! What do you know? Come here," immediately giving the wee Irish lass a hug.

"Bless ya's, Gary. Always great to see ya's."

"You too, Connie. You too. And hey, thanks again for this."

"Auch, away with ya's, son."

I left Connie to busy herself readying for another soccer morning at Conors and carried on through the front door to greet my guest.

I noticed a line of fans had gathered on the sidewalk in the few minutes since I had left Ted. There was a definite extra buzz in the air.

As everyone began to file in, there on the road in front of me was Ted, struggling to transfer himself from his vehicle to his wheelchair.

"Ted! Do you need a hand there, mate?"

"Hey there, Gary lad. No, I'm fine. Done this a million times, son, so I have. I am almost away from this bloody piece of junk anyways now. Give us a wee minute, will ya?"

I observed a man fully focused on his arduous task at hand.

"Of course, mate. No worries. What a beautiful morning," I replied. "A beautiful morning to see the greatest team in England bring home another Premier League title, eh?"

"Ah, yes, Gary son. I am so looking forward to this, so I am. Can't thank you enough there, son."

With a slam of his car door, my determined friend was onto the road, a deft maneuver up the curb and then wheeling himself to the door of Conor O'Neill's.

The two of us entered the pub and, all of a sudden, I was seeing all before me in a different light—a Ted perspective, perhaps—as I tried to plot the best path for my wheelchair-bound friend through the gathering crowd.

"Fellas, this is Ted, a mate of mine."

"Hey, Ted!"

"What's up, Ted?"

"Great to meet you, Ted!"

To a man, they all greeted the excited Irishman warmly.

Introductions complete, I glanced over at Ted as he became transfixed with the screen in front of him. Wriggling out of his coat, he rolled his sleeves up and then turned to me, smiling.

"This is magic, Gary son! Pure magic."

Red and my Irish friend appeared to hit it off right away as the lanky American became intrigued with the story of an Irishman's opinions on soccer and the early days of the North American Soccer League. It did not pass me by that Red, Fred, and all of our early morning crew had gone out of their way to make Ted feel welcome. It was almost always the case at

Conor O'Neill's; soccer fans, regardless of allegiance, instantly engaging in conversation, brought together through a mutual love of the beautiful game.

A huge roar filled the room as Old Trafford — the Theatre of Dreams — appeared on the big screen in all its glory. Instantly I received a high five from Ted, beaming with excitement at what lay ahead. No further words were required.

We were also to be treated to real-time highlights of developments at Highbury where Arsenal were taking on Aston Villa — a simultaneous broadcast as the two title contenders battled for glory. Given the circumstances, there were apparently two Premier League trophies, one at Old Trafford and one at Highbury. The big question was — which one would see the light of day? A win at Old Trafford for Manchester United against Tottenham Hotspur and there was nothing that Arsenal could do. But if United failed to win and Arsenal emerged victorious, then a poxy replica, no doubt, would be held aloft in North London.

The stage was set.

The atmosphere inside Conor O'Neill's was absolutely brilliant.

Right before kick-off, I heard a voice calling my name from across the bar, and, as I looked up, I saw Dave and his girlfriend, Sandy. Just as they had promised, they had got up early and driven over to Ann Arbor for a taste of the British soccer fanatics enjoying their fix. I gave Dave a nod and shouted "Catch you at half-time, mate."

Dave mouthed the words "Go United! Good Luck!"

I loved that!

I nudged Ted "Look who's here, mate."

"Well, look over there then, eh" said Ted, raising a hand to acknowledge a fellow patient.

Eleven o'clock arrived and, with it, the intensity inside Conor O'Neill's reached new heights.

"Come onnnnnnn you Reds!"

As the teams readied for kick-off, Fred nudged me and pointed toward the front door. A huge smile came across his face as, right on cue, Cliff Miller entered the fray at the very last minute with his usual stooping swerve matching that tilt of the head towards the big screen in the corner. He made his way over to the paddock to the backdrop of raucous applause. His response was wonderful as he immediately held his tattered old Arsenal scarf aloft, reminding us all, as if we needed it, of his unerring allegiance to the Gunners.

"I gather this means that you'll be staying today then, hey Cliff?" exclaimed Fred.

The American Gooner didn't rise to the bait, firmly ensconced in his own Arsenal world.

"Come on the Arrrrsssennnaaaal!"

Clifford Miller was in his very own Gunner zone!

I was all eyes on Old Trafford.

The cameras panned over the crowd. The sense of urgency on the faces of the United faithful was clear for all to see, and looking around at Conor O'Neill's own United clan, it was the same. Battle was about to commence. It had all come down to one final game.

Connie dimed the lights. For the next ninety minutes, I felt as though I was inside Old Trafford, connected with the expectant crowd in Manchester.

The game got off to a flying start with a dreadful mistake from Ian Walker in the Spurs goal, his attempted kick swiftly closed down by Dwight Yorke. One second, the camera was focused squarely on David Ginola's butt as he received treatment on the sidelines and the next, a sudden surge in Ian Darke's voice and the cameras shot to the ball as it rolled its way toward the corner of the open goal. Den and Don were punching the air, red faced and unreserved as ever, eager for the ball to bobble its way over the line. Instead, it hit the post and returned to the hands of the thankful goalkeeper.

"Aha! No! No! No!" exclaimed Clifford Miller, attempting to convince himself and any of the other non-United clan around him that all was still well. It was a most bizarre start to proceedings. I sat quietly. My game head was on. I reverted to Hotel Hairpiece watching mode, slipping into my United zen, as I did when I watched the VHS recordings from Dearborn Dorothy alone in my apartment. I was fully aware of the vibe around me but totally zoned in on the match, willing my team on, kicking every ball, emotionally fully invested.

Twenty-five minutes in, however, as United continued to pressure the Spurs goal, disaster struck. A sudden sense of disbelief and anguish engulfed Old Trafford along with a certain Irish soccer pub in the American Midwest. With only their second attempt on goal, Les Ferdinand, the big Tottenham striker, nipped in between two United defenders and flicked a looping ball over Schmeichel, leaving the United goalie flapping at thin air as both ball and, indeed, the great Dane, fell into the back of the United net.

The cameras panned over the Stretford End—a mass of United devotees, blank stares, fans looking at each other in shock. Surely not?

Ferdinand's brilliant goal had caught the United defense and our great keeper totally off guard. The crowd inside Old Trafford, the manager and the United contingent in Ann Arbor were stunned.

Silence fell over the Conor's paddock, except, of course, for the cries of joy from Clifford Miller and a couple of other Arsenal fans.

"Yes! Yes! Get in there! Come on you Arsennnnalll!"

The American Gooner rattled the table in front of him. The broadcast immediately switched over to Highbury where, to a man, there was the chorus of "Come on you scum," an irony if ever there was one, as Arsenal fans inside the stadium were all willing on their number one enemy—Tottenham Hotspur—to produce the win they needed at Old Trafford.

"Come on, Arsennnallllll! Come on, you Gunnerrrs!" Cliff had embedded himself firmly among the Highbury faithful in North London.

It was pure theatre!

"Bloody hell, mate. That wasn't meant to happen," Jack said to me.

"Understatement of the year, mate" I quietly responded.

The picture returned to Old Trafford and our clan raised the decibel levels. United responded well and continued to pressure the Spurs defense with Ian Walker making save after save. United were spreading the ball around, Giggs and Beckham rifling cross after cross into the Spurs penalty area.

"Looks like it could be one of those days for United" Fred uttered.

"Hey, none of that, mate," I replied.

I still believed.

"Scholesss! Great save from Walker," exclaimed match commentator, Ian Darke, confirming another brilliant stop from Ian Walker in the Spurs goal.

"Sheringham in again. Scholes again denied by Walker. Can you believe it?" Darke again confirming the defiance of Tottenham's keeper.

"One of those days?" Maybe Fred was onto something.

Scholes's face portrayed agony.

"Two huge saves by the Tottenham goalkeeper. It just won't happen for Manchester United," Darke exclaimed.

"Hey, you've won nutin' yet, Gary la," shouted Gerry George adding that all-too-familiar refrain from somewhere across the bar. I had wondered where Gerry was and, indeed, what had taken him so long. My right hand immediately shot up in acknowledgment.

"Yeahhh, Gary la" another verbal volley from the happy Scouser.

And then, right on cue, Beckham sprinted into the Spurs box to meet a beautiful cross from Giggs. Beckham's bullet of a header should have broken the Spurs net.

"Point blank range. And he's put it over. Can you believe it?"

Keane drove through the middle of the Spurs midfield. Another chance blocked by the Spurs defense.

"United now have opened up all cylinders." Darke continued nailing the dynamic.

We were on our feet, united as one, urging our team forward.

Spurs then countered, and if it wasn't for a last ditch tackle from Gary Neville, Iversen could have easily made it two-nil.

It was a brilliant game for the neutral; agony for United and Gunner's fans.

"Bloody hell! We should have had at least four by now," exclaimed Eddie.

"I can't believe this, man," added Ahmed, both arms in prayer position, elbows protruding out to his side as the rhythmical pumping of his hands expressed his frustration. Ahmed always communicated his thoughts via his upper extremities!

Darke reminded us once again, "and over at Highbury, it's still scoreless. Arsenal 0, Aston Villa 0."

"Come on the Arsennaalllll," responded Cliff as he stood tall with his scarf high above his head.

Iversen again pulled a fine save out of Schmeichel.

The game was now wide open. Spurs, relying on the counter, could quite easily have squeezed another one in.

"Ouuff!" Jack looked at me. I looked at Eddie. Den, of course looked at Don!

"Hey, Gary la! Hey Gary . . . how ya doin' over there, son?"

Once again, I raised a hand high into the air, my gaze remaining firmly focused on the screen.

"Yeeehheeyyyy! Youse haven't won nuttin' yet, Gary la! Nuttin'!"

"Cheers Gerry!" I yelled back "Much appreciated, mate"

"You're welcome, son! Very welcome!"

And then . . .

"Giggs, Scholes, Beckham . . . a real chance here for United. And David Beckham has scored an equalizer for Manchester United! It's 1-1!"

David Beckham sent a viciously curling shot into the top far corner of the Spurs goal.

Old Trafford went nuts! The Conor's paddock erupted!

I almost had the life squeezed out of me with two bear-hugs, first by Den and then by Don, along with the usual high fives from all my United brothers.

Ted yelled "get in there, my son! What a goal! What a goal!"

I shook the Irishman's shoulders in delight, glad to know that he had his wheelchair brakes applied!

And so, there we were.

1-1 at half-time.

0-0 in the Arsenal/Villa game.

Advantage United as it stood. However, one goal from Arsenal and it would suddenly be advantage Gunners.

Dave and Sandy wandered over. They appeared to be enjoying the atmosphere, Sandy commenting again that she thought the British soccer players were "pretty cute" with "great legs."

"I just love that Beckham guy."

"How ya doin there, Ted?"

"Hey, what about ya's, Dave. And would you look at that? Yer young lady is here too? Lucky lad you are there, son!"

"Thank you so much, sir" Sandy replied, blushing.

The half-time conversation was all about the nail-biter that lay in store. Forty-five minutes to go and everything to play for. It was a final match day worthy of its billing.

Andy Cole came on for Sheringham at the start of the second half.

And within a couple of minutes . . .

"Gary Neville floats it in. Cole in space. Brings it down. It's Andy Cole . . . oh and it's a brilliant goal from Andy Cole."

Old Trafford and Conor O'Neil's were in raptures once more as Cole controlled the long ball into the area before lobbing it over Ian Walker and into the Spurs goal.

"Yes! Yes! Yes!" I danced with Red and Jack, Eddie diving in to seize the moment.

Moments later, it was hearts in mouths as Iversen once again tested Schmeichel, the replay showing what a brilliant chance it was for the Spurs player to pull his team level.

Ian Darke increased our tension.

"And as that was happening, news has come through that Arsenal have taken the lead against Aston Villa through Kanu . . . so United, as things stand, will have to hold on for the win here!"

As promised, cameras were providing up to the minute action, the brief clip of the Arsenal goal sending our Gunners comrades into raptures.

"Yes! Yes! Come on Arsennnallllll!"

"United! United! United!" came the louder response.

Cliff surged forth, stood arms aloft:

"Come on, Arsennnalllll!"

Red looked over at me. "I don't think I can take much more of this, man."

The satellite feed was now split between Highbury and Old Trafford.

"Come onnnnnn!"

"Arggghhh!"

"United! United!"

"Come on, you Gunners!"

As the final seconds ticked down, the expressions on the faces in the crowds at both grounds said it all.

Ted was loving it! "Son, this is unbelievable, so it is. I've got meself two games for the price of one now, eh!"

"United are almost there, Ted," I replied, willing the game to end.

"So they are, son. So they are!"

"You wanted drama, eh Chinny," I yelled at my American friend.

You could feel the tension and the excitement among our United cohort. Our Red Devils were almost home and dry.

And then, both final whistles blew.

It was over!

"Yes! Yes! Yes! Championes!" Jack yelled, his right arm aloft.

"Get in there!" shouted Eddie, arms held high, exultant in victory.

"Gary, you wanker! You bloody wanker! We did it! We bloody well did it, mate! United forever, dude!" exclaimed Red standing tall beside me, arms aloft.

"We sure did, Frank. We sure did, mate!"

"I am breathless after that, you tosser! What a finish!"

The pictures on the screen above our heads showed an ecstatic Alex Ferguson sprinting onto the Old Trafford pitch to embrace Roy Keane. Contrast that with the resignation on Arsene Wenger's face as he left the Arsenal dug out, Gunners fans at Highbury stood, radios to their ears, now surely aware that their chance had gone.

Manchester United had won the title by a solitary point and had just a one goal better goal difference.

"We did it Fred!"

"Worthy champions, Gary. Wow that really was exciting stuff!"

I stood up and walked over to Cliff. There was a small congregation of Gooners around him, gathered together in mutual mourning.

"Well played, mate. That was quite some finale, eh, Cliff?" I said reaching out to shake his hand.

"Hey, congratulations, Gary. It pains me to say this, but well done to United. Damn! We almost made it. What a finale. If it wasn't for that Leeds United match . . ." Cliff was already deconstructing the incredible events of the last few weeks in his very own Gunnerland.

"Not good for the heart, right, Cliff?"

"Yeah, but you gotta love this game, what it can throw out there. There's nothing like it."

"Sure isn't Cliff" I replied, adding "all the best mate" as I gave our American Gooner a pat on the back.

I realized I had someone else to chat with, but not before Ahmed tried to jump on me and Den and Don burst into a rousing chorus of "Glory Glory Man United" inches from my face, their facial expressions suggestive of having suffered from constipation over the last couple of days.

"Well done, United!" Chinny shouted as I passed by him, reaching over to shake my hand.

"Yeah, congratulations, Gary," added Jake and Scouse Carl, both gracious, reaching out to shake my hand.

It was true camaraderie between a special bunch of soccer fans. We all had an honest realization of just how fortunate we were, fortunate to have been able to find our soccer connection — our soccer community.

I made my way to the back of the bar. I caught Gerry George's eye en route. He gave me a huge smile and simply nodded his head in recognition, his eyes closing as he took a long drag on his cigarette.

I reached the payphone area and carefully dialed in the long string of numbers.

"Yesssssss! Mate! We did it!"

"Brilliant! What a team, eh, son? What a team!"

"It was incredible here, dad. Can you believe it? I saw it all, mate!"

"Bloody incredible, son. So far away and still you manage to catch the game. Look at that, eh!"

"They even had a split screen simultaneously showing the United and the Arsenal matches, mate."

Des was gobsmacked, once again resigned to listening to the whole affair on BBC Radio Five Live—the irony again recognized by us both.

"One down, two to go, dad!"

"Son, this team is . . . I think they really . . . ya know, son."

"What was that, dad?" The noise in the bar was so loud that I could hardly hear my father.

"I said that this team is pretty special, son. I think they can pull off this treble, ya know. Here they come. They've just said on the radio that Keano is leading them out to get the trophy."

"Oh right. Cheers, dad. I'd better fly. You're a few seconds ahead of us so I should be able to catch it over her, mate."

"You'll see it before I do, lad! Bloody mad that is! Good luck."

"Look after yourself, dad"

"You look after yourself, son. Keep goin and . . . come on United!"

I shot back to our paddock area and, sure enough, the live pictures beaming into our haven showed Roy Keane leading his team out once again onto the Old Trafford pitch, ready to receive the English Premier League champions trophy. We all stood applauding and raised the roof as Keano lifted the trophy high.

Immediately, a glass was thrust my way. Johnny and Connie had brought out a couple of bottles of champagne. The corks popped and toasts rang out as we all celebrated. It was a great gesture from the manager of our soccer pub, a real surprise. I sipped my glass of "champers" and leaned over to Fred.

"No fat lady singing yet, mate!"

We toasted Fred's health and the very best for his upcoming surgery.

I took in the scenes around me. It was as if our toast not only signified United's magnificent achievement, but also it was a celebration of everyone present being able to maintain an important link to home; it was a commitment to each other, to our special clan of soccer fans. And it also represented the finale to our first season of Premier League soccer watching at Conor O'Neill's.

As we all started to filter out and the handshakes and well wishes for the week began—Cliff was by now understandably long gone—I couldn't help sense that Part Two of the "Impossible" Treble was now on the minds of our United clan.

"In a week's time then, eh, Gary?" Jack acknowledged.

"Part Two," said Eddie shaking my hand.

"See you next week, Red." I shook Red's hand.

"The Treble lives on, you wanker!" Red had nailed it.

I then wandered over to Gerry George for a quick word.

"What about that then, mate?"

"Yeaahh. Credit where credit is due son."

"How are you feeling, mate?" I asked the Liverpudlian.

"Oh, I keep going, Gary son. Always keep chuggin' along. Otherwise, what's the bloody point, hey la?"

"True. Well, look after yourself, eh, Gerry. Hope to see you in here next week."

"I am thinking you might well, son. Anything to keep avoiding the bran flakes and water, sat bored silly at home on a Saturday morning. Go easy, eh la!"

After a quick thank you to Connie and the crew, I shot outside to check on Ted's progress.

No need to have worried, he was already in his car.

"I am away now, son. Thanks. I loved that. I really did, son!"

"So glad you made it, Ted. You know where we are now, right?"

"Aye. That I do, son. That I do."

I gave the trunk of Ted's car a slap as he steered himself away from pole position and off home. I noticed the huge smile on his face and didn't doubt we would see him at Conor O'Neill's again in the not too distant future. We were certainly going to have plenty to talk about at our next physical therapy session.

Just as I had waved Ted off, Dave and Sandy stepped up next to me on the pavement outside.

Dave offered his hand.

"Gary! That was freakin' awesome, dude."

A hug from Sandy and our well wishes were complete. Another couple of American converts to the English Premier League, I immediately thought to myself. I wished them both well.

I stood for a few seconds on my own on the sidewalk outside Conors. United had just won the English Premier League and, yes, again, I had witnessed it live from the Midwest American outpost which was my home away from home. In a mere six days' time I was planning to return, because, on May 22, Conor O'Neill's would screen the 1999 FA Cup final: Manchester United versus Newcastle United live from Wembley Stadium, London, England. All of the United faithful in our Conor's paddock were well up for it. Fred, too, hopefully less one angry prostate, ready to witness a certain Fat Lady continue her warm up, ever closer to finally singing her heart out.

53

Peeing Red!

May 22, 1999. FA Cup final day!

Three FA Cup finals had taken place during my time in the States. All three had provided an opportunity to celebrate English soccer tradition — tradition that accentuated ties with the old country, prompting most of us that day to think of "home." This historic day in England's soccer calendar brought up fond memories for most of the British expatriate community.

I couldn't help but drift back to my earliest memories of those FA Cup finals past: the ITV battling the BBC to grab the highest viewership; my uncle Jack chomping on his tongue sandwiches; my United shirt dangling from atop the television cabinet; the interviews on the team buses allowing a young passionate Manchester United fan the ability to ride along with his team to Wembley; that first sight of the Twin Towers and the crowds filing along Wembley Way; the players walking onto the pitch prior to kick-off; over 100,000 fans singing "Abide with Me"; British royalty meeting and greeting each team — and British royalty also providing that outlet for my mother's ire, as one of its members stood ready to hand the FA Cup trophy to the winning captain.

As I drove to Ann Arbor, the FA Cup final kick-off was only an hour or so away and its significance could not be understated. A win against Newcastle United would provide the Red Devils with a second piece of silverware and the domestic double — a brilliant achievement in itself. Should that be the final outcome, then surely United fans the world over could dare to dream even more of a third trophy and, ultimately, an unprecedented Treble. Conor O'Neill's opened early, once again demonstrating its commitment to soccer by providing us with the Sky Sports pregame show.

As I stepped into Conor O'Neill's that morning, it was as if a switch had been flicked, propelling me back in a time warp to a time when I first fell in love with soccer and Manchester United. Did I ever consider that I would one day be watching the final thousands of miles from Lancashire, still filled with that same excitement and expectation that I had back in the day? The FA Cup final was *the* day when a soccer match was available to one and all across the length and breadth of the country. Oh, how far we have truly come since then.

Ted was back for more. I met up with him outside again and made sure that he got installed in the paddock. "This is just lovely, son! Just lovely," he noted, appearing thrilled at the prospect of being able to watch an FA Cup final again after all his years as an expatriate in Michigan. It was two matches in less than a week for Ted. His soccer-watching world had suddenly taken a most positive turn, to say the least.

The soccer crowd began filtering into our den.

Eddie had made the break from the bakery early and arrived with his mate, Jack, swelling our Manchester United supporter ranks. It appeared that some sort of vanilla delicacy must have been the order of the day, judging by the waft emanating from Eddie's clothes. I welcomed the change from the usual cinnamon sensory overload.

I smiled at the excitement on the big Jordanian student Ahmed's face as he sat proudly in anticipation for the game, his tightly clad United shirt bursting out over his pants as he had once again acquired an early plateful of "full Irish." He had truly found his very own pregame tradition. Not a smidgen of fattoush in sight.

Red, Chinny, Den and Don all arrived. Carl, the Liverpool fan, had acquired the only cushioned chair in the building for Fred—and it looked quite regal too. We all agreed that it would provide the ideal soft landing for our elder statesman and his tender, post-surgical rear end. Indeed, just as the makeshift recuperation throne had been carefully positioned, a big cheer echoed around the paddock. Looking a little tired and walking with a definite air of fragility, a smiling Regal Fred entered the fray.

"Your seat, m'lord" Carl quipped, a huge smile on his face as he gestured to Fred, his right arm wafting Fred towards his throne.

"Ah, that is just perfect, Carl. Thank you!" Fred responded.

"Told you I would make it," Fred said, leaning in toward me and placing his hand on my shoulder to aid his slow and measured descent.

"Doing alright there, Fred" I enquired.

"Not too bad thanks, Gary. Now let's get through the game lads and then maybe we can all have some medication on my behalf."

I marveled at the man's speed of recovery, having been in surgery just seventy two hours earlier. He had promised that he would make it. And he had.

At exactly ten o'clock local Michigan time, the lights dimmed.

Game on!

I couldn't help but sense a slightly strange air to the proceedings. United had won the English Premier League title a mere six days earlier and looming large on the horizon in four days' time was the chance of European glory against Bayern Munich. Was the Champions League final overshadowing our 1999 FA Cup moment? Excitement filled the building for sure, but, in some ways, it felt like a case of let's get this one done and dusted and then we can dream even bigger. With all respect to Newcastle United, losing finalists in the previous year's final against Arsenal, Manchester United's players had to focus hard on the immediate prize and not fall into the trap of looking beyond the moment. I felt that the United crowd inside Conor O'Neill's was trying to do the same.

The cameras were in the tunnel and we witnessed a warm handshake between Ruud Gullit, the Newcastle manager, and Alex Ferguson. The teams entered the pitch through a firework fog, the roar of the supporters willing their heroes forth and prompting our Conor's United clan to respond.

The atmosphere was electric inside Wembley Stadium. The sun beamed down on both sets of fans, the black and white of the Geordies contrasting with Manchester United red. The national anthem started and the crowd inside Conors immediately burst into song along with over 100,000 fans inside the stadium. Expatriates needed no prompting on that front.

I smiled to myself as Prince Charles appeared, ready to greet each player in the lineup. A penny for my mother's thoughts at that very moment. It was no surprise that both Roy Keane and Paul Scholes were in the lineup, both ruled out of the upcoming Champions League final due to suspension.

"Got to be careful of Shearer here, Gary."

Red was on the money. On his day, Alan Shearer, the Premier League's runaway top goalscorer, could punish any team. David May and Ronny Johnsen would have to keep a close eye on the prolific English striker. In the first ever FA Cup final between two Uniteds, the form book pointed to a Manchester United win. However, FA Cup finals had a sneaky habit of throwing the form book out of the nearest available window.

A sudden elevated roar filled Conor's as the referee blew his whistle. "That's more like it," I thought to myself.

Shearer surged into Manchester United territory but he was met by

Keane who laid down his marker. Two captains full of intent. The 1999 FA Cup final had well and truly begun.

Newcastle started well. With only three minutes gone, a lively Nolberto Solano attempted an audacious volley, Schmeichel scrambling to his left in order to gather.

"I tell you what, mate, Newcastle look well up for this," said Jack, my United cohort.

Roy Keane continued getting stuck in at every opportunity, leading from the front as he so often did. Then, with only minutes into the match Gary Speed caught our captain. The Irishman fell awkwardly. The commentary team continued to remind us that he was in trouble as he continued to try and run off the knock. Eventually, the physio sprinted onto the pitch and headed towards Keano.

"Ankle, Gary?" I had expected the inquiry from Fred.

"Looks like it, Fred," several replays of Gary Speed's tackle confirming the possibility.

"We'll make a physio out of you yet, eh, Fred?" I added.

After a delay of several minutes, the physio left the pitch and pictures on the screen above our heads portrayed Keane trying to regain his normal gait. It didn't look good. Newcastle United were not giving the Reds a moment on the ball. It appeared a definite game plan from the start. Dietmar Hamman left a little naughty "afters" in on Phil Neville and was duly booked as a result. Gary Neville was clattered and, of course, the Gary Speed tackle on Keane were all evidence of how the Magpies were trying to interrupt the Red Devils' flow.

With only eight minutes gone, Keane had decided that his race was run. The Irishman's luck was seemingly in short supply. His contribution to United's end of season run was instantly recognized by our Conor's Reds as applause rattled around our paddock to the sight of our captain hobbling toward the touchline. Manchester United's Wembley contingent responded as one, on their feet to applaud him.

"Tough for the lad so it is, eh Gary son," Ted commented.

"Just hasn't had much luck lately has he, Ted."

"Gotta go for Teddy now, right?" Red chimed in.

Alex Ferguson responded positively. Maybe he had heard Red?

Teddy Sheringham entered the fray. I noticed Beckham moving into a more central midfield position and Solskjær adopting Beckham's normal wide right birth. Sheringham's impact was immediate.

"Cole, Sheringham . . . beats two, into Scholes . . . to Sheringhaamm! 1-0!"

Eleven minutes on the clock and Teddy Sheringham, minutes after entering the field of play, had broken the deadlock.

The Red throng inside Conor O'Neill's rose collectively to its feet.

Regal Fred muttered in my ear. "That's marvelous! Simply marvelous! He is such a skillful player, Gary!"

Fred then stood, maneuvering awkwardly around a couple of chairs to make one of several rather uncomfortable looking adjustments, carefully stepping through the watching hoards. He was quite obviously in some degree of discomfort. A few minutes later, he returned from the bathroom, looking none too happy.

Meanwhile, we had a pretty decent game on our hands. Solskjær could have done better near post, Cole also should have done better with only the Newcastle goalie to beat. Then, at the other end, Hamman let loose from just outside the penalty area, pulling a fine save out of Schmeichel. Sheringham again came close, rising well and powering a header just past the Newcastle upright. The commentary team continued to reference the match to come in Barcelona, almost to confirm that we were all just passing through Wembley Way, with more important matters on the horizon.

The half-time whistle blew.

"Just forty five more minutes, dude." Den offered his usual high five.

I stood for a moment as the cameras panned Wembley Stadium from above. It looked like a glorious spring day in London as the old stadium dominated the screen. I thought of home once again and of FA Cup finals past.

I wandered to the back door and grabbed the telephone.

"What do you think then, son?"

"They seem pretty much in control, don't they, dad?"

"They do, son. Pity about Keane, but Sheringham is playing well."

"It's a great turnout in here again, dad. The pub has a few of those new high definition TVs in place now, too."

"Bloody hell Gary! Sounds like you've got it made over there. Well, I won the vote over here. We've got BBC on. Your mother must be in a good mood today. It's bloody great to be able to watch the match live instead of having to wait for Match of the Day."

"What do you think second half, mate?" I asked my father.

"2-0 United!"

"Love it, mate. Come on!"

"Look after yourself, son. Enjoy the rest of the match, eh."

"You too, dad."

Once again, the miles had melted away.

Newcastle made a change at half-time, Hamann taken off, allowing Duncan Ferguson to enter the fray. The Magpies were showing their intent. Their fans were buoyed as the Geordie faithful roared their approval at Gullitt's positive change.

The second half commenced and the game opened up. Newcastle started well. For the first few minutes, they were quicker into the tackle and spreading the ball about nicely. Duncan Ferguson was fired up and several balls were looped into the Red Devils' area, increasing the decibel level from the Newcastle fans behind Schmeichel's goal.

Then, out of nowhere, as Dabizas was pressed in the opposite corner by Giggs, the Greek player's clearance was picked up by Solskjær whose acceleration took him into the Newcastle penalty area to fire a pass into the feet of Sheringham. With his back to goal Sheringham then calmly dispatched a simple lay off into the path of Scholes, who slotted a delightful left foot finish low to Harper's right.

"We shall not, we shall not be moved" echoed loudly around Wembley.

Had Scholes sealed victory for Manchester United?

With fifty-three minutes gone in the match, the fans of the United of Manchester appeared to feel that, indeed, he may well have.

The game then seemed to take on a new dimension. Cole was replaced by Yorke, and from that point forward Manchester United began to dominate. Stam came on for Scholes, the United midfielder leaving the Wembley turf to a huge ovation. Shortly after that, Giggs broke into Newcastle's box, slotted a pass to Sheringham and the United striker executed a wonderfully delicate chip over Harper only to watch the ball hit the crossbar.

"What a player, Gary. That was so poised," commented Fred, who once again had the chance to laud a player he had come to admire.

"What a goal that would have been, you tosser," said Red, adding his rather less refined opinion.

I watched Fred take another walk around the bar before shuffling back into his seat. He tilted his head over his shoulder and spoke in my ear. "Gary, talk about it being all United today. Would you believe it, my friend, I am even peeing red!"

A sneaky snapshot of Fred's catheter coming into view as the FA Cup final came to a close, was not something I had expected. Sure enough, the small, discreet catheter revealed a collection of fluid most definitely of a United red!

"Alright! Thanks for sharing, Fred," I replied, sarcastically.

"Most welcome, Gary. Just wanted to fully verify my allegiance today."

I patted my good friend on his shoulder, exclaiming that maybe, just maybe, he was, after all, becoming a Red Devil convert.

As the match reached time added on, the television pictures focused on the Manchester United bench. Ferguson and his assistant, Steve McClaren, were both smiling, waiting for the referee to blow his whistle.

The referee raised his arm aloft and it was game over.

A third domestic double in five years for Manchester United. That, in istelf, was an incredible feat, but now for United, an even greater challenge loomed on the horizon.

I noticed a banner that read "Two Down, One to Go!'

That said it all.

Schmeichel passed the captain's arm band to Roy Keane and United's captain led his team up the Wembley steps.

The United clan in Conor O'Neill's stood and applauded as Keane raised the trophy high above his head. As he exited stage right, a smile came across my face as the camera focused in on the Duchess of Kent. For a split second, amid the noise, I could hear my mother's voice!

High fives all around from the Conor's United clan emphasized the joyous realization that our beloved Reds were now just one game away from glory. The celebrations among our United faithful were, indeed, a tad less jubilant than the week prior. Don't get me wrong, it was undoubtedly a huge achievement in itself—winning the English domestic double—and for that third time too, but as soon as that trophy had been lifted and those congratulations had been passed around in Conor O'Neill's, it was almost as if everyone present was immediately thinking ahead four days to that final historic hurdle.

I stepped away to assist Ted once again as he bid farewell to all and, with minimal fuss, he transferred into his car.

"Thanks again, son! Terrific morning, that."

"No worries, Ted. Be safe my friend" I replied.

"Always am, son. I always am."

After waving Ted off, I wandered back into Conor's and noticed the rest of our paddock was also beginning to drift away.

"Till Wednesday, Gary. I cannot wait, you wanker!"

"Me neither, Red. Can't come quick enough, eh mate," I replied, shaking the American's hand before he headed for the door with Chinny.

"Well done, United" Chinny declared as he went around to every United fan in our crew, Eddie attempting to convince him to "leave the dark side" and become a Red Devil.

"No way man. Not a chance!" I expected nothing less.

Jack, Eddie, Ahmed, Den, Don, and myself all shook hands with that job-done vibe filling the air.

Two down, one to go.

The pub soon returned to its non-soccer state. Saturday lunchtime had arrived and, with it, a new group of punters were now in the building, looking, perhaps, for a sports fix of a more traditional American nature.

Fred and I remained and settled in for a wee bit of medication time.

Fred decided that under the circumstances, a much milder medication than the usual black stuff was the order of the day and with a reduced fluid ounce intake at that. I took full responsibility and decided that it was only right that I have one for the both of us.

After a swift reflection on the match, Fred still lauding Sheringham, our conversation veered toward the subject of previous FA Cup finals. I asked Fred about the first final he had seen while living in the U.S.

"Well, as you know, Gary, I left England in 1957 and would you believe that I didn't see a soccer match for years after that, as they weren't carried on either Canadian or U.S. TV. While I was living in Southfield, I somehow got wind of the fact that the Canadian Channel, CBC Windsor, would be showing the FA Cup final between Chelsea and Spurs."

Fred's tired looking face suddenly projected a broad smile, as an old memory came flooding back.

"My family and I were scheduled to visit the dentist that day. My wife, my two kids and I . . . and a small thirteen-inch Portable TV!"

"What?" I exclaimed, a little thrown with the mention of a portable TV and a visit to the dentist in the same sentence.

"Yes, a thirteen-inch portable television, Gary. I had realized that the game was to be shown right at the time of our appointment so I decided to bring the TV with us. As soon as we got there, I spotted a socket and placed the TV up on a chair in perfect position for viewing. There was only one other person waiting, and they didn't object in the least, so I went ahead and tuned in. And there it was, Wembley Stadium, coming to life inside a dentist's waiting room, via a broadcast from across the Detroit River over in Windsor. It was the first game I had seen in ten years. I was thrilled. It was also the first all-London final. I was happy to see Spurs win. They were the team of the sixties, Gary."

"I didn't get to see another FA Cup final until 1979. What a game that was! I was in Canada for the weekend and happened to flip on the TV in my hotel room. And there it was in front of me—Wembley Stadium! I must have cancelled whatever plans I had for that afternoon because I remember watching the rest of the game. Thankfully I had only missed the first few minutes. I'm sure you must remember that crazy end to the game Gary, Manchester United scoring two goals in the last few minutes to equalize against Arsenal who then went on to score right at the death!"

"Alan-bloody-Sunderland. Oh, please, don't remind me, mate!"

Fred and I continued reminiscing for a while longer. I learned that it had taken almost fifteen more years before he was able to see another FA Cup final—the 1994 final between Manchester United and Chelsea, his first game experienced live via satellite in his own home. He had not missed a final since.

I finished off my last mouthful of medication as we once again reflected on the current day's events. We both agreed that in light of the intense expectation of what lay ahead for the Red Devils, it had been somewhat of a rather more laid back ending to an FA Cup final for many a year.

"Fred, I can't believe it, mate. United win the double and still I'm dreaming of more."

"It sure is one heck of a season, Gary, isn't it?"

"The crazy thing is, Fred, that final just seemed quite a stroll in the end, didn't it?"

"Gary, FA Cup finals are still to be savored though, aren't they. Look at us, miles away and still able to watch it and United have their hands on that old trophy for another year now."

"In a nutshell mate," I responded, smiling at how Fred had put it all in perfect perspective.

I began to notice that Fred was starting to look more pale and tired. I could tell that he was ready for home and some much-needed rest.

"I'm so glad that I could make it to the game today, Gary. I told you I'd do my best to get out of that hospital in time. Time now, though, to get home for some shut eye. Wednesday will soon be upon us, my friend! What a day to look forward to."

I walked with Fred to the back doors of Conor O'Neill's. The immediate impact of the bright sun hit us—the usual adrenaline comedown upon leaving our soccer den hastening our adjustment to the outside light of the day.

I, too, felt somewhat tired: the early morning start, United's victory, and its significance having sapped some energy for sure. God knows how Fred must have felt so soon post-surgery.

With a shake of my old friend's hand, I told him I was looking forward to seeing him in four short days and sharing with him the historic moment when United would usher out a certain chubby lass to help them hoist high the European Champions League trophy.

Fred simply shook his head and made his way gingerly down the steps. He ambled slowly towards his car, looked back at me, smiling, and, in a somewhat weary voice exclaimed:

"You just don't give up, do you, lad?"

54

And So It Goes

Manchester United fans the world over will have their own memories of where they were on May 26, 1999—the chosen few and envy of the rest of us, able to recall it all as they stood inside the iconic Camp Nou stadium in Barcelona.

"I'll call you at half-time, dad. Sing loud, mate . . . and as I've got used to saying over here, Go United!"

"Enjoy the game, son. What a day to be a United fan, eh?"

My day had started well with an early morning transatlantic call.

Des was full of it and ambled straight down memory lane.

"I keep thinking back to '68, son!" he chimed in.

"Go on, dad!" I replied, perfectly happy to hear my father tell his version of the greatest night in Manchester United's history.

"Just two years since the country had enjoyed the 1966 World Cup, millions tuned in to witness United at Wembley in their quest to defeat Benfica and become the Kings of Europe. The game was magical, son, and of course the teams were deadlocked at 1-1 after ninety minutes. Our black and white TV hid nothing of the drama and your mother and our friends all huddled closely in front of the screen cheering the Reds on as extra time began. I later heard about the country struggling with its electric grid at that moment, with so many people making cuppas at the same time. Oh son, those goals from Bobby Charlton and Besty and nineteen-year-old Brian Kidd on his birthday. United hammered Benfica in that last period. And Matt Busby received a knighthood a month later!"

I had seen countless replays of those goals, but I let my father continue his reminiscence.

"So where was I, dad? Did I get an early sniff of the Reds along with you that night?"

"You were only four years old then, son. We had you tucked up in bed, safe and sound."

Terrific!

Des returned to the present.

"No Keano or Scholesy tonight, lad. Big hole in that midfield. It's not going to be easy. Your mum and I are going to watch it above the Post Office with Sandy and Marnie."

I smiled to myself as I envisaged a small flat in the tiny southern Scottish village of Drummore becoming rather raucous at around eight o'clock that evening. A week prior, I had somewhat impulsively offered to fly my dad out for the occasion. He had graciously declined, instinctive in his duty, staying home and keeping watch over his elderly mother and aunt for whom he had cared for so many years. I couldn't fault him for that.

Conor O'Neill's in Ann Arbor, Michigan—my venue for the 1999 European Champions League final—was, in more ways than one, a world away from being huddled around a tiny black and white TV set in Hesketh Bank, Lancashire in 1968.

I left Hotel Hairpiece around 7:30 a.m. and hit the road for work. Tuning in to the radio, there was, of course, no mention of the game that would hold the attention of an entire soccer-mad continent across the Pond later in the day. I continued to miss those extended prematch moments.

I moved the radio dial to my trusted musical avenue, courtesy of 89X. The speakers blared out "All Around the World," an Oasis anthem—such irony as the Gallagher brothers, staunch supporters of the Blue side of Manchester, were fueling the energy of a most passionate United fan abroad. The Gallaghers' allegiance to the dark side did nothing to deter my excitement. I couldn't help but reminisce about an incredible night when the band had played in Detroit back in 1996.

The Britpop scene had exploded over in the States. In a funny way, I felt like it accentuated our identity while living on American soil: British Resident Aliens surrounded by a musical vibe all their own and most definitely in vogue with Southeast Michigan as bands from dear old Blighty flocked to Detroit and Ann Arbor.

My old Pontiac merged swiftly with the highway traffic and flapping in the breeze from the passenger side window, the red, white, and black of my Manchester United scarf announced my arrival onto the US Interstate. My head tilted back and I sang along to the music of a group of diehard Manchester City fans.

Upon my arrival at the hospital, I stepped out of the car, draped my scarf around my neck, picked up my United shirt, and strolled into the clinic on full Red Devil Alert.

Today's mission: let everyone know exactly what was going to be taking place at the Camp Nou in Barcelona!

I had requested the afternoon off the day after United had beaten Juventus in the semi-final, but wanted to let my boss Kathy—and basically anyone else who would listen—know all about the significance of Manchester United having reached the final of Europe's premier cup competition for the first time in thirty-one years. I decided to opt for a Detroit Red Wings comparison, liking my situation to how a fan of Detroit's finest on ice might well be feeling if the Wings are about to play the final game of a seven-game series in the Stanley Cup final with *everything* on the line! Kathy adored the Red Wings and that comparison seemed to strike an emotional chord.

"Hey, why don't you wear that Manchester shirt of yours, Gary? No need to just hang it at your desk. We can always use a little more excitement around here, don't ya think?"

I proceeded to spend the rest of the morning explaining my new uniform to my patients, the Manchester United crest prominently displayed on the front left of my chest. At one stage, however, my shirt did end up laying across Mrs. Rossi, my 80-year-old patient, as she sat on a treatment table.

"Go United!" she declared after a round of coaching from yours truly while she lay there with an ice pack on her left hip. 80-year-old Sophia Rossi, Manchester United's latest fan, her beaming smile accompanied by a beautifully executed Stuart Pearson style fist pump and surrounded by four burly men, is a vision that will remain with me forever!

"So what's all this about again, Gary?" Sandy, my work colleague and link to Dearborn Dorothy, enquired.

"Well, in plain English, Sandy . . ."

"Ha! I love that. Gary. Plain English. I've never heard that phrase before."

"Yeah, plain English, Sandy! My team, Manchester United . . ."

"Oh, I know who your team is alright, Gary!"

"I guess so," I replied smiling. "Anyway, today is arguably *the* biggest match in the club's history. Not only could they become champions of Europe, but they now have a chance to win three trophies in one season! Nobody has ever done this before, Sandy! They would be the English premier League champions, the English FA Cup winners, and, hopefully, the champions of Europe!"

"Wow. That sounds pretty awesome to me, Gary."

"I've supported United since the mid-seventies, Sandy, and I've not known anything quite like this day."

"So what on earth are you doing here, then?"

"Working!"

"No, I get that, but surely you need to get outta here and build up the excitement?"

"In a couple of hours, Sandy. Two more hours and then I'll be on my way to Ann Arbor."

"Oh, that Irish pub, right?"

"That's the one. Conor O'Neill's. No need for Dorothy's mailbox today!"

"Awesome! I am watching the clock for you Gary. Oh, and Go Man U, right?"

"Love it, Sandy! Love it!"

"Hey, Gary, put one of your tapes on, buddy. It will help get you in the mood. I love all that British stuff!" Randy, one of our patient aides enthusiastically declared.

"Come on, maaan. I *love* it!"

Randy "loved" everything!

"Give me a minute, Randy. Crikey, you're on fire today, mate!"

"Oh, my God! *Crikey!* I just *love* that word! And you called me 'mate' again. I can't take it, Gary. I can't take it!"

Although his heart was in the right place, my interactions with Randy were mostly insufferable.

"Here you go, mate. Wrap yer ears around this lot," I replied as I placed my latest mix tape into our clinic's boombox.

"Bittersweet Symphony" by the Verve echoed througout the room.

At this point, Randy was stood center of the gym, feet together, head tilted high, eyes closed, both palms facing outwards with his elbows tucked into his side and swaying back and forth, floating on his very own Britpop cloud.

"God, Gary. I simply *love* this stuff! These tapes make my day so much more tolerable."

"Passes the time, doesn't it, Randy."

"Oh my God, does it evva! Oh, and that shirt, Gary. I simply *love* your shirt!" Randy had now shifted his attention to my United shirt.

"Your team has the most beauuutiful logo, Gary!"

"Cheers, mate. Hey, don't you have a patient to tend to back there?" my subtle hint that I had just about reached my Randy limit.

"Oh my God, Gary! I forgot! I have Mrs. McLean on a hot pack. She will be like a fried turkey if I don't get back there! Thanks, dude."

"La la la la la laaaa la ... mmm ... mmm. Oh God, Gary I loooove it!" Randy exclaimed, exuberantly waltzing away to tend to his prospective burn victim.

At that point, Sandy declared, "Randy has left the building." We all raised a smile.

I took a moment to once again contemplate my situation. The Champions League final was a mere two hours away and here I was still at work in a physical therapy clinic surrounded by clients that needed treatment and "Bittersweet Randy" bouncing his rather ample 250-pound frame around, high on his toes to the sound of the Verve and all things Britpop. Life's journey can certainly be a most surprising experience.

Just as I was starting my functional strength training session with Mr. Santoni, Kathy wandered into the main gym area.

"Gary, why don't you wrap things up with Mr. Santoni. I've been chatting with Amber and she will cover your last couple of clients."

"Are you sure, Kathy?"

"No problem. You have a soccer match to watch. And a pretty important one at that it seems. Get outta here whenever you're done, okay?"

"Brilliant! Cheers Kathy. That's so kind of you. That will get me out to Ann Arbor in good time. I truly appreciate it."

"What is it you say? *No worries, mate!* Oh, yeah, and Go United!"

"Hey, you're catching on there, Kathy. Michigan's latest Red Devil!"

"Well, hold on a minute. I don't know what you mean there, but anyways I will be rooting for your team today for sure." Kathy was not yet quite up to speed when it came to English Premier League team nicknames.

Final paperwork complete, client treatments documented, I grabbed my jacket to leave the department.

"Go United! Go United! Go United!"—a communal cheer from my co-workers, with Kathy leading the chorus.

"Go Beckham! I love Beckham!" Trust Randy to add his own spin.

My co-workers looked like they were about to break into an incredibly complicated cheerleading maneuver. It was the most surreal of moments.

Talk about feeling like a fish out of water and yet most appreciated at the same time. It was a great touch.

I left the clinic just before 12:15 p.m. and headed straight for Conor O'Neill's.

New Order were busy raising the musical bar as I sped along the I-94 freeway on my journey west. My adrenaline was now firmly kicking up a notch and the anticipation for what lay ahead was at full tilt. I couldn't wait for *the* moment, for the moment that I would witness Manchester United walking out onto the field for the biggest game in their history!

I exited onto Main Street, hardly able to contain myself as I parked at the back of the pub. I ran up the steps and straight into Conor O'Neill's.

I could not believe my eyes.

There was hardly a soul in the place.

The pub was dead except for a couple of people enjoying an extended lunch. I didn't even recognize the staff on duty.

With only ninety minutes to go before kick-off, the atmosphere I craved, the prematch vibe, the buildup, was completely non-existent.

I couldn't see Tim or Connie anywhere, and after a short time stood rooted next to the kitchen entrance, I simply wandered straight through the building, past our empty paddock area, and exited out the front door and back onto Main Street.

I had left a message for Fred earlier that morning to suggest a chance to chew the cud before the game and to arrange for us to meet "early doors." There was no sign of the man as yet.

Not exactly the start to the afternoon that I had envisaged.

I had been thrown a curve ball. As I watched the clock tick towards 1:15 p.m., I stood for a second and thought. I decided there and then that a walk up to the University of Michigan campus, opting for some quiet prematch contemplation, was the way to go—a few moments of solitary time to focus on what lay ahead and to move myself further into the moment, despite my complete detachment from events across the Pond.

Taking a seat on a bench, I considered once again just how intense the prematch build up would be back in Britain at that moment and just how packed out the pubs would be, everyone waiting for kick-off, joyous in the sheer anticipation of what could be. After about fifteen minutes or so, I headed back down Liberty Street towards Main and Conor O'Neill's.

Half way down Liberty, I heard a shout from behind me.

"Go Manchester!"

As I looked back, I saw a group of Asian students sat on a wall outside the Ann Arbor post office. Below them on the sidewalk a tramp appeared to be sleeping the afternoon away, oblivious to their magnificent call.

I raised a clenched fist high, garnering an immediate response from the lads as they too thrust their arms aloft in recognition:

"United! United! United!"

Smiling, I suddenly felt more at home. You get it where you can, right?

As I made my way back to Conor O'Neill's, I could see a number of fans in Man United and Bayern Munich shirts and scarves filing into the pub. My pace quickened.

Inside Conor O'Neill's, our paddock area was steadily transforming, readying for the biggest game of its young, soccer pub life. A few of our regulars were now present, along with a number of other fans I didn't recognize. A huge Manchester United banner was being tacked up right below the big screen, courtesy of our two United-mad Yanks, Den and Don. Even better—and thankfully—considering the crowd now gathered inside, the lads had saved seats both for me and Fred.

"Gary, mate! Get in here," Eddie shouted.

"How's it goin' Gary?" asked Jack, my fellow Red Devil, calmness personified, as he greeted me with a firm handshake.

"Lads! How's it goin'?"

"For the glory, Gary!" Don shouted to me, finishing up his shrine to the Reds.

"Looks great, Don" I replied.

I slid into my seat, leaving the only cushioned seat in the house ready for our elder statesman.

More of our morning crew of fanatics were now filing in: Scouse Carl, Chinny, Jake, Blue Peter and Robbie, the latter pair appearing happier with an afternoon kick-off as opposed to an annoying "early doors" it seemed. Even Gerry George was in, stood in his usual place, tucked away at the corner of the bar, raising his hand high and shouting "Hey, Gary la!" just as I was taking my seat.

"Glory Glory Man United" rang out through the bar as I continued with my hellos. Ahmed had brought his United CD and Connie and Tim, both now present, had kindly obliged, playing the United anthem over the pub's PA system—the smattering of Bayern Munich fans appeared none too impressed.

"Hey, Gary la!" It appeared Gerry was already warming up his vocal chords. I turned around once again and noticed the Liverpudlian gesturing over to the front door.

I turned to look at the Conor O'Neill's entrance.

There, looking most isolated, was the sight of Ted in his wheelchair attempting to make his way inside.

Bloody hell! I hadn't seen Ted since the FA Cup final. His treatments were on hold. We hadn't tied down any firm arrangements and with the Champions League final being shown on ESPN2, I figured that he would be tucked in at home ready for kick-off.

"Chinny, save my seat please, mate,"

"Yeah man, no problem."

I shot over to the front door.

"Auch, Gary son. How the hell are ya's?"

"Ted, I can't believe it mate! Where on earth did you park?"

"Oh don't be worrying about that, Gary. I got meself all sorted. This isn't my first rodeo now remember, eh. I am here and we have a soccer match to watch."

"Come here, mate. Let me help you through." I slipped in behind Ted's wheelchair and everyone stepped aside allowing us a clear path to the paddock ramp.

"Teddy's in the house!" Eddie declared, offering the Irishman a strong slap on the back before Ted could even apply his wheelchair brakes.

"Nice one, Ted!" Chinny noted.

"Great to see you again, Ted," Scouse Carl and Jake acknowledged the Irishman with a warm welcome.

"Ok here, Ted?"

"Ah, that's just perfect, so it is Gary."

"Hey Ted! Gary!" Red suddenly appeared, out of breath.

"Well hello there, Red" replied Ted. "Great to see you again, son."

Red appeared somewhat bewildered at having been called "son" for the first time in a while I am sure.

Given the enormity of the occasion and the overwhelming enthusiasm from the crowd gathered inside the pub, I couldn't help but notice that Red appeared a tad subdued.

"Red! You doin' alright there, mate?"

"Yeah, ya wanker. Not bad," Red replied in a rather less enthusiastic manner than usual.

"You sure, mate?"

"Well, no. Not really," replied Red, cutting straight to the point.

We pulled to one side for a second.

"What the fuck's up, mate?"

"Stupid really. I dunno. Just had a big row with, how do you Brits say it, the missus . . . all over something and nothing really."

"Bloody hell mate. I can see it's bothering you."

"Yeah, ya wanker. Money's been a bit tight lately. Often is. We got into it and, of course, I'm watching the clock to get down here to support the Reds, next thing you know Nina goes ballistic and I know I have to head out. That didn't go down well at all to be honest. Load of bollocks for sure, Gary."

"Mate! I'm sorry to hear that. These moments happen, eh."

Red was one of the most passionate Manchester United fans I have ever met. And this was one of the biggest days in the club's history. It was time for a swift pep up!

"Thirty-one years, brother. A whole generation since our lads won the greatest prize in European football! And here we are, about to see it happen once again, mate!" I raised my voice even louder into Red's earlobe as the "Glory, Glory" of United rang into the air.

"History is in the making, mate. The Treble! I hear your pain, Red. But for the next two hours, forget about it and soak in every minute of this game. It could well be a long time before a moment like this comes around again. All those times you struggled through ice and snow to make it over to the Britannia Club. Those freezing mornings you dragged yourself down here to watch United. Even the time you picked me up in Dearborn! Fuck me Red, I'm still recovering from that one and I'm sure you are too! So, mate, come on, this is the biggest game of the lot! Your good lady will come around. You know she will. She's top draw. But for now, for the next two hours, brother, we stand United!"

"Mate! You're right! You're so bloody right, you English wanker! Thanks Gary!" Red's demeanor changed before my eyes as he responded in a rather dodgy attempt at an English accent.

"Ouuff! Steady on there, Red!" I joked.

The tall Yank grabbed my right hand firmly. "Thanks, dude! Really appreciate it!"

"No worries, mate! Come on! Game on! Let's do it!"

As if on cue, the lights dimmed, and with a huge roar, our Ann Arbor soccer den instantly became one with the Camp Nou more than four thousand miles away in Barcelona. Such contrast to outside of Conor O'Neill's, where it would remain just another spring "hump day" afternoon, business as usual as most people, oblivious to the fans packed inside the town's newest pub, all set to witness the game of their lives.

As the two teams readied themselves to enter the pitch, I will never forget, just minutes before kick-off, Blue, Chinny, Jake and Scouse Carl shaking hands with all of the United faithful, wishing us all good luck. At that moment, we were all simply British expats abroad. We were all soccer fans. We were all about to watch an English team in the European Champions League final. It was another chance to celebrate our community, our friendship, and not having given up on the game we loved no matter how far away from home.

I was beginning to feel a little anxious as to the whereabouts of Fred when, all of a sudden, the door burst open. Like clockwork, it was another of those patented late entries from Clifford Miller—but this time he was here to stay. This was one of the first times that our American Gooner would have known in advance that his beloved Arsenal were not playing and yet he still showed up—and indeed was fully intent on staying.

Ridicule rained down on the man and he duly responded.

"Well, I had nothing else to do, lads. Business is kind of slow today," his immediate wry smile obvious to all. With a few quick handshakes, Clifford squeezed himself into a corner of the paddock.

Our corner of Conor's roared loudly as the two teams strode forward, out into the Spanish air and onto the Camp Nou turf.

"United! United! United!"

I thought of home. I thought of my father and mother. My brain began flitting through random moments of United glories: the 1977 FA Cup win over Liverpool that had prevented the team from Merseyside from completing their own historic treble; the presentation of the Premier League Championship trophy in 1993; Cantona's late winner against Liverpool in the 1996 FA Cup final. The Red Devils were now on the cusp of their greatest achievement. Standing between them and glory were the German Bundesliga champions, Bayern Munich.

The noise inside Conor's was deafening. I zoned in on the big screen in front of me.

Red patted me on the shoulder. I turned back to look at him and nodded. As I did so I also caught Jack's attention and he too nodded, mouth closed tightly, pumping his right fist with a small sweep in front of his torso. Eddie stood arms aloft, declaring his undying devotion to "his" Manchester United. We were ready.

I leaned in and shook Ted's shoulders. The Irishman looked back over his left shoulder, a huge smile on his face.

Italian Referee Pierluigi Collina was holding court in the center circle as the two goalkeepers met for the coin toss. I focused on the United players as the camera picked them out, taking their positions ready for kick-off. A young David Beckham bent down to ensure his boots were tied properly. He then stood, turned to his right, and, from what I could tell, mouthed the words "Come On!" in the direction of Ryan Giggs who appeared to be lining up wide right, allowing Beckham to move inside to a more central midfield role in the absence of Roy Keane.

"Coooooome Ooooonnn!"

The same phrase thrust forth from the mouths of our own United clan as Collina moved the whistle to his mouth and blew to signal the start of the 1999 European Champions League final.

Game on!

All eyes were firmly focused on the big screen as the Conor O'Neill's soccer clan erupted into rapturous applause.

Suddenly, Fred's daughter, Lara, appeared out of nowhere, prompting a few heads to turn. Lara worked her way through the crowd and reached me just as Giggsy attempted a swinging cross in toward Andy Cole.

"Ouuwwwwww," the shout from our crowd.

I acknowledged Lara amid the mayhem.

"Lara! What the hell are you doing here? Where's your dad? This is the game of the season, the one we've all been waiting for."

"Oh, we know, Gary. Believe me, it's all he's been talking about," Lara replied, the anguish on her face obvious.

"He isn't well. He isn't well at all. He spent last night in hospital."

"What? You're kidding. How is he? Where is he?" I exclaimed.

"What's up, Lara. Where's your father?" Red chimed in as he leaned in to listen. This was our elder statesman, our Regal One. He had to be OK.

Raising her voice to be heard above the noise, Lara continued.

"It's the operation. The doctors feel that he left hospital too soon. Of course, he stubbornly put off going until last night and only then because I insisted. He looked terrible, Gary. He was as white as a ghost. This has taken more out of him than he thought."

"Is he home now Lara?" I asked, my question barely audible over the commentary. Cries of "sit down" flew from the mouths of some of the punters, ignorant as to the contect of our conversation.

"Yeah. He got back a couple of hours ago. He said that there was no way that he was going to miss the game. You know what he's like about his soccer, Gary. I've brought my mobile phone with me. Can you speak with him? It will make him feel a whole lot better!"

Lara dialed the number and the faint ringing in my ear preempted a click. Sounding frail and subdued, I could just make out Fred's voice.

"Gary! So great to hear your voice, my friend! I have the game on. It's live on ESPN2. You know I wish I could be there."

"Fred, mate, you'd be in your element. I'm sitting next to the cushioned seat we saved for you. You are being sorely missed my friend."

"This has really knocked me for six, Gary. The FA Cup final was what did it. I should have listened to the docs and waited to return for the big one. You live and learn, right?"

I smiled.

On realizing that our elder statesman was on the end of the line, the next few seconds had all the lads in unison, momentarily diverting their attention from the big screen above them to give an impromptu, rousing rendition of a terrace favorite, "Montague for England! Montague for England!"

"Can you hear that, Fred?"

"Ah, that's terrific. That's terrific!"

"Mate! Enjoy the game. The Fat Lady is warming up remember!"

With that I wished our friend a swift recovery, telling him that we would leave his cushioned seat empty in acknowledgment of his absence.

After all of the games we had viewed together, after all of our medication times, this would have to be the day that Fred was lying in bed, home alone. The man's passion for the game had been reignited with the arrival of our Irish haven, giving him a soccer home for the first time in over thirty years. It saddened me to think that he was missing for the biggest game of the lot.

I returned the mobile phone to Lara. We hugged. Several of the lads reached out to her and then she made a hasty retreat.

"Hey, Lara!" I shouted after her. "Take good care of him, okay?"

"I will, Gary," Lara replied as she exited the pub.

I returned my focus to the big screen.

Bayern Munich had been awarded a free kick on the edge of the United penalty area. Effenberg and Basler were both sizing up their options. Beckham and Schmeichel debated the best placement for United's four-man wall. I could feel the tension build.

Basler put his foot through the ball and curled it via a channel opened up by Markus Babbel as he rolled inside from the left edge of the wall.

Peter Schmeichel stood rooted to the spot. A fierce clap of his huge gloved hands signified his disgust.

Bayern Munich had taken the lead with only six minutes gone!

It was the worst possible start. Once again, United would have to come from behind in Europe, to do it the hard way.

The loud cheers and celebrations of the small group of Bayern fans, all clad in the official shirts of their own beloved team, filled the pub. Outnumbered at around four to one, the noise they made at that moment suggested otherwise.

Early days, early days. Lots of time to go, I told myself.

There were, in fact, at least eighty-four minutes of play left.

United responded well with Yorke and Cole looking lively up top, Beckham spraying passes and playmaking in midfield. Cole came close from a long throw from Gary Neville, but, in the end, neither he nor the Bayern defense knew little about the outcome as the ball trundled over the Bayern line for a goal kick.

"United! United!" rang out the chorus led by Den and Don, the latter swirling his United scarf high above his head, much to the chagrin of the Bayern fans stood directly behind him.

"It's not happening, Gary. The final touch isn't quite there," Red commented.

"Plenty of time yet, Red. They just need to hang in right now, eh."

"I tell you what, those Germans are some big feckers so they are."

Ted was not wrong. Carsten Jancker, at six foot four, was a giant and he was causing all kinds of problems for the United back line each time the ball was played in.

Right on cue, Ronnie Johnsen went through the big German and Bayern had another free kick, this time from the right.

Basler again . . . but this time, thankfully, it was high and wide. I gave Fred an immediate thought as I knew he would be muttering the words "three points to Wigan" at that very moment.

Moments later, Jancker clattered Beckham and referee Collina let play roll on. A huge response from our paddock followed as the cameras picked up on Gary Neville having a go at Jancker for the tackle.

"He'd eat Neville up for breakfast," Eddie declared. It certainly did appear somewhat of a mismatch. I loved our right back's aggression. It said everything about the Red Devils' attitude.

Minutes later, Yorke and Cole almost beat Kahn in the Bayern goal after successive Beckham corners and a throw-in for United from deep inside the Bayern half.

"They are flying in on Beckham any chance they get, eh, Gary."

I fully concurred with Jack's observation. The England man had settled well, looking confident in the role he had always craved. Bayern Munich appeared to have marked the young Englishman as the main outlet to the front three. Beckham continued to be fully involved and was at the center of everything, hitting long balls left and right into the feet of Cole, Giggs, and Yorke. He had several corners, too, as United continued to create, but without any real final product. They were definitely matching Bayern, possibly with a greater percentage of possession, too.

With just minutes to go before half-time, Yorke and Cole combined and Giggs ended up in a foot race into the Bayern penalty area, Kahn quick off his line to smother the ball. Yet another Beckham corner swung into the Bayern box, with Kahn again sharpest to react.

With the United crowd inside the Camp Nou raising their voices once again, Collina blew his whistle as the one extra minute of added time concluded, signaling half-time.

We were instantly bombarded by a group of loud and obnoxious commercials and infomercials. I decided to pull away away from our fanatics and stood back to take it all in. Another momentary United zen. Ted and Red were deep in conversation and several of the others had started the toilet run or were on their phones.

"Hey Gary, la!" I welcomed the cry from behind me.

I wandered over to Gerry George.

"What do you reckon, eh, Gerry?"

"What do I think, son? I think United are well in this. I think they need to hold their nerve and this game is not over by any means."

"I have to say mate, I feel the same."

Gerry knew his soccer. He loved his soccer. I could also sense that, deep down, this Liverpool fanatic was willing a team from his home shores on to victory.

"Send those vibes over to Spain, eh, Gerry."

"Whoa, steady on a minute there, Gary la. Let's not get too carried away now."

The two of us smiled as I turned to head over to the payphone.

"They're looking second best at the moment, don't you think, son?" said my father "But Sandy reckons they'll come back and win it."

"I think we are holding our own, dad. Besides, we've had to come back before and we'll do it again. A whole half still to play. It's gonna be our day, dad. Believe!"

God, I hoped I was right.

"Ever the optimist, eh, son. We're all willing them on up here, lad. Here, let me grab yer mother."

"Come onnnnnn United! Hey, Beckham's getting stuck in there, isn't he, Gary? I think Fergie should bring on Babyface! I love him. I always feel like he needs a decent jam butty."

My half-time analysis from above the Post Office in Scotland's southernmost town was rather unique. My mother certainly had a way with words. The brandy bottle must have been well and truly opened.

"Hey, mum. We have to do it. United are going to win!"

"Of course, son. Of course they are!"

"Say hi to Sandy and Marnie, eh. And go easy on the brandy!"

"Yes and no! Behave yourself son. Come onnnnnnnnn United!"

I tried to visualize the scene in the flat in that sleepy Scottish village. I knew the intensity of my parents' support would not have been in doubt. Throw in a mad Glaswegian and his wife who both loved their soccer, too, and I was certain they were all doing the occasion justice.

I weaved my way back to our paddock and returned to my seat. Fred's cushioned throne was still prominent. Nobody was claiming it, the lads showing their continued respect for our absent elder statesman.

I looked around at the faces of my compatriots and friends, the wonderful people who were all such an integral part of our clan. I could feel their emotion, their intense yearning for United to come back and win the biggest game of all and to claim the impossible Treble.

As the whistle blew for the start of the second half, I smiled to myself, knowing how fortunate I was to be watching this game live and in such brilliant company. Once again, the lights dimmed and all eyes focused in on the big screen. Forty-five minutes—plus injury time—that would define history for Manchester United Football Club.

Den and Don were busting blood vessels left, right, and center as they fired themselves up for the final assault. Jack and Eddie were staring intensely at the screen, and a simple thumbs-up in my direction from the latter said it all, acknowledging the fact that we were United lads and we were in our element.

Red had seemingly long forgotten his marital woes and was as animated as I had ever seen him, randomly shouting all of the English phrases he had learned over the past couple of years.

"Bollocks! You wankers! Bayern you bag o' shite!"

Twinkle Toes Robbie had spent most of the half-time break unable to stand, still flowing from one person to the next in a groove all of his own.

As I watched our United clan and their reactions, I could tell that they were, without question, among the most ardent and enthusiastic fans I had ever seen. Consider the location, the lengths to which one and all had gone to for so many seasons past, now all gathered together willing "their" United to glory.

Bayern's Carsten Jancker started the second half on the front foot. He burst into the United penalty area, managing to stretch Schmeichel and forcing another corner. Mario Basler was coming more and more into the game. After some terrific defensive work to thwart a Giggs break, he attempted an audacious long range effort, seeing Schmeichel off his line. Thankfully, the United keeper remained alert.

"Bloody Blomqvist is giving it away every time," Jack commented. We both agreed it wouldn't be long before the Swede would give way for a United substitute.

Cole and Yorke continued to look lively, but Bayern's back line continued to keep the door firmly closed. Giggs started seeing more of the ball and shortly after a neat pass into Yorke, who was closed down immediately by Bayern's defense, the Welshman once again played a lovely low cross into the Bayern penalty box. Sprinting to meet it was Blomqvist, but again, Markus Babbel did enough, forcing the young swede to loop the ball over the Bayern bar.

The United fans inside the stadium raised the decibel level, knowing that United were pressing, giving everything to get back into the game.

"United! United! United!" the response rang out from the Conor O'Neill's Red contingent.

Basler then burst forward down United's left, Stam meeting him head on and forcing him all the way back into his own team's half.

"Gary, you wanker. Stam? What was I thinking? He has been immense today!" Red called it.

Giggs suddenly broke from midfield and was blatantly fouled by a Tarnat and Effenberg combo, the Welshman's pace too much for the Bayern players.

I was happy with my boys. They were seeing a lot of the ball. But every time the ball entered the Bayern box, it just wasn't happening for Cole and Yorke, the Bayern defense for their part continuing to hold firm.

Basler continued to impress and again from long range, caught Schmeichel off his line. The United keeper scrambled and was glad to see the ball dip over the crossbar.

Another flowing move developed, with terrific link up play between Butt, Beckham, Cole, Irwin, and Yorke, Beckham eventually swinging in a cross that a Bayern defender blasted into touch. Corner to United.

Sixty-six minutes gone and it was time for Teddy Sheringham to enter the fray. The United fans in the Camp Nou increased the volume once more. The United clan inside Conor's responded.

Beckham moved onto the right flank; a reshuffle for United as they played a new attacking hand. Within minutes, Yorke flicked the ball on, and a huge roar erupted as Andy Cole attempted an overhead kick. He completely fluffed his lines, but we could sense it; the crowd inside the stadium could sense it. United were getting closer.

Mehmet Scholl entered the fray for Bayern with twenty minutes left on the clock. His impact was immediate, combining well with Effenberg, whose shot flew past the United post. Moments later, Effenberg tried to lob Schmeichel, the Great Dane pulling off an instinctive save. It was Bayern's turn to up the pressure.

Fifteen minutes remained. United needed something. They had averaged at least two goals a game for the season. Our Reds in Conor's that day would have given anything for fifty per cent of that statistic to hold true.

Ten minutes to go.

I was happy with United's movement, their interplay. Another fine move was in the offing down United's attacking left, a back heel, one touch stuff and then, just one misplaced place pass on the edge of the Bayern box, and Basler was away, skipped over Beckham, running at Johnsen, past Neville. Scholl took over and produced a delicious chip, leaving the whole United defense, including our goalkeeper for dead.

It rattled the upright.

United had escaped certain defeat.

"Bollocks, Gary! That was close!"

Ted turned to me "Time is running out, son"

I remained silent and stoic, eyes fixed on the screen above me.

Moments later, Beckham and Sheringham combined at the other end, Butt burst into the penalty area and lofted a chip that floated agonizingly right across the Bayern goal, no United player able to connect.

"Come on United, for fuck's sake!"

Corner to United.

Enter Solskjær.

I knew my mother would be happy to see "Babyface!" So it seemed was our United clan as a communal cheer filled the bar.

A corner was floated over, dealt with by Bayern, recycled by Neville right side and Solskjær rose to pull a fine stretching save out of Kahn in the Bayern goal.

I looked over at Eddie and we both rolled our eyes.

Time was running out.

"Come on United!"

Scholl responded and let fly from twenty yards, pulling another fine right-handed save out of United's goalkeeper.

Corner to Bayern Munich.

Basler floated it in. The ball found Scholl, his header looping up and Jancker unleashed an unbelievable overhead kick that slammed against the United upright.

United's luck was still holding.

The Bayern fans inside our pub, to a man, had hands on heads.

It was looking like Bayern's day.

Their fans began singing, sensing they were almost home and dry. Their chants collided head on with the yearning pleas of our United lads.

"United! United! United!"

There was still time. There had to be. I still believed.

It had been twenty-four years since Lou Macari had won me over, since the day that I "became United" and now here I was, sat in an Irish pub in Ann Arbor, Michigan, surrounded by United diehards, desperate to see "their" United become Champions of Europe.

That sense of do-or-die among our crew was palpable.

Den and Don were stood atop their chairs.

Twinkle Toes was actually stood still, both hands running through his hair, beads of sweat covering his face.

"Hey, Gary la! Hey, Gary la!"

Not now, Gerry. Shut the fuck up.

"Hey, Gary la!"

I had to turn around.

"You're not done yet son. There's still time!"

A smile lit up my face. The Scouser was still willing the Red Devils on!

Less than five minutes of normal time remained.

The TV cameras panned over to the prized trophy which was now being adorned with ribbons in the colors of Bayern Munich. Was the UEFA official being presumptive or simply hedging his bets?

Solskjær's backheel found Sheringham and Teddy put his laces through it. Kahn dived to save low to his right.

"Ouuuwwww! United! United! United!"

"Last chance, Gary son?" Ted tilted his head back to offer his opinion.

"Still time, Ted! There's still time!" came my response. It was how I was wired. I wasn't about to change any time soon.

United surged forward again.

Beckham into Yorke . . . who completely miscued.

"United! United! United!"

Solskjær with a header.

Kahn saves.

United were throwing everything they had at the Germans.

One minute to go.

United earned a throw-in deep into Bayern territory, down the German's left flank. Gary Neville sprinted across the pitch.

All about route one now.

The fourth official held up the board to indicate a bright red number "3." Three minutes of injury time. It was do or die.

Neville took a long throw-in. Beckham picked up the loose ball and drove forward. He passed back to Neville whose low cross was deflected out for yet another United corner.

We are now into the first minute of the three minutes of injury time.

I looked down at Fred's empty chair.

"Look! Here comes Schmeichel!" yelled Den as he still stood atop his chair. It was Peter Schmeichel's last two minutes as a Manchester United player and there he was in the Bayern Munich penalty area doing everything he could to help United pull level and take the game to extra time.

Everyone was on up their feet, willing the ball into the Bayern net.

As the corner came over, Schmeichel's menace was immediate as he fought with all he had to get his head onto the ball. It flew past him, landing close to Yorke, who battled with a Bayern defender, but lost out as the ball moved away from the goalmouth.

"Bollocks, Gary! I can't take this!" Who else but Red?!

An attempted Bayern clearance landed on the edge of the box where a tame volley from Ryan Giggs bobbled forward towards the German goal.

. . . and then it happened!

The right foot of Teddy Sheringham connected, sending the ball spinning into the corner of the Bayern goal.

Mayhem!

Absolute fucking mayhem erupted inside Conor O'Neill's!

The United fans in the stadium behind the Bayern goal were going nuts!

The United fans inside Conor O'Neill's were going nuts!

What a moment!

What an experience!

Chairs were all over the place in our paddock, including a certain cushioned one.

United had done it!

Thirty minutes of extra time on the way!

United were still alive!

In that split second, the game had taken a massive swing and the looks of determination and belief on the faces of the United players was clear. The Bayern players looked down and out.

The game restarted.

A corner of the Camp Nou was now enveloped in red smoke.

I had no idea where Red was. He was on the other side of the bar somewhere, lost in the mayhem, cheering his men on to victory. I don't think he had ever known such excitement during a sporting event. Had any of us?

With only seconds left on the clock, United's constant pressure resulted in another corner.

Beckham again sprinted over to the corner flag and placed the ball.

. . . then, everything seemed to happen in slow motion.

A perfectly lofted corner into the box where once again Teddy Sheringham was influential as he beat all around him to the ball. Sheringham's header flew toward Ole Gunnar "Babyface" Solskjær who stuck out his right foot, his glorious right foot, and connected with the ball—for *that* moment . . . that most glorious Red moment!

The Conor's paddock exploded!

I watched in disbelief as the whole United bench converged on the baby-faced assassin.

Schmeichel was turning cartwheels in his goalmouth as a cloud of red smoke filled the Camp Nou.

Manchester United 2, Bayern Munich 1!

Two goals in two minutes!

British commentator Clive Tyldesley framed it best: "Memories were made of this. Forever and a day United fans will ask where did you watch the 1999 European Cup Final? Where did you see Ole Solskjær win it with virtually the last kick of the final?"

Well, I was in a small Irish pub in a sleepy Midwestern U.S. town surrounded by a crowd of diehard United fans—friends that had travelled that Treble Dream journey along with me, every step of the way.

And I will NEVER EVER forget it!

The Treble!

United had won the Treble!

Premier League Champions, FA Cup winners . . . and now, after thirty-one years, Manchester United were once again Kings of Europe!

I unleashed a yell of unbridled jubilation as I struggled to take in the unbelievable scenes playing out in the Camp Nou.

I scrambled over the mass of bodies in an effort to see the replay — to see *the* moment of Manchester United history! Every hair on the back of my neck stood on end as I watched Solskjær react before anyone to score *the* goal that crowned United Champions of Europe.

Nicky Butt cleared long and the final whistle blew.

"Give me that camera mate! Get in there!" Scouse Carl yelled. Oh, the irony, as I handed the small camera that I had in my back pocket to a Liverpool fan at the moment Manchester United won the Treble!

I immersed myself deeper in the throng that was now dancing all over our paddock.

I will never forget seeing Ahmed, the Jordanian student and gentle giant, in tears and on his knees as the significance of the moment sunk in.

I broke away from the crowd, instinctively. I had a phone call to make. As I approached the payphone, I could see Den, who was deep in conversation on his cell phone, dancing as he described the victory. The back door adjacent to the public telephone was open and I could see Don running around, shouting into his mobile, along with several other fans excitedly reliving the moment, oblivious to the Ann Arbor locals who were going about their usual business. Outside in the streets, it was just another regular Wednesday afternoon in a town that was, for the most part, oblivious to what had just transpired.

I eventually got through to the small flat above the Post office in Scotland.

"Championes! Championes! Olé, Olé, Olé!"

My father's hoarse voice, as animated as I've ever heard him, came in over the phone line.

"I've never seen anything like it before, son! What a team! What a team! They just never ever give up!"

I could hear my mother in the background shouting "United!"

Next thing I knew, she was screaming down the telephone "Oh my little Babyface! Give him that jam butty!"

My mother was one of a kind.

My father came back on the phone: "Sandy's got the whisky out son, and Marnie's warming up for a few songs. God help us all, lad!"

I guessed that a rendition of "Flower of Scotland" could be deemed appropriate, given the nationality of the United manager, Alex Ferguson.

I eventually managed to get a word in.

"Dad. Can you believe it mate? We did it! We bloody well did it!"

"And who would have thought, eh lad? You calling me all the way from America on the night United win the European Cup. Bloody mad, that is."

"We always manage to get a chat in when it matters, eh mate?"

I pressed the receiver tighter to my ear, battling the mayhem inside Conor's as my father continued.

"Where have all the years gone, son? Where have they gone?" He paused for a moment before adding "You keep going, eh lad. Keep going, son."

"You know I will, dad. You know I will. All the best to you, mate. Speak soon, OK?"

Des and I had once again shared in the moment—and this was *the* moment of United moments, the one we'd be talking about for years to come.

I was then compelled to call my old mate, Tom Skinner. I knew he would have been in front of the television back home, despite his allegiance to Leeds United. The phone rang twice before he answered.

"Hello!"

"Yeeeaaaaaaahhhh!"

Calm as you like, knowing it was me, he replied.

"You know what mate? I am not kidding, I just got back from watching the game round at the neighbor's. When that second goal went in, I looked at him and said there's a bar in Michigan at this very moment that's just lost its bloody roof!"

"Unbelievable, mate! Un-fucking-believable! You know how much this means mate, don't you? You know how much this means to me, lad?"

We chatted a tad longer before I wished Tom and his family well.

I had one more important call to make before returning to the celebrations inside Conor O'Neill's.

A quiet and tired sounding voice answered my call.

"Fred Montague speaking."

I smiled for a split second, took a breath, and said:

"My friend! She has finally arrived! Let her sing her guts out, pal!"

"I am so pleased for you, Gary! Fantastic! I was thinking of you all over there. What a game this soccer is. And what a simply breathtaking finish.

They did it, Gary. By God, they did it! Go and have some medication for me, my friend."

I quickly returned to the festivities, the big screen still lit up with the scenes from Barcelona, United ready to lift the trophy.

I arrived back into the fray to see Beckham kiss the beautiful silver trophy. Schmeichel disappeared from view for a second. Moments later, he returned with Fergie in tow. All of the United fans in Conor O'Neill's stood glued to the screen and then . . .

"Manchester United! Champions of Europe!" as our captain and manager thrust the Champions League trophy high above their heads.

The camera panned to a smiling Bobby Charlton, applauding the current United team, and perhaps reflecting back on the night when he had become a European champion as a member of Matt Busby's 1968 United team. On what would have been Sir Matt's ninetieth birthday, Manchester United had achieved European glory once again.

Unbelievable!

Maybe, just maybe, at that very moment, Sir Matt was smiling, too, as he looked down on the Camp Nou.

I spent the next few minutes shaking hands and celebrating with the United crew, even the likes of Blue Peter, our usually gruff Chelsea fan, and Chinny, United-hater extraordinaire, conceded their admiration for United's incredible comeback and achievement.

Gerry George once again caught my eye. I headed over to him. He reached out his right hand and began shaking mine countless times, between several large swigs of beer—no evidence of cardiac arrhythmia at that moment it seemed, for which I was thankful.

"Hey Gary, la," he kept repeating, "Tell you what! You're still a jammy fucking bunch of mank bastards . . . but you're champions of Europe, pal! Can't deny you that one. What a performance at the end. Well done. Really pleased for you, la." Were my ears deceiving me?

I walked away to a further pat on the back from Gerry, heading over to the continuing celebration in our paddock corner of the pub.

An impromptu medication time—tempered only by the absence of Regal Fred—and to the back drop of "Glory Glory Man United" became the order of the day in recognition of an incredible season. We had shared so many twists and turns. The English Premier League. The FA Cup— Schmeichel's injury time penalty save and Ryan Giggs' wonder goal. And now, the mother of them all—the European Champions League.

We realized that it could well be a long time before we ever saw another season quite like it—if ever.

I sat among my own: Eddie, Jack, Red, Den, Don, Ahmed, Twinkle Toes, and an elderly Irishman in a wheelchair reliving it all, joyous in United's triumph.

"Son! I have never ever seen anything like that on a soccer pitch!"

"Just think, Ted, if you hadn't had that leg amputated, you still may never have seen anything like that on a soccer pitch!"

"Well, right you are there son, right you are," replied Ted, smiling at the thought.

"I think I'd better be shooting away now, Gary," Ted added.

"No worries, Ted. Can I help you out of here," I replied, offering my patient a hand to exit the pub.

"No, son. I am in good shape. High as a kite, truth be told. I'll be managing just fine from here now."

Several of the lads stood to wish Ted farewell.

"Glory Glory Man United" still echoed throughout the pub, matching the sounds from the Camp Nou.

"All the best, Ted, mate! Take care! We did it Ted!" Eddie, Jack, Red and the rest sending the Irishman on his way.

I watched closely as Ted exited the main front doors and then stepped away from our crew, taking a peek out of a window to ensure his safe transit along Main Street, his car clearly visible just yards away. Ted was all set.

I remained behind at Conor's well into the evening. Time was spent chatting with Tim and Connie, reflecting on such a phenomenal first soccer season for the pub. Cliff the Gooner, Scouse Carl, Crown Paints Jacob, and my friend from those early days at the Britannia Club, Chinny, had all hung for a while postmatch, but, in the end, the Red Devil overload had become too much even for their gracious acknowledgement of United's incredible achievement. Our very own Gooner, his Arsenal scarf wrapped around his neck as he wandered toward the exit, couldn't help himself, "Next season! Next season!" Coome onnn the Arrrrsennalll."

I expected nothing less.

Cliff's chant was met with a round of applause and cheers as he exited the building.

Eventually, I, too, decided to bid the remainder of the fanatics farewell, but not before standing with Jack and Eddie on the very same spot that we had watched the game, the beer-stained sticky floorboards on which we had witnessed Ole Gunner Solskjær win the match. Gerry George was still hanging out and took a photo of the three of us pointing to the now sacred Conor O'Neill's floorboards, our Irish soccer heaven in the American Midwest, thousands of miles from home.

I was just about to leave, when Red, who had left an hour or so earlier, burst in waving a brand new United shirt high above his head. He excitedly explained how he had been greeted at home by his wife, Nina, holding aloft a new United home shirt.

"I told you it would all work out, didn't I, Red?"

"It all worked out, Gary! It most certainly all worked out, you English tosser!"

ACKNOWLEDGMENTS

When relocating alone to a new country, you hope to be fortunate enough to meet people with whom you get on and with whom you have something in common; people who will help make that transition easier and your experiences richer. This is a story that is full of such characters: some real, some a meld of several I met along the way. It would not be the same without any of them. They lit up a journey. I thank ALL of them!

Thank you to Jon and Laurie Wilson for believing in my story. What an incredible ride this has been. Who says that friends can't work together?

To J. Caleb Clark: you knocked it out of the ballpark, or, should I say, soccer field. To Bob Wood, your dedication, opinion and commitment to a "United" cause blew me away. To Frank Morelli and Bill Rouster, thank for your valued opinion and support. Thank you to Steve Heptinstall, Stuart Marley, Les, Chul, Colin, and Jukka, for taking the time.

Thank you Tom, manager of a certain Irish Bar: this book would not have been possible without you having achieved your dream. I was there when it began and there when "it" happened.

To Jim Menlove: a most valued friendship, all thanks to the beautiful game.

For the family I am so blessed to have. My wife Julie, for your love, support, understanding, and patience as you listened to yet another read through. My beautiful daughter: what a gift you are. My late mother: you always said that I would write. My father: for all of those late night taxis and, of course, for bringing football, or, should I say, soccer, into my life. Elaine: it was great to grow up with you. Joanne: you inspired me. My Uncle Jack: sorry I ruined your garage doors practicing all of those free kicks and penalties. Not forgetting Frances and Annie for your support and encouragement.

And finally—to Manchester United and the game of soccer itself. None of this would have happened had it not been for that day back in 1975.

Thank you!

ABOUT THE AUTHOR

Gary B. France is a native Englishman and "naturalized" ("sounds rather like I've been dipped in vinegar," he suggests) American. His daily existence is one of self-proclaimed varying degrees of confusion.

Growing up in rural North West England, France developed his wanderlust at a young age, prompting him to backpack around the globe before eventually settling across the Atlantic. A northern outpost along the coastline of Michigan's Great Lake Huron is where he now resides—for the time being anyway!

France has always written. A common thread throughout his work over the years has been his reflections on journeys and life experiences—stories waiting to be told. France has been a medical health professional for over thirty years. He has worked in various settings. Traversing northern Michigan's terrain specializing in home health care is among one of his favorites. Experiencing the eccentric, bizarre, sometimes sad, sometimes uplifting, France describes the job as a "northern exposure" where there is never a dull moment.

France also has a passion for music. He has produced and hosted "The British Invasion" radio show in Ann Arbor, Michigan. He continues to enjoy discovering and researching new and old musical artists.

It is said that you don't choose your team—your team chooses you. In 1975 Manchester United chose a ten-year old Gary B. France. His dedication in support of his team, whenever and wherever, continues to endure.

Visit www.garybfrance.com.